After starting life as an economist, Phil spent the next [illegible] years working in business and management consulting, where he specialised in strategic planning and business improvement. He has worked for many of Australia's largest companies in mining & resources, manufacturing, utilities, telecommunications, finance, professional services and all levels of government across Australia and the Pacific.

Phil maintained an active interest in economics and was one of the few analysts globally to publicly predict the GFC.

The Great Depression of the 2020s

Its Causes and Who to Blame

Philip Williams

First published by Philip Williams in 2019
This edition published in 2019 by Philip Williams

The Great Depression of the 2020s

EPUB: 9781925786422
POD: 9781925786439

Cover design by Red Tally Studios
Good faith effort was made to contact all copyright holders for permission for any content reproduced in this book.

Publishing services provided by Critical Mass
www.critmassconsulting.com

To Brenda and Richard
My sincerest love and gratitude for putting up with me while I worked on the book

To Catherine
Thank you for all your encouragement and support throughout the journey

To Mum and Dad
My sincerest gratitude for everything you have done for me

May life always be filled with *'Love and Laughter'*

Contents

List of Figures

About the Author

I was born in Sydney, Australia and graduated with an economics degree from the University of Sydney.

After graduating, I joined a major Australian bank as a graduate trainee, working in branch banking before transferring to its economic department. Here I worked as a research officer, focusing on a range of subjects including international trade.

I left banking and joined Shell Oil. Throughout my 14-year career, I worked in retail management, sales, finance and administration, network development, manufacturing, logistics, business improvement and strategic planning.

I left Shell and worked for a leading global management consulting firm, specialising in strategy and business transformation. It was here that I learnt how to analyse and restructure businesses.

For the next 20 years, I worked as a management consultant across a range of industries including mining, heavy industry, telecommunications, all tiers of government, utilities, agriculture, entertainment and railways. This work included strategic and business planning, business transformation, change management, procurement, IT, operational improvement and program management.

This broad business experience gave me a unique insight into how businesses operate, how managers allocate capital and make business decisions, and how corporations grow, thrive, stagnate and die. It also impressed upon me the inefficiency of government bureaucracies and how out of touch government bureaucrats are.

In addition to my career, I was also active in politics, serving for a number of years on the governing body of the Liberal Party (conservatives) in Queensland. Here I worked on numerous local, state and federal election campaigns and got to mix regularly with senators, federal and state politicians, cabinet ministers, mayors and local councillors.

My involvement in politics left me with an enduring sense of cynicism towards politicians and the political process. With few exceptions, I found politicians to be self-serving, conflicted, reactive, short-sighted, cunning and, often, not particularly smart. It also re-enforced that the higher the level of government, the more detached and remote politicians are from their constituents. I came away supporting Aristotle's view that the most responsive form of government occurs at the local level.

While no longer working as an economist, I maintained an interest in economics. In the mid-2000s, I became a guest commentator on economics on the Australian Broadcasting Corporation's evening radio show – Australia's version of Britain's BBC. In July 2007, I was on the public record stating that U.S. house prices were in a bubble and that the world would experience a financial crisis. Three months later, the world's financial system was bought to its knees when the Global Financial Crisis (GFC) struck in September 2007.

In subsequent interviews, I argued that extreme money printing by central banks (counterfeiting) would not restore prosperity; the European Union (EU) would eventually break up; and that a deflationary depression was the most likely outcome from irresponsible bank lending and central bank activism.

The fact that so many mainstream economists – the so-called experts that the mainstream media loves to quote – got it wrong not only surprised me but caused me to question the very foundations of modern economic theory. I also pondered why my analytical framework allowed me to see so clearly the looming economic problems and yet so many famed economists couldn't.

Which brings me to the reason for writing this book.

Reasons for Writing the Book

Economics plays a vital role in our prosperity, standard of living, health, mental well-being and safety. It enables us to not only meet our basic needs but to live the more affluent life we've become accustomed to. And yet very few people, including many economists, have a good understanding of how economies function, and what drives the endless cycle of boom and bust.

Our general economic illiteracy has enabled the banking elite to take control of the world's financial systems. In key areas of the economy, free-market capitalism has been replaced by a hybrid of central planning, corporatisation and protection of favoured industries. This, together with globalisation, has led to the hollowing of the middle classes and the massive transfer of wealth to the elite. A large underclass of financial serfs has emerged who are beholden to the banks.

Alongside this, the west's prosperity is threatened by the rise of China as an aggressive, strategic competitor. China has achieved the status of a global economic powerhouse through illegal means and unfair trade practices.

Economists' reliance on flawed mainstream economic theories, fiscal stimulus and central bank activism have sown the seeds for an economic collapse of a magnitude as great as, if not greater than, the Great Depression. This event will shake the very foundations of the world as we now know it.

*

One other reason for writing this book is personal. Based on financial advice, I was fully invested in managed funds through the 1990s. I was mortified when the dot-com bubble collapsed. I can still vividly remember the fear I suffered every morning as I tuned in to see how much the Dow Jones had fallen the previous day. Five years later I was diagnosed with cancer. Fortunately, I have made a full recovery but I put this bout of cancer down to the extreme fear that I suffered in the 2000 stock market collapse, and the possible loss of our life savings.

The reality is that booms and busts are not just esoteric events. They have real world consequences, sometimes dire.

The purpose of this book is to demystify economics so that people can use the knowledge gained to actively engage in debate. From this position of power, our society can challenge the fraud perpetuated by the elite – banks, mainstream economists, central banks, politicians, bureaucrats, corporate executives, financial commentators, the mainstream media, the real estate industry and special interest groups – and return some balance and fairness to society.

Introduction

Greed, hubris and flawed economic theories have led to a massive build-up in debt, malinvestments and distortions in the global economy, at levels far greater than at any other time in human history. Not only has this led to a massive redistribution of wealth from the poor to the elite, but it has sown the seeds for a calamitous deflationary depression and economic collapse of a magnitude as great as, if not greater than, the Great Depression.

We are now at a tipping point where the economy is so distorted that only a depression can cleanse the system of its malinvestments and distortions before sustainable economic growth can resume.

So how did we get to this point, and who's to blame? Turning to the second part of the question first – the answer is simple. Politicians, bureaucrats and the general public have taken for granted that mainstream economists and central bankers are experts and know what they are doing. As I shall demonstrate, they don't.

Not only have mainstream economists failed to properly analyse economic history and therefore develop a proper understanding of how economies function, they have also failed to learn the lessons of history.

They have failed to heed the warnings which highlight that boom and bust cycles have been a regular feature of the economic landscape through the ages. With few exceptions, booms have been brought about largely by poor banking practices, excessive debt, runaway inflation and credit-fuelled asset booms. And surely as night follows day, booms have been followed by busts, often with catastrophic consequences.

History clearly demonstrates that the best way to handle a financial crisis if it does arise is to let the debt implode, let bad banks fail or be reconstructed, and let asset and consumer prices and wages deflate to more sustainable levels. This ritual cleaning of distortions and malinvestments sets the foundation for renewed and vibrant growth.

Mainstream economists have eschewed this evidence, instead promoting policies that encourage government meddling and intervention in the economy. Intervention that actually prolongs economic depressions and human suffering while failing to cleanse the system of structural imbalances.

In recent years, mainstream economists and politicians have taken economic meddling to an extreme, undertaking the greatest monetary and fiscal stimulus in history and in so doing running up record levels of debt. And yet despite this unprecedented monetary and fiscal stimulus, the rate of real economic growth in the west has been in inexorable decline for the past seven decades.

In other words, government intervention in the economy not only causes imbalances and exacerbates financial problems, it prolongs human suffering while doing little to support real economic growth.

And while they have been pursuing these flawed policies, they have failed to promote policies that actually support economic growth and prosperity. Policies that encourage sound money, that encourage laissez-faire economics and support increased productivity.

It is nothing short of scandalous. Mainstream economists have perpetuated a gigantic fraud on the working people of the world: firstly, by suggesting that they understand how a modern economy works; and secondly, by implying that they can control economic outcomes. If mainstream economists had such wisdom and power, the world would be on a trajectory of sustainable economic growth rather than standing on the edge of an economic precipice.

In perpetuating this fraud, they have also created a number of myths, for example that inflation and low interest rates are necessary precursors for economic growth, and deflation is bad for the economy. Myths that are not only incorrect, but are actually damaging to economic growth.

These flawed economic theories have allowed politicians and others to hide behind a chimera of respectability while wreaking havoc on the economy and the well-being of millions of innocent people.

More importantly, it has exposed a dark underside to humanity, insofar that politicians, when faced with economic difficulties – generally of their own making – will say things that are often misleading and will implement draconian measures that impact directly on the rights, freedoms and lives of their own citizens. This time will be no different.

The banking and corporate elites have exploited these failures to hijack the economy for their own benefit. In so doing, they have massively increased the size of the banking sector relative to the real economy. This has not only created huge asset bubbles, but transferred hundreds of billions of dollars of wealth from the low and middle classes to the elite, while creating a massive underclass of serfs financially beholden to the banks. It's now a matter of: 'I owe, I owe: it's off to work I go.'

Of course, the elites aren't the only ones to blame. Ordinary folk have been caught up in speculation and the borrowing binge, hoping to get rich on the asset boom, or living beyond their means. But none of this would have been possible if credit hadn't been so readily available, and at such low interest rates.

The elites have also created the pre-conditions for a depression through the creation of fractional reserve banking and fiat currencies, and through the actions of central bankers, all of which have undermined the concept of sound money.

While this book seeks to expose how the elites have exploited the fraud that is mainstream economics, there is a glimmer of hope.

There are minority groups of non-mainstream economists who do have a clear understanding of how economies work, what causes booms and busts, and what policies can deliver prosperity. They are also very clear of the limitations of economics in solving world problems. Until now, their theories have been largely ignored as they haven't supported the narrative of the political classes and the elite. It's time to change that.

*

The book is divided into five parts. Part 1 introduces basic economic and financial concepts, while highlighting how mainstream macroeconomics is not a science, but rather a jumble of disconnected, unproven and failed theories. It also provides several examples of financial crises through the ages.

Part 2 covers the creation of the U.S. Federal Reserve – the worst financial decision in U.S. economic history, together with analysis of the 1920–21 Depression, the Roaring Twenties and the Great Depression. It also critiques the different theories put forward as to the causes of the Great Depression and demonstrates clearly how these theories, which form the basis of current mainstream economic thought, are not only deeply flawed but are at the heart of most of today's economic problems.

Part 3 uses the post-war U.S. economy as an exemplar to support my arguments of economic malfeasance by mainstream economists. This looks at key stages in the growth and development of the post-war U.S. economy before delving into how banks have taken control of the world's financial system; and how misguided U.S Federal Reserve monetary policies, such as inflation targeting, have led to the financialisaton of the economy. These policies have not only created structural imbalances, but have contributed to the transfer of billions of dollars in wealth to the global elite, especially bankers.

Part 3 also describes how excessive credit growth led to the credit crisis in Japan in the 1980s, how China has exploited mercantilist policies to take unfair advantage of freer trade in the west, and how structural problems in the EU have been caused by flawed economic and geo-political policies that favour France and Germany at the expense of peripheral nations.

Part 4 identifies measures that suggest that the global economy is at a tipping point of another financial crisis. It also introduces four scenarios as to how the financial crisis may play out, with a detailed explanation of the most likely scenario – a devastating and prolonged global deflationary depression. It paints a picture of untold misery, pain and suffering, and massive social upheaval.

Finally, Part 5 looks at how we, the people, can wrest control of the global economy from the elite, before detailing a range of factors that are crucial to deliver economic prosperity moving forward.

It is now time to challenge the elite and their reliance on quack economic theories that have created this ungodly mess.

I hope you enjoy the book and that it will help protect your savings in the ensuing global meltdown.

Part 1
Key Concepts

Chapter 1

Key Economic Concepts

'Economics is extremely useful as a form of employment for economists.'

John Kenneth Galbraith

Economics plays a vital role in our prosperity, standard of living, health, mental well-being and safety. Without the products and services provided through modern economic activity, we would be unable to meet our basic needs, let alone support our modern way of life.

One only needs to compare the standard of living in the west to those living in developing nations, or to the lifestyles of our forebears, to understand the benefits of economic progress.

Unfortunately, the field of economics has become a political football, open to abuse and manipulation by vested interest groups towards their own ends.

Many people – including politicians, unionists, church leaders, academics, the media, social activists and even economists themselves – have difficulty separating economics from other disciplines such as finance, politics, psychology, anthropology and sociology. Many suggest that economic growth can solve all of life's problems. Others blame economic growth for all of life's ills. Both groups are wrong.

Another problem is the relentless battle that rages between the aspirations, goals and objectives of diverse groups within society, requirements that are often at complete odds with one another. This is no better exemplified than the ongoing ideological battles between environmentalism and development, socialism and capitalism, collectivism and liberalism, democracy and authoritarianism.

A further problem relates to short-term political and economic needs versus the long-term needs of current and future generations.

Unfortunately, some prominent economists have adapted and sponsored economic theories to support partisan political and social views. Worse still, some have been willingly co-opted by the elite to support economic theories which favour the elite. This has resulted in massive financial and social distortions which will blow up in our faces.

This is not only an indictment of the economics 'profession' as a whole – and I use the word 'profession' very loosely – but of those prominent mainstream economists who have sold their souls for twenty pieces of silver.

Economics does have a place in supporting social and political debate. Economists can provide the theoretical and analytical frameworks to help policy-makers and the public make informed decisions against the complex trade-offs between competing interests.

But it cannot solve all of life's problems. People need to make decisions which reflects society's needs and wants. Such decisions may have good economic outcomes, or they may have very poor social and economic outcomes. The best economists can do is provide the analysis to support debate in making these decisions.

Ideally, economics should be agnostic and neutral to all groups within society. Sadly, it never will be as economists are driven by the same primordial psychological factors that drive the rest of us – self-interest.

Given these shortcomings, the best I can do is highlight the gross deficiencies in current mainstream economic theories so that people can participate in the debate on how society and the economy should function to the benefit of as many people as possible.

*

The following provides a brief introduction to the field of economics before moving onto the main chapters in the book.

Definition of Economics

The first problem with economics is that economists can't agree on a common definition of economics. The definitions range from a focus on the study on wealth; how individuals and society choose to employ scarce productive resources; to how society goes about organising the production and distribution of the goods and services it wants.

Despite the multiplicity of views, five underlying principles and commonalties seem to emerge from these definitions.

Firstly, the study of economics arises out of the need to use resources to satisfy human needs and wants.

Secondly, they identify key aspects of economic activity, namely: production, distribution, consumption and savings of individuals and groups within society.

Thirdly, they raise the critical role that time plays in relation to economic activity. For example, do we consume everything now and leave nothing for future generations, or do we have some form of moral obligation to future generations?

Fourthly, economics deals with scarcity and choice – and how resources are allocated, now and in the future.

Finally, economics should help people establish frameworks of how economic systems work to help solve everyday problems.

What Problems is Economics Trying to Solve?

Global economies are highly complex systems that handle literally billions of economic transactions every hour. That the system works at all is a miracle. Can you imagine, for example, trying to design and maintain a machine that could handle so many components and transactions in an environment that is continually changing? And yet, the global economy, for better or worse, does exactly that.

Lipsey et al[1] identify six types of problems that economics is trying to solve. The first three questions fall within the realm of microeconomics while the latter three questions fall within the field of macroeconomics.

1. *What goods and services are being produced and in what quantities*?

This question addresses the issue of scarcity, that is how an economy allocates scarce resources to meet insatiable and unending human needs, where demand will always outstrip supply.

There are various mechanisms for allocating goods and services. In a centrally planned economy, the decision to allocate resources and at what prices is determined centrally, either by bureaucrats or by decree. This is often undertaken without regard to the prevailing market conditions, or to consumer needs and wants. In contrast, in free-market systems, resource allocation is determined in competitive markets through the price system. In such cases, the relative prices of goods and services will adjust over time to reflect changing consumer preferences, which in turn impacts on the supply and demand for goods and services.

In reality, most economies are a hybrid of centrally planned and free-market systems with a leaning towards one or the other of the two extremes.

2. *By what methods are goods and services produced?*

Generally, there is more than one way to produce goods and services. These range from labour intensive to highly automated methods. Unfortunately, there is no simple formula to determine the optimum mix as the answer will depend on a range of local and international factors.

3. *How is the supply of goods allocated amongst the members of society?*

This question seeks to address issues associated with the allocation of income, wealth and resources throughout society. There are two aspects to this question. The first relates to purely economic forces, where resources are allocated on the basis of economic factors, independent of any other considerations. The second aspect transcends economics to look at other areas such as sociology and politics to determine how income and wealth should be distributed.

In recent times, there has been a great deal of debate around income and wealth inequality. Whatever one's social and political leanings, history would suggest that wealth and power tend to concentrate amongst a few, highly powerful individuals and families while invariably there will be a middle class of varying proportions and a large underclass. This is true whether the prevailing political and economic system is socialism, Nazism, communism, tribalism, autocracy or capitalism.

Moreover, despite the recent debates, human nature being what it is, I believe this disparity in income and wealth will continue well into the foreseeable future.

4. *Are the country's resources being fully utilised, or are some of them lying idle and thus going to waste?*

In recent times, politicians and economists have focused almost exclusively on economic growth at all cost. Unfortunately this debate has been driven largely for political considerations, that is to keep the incumbent government in power, rather than for purely economic reasons.

The argument goes that if a nation's resources are under-utilised then a nation's economic output will be reduced, unemployment will be higher and the economy will be less able to satisfy society's needs and wants. But more importantly, politicians will be less popular and therefore less likely to be elected.

But there are many legitimate reasons why an economy might be underperforming. For example, is the under-utilisation due to short-term cyclical problems or is it due to longer-term structural problems, for example industries becoming uncompetitive or major changes in consumer needs? Equally, by running at peak utilisation, are a nation's resources such as land and the environment sustainable? Or are they being depleted, making them less productive or unusable in the future?

These are complex problems with no easy answers. While long-term economic growth is desirable, focusing on short-term economic growth at all cost just to get politicians re-elected or maximise company profits is fraught and will not always lead to the best economic outcomes in the long term.

5. *Is the economy's capacity to produce goods and services growing or remaining the same over time?*

Like question 4, this question is more complex than it might otherwise seem. The mantra that 'Growth is Good' parodies the famous line from the 1980s movie *Wall Street* that 'Greed is Good.'

There is no doubt that economic growth has been very beneficial for vast numbers of people. It has lifted millions out of poverty, raised living standards, increased lifespans, provided better education outcomes, given people more choice, led to the eradication of deadly diseases and helped people overcome chronic suffering through improved health services. Those who criticise economic growth seem happy to reap its rewards while failing to acknowledge its benefits.

On the other hand, the relentless focus on growth by politicians and economists is not always good. This question assumes, for example, that the world has infinite resources to meet all current and future needs. But we know intuitively that this is not possible.

Secondly, there seems to be an underlying assumption that economic growth leads to greater happiness. Politicians surmise that if the people are happy, they are more likely to be re-elected – probably a fair assumption. However, if economic growth was the primary cause of happiness, then the U.S. should be one of the happiest places on earth. But this is not the case. The U.S. has major social issues including some of highest levels of incarceration, drug use, mental illness, murder and gun crime in the world, unaffordable health costs and falling education standards. And, all of this despite increasing levels of debt and deficits.

Other problems include that the fruits of economic growth have not been shared equitably across the diverse groups, while unbridled economic growth has led to environmental problems.

Thirdly, the ability to expand an economy's capacity to produce goods and services depends largely on having the right economic policies in place: policies such as having sufficient savings, capital investment and improved productivity. As I will demonstrate later, many of these factors have been diminished over the past four decades.

So, while economic growth plays a vital role in improving our standard of living, we also need practices and processes that balance the needs of different stakeholder groups and that balance the needs of current and future generations.

6. *Is the purchasing power of money and savings constant, or is it being eroded due to inflation?*

Currency debasement (a.k.a. unsound money or inflation) is one of the most pernicious forces in economics. Inflation has been central to almost every financial crisis throughout history. For example, chronic inflation over many decades was one of the primary causes for the decline and subsequent collapse of the Roman Empire. Equally, hyper-inflation in Germany during the 1920s played a major part in the rise of Adolf Hitler. Inflation was also one of the primary causes of the Great Depression and the GFC.

Rampant inflation has also been one of the primary reasons for the massive increase in wealth of the elite and will be central to the looming Great Depression of the 2020s, as the chronic inflation of the past three decades turns into a deflationary spiral.

The topic of inflation and the problems it causes will be a central theme throughout the remainder of this book.

Lipsey's six types of problems highlight two further points. Firstly, economies are very complex, dynamic systems which are beyond the capacity of anybody to fully understand, let alone control. Secondly, economies are natural systems which ebb and flow over time. As I shall demonstrate, constant interference by governments and central banks in recent years has led to massive distortions in the effective functioning of the global economy, and will be at the heart of the looming economic crisis.

How an Economy Functions

There are three primary groups within an economy: households, government and firms. Each group has two roles. Firstly, as a consumer, and secondly, as a provider of goods and services. Figure 1 shows the key components of an economy as well as the flow of resources through the economy.

Households provide resources in the form of land, labour and capital, while they receive income in the form of wages, rent, interest and dividends. Wages and salaries, which comprise the majority of household income, are primary drivers for consumption in an economy.

Firms use factors of production as inputs to provide goods and services. The primary inputs are land, labour, capital, finance and entrepreneurship.

Governments provide a range of goods and services on behalf of their citizens while paying for its services by levying a range of taxes on citizens.

Countries also trade with other countries through imports and exports.

Modern economies are also underpinned by the finance sector which houses a nation's savings while providing money and credit to facilitate economic transactions. It is important to note, however, that while the finance sector is inextricably linked to economic activity, as we shall see later in this book, it is a separate system to the real economy and operates by a separate set of principles.

Figure 1 Key Components of an Economy

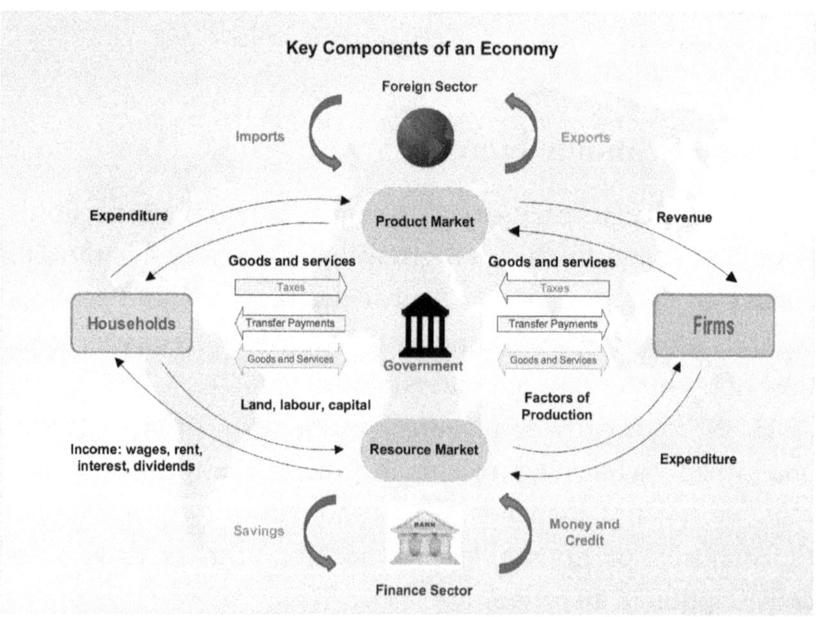

Economists use a variety of measures to measure economic activity, the most important being Gross Domestic Product (GDP), which measures an economy's output over a specific period of time.

It is perhaps worthwhile noting at this time that although GDP and its related concepts are useful in measuring a country's output, income and standard of living, they do have their drawbacks.

Firstly, they only measure transactions in legal markets. Hence, they exclude transactions on the black market, which in some countries can be quite substantial, and services provided by people themselves, for example mowing your own lawn or the contribution of stay-at-home parents. Secondly, as aggregate measures, they don't show which economic sectors are growing or in decline, whether the increased income results from more or fewer hours worked, nor do they show how the income and wealth is being shared. Thirdly, they don't show the impact of economic development on the environment, the depletion of resources, urban amenities, and so on, nor do they measure changes in people's quality of life.

Having said that, GDP and GDP per capita are useful measures to indicate economic progress over time and we will use them extensively in the book.

Economics and finance are like two sides of the same coin. They are different, but joined at the hip. Therefore, to understand how a modern economy functions, and how economic problems might arise, we also need to have a clear understanding of the basics of money and credit.

Chapter 2
Money and Credit

'Debt is the slavery of the free.'

Publilius Syrus

The abuse of money and credit has been at the core of almost every financial crisis throughout history. Therefore, it is essential that people have a good understanding of key concepts of money and credit, as well as how governments have harmed their citizens by eroding the value of money.

In this chapter I will briefly discuss the functions of money and look at how money and credit have evolved over time, especially the transition from sound to unsound money, before providing several examples of financial crises through the ages.

Money has three main functions.

- Money acts as a *medium of exchange* that facilities the exchange of goods and services. Without money, we would need to use barter to exchange goods and services. Economic progress would have been impossible without the development of money.

  One of the key characteristics of money as a medium of exchange is that it is divisible into different denominations. This allows trade to occur at the micro and macro levels.

Another characteristic of money is that it must not be easily counterfeited. If people lose trust in the integrity of the money, then it loses its usefulness as an accepted medium of exchange.

- Money provides a *store of value*. Of course, many other items can act as a store of value, including stamps, art, rare books and precious metals, as well as land and buildings. However, the advantage of money is that it is very liquid, meaning that its value can be realised instantaneously.

  To be of any use, people must have confidence that the money they are holding today will have the same value in five, 10 or 50 years' time.

  Importantly, it is this very function of money that countless generations of monarchs, politicians, bureaucrats and bankers have sought to undermine through devious means.
- Money is a *unit of measure*, which means that every product, good, service and asset traded throughout the world is assigned a specific value measured against a specific yardstick. It is this unit of measure function that underpins the workings of the pricing system, which in turn allows the efficient allocation of scarce resources.

  The unit of measure expresses prices in both relative and absolute terms. For example, it allows the prices of, say, apples or bananas to be set at a particular time. However, it also highlights the difference in relative value between those apples or bananas and all other types of produce, and in fact all other goods, services and assets.

  This unit of measure concept even extends to money itself, where different currencies are assigned a specific value against all other currencies.

A Brief History of Money

The existence of money dates back at least 10,000 years when our ancestors traded using barter. In earliest times people used livestock and farm produce, such as grains and vegetables, to trade. Since then, the types of money in use have evolved but, as we shall see, not always for the better.

Our early ancestors used a variety of independent objects as money. The original objects, known as *commodity currencies*, ranged from precious and base metals to barley, beads, shells, salt, pigs and tea. In early Australian colonial times, for example, rum served as the main currency due to a shortage of coins, while opium featured prominently in trade between China and Great Britain during the nineteenth century.

The important characteristic of commodity currencies is that they consist of objects that have value in and of themselves (intrinsic value) as well as value in their use as money.

Gold and silver have been particularly favoured forms of money, principally because of their relative scarcity, portability and durability. Base metals such as copper and iron were also used as coins instead of precious metals. The problem with base metals, however, was that the higher value tokens became too heavy to carry around to be of any great use.

The introduction of money was crucial to economic progress and spawned development of a range of factors critical to economic development. These included rules on debt, legal contracts and codes of law relating to business practices and private property, as well as a standard form of weights and measures.

The next step in the evolution of money arose out the widespread use of *paper money* as a medium of exchange. The Chinese were at the forefront of money innovation when in around 100 BC, they invented an early form of money fashioned out of brightly coloured pieces of deer-skin. From the ninth to the fifteenth century, the Chinese used paper money as currency. The use of paper money disappeared in China in the middle of the fifteenth century, however, as the economy was ravaged by inflation brought about by excessive money-printing.

In the thirteenth century, news of paper money made its way to Europe following the exploits of travellers such as Marco Polo. In medieval Italy and Flanders, money traders introduced promissory notes as a way of overcoming the impracticalities and security involved in transporting large sums of money, especially gold, over vast distances. In the beginning, promissory notes were personally registered, but they soon became a written order to pay the amount to whomever had it in their possession,[2] thus making it not only easy to trade, but also open to theft. These notes were the precursor to regular banknotes.

Bills of exchange became prevalent with the expansion of European trade towards the end of the Middle Ages. A flourishing Italian wholesale trade in cloth, woollen clothing, wine, tin and other commodities was heavily dependent on credit for its rapid expansion. Goods were supplied to a buyer against a bill of exchange, which constituted the buyer's promise to make payment at some specified future date. Provided the buyer was reputable or the bill was endorsed by a credible guarantor, the seller could present the bill to a merchant banker and redeem it in money at a discounted value before it became due. Like promissory notes, the main purpose of these bills was to reduce risks associated with traveling with large amounts of cash.[3]

Goldsmiths in England had been craftsmen, bullion merchants, money changers and money lenders since the sixteenth century. Due to the nature of their business, they stored their inventory in very secure vaults. Because of this security, it also became customary for their customers, for a fee, to store their surplus gold in these vaults. The goldsmiths acknowledged receipt of the gold by issuing a receipt, certifying the quantity and purity of the metal, together with a promise to return the gold on demand. Over time, merchants found it more convenient to exchange these gold receipts rather than physically transfer the gold.

The success of this monetary system was totally dependent on the reputation of the institution storing the gold and issuing the receipt. Generally, these were either goldsmiths or the larger banks. The paper money in such instances was said to be fully convertible, meaning that it was fully convertible into a specific quantity of gold on demand. The system itself was said to be based on the gold standard, because the money in circulation was underpinned by something of value, namely gold.

In the ordinary course of business, the level of gold redeemed generally equalled the level of gold deposited so, in normal times, the physical stock of gold held in storage remained constant. The goldsmiths and banks took advantage of the stability in physical gold stocks to increase the level of money in circulation at a far greater rate than the actual increase in their holdings of gold. The amount of leverage varied over time, but it settled at around 10 to 20 per cent of gold to the total value of money in circulation. Thus, a gold holding of $1 million supported actual money in circulation of $5–10 million.

The use of leverage gave rise to two monetary gold systems. A *100 per cent gold standard* exists when all the money in circulation can be exchanged for an equivalent amount of gold. The international monetary system, which operated in the immediate aftermath of World War II, operated as a de facto 100 per cent gold standard insofar that countries settled their international balances in dollars, and U.S. dollars could be converted into gold at any time at a fixed exchange rate of $35 per ounce.

A system where the total amount of money in circulation is backed by less than the equivalent value in gold (or bank deposits) is known as a *fractional reserve system.* The international gold standards of the nineteenth and early twentieth centuries were typically fractional reserve systems, where the money supply was a multiple of the actual gold stock.

The major advantage of a gold standard is that because of the scarcity of gold, it acts as an automatic break on the amount of money that governments can artificially create. In turn, this acts to maintain confidence in a currency by preserving the value of the money over time.

Not surprisingly, politicians, bankers and the elite don't like the gold standard because it restricts their ability to conduct ill-disciplined military expeditions and undertake excessive government expenditure, while also limiting the growth in banking.

Historically, money was typically issued by privately owned banks. The acceptance of these banks' notes as a medium of exchange was determined largely by people's confidence in the strength of the issuing institution. If people questioned the institution's ongoing viability to honour these notes, then the underlying value of the notes was devalued, thus prejudicing the very survival of the issuing institution. This forced issuing institutions to conduct business prudently, rather than put the ongoing viability of the business at risk. In contrast, when people lost confidence in the credibility of management or the institution, people either withdrew their funds or demanded higher interest rates to cover their risk. This was what the free market is all about.

Central banks arose as a natural outcome of the evolution of the financial system. Initially most central banks were private institutions which provided a number of services to the commercial banks, including the safe-keeping of excess reserves of money.

Over time, central banks forged a closer relationship with governments and were progressively either taken over by governments, or in some instances created by government as special purpose intuitions. Today, the stated goals of central banks are characteristically to control inflation and to maintain stability of the financial system.

In normal times, a fractional reserve system works well, provided that the overall supply of money and credit remains well calibrated to the demand for money necessary to support trade and commerce in the real economy. However, as we will see later, fractional reserve banking is especially open to abuse as governments and banks increase the amount of leverage by reducing the percentage of reserves relative to the total money supply.

The next evolution in the development of money came with the introduction of fiat currency. *Fiat money* or *fiat currency* is a modern form of money that differs from commodity currencies in that it is not backed by anything of intrinsic value, for example precious metals or pigs. Instead, fiat currencies are created either by printing notes, which have virtually no intrinsic value in and of themselves other than the cost to produce the note, or by creating billions of dollars electronically through the wonder of modern computers.

Fiat money derives its value only because governments mandate it as legal tender – the only medium of exchange – and because consumers have confidence that governments will maintain the value of the currency. Today, all major currencies are based on fiat money.

Inflation

Inflation, also known as currency debasement, occurs when the value of money is diminished, or devalued, through the actions of authorities – rulers, governments and central banks. It occurs when the quantity of money or credit in circulation increases at a faster rate than the supply of goods and services.

Currency debasement was traditionally associated with commodity currencies, such as gold or silver coins. A coin is said to be debased if the quantity of precious metals within the coins is reduced, while the coins continue to circulate at face value. Governments used a variety of means to debase their metal currencies including melting the coins down and adding less valuable materials such as alloys and in reducing the physical size of coins by shaving metal from the coin's edges, punching holes in the coin and sweating, which involves shaking the coins in a bag and collecting the metal filings. However, governments using the gold standard have also debased their currencies by moving from a 100 per cent-backed gold standard to a fractional reserve system, or by taking them off the gold standard altogether.

Inflation is particularly rampant today with fiat currencies. This has been achieved by a variety of means including fractional reserve lending, where banks lend multiples of their reserves; government deficit spending, which is financed by central banks 'creating money out of thin air'; or by redenomination, which occurs when authorities alter the face value of a currency without changing its foreign exchange rate. Redenomination is common when countries experience hyper-inflation.

Inflation undermines the utility of money in several ways. Firstly, it undermines its ability to act as a store of value as the purchasing power of money is eroded over time – a dollar will buy you less in five years' time than it will today. Secondly, it undermines the working of the pricing system by distorting the relative prices of assets, goods and services.

No matter which method is used to debase the currency, the purpose is always the same: to increase the amount of money in circulation relative to the supply of goods and services, and thus allow governments to spend more money, or to allow banks to lend more money than they otherwise could.

As an aside, it is a strange irony that while the public is prohibited from counterfeiting money, governments, through their central banks, have been engaging in counterfeiting money at unprecedented levels through the practice of 'creating money out of thin air', with barely an utterance of protest from politicians and economists who espouse the principles of free markets and capitalism. Go figure. Moreover, the recent actions of banks and central banks to debase their currencies is at the epicentre of the looming financial and economic crisis.

Financial Crises Through the Ages

Financial crises have been a feature of the economic landscape since earliest times. While some have resulted from natural causes such as disease, pestilence, floods and famine, more often than not they have resulted from man-made causes such as revolution, war, inflation and credit-fuelled financial manias.

Unfortunately, governments and politicians have proven time and again that they cannot be trusted to preserve the value of money. Desperate to cling to power at any cost, self-serving politicians have invariably resorted to printing money to meet spending commitments beyond their government's capacity to pay. Whether it be to fund their wars, pander to the electorate or special interest groups, or to cover for government waste, incompetence and corruption, politicians will invariably turn to currency debasement as an 'easy fix'.

Some of the more noteworthy financial crises throughout history have included the decline of the Roman Empire, the Mississippi Bubble (1716–20), the South Sea Bubble (1720), the European credit crisis (1772), the U.S. Panic of 1792, hyperinflation in the Weimar Republic in Germany (early 1920s) and Zimbabwe (2008–09), the Latin American Debt Crisis (1980s), the Asian (1997) and Russian (1998) financial crises, the dot-com bubble and the 2008 Global Financial Crisis. (Interested readers can find details of these financial crises, and more, on my website: www.philipwilliamsauthor.com).

So, what can we learn about financial crises?

Inflation has been at the core of almost every financial crisis and, once again, will be at the core of the looming great depression of the 2020s. Recent examples of crises caused by excessive money printing include the Weimar Republic and Zimbabwe, while the dot-com bubble and the GFC are examples of financial crises caused by runaway credit growth. Moreover, financial crises have not been isolated to any ethnic or cultural group, nor to any specific epoch. Rather, they have occurred throughout the ages and on most continents.

While inflation impacts diverse groups in different ways, it invariably benefits the wealthy while doing the greatest harm to the poor and middle classes. Inflation is highly destructive and can have major political and social consequences. For example, the hyperinflation in Germany during the Weimar Republic was a major contributing factor in the rise of Adolf Hitler, while inflation played a major role in the collapse of the Roman Empire. Moreover, the greater the excess, the greater the hangover, as inflation unwinds through deflation.

The introduction of fiat currencies and fractional reserve banking has made currency debasement far easier than when governments had to resort to physical means to debase their currencies. Without the discipline imposed by the gold standard, politicians and central banks can inflate the money supply far more easily to pay for their excessive expenditure just by 'printing money'. In fact, it has become mainstream economic policy to help governments debase their currencies in the delusional belief that this leads to economic growth and prosperity. It does neither.

Speculation and poor banking practices have also featured prominently in financial crises, for example the credit crises of 1772 and 1792, multiple financial panics in the U.S. in the nineteenth century, the Latin American debt crisis and the GFC.

Finally, although inflation has been at the core of most financial crises, two human emotions – fear and greed – have also played central roles in all financial crises. Greed! The pure, unadulterated greed of unscrupulous people who will stop at nothing to realise their misguided ambitions has led to the inflationary abyss. Greed, fear, panic and loathing has resulted in unfathomable anguish and suffering of tens of millions of everyday people as the economy has collapsed under the weight of imploding money. This is no better illustrated than looking at the factors that led to the fall of the Roman Empire and the 2008 GFC.

The slow collapse of the Roman Empire has several parallels. Excessive government expenditure on non-productive activities such as the military and bureaucracy, currency debasement, destroying the productive middle class, excessive state control and allowing the wealthy to evade tax culminated in the inevitable: economic decline, inflation and ruination. Inflation is like an addictive substance: the longer it continues, ever greater levels of inflation are required just to keep the patient stable. Not only does it mask structural problems in an economy, over time, inflation creates ever-greater problems, destroying the patient from within.

Let's look at some of the details.

Rome used a tri-metal monetary system based on gold, silver and copper coins. The monetary system, including minting, quality control and determining the amount of money in circulation, was controlled by the government. In an economy with a currency backed by precious metals, the money supply was totally dependent on the supply of the underlying metals. If the supply of metals failed to keep pace with economic growth, the economy slowed. Conversely, if the supply of currency outstripped the supply of goods and services, either because of new discoveries, military conquest or manipulation through currency debasement, the economy grew and predictably resulted in inflation.

The tri-metal system had several inherent weaknesses. Firstly, the relative values between the various metallic coins depended on a steady increase in the supply of each of the metals in proportion to each other. A disproportionate increase in the supply of one metal over another disrupted the relative values between the units of account.

The greater problem, however, lay in the tendency of emperors to debase the currency in times of war, and during social and political unrest. They did this either by reducing the size or weight of the coin, while leaving the face value of the coin unchanged, or by reducing the actual metal content in each coin. This allowed officials to mint far more coins then they had in available metals.

Currency debasement is best exemplified by the devaluation of the silver denarius which was the most popular coin in circulation during the Roman Empire. Throughout the first century AD, the denarius contained over 90 per cent silver, but by the end of the second century, the silver content had fallen to less than 70 per cent. A century later, there was less than 5 per cent silver in the coin and, by 350 AD it contained barely any silver at all.[4]

This prolonged and extreme period of currency debasement had several grave consequences. Firstly, it led to runaway inflation as the increase in the money supply outstripped the physical increase in the supply of products and services – more money chasing the same amount of goods led to increasing prices. This not only increased the cost of government, but it also reduced the living standards of everyday citizens as the purchasing power of their money and savings declined.

Secondly, people came to lose faith in the currency as a store of value. For the most part, Rome ran a trade deficit with its trading partners. Because trade was settled in the physical movement of gold or silver, this led to a drain on the available stock of gold or silver within the empire. As Rome continued to debase her currency, foreign traders began to refuse to accept the debased currency as payment. This put more pressure on the economy and encouraged further currency debasement.

But most importantly, it helped undermine the social fabric of the Roman Empire. Of course, it would be wrong to suggest that currency debasement was the sole cause of the fall of the Roman Empire. The fall of the Roman Empire had many causes including never-ending political infighting, the cost of financing endless wars, defending an empire which was too large to defend, maintaining a bloated bureaucracy, plague, fatigue, decadence, corruption, social dislocation and taxing the lower and middle classes into oblivion. Not surprisingly, these actions eerily parallel the decline of many empires throughout history.

Initially, Roman authorities responded to their financial problems by running down accumulated reserves, selling off state assets and debasing the currency. When problems persisted, the government responded by introducing new taxes such as inheritance and other wealth taxes and increasing the number of citizens subject to the tax base. However, as conditions continued to deteriorate, rulers resorted to ever more draconian measures. These included using trumped-up charges to confiscate the assets of the wealthy, implementing wage and price controls, restricting citizens' rights and persecuting minorities, including Christians.

The faltering economic conditions led to a vicious downward spiral that fed on itself. Inflation and a relentless increase in taxes decimated the productive sector. In turn, this led to more currency debasement, increased taxation, greater efforts to avoid tax, and a further erosion in economic activity. The wealthy and middle classes were so decimated that the tax burden fell even further on the lower class. In the end, things got so bad that the government was forced to requisition goods and services directly from farmers. Food production was greatly affected as large tracts of land were abandoned and remained fallow, or fell into the hands of the state, whose mismanagement generally led to a further decline in production.[5]

And yet, ordinary people showed extraordinary resilience in their response to these unforgiving conditions. A thriving black market developed as goods were withdrawn from sale and traders resorted to barter. Others fled to the countryside and took up subsistence farming or attached themselves to the estates of the wealthy. Large, powerful landowners, able to avoid taxation through legal and illegal means, began to organise small communities around them. Small landowners, crushed into bankruptcy by the heavy burden of taxation, threw themselves on the mercy of the large landowners, signing on as tenants or even as slaves – slaves, of course, paid no taxes. The latter phenomenon became so widespread and injurious to the state's revenues that in 368 AD, Emperor Valens declared it illegal to renounce one's liberty in order to place oneself under the protection of a great landlord.[6] The result was increasing feudalisation of the economy, loss of freedom, centralisation of power and the imposition of autocratic rule.

Of course, not every group fared badly. An army of bureaucrats was required to administer the new laws and regulations. The military also did well as the emperors became reliant on the army to retain power. And while the Roman senate extended taxes to include new regions, it exempted Rome itself, where most of the senators resided.

As Rome was being destroyed from within, it eventually fell when the empire was overrun by the Germanic Visigoths in 410 AD.

Rome shows us that unscrupulous and self-serving leaders will do whatever it takes to remain in power, even if it means appeasing powerful vested interest groups, reducing freedoms, impoverishing the majority and destroying the economic system. The Global Financial Crisis in 2008 is another example.

The collapse of U.S. financial services firm Lehman Brothers in September 2008 triggered the largest economic crisis since the Great Depression. In the ensuing months, credit markets froze, stock markets collapsed, millions of people lost their jobs, and governments and central banks were forced to undertake the largest bailout in history to save the financial system from collapse.

Although the global economy has recovered somewhat since 2008, the GFC has left countries saddled with anemic growth, high unemployment and substantially higher debt. And, because of their extraordinary and unprecedented stimulus measures, central banks have been left with a monumental problem of how to unwind the greatest financial experiment in history. So, how did the failure of one U.S. financial institution threaten to bring down the entire global financial system?

The answer to this question is both simple and complex. In simple terms, the GFC was just another in a long line of financial booms and busts that has plagued society since money was invented. It was triggered by a period of excessive optimism which encouraged borrowers to borrow too much, lenders to lend too much, and policy-makers to turn a blind eye to blatant flaws in financial governance. In this instance, the poison was real estate, but it could well have been any other asset class such as shares in technology, mining or energy companies.

The more complex answer has its origins in the 1990s when President Clinton enacted a suite of measures which undermined governance in the finance industry. This included measures to repeal the Glass-Steagall Act, a cornerstone of Depression-era regulation, exempting 'credit default swaps' (CDSs) from regulation, and loosening housing rules by rewriting the Community Reinvestment Act, which put added pressure on banks to lend in low-income neighbourhoods.[7]

The creation of a financial bubble was also encouraged by prominent mainstream economists such as Paul Krugman who in 2002 suggested:

'To fight this recession [the aftermath of 2000 dot-com bubble], the Fed needs more than a snapshot; it needs soaring household spending to offset moribund business investment. And to do that...Alan Greenspan needs to create a housing bubble to replace the Nasdaq.'[8]

Well, we know how that ended. A financial collapse and millions unemployed. But hey, the elite were bailed out, so that is all that matters.

Moreover, despite his sage advice that the way to kickstart an economy is to create an asset bubble – with all the attendent risks that a financial crisis will inevitably arise – Krugman got a Nobel Prize in Economics, is still employed and is still influential amongst the elite. Go figure, but that's how the world works.

In the aftermath of the dot-com bubble, banks began to expand lending, this time targeting real estate. The bubble began when mortgage brokers started issuing loans to families, often with low credit scores, on terms that were often unfavourable to borrowers. Some of these so-called subprime mortgages carried low 'teaser' interest rates in the early years that ballooned to double-digit rates in later years. Some also included prepayment penalties that made it prohibitively expensive to refinance the loans.[9]

Mortgage originators typically didn't hold onto these loans, but instead sold them onto banks or the government-sponsored enterprises, Freddie Mac and Fannie Mae, whose role was to expand the secondary mortgage market by securitising mortgages in the form of 'mortgage-backed securities' (MBSs). This allowed banks to expand lending far beyond what they could have otherwise done if they had been required to hold the loans on their own books. In turn, Freddie Mac and Fannie Mae onsold the mortgages to investment banks, which would bundle them with hundreds or thousands of other mortgages into a MBS that provided an income stream comprising the sum of all the monthly mortgage payments. The security would then be sliced into perhaps 1,000 smaller pieces that would be on-sold to investors, often with a AAA rating.

Insurance companies also got into the act by trading in CDSs. What initially began as insurance quickly turned into speculation as financial institutions bought and sold CDSs on assets that they didn't even own. From 2001 to 2008, the amount of credit insured by these derivatives soared from around $900 billion to an astonishing $62 trillion,[10] more than four times the size of the U.S. economy. All of these actions led to a massive increase in the money supply, which in turn fuelled the asset boom.

By 2006, however, the housing market had entered a mild slump, forcing some people into foreclosure and others into arrears. By 2008, the slump in housing prices had turned into a free fall. While the downturn had been orderly up until then, panic set in after financial services firm Lehman Brothers declared bankruptcy after being unable to find a buyer, and insurance giant AIG was unable to secure credit through normal channels. Faced with massive losses on CDSs, the U.S. central bank provided an $85 billion loan to AIG. When this proved insufficient, Treasury tipped in a further $38 billion in return for a near four-fifths stake in the company.[11]

With fear, panic and mistrust at extreme levels, the overnight inter-bank lending markets froze. The Fed responded by injecting liquidity into the financial markets and slashing short-term interest rates to a range of 0–0.25 per cent. When this failed to boost economic growth, the Fed injected money into the economy by embarking on an unconventional array of policy experiments including loan guarantees, and purchases of government securities. By December 2008, it had injected more than $1 trillion into the financial system and promised to do much more.[12]

In addition to the $1 trillion that the Fed disclosed, it has been claimed that in the lead-up to the financial crisis, it made commitments of up to $7.77 trillion in undisclosed loans to struggling banks and financial institutions. According to reports, the loans came with virtually no strings attached. In one month, Morgan Stanley – one of the most vulnerable financial companies at the time – took $107 billion in secret loans, enough to pay off a tenth of the nation's delinquent mortgages. The loans, like those made to other institutions, were never reported to Morgan Stanley's shareholders nor to the taxpayers who subsidised them.[13]

The U.S. Treasury, under the control of Hank Paulson, former head of investment bank Goldman Sachs, also chipped in with the $700 billion Troubled Asset Relief Fund (TARP). TARP was originally designed to buy illiquid MBSs and other assets from key institutions and to inject funds directly into banks that held the toxic securities. It was subsequently extended to include loans to bail out other organisations such as the big three American automakers. By the end of 2008, the government owned stock in 206 banks.[14]

The GFC hit the real economy and stock markets hard. U.S. GDP fell by over 2 per cent while the Dow Jones Industrial Average (DJIA) fell by more than 50 per cent. Unemployment soared as workers were laid off, further exacerbating the downturn. While no industry was spared, those industries such as financial services and real estate that had benefited the most during the boom were especially hard hit. While the recession officially ended in June 2009, the ensuing recovery was one of the most anemic on record.

Interestingly, neither the central bank nor the government bailed out struggling householders. Just their mates who had lived high on the hog in the boom times, but now demanded protection when things went pear-shaped.

Although the GFC was 'Made in America', this didn't stop the crisis from spreading to other parts of the world. Governments across Europe were forced to prop up major financial institutions either by buying stakes in banks or providing loan guarantees. Stock markets collapsed, companies failed, and unemployment soared to double-digit figures as economies fell into recession. The slumping economy drew hundreds of thousands of protesters out onto the streets to protest the loss of jobs and the so-called austerity measures, as governments attempted to cut spending in the face of dwindling revenues. Of course, the alleged austerity measures were a chimera insofar that governments continued to run large budget deficits throughout the downturn. But in a welfare-dependent society with a strong sense of entitlement, any attempt to cut government services or raise taxes will be met with strong opposition.

So, what caused the worst financial crisis since the Great Depression?

Put simply, the GFC was a debt-fuelled bubble in real estate which drove asset prices to unsustainable levels. The resultant collapse in stock and housing prices was the economy's way of cleansing itself of malinvestments and excessive asset prices. More specifically, the housing boom had all the hallmarks of a typical mania driven by greed, arrogance, fraud and stupidity.

The use of low teaser rates allowed subprime borrowers to enter the market, and for borrowers to borrow more than they otherwise could. Speculation was also rife as people bought multiple houses with high debt and low deposits and engaged in 'flipping'. All of this helped drive up house prices across the nation. Mortgage originators and financial institutions also created massive amounts of credit by making loans, and then selling their loan books off to banks and GSEs.

Risk assessments went out the window as financial institutions chased market share and profits. In other instances, financial institutions knowingly committed fraud by slicing and dicing loans of dubious value, and then selling them off to other institutions who should have known better. Credit agencies also suffered extraordinary conflicts of interest by providing services to banks and companies that they were supposed to rate objectively. And to add insult to injury, central banks turned a blind eye to the looming crisis, wrapped up in their own importance, hubris and misguided policies.

Finally, in 2015, in somewhat of a mea culpa for the economics 'profession', prominent mainstream economist Joseph Stiglitz, announced the first Stiglitz Essay Prize.[15] The prize was open to any fulltime student and the essays were to focus on one of two broad themes: the causes and policy consequences of growing inequality; and the reconstruction of macroeconomics and proposals for new approaches that speak to the weaknesses in modelling revealed by the 2008 global crisis. In short, what Stiglitz was saying was: economists got it wrong, our models are not only flawed but our approach to modelling is flawed. I'm not quite sure that Stiglitz got any insightful responses that may actually improve mainstream economists' understanding of macroeconomics, but I suspect not.

Chapter 3

Economics: The Science That Isn't

'The purpose of studying economics is not to acquire a set of ready-made answers to economic questions, but to learn how to avoid being deceived by economists.'

Joan Robinson

Economics has long been regarded as the dismal science for good reason: it is. Not only is it dismal, but it is not a science. In science, we have the immutable laws of gravity, thermodynamics and planetary motion, amongst others.

So, what do we have in economics? Not one coherent and widely accepted theory of how an economy works over the business cycle. Worse still, economics is littered with the corpses of theories that have proven popular for a period, only to be jettisoned when put to the test of whether their descriptions of the real world work in practice. In short, mainstream economics, especially macroeconomics, is an assortment of disparate thought bubbles masquerading as a science. This should not be unexpected, however, given the complexity of local, national and global economies as well as the wide-ranging inter-relationships between economics and other disciplines such as finance, politics, religion, psychology and sociology.

In contrast, scientific method is at the core of any science. Scientific method has four steps: observe and describe the phenomena that needs explanation; develop a theory; design an experiment and predict the results; undertake the tests and measure the results against the hypothetical results. Scientific method then requires that the experiments are repeatable and verifiable by independent sources.

Economics fails on all counts.

The problem with economics is that there are plenty of theories. In fact, the field of economics is brimming with theories. Unfortunately, many of them are abstract concepts or opinions cloaked in a modicum of respectability. But economics breaks down after that inauspicious beginning, when such theories fail in practice. Worse still, people treat economic theories as proven facts rather than as theories. Economics has become the religion of the twentieth and twenty-first centuries, replete with their high priests, namely, central bankers and financial commentators. But just as Catholicism was shown to be full of falsehoods through the Scientific Revolution and the Enlightenment, so economics will also be exposed for the fraud that it is.

Plain and simple: economics is not suited to the laboratory nor to the rigours of scientific method. The very nature of the social sciences requires a different approach to studying how the physical world operates. In studying the physical world, scientists can test their hypotheses using controlled experiments in laboratory conditions. They can conduct experiments by holding some variables constant while allowing other variables to move, recording the results in minute detail to determine scientific outcomes with a degree of precision and confidence that can only be dreamt of in the social sciences.

In contrast, economic activity is impacted by the interaction of millions of variables, which can and do change over time. Because of the inability to study economics in the laboratory, economists are forced to study historical and statistical data to develop theories on how economies operate. From there, they must extrapolate what occurred historically and seek to integrate their hypotheses with the prevailing cultural, religious, social, political and technological factors – factors which invariably will have changed.

Simplification, abstraction and formulation of economic theories is also subject to limitations. Firstly, researchers are often swayed by their own value judgements and worldview. Take, for example, the conflict between Marxist economics and capitalism. Neither group can plausibly develop an economic theory or model of how an economy works without being swayed by their ideologies, many of which have more to do with politics and sociology than they do with economics.

Secondly, a theory is only as good as its ability to represent the real world and to accurately predict outcomes. And, as we know, economists have a woeful track record in predicting events. This is no better evidenced then the failure of most mainstream economists to predict the housing crisis and GFC.

Finally, economic theory has not been one constant throughout history. Rather, it has evolved in line with the prevailing economic, social, military, religious, technological and political conditions.

If economics was a science, then economists could establish the objectives and measurable outcomes for their policy initiatives, and the public could independently verify the success of such policies. For example, rather than suggesting broad economic measures such as running much larger deficits or reducing interest rates, proponents of these interventionist policies could state exactly the results they would achieve with different levels of stimulus and intervention using key economic measures such as GDP and unemployment. Without such precision, the broad generalisations about the effectiveness of their policy prescriptions are vacuous.

So, why is this discussion on economics and economic theory important?

Over the past four decades, economics and economists have played an ever-increasing role in government policy and social discourse. Prior to that, people rarely heard economists speaking on TV or radio. These days it's hard to avoid them and the continuous babble from talking heads. More importantly, central banks have now assumed a far more dominant role in global economies than was ever envisaged.

What this means is that economists have a far greater influence on our everyday lives than ever before. And personally, I find this most disconcerting given their woeful track record.

For example, the world has suffered a series of crises such as the GFC and the dot-com bubble brought on by central bank policies, while economic dogma has played a key role in the loss of millions of higher-paying jobs in western nations as their jobs have been exported to low-cost countries. Income and wealth inequality seems to have grown while the world has been saddled with extraordinary levels of debt and dangerous asset bubbles.

The problem for us common folk now suffering the fallout from economic and political mismanagement is that for many years economists, politicians and central bankers have peddled the lie that they understand what is going on, that they have their hands planted firmly on the economic levers, that they can control economic outcomes and, most importantly, that they are working for the good of ordinary people. Of course, none of this is true.

As we know, many people are driven by self-interest. And politicians' self-interest lies solely in getting elected and serving the people who fund their campaigns, while the elite just want power and wealth.

Economists are no different as they are beholden to their masters, typically the major institutions such as banks for whom they work, the government or the people who fund their research. In reality, many high-profile economists have been co-opted into becoming mouthpieces for the elite.

More disturbing, however, is that not only have these people and institutions created this unholy mess, but they are still in control of the economic levers as they seek to steer us out of the economic and social malaise of their making. Talk about the inmates being in charge of the asylum.

If some perceive that I am being too harsh on mainstream economists, let's consider some disturbing facts:

1. Why did such a tiny minority of economists predict the GFC in 2008?
2. Why were central banks and governments forced to undertake the largest bailout in history?
3. Why have economists not learnt anything from history about the causes of financial crises and how to prevent them from occurring?
4. Why has the rate of economic growth fallen over the past seven decades despite massive financial stimulus and record levels of debt?
5. How can anybody regard as fair, equitable or reasonable, the massive redistribution of wealth away from the lower and middle classes to the financial and political elites over the past 20–30 years? How could any politician with any sense of morality not only not rail against it but, more importantly, promote fiscal and monetary policies that support such outcomes?
6. Why are we on the brink of another global depression if economists, governments, banks and large institutions can control events at whim?

7. If governments can't control future events, then why do they portray that they can, or set up institutions such as central banks to do so?
8. How can we have any confidence in modern economic thought when economists can't agree on a common theoretical model for how an economy works?

In this chapter, I will take a quick journey through the evolution of economic development and economic thought through the ages. This will cover ancient times through to the Middle Ages, and the early modern era up through to the nineteenth century. It will include a summary of the key economic philosophies including feudalism and manorialism, mercantilism, and classical and neoclassical economics.

While brief, this will highlight how disparate the thinking on economics is, and has been through the ages. In particular, it will demonstrate how, with few exceptions, economic theory has been unable to explain how an economy functions. Sure, it will get certain elements right, but not the system as an integrated whole.

The chapter will also highlight that economic theory is often a product of the prevailing social, political, technological and economic environment within which people find themselves. Moreover, rather than leading economics in action, economic theory trails economic evolution as scholars seek to explain the evolving economic system. It will demonstrate how, over the centuries, popular economic theories have been proven wrong or redundant within a very short period of time. And, it will show how, as the ancient philosophers observed, economics cannot be divorced from other disciplines including politics, philosophy, science and social studies.

I will also use the discussion on neoclassical economics, from which key elements of modern macroeconomic theory are derived, to highlight some of the fundamental flaws in modern mainstream economic theory.

Because most current economic theories arose out of analysis of the Great Depression, I will leave the discussion on developments in economic thought in the twentieth century to Chapter 7.

Ancient Economic Thought

Economics is often traced back to Hebrew and Jewish times around 2500 BC. The philosophers of those times wrote about a range of economic concepts including the division of labour, money, interest, property, wealth, trade and taxes. The Old Testament, for example, includes passages which describe characteristics of modern capitalism and private property.

Ancient economic thought was inextricably linked to political and social customs, ethics, religion, philosophy and to the basic economic structure which was primarily based on agriculture, trade, defence and war. It was also dominated by the needs of the ruling emperors and their courts, with economic life being controlled by priests and rulers.

Leading Greek philosophers such as Plato and Aristotle also talked about economics. Their contribution was not so much in the form of a cohesive economic framework, but rather in terms of economic principles that formed part of a broader philosophical, political and social discourse on creating a better society.

Power and wealth were based on control over key resources such as land, gold, silver and access to cheap labour. Slavery was common place, and most families had one or more slaves.

Aristotle favoured private ownership of property and resources over public ownership as he believed private ownership better aligned with people's self-interest and would therefore lead to greater economic progress.

In contrast, he argued that goods owned in common will receive little attention, as people pursue self-interest and neglect communal work. He also believed that communal property would lead to continuing and intense conflict, since each will complain that they have worked harder and obtained less than others who have done little and taken more from the common store.[16] Aristotle's observations have certainly been borne out through experiences in socialist countries such as Venezuela, Stalin's Soviet Union and Mao's China.

Aristotle's contribution to philosophy, ethics and economics cannot be understated as his works were widely studied by Islamic and European scholars in the Middle Ages. His focus on simplicity and ethics was very different to today's focus on self, ego, material possessions and instant gratification.

The Middle Ages

The Middle Ages were a mixed bag in terms of economic development and economic thought, giving rise to scholasticism, feudalism and its bedfellow, manorialism.

The Early Middle Ages (500–1000 AD) was characterised by population decline, decentralisation, invasion, large-scale immigration and the mass movement of peoples following the collapse of the Roman Empire. This prompted many people to seek security and shelter under the economic and military protection of lords and nobles.

Feudalism was a contract freely entered into between the lord and the vassal, which imposed mutual obligations on both parties. In return for the lord granting the fief (a parcel of land), the vassal agreed to provide military service on behalf of the lord, as well as general counsel. While many peasant workers resented being unfree, they were left with the difficult choice of either freedom but no access to land, or servitude. Most chose servitude.

Feudalism reached its peak in Europe during the thirteenth century. After this period, subinfeudation – subletting a part of the land to sub-tenants – meant that lords found it increasingly difficult to obtain the services they needed. In addition, vassals preferred to provide money rather than military service, while lords preferred to use the money to employ more professional troops. Many lords also found that the productivity of tied labour was significantly lower than that of free labour employed to do the same task.

Manorialism differed from feudalism in that it was an economic, rather than political and military, system. In effect, manorialism was a barter system where villagers traded their labour for food, shelter and security. The serfs held land from their lord, who could be a king, duke, bishop, abbot or lessor noble. In return, they paid dues in kind, service or money. Unlike fief holders, the serfs were not obliged to provide military assistance to their lord. On the contrary, it was the lord who provided military protection to his serfs.[17]

Karl Marx was particularly critical of feudalism. For Marx, what defined feudalism was that the power of the ruling class (the aristocracy) rested on their control of arable land, leading to a class society based upon the exploitation of the peasants who farm these lands, typically under serfdom.[18]

In some ways, Marx was correct. It was exploitation of the working class by the elite. But this was not a new phenomenon. Exploitation of the masses had been a feature of life since ancient times. Moreover, given the rural nature of the economy, ownership of land bestowed great wealth and power onto the aristocrats.

On the other hand, given the chaotic and often violent times, feudalism and manorialism provided the common people with security and stability as well as the opportunity to make a living. While there was no upward mobility, in such turbulent times, perhaps this wasn't a high priority for our forebears.

During the High Middle Ages (1000–1250 AD), the population of Europe increased greatly as technological and agricultural innovations allowed trade to flourish and the Medieval Warm Period increased crop yields. Improved security and stability led to a revival of trade and commerce, while the rise of larger towns and cities contributed to the gradual demise of manorialism throughout most parts of western Europe. Manorialism continued to exist in other parts of the world, particularly in large parts of Russia and Eastern Europe, until the nineteenth century.

The Late Medieval period (1250–1500 AD) represented a return to the bad old days, as Europe was ravaged by famine, plague, social unrest and war. Between 1347 and 1350, the Black Death killed around a third of Europeans. Controversy, heresy and the Western Schism within the Catholic Church added to the chaos, as civil strife and peasant revolts swept the kingdoms.[19]

The Early Modern Era

The early modern era was one of the most dynamic periods in mankind's brief history. Nestled between the Middle Ages and the Modern Era, it was a period of great change and transformation. It was a period when people in the west started to question authority, to seek answers beyond the constraints of religion and monarchical authority, and modern thinkers reached out to the ancient Greek philosophers to search for meaning. It was a time when courageous seafarers explored the world in search of adventure and riches, and where the old world discovered the new world. It was also a period where, for the first time, people started to see the world as it is, its existence in a broader cosmos, rather than through some ignorant, restricted religious worldview.

It was a period which included some of the most extraordinary events in history: the Age of Discovery, the Age of Colonisation, the Golden Age of Piracy, the Reformation, the Religious Wars, the Renaissance, the Scientific Revolution and the Commercial Revolution. It was a period where economic life moved beyond the farm-gate to encompass global economic trade, and where there was a major shift in population and influence from the farms to the cities.

It was also a period of great contrast, where some areas in the western sphere started their move towards democracy, while others remained mired in autocracy. It also ushered in the beginnings of modern-day nation states. It was a period where Spain and Portugal gave up their pre-eminence to emerging powers such as Holland, France, England and Russia. In other spheres, the Ottoman and Far Eastern empires continued their dominance over their domains.

The changing economic circumstances gave rise to innovation, including improvements to banking and commercial practices, and new economic theories. Despite progress, governments continued to spend up big on mindless, narcissistic pursuits such as war and excessive consumption. This over-expenditure of course led to the inevitable cycle of inflation, recession and default, a cycle that continues to this day.

And finally, the early modern era set the world up for the Modern Era.

Economic development during this period is probably best described by the term the Great Divergence – a period when the western world overcame pre-modern growth constraints to become the most powerful and wealthiest civilisation of the time, eclipsing Qing China, Mughal India, Tokugawa Japan, and the Ottoman Empire.[20] In Europe, it also ushered in the Little Divergence, a period where the British and Dutch economies outstripped growth in other areas of Europe.

Many factors contributed to this growth including positive social mood, an outbreak of peace following the end of the Eighty Years' War, growth in European trade, the existence of a motivated and skilled workforce, a more open and tolerant society unhindered by the rigidity of religion and class structure, social mobility, a strong merchant class, a rising and affluent middle class, an extensive and reliable transport network, cheap energy, political stability, a favourable regulatory environment, innovation in agriculture, industry and commerce, advances in science and technology and, finally, a supportive and increasingly sophisticated financial system.

Two schools of thought dominated economic thought at the time: mercantilism and physiocracy.

Mercantilism was the prevailing economic system in Europe from the sixteenth to the eighteenth century before it was eventually replaced by policies that favoured freer trade. It was never one coherent theory, but rather a series of principles that developed over time to support government policy in areas relating to trade, government regulations, taxes, tariffs and international relations. It is the antithesis of free trade.

Mercantilism is an economic system where governments impose strict controls on crucial parts of the nation's economy to increase the nation's wealth and enhance military security. It is a beggar-thy-neighbour policy aimed at benefiting your own country at the expense of other nations.

Mercantilists viewed the economy as a 'zero-sum' game, which made it impossible to maximise the common good (on a global scale). It assumes that the wealth of a nation depends primarily on the accumulation of treasure in the form of precious metals, such as gold and silver. They also believed that world trade was fixed. Therefore, the only way to increase wealth was to take it from another country.[21] As a result, economic policies were directed towards increasing exports and reducing imports.

This assumption was rational for that period because with little money in circulation, gold and silver acted as both a medium of exchange and a store of wealth. As such, the more gold and silver a country could accumulate through trade, the more it would enrich the merchants and government. Conversely, a drain of gold and silver directly weakened a nation's economy and the government's ability to wage war. Mercantilism was a practical and successful economic approach because western nations were in a perpetual state of war and therefore it seems natural that they would seek to leverage economic advantage as part of their armoury over their enemies. In fact, it would seem strange that they would do otherwise.

Mercantilism was also a key driver of colonial expansion as European nations scrambled to secure new territories, both as a source of raw materials and to provide markets for manufactured goods. Unfortunately, this meant that the colonial masters treated indigenous populations in many instances in a cruel and inhumane manner.

Mercantilism is especially important in a modern-day context, as it underpinned the export-led growth strategies of both China and Japan in the late twentieth century. We will cover this in far greater detail in later chapters.

Josiah Child (1630–1699)

Josiah Child was an English merchant, economist, a proponent of mercantilism and governor of the East India Company. His theory on interest rates is a good example of how people can so easily draw the wrong conclusions about economics based on faulty analysis of cause and effect. This has been a regular feature of economics throughout the ages and exists to this day.

The debate about the link between interest rates and economic prosperity raised its ugly head as far back as the late seventeenth century. Child observed that interest rates were much lower in Holland, their arch economic rivals at the time, than in England. English merchants incorrectly jumped to the conclusion that low interest rates were the cause of Dutch prosperity, and therefore it was the role of the British Government to force the maximum rate of interest down until interest rates were lower than in Holland.[22]

Child suggested lower interest rates as 'virtually a panacea for all economic ills. A lower rate would vivify trade and raise the price of land; it would even cure drunkenness.'[23]

Child's critics attacked his arguments on two fronts. Firstly, they pointed out that low interest rates are the consequence of wealth, not the cause of it. As Edward Waller noted during the House of Commons debate: 'It is with money as it is with other commodities, when they are most plentiful then they are cheapest, so make money [savings] plentiful and the interest will be low.'[24]

Others also pointed out that the Dutch had been able to achieve lower interest rates through market forces rather than through statute. Child countered with a rather lame and baseless retort that if market forces hadn't driven interest rates lower, then they would have done so by statute.

Such a debate about the desirability of low interest rates would become a lightning rod for debate and the goal of central banks more than 300 years after Child's death.

The study of physiocracy illustrates not only how economic theorists can conflate economics with other fields such as politics and sociology, but how quickly such theories can fall in and out of favour. Of course, this is not to say that the theory doesn't have some positive aspects, but it does mean that overall it is flawed.

Physiocracy developed in eighteenth-century France. Physiocrats believed that the wealth of nations derived from productive work, and especially labour associated with agriculture and land development. The movement was built largely around the work of Francois Quesnay, King Louis XV's physician, and Anne-Robert-Jacques Turgot, an economist and politician. It developed at a time when agriculture represented 80 per cent of the country's wealth, wealth inequality was at extreme levels, French agriculture was mired in Medieval regulations, key public infrastructure was in a pitiful condition and merchant guilds exercised monopolist powers.

Physiocrats believed that economies were driven by self-interest where each individual was best suited to determine what goods he wanted. They favoured a laissez-faire approach which called for the removal of restrictions on internal trade and labour mobility, and the removal of state-sponsored monopolies and the guild system. They also recognised the importance of capital in production as well as the need for strong legal support to secure individual property rights.

Despite being accurate in the above assessment, physiocracy was deeply flawed in other ways. For example, its proponents argued that manufacturing added no net wealth to an economy as the level of inputs used to produce goods resulted in the same level of outputs, so there was no net gain. Their focus on productive versus unproductive work also took on a political flavour and grew out of their immense dislike of the waste and idleness of the nobility, aristocracy and church leaders. Physiocrats used their ideas as a veiled attack on the upper classes.

Finally, physiocrats confused economics with ideology, where they envisaged a society in which natural economic and moral laws would have full play and where economics would be in harmony with natural law. They also pictured a predominantly agricultural society and therefore attacked mercantilism not only for its mass of economic regulations but also for its emphasis on manufacturing and foreign trade.[25]

Like many other economic schools, physiocracy was quickly discredited as having little enduring value and represented just another in a long line of short-lived thought bubbles that is the 'science' of economics.

Nineteenth-century Economics

The nineteenth century was a period of extraordinary social and economic development, boosted by major advances brought about through the Industrial Revolution. As a result, the global economy almost tripled in size between 1820 and 1900, and GDP per capita doubled.

Growth in the west continued to outstrip growth in other regions, with western Europe and North America contributing 65 per cent of total global growth. The U.S. showed the most spectacular development, with her economy growing twenty-five-fold, while Europe's economy quadrupled.[26] In contrast, China's economy went backwards due to political instability, social unrest, famine and colonisation.

The changing nature of economic activity necessitated advances in economic theory, which was dominated by classical and neo-classical economics. Marxism was also developed at this time.

Classical economics was an English school of thought which originated during the late eighteenth century and focused on economic growth and free markets. Its key proponents included Adam Smith, David Ricardo, Thomas Malthus, David Hume and John Stuart Mill. It dominated western economic thinking until around 1870 when it was replaced by neo-classical economics.

Much of their work looked at the way markets and market economies work. Coming at a time when mercantilism held sway, they believed an economy was best able to maintain equilibrium through market forces, while government intervention, in the form of artificial tariffs or other barriers that disrupted the free flow of goods and services, was harmful to the economy.[27]

They criticised special interest groups who seek to use political power to coerce the authorities into favouring their members at the expense of the wider community. They also believed in small government, and that government should not interfere in the economy.

Richard Cantillon (1680–1734)

Richard Cantillon was one of the more influential thinkers on classical economics and is perhaps one of the most insightful economists of all time. While he lived before the development of classical economics, his contribution to the school is important because of the impact his writings had on other economists including Adam Smith and Jean-Baptiste Say.[28]

Cantillon was one of the first to acknowledge the vital role that entrepreneurs play in economic development. He argued that any profits they earn, even outsized profits, are fully justified given the uncertainty and risks they take.

He was also one of the earliest thinkers on the causes and perils of inflation. Cantillon accurately determined that increases in the money supply lead to inflation, and that inflation benefits those closest to the initial source of the increase in the money supply. However, increases in the money supply will not impact the prices of all goods at the same rate, but rather at differing rates. He also argued that when the elite debase money or issue imaginary money, this hurts the economy, and that war increases interest rates due to increased expenditure, while peace reduces interest rates.

Cantillon also attacked the role of central banks, including the Bank of London and the Bank of Venice, for the practice of inflating the money supply to reduce interest rates, opining that any increase in stock prices associated with the reduction in interest rates will end badly, as stock prices decline.

What Cantillon was doing was forecasting the carnage that central banks would bestow on unsuspecting citizens in the twentieth and early twenty-first centuries. And he was in a privileged position to comment having lived through, and profited greatly from, one of the largest financial calamities of the early modern era – John Law's 1720 Mississippi Bubble in Louisiana.

Cantillon was also the first to show in detail how an economy works. He demonstrated how all parts of the market economy fit together in a natural, self-regulating, equilibrating pattern with existing supply and demand determining prices and wages, and ultimately the pattern of production. Consumer values determine demand, with population adjusting to cultural and economic factors. The equilibrators of the economy are the entrepreneurs who adjust to, and cope with, the all-pervasive uncertainty of the market. He also extended his model to international trade.

Finally, Cantillon provided a description of why skilled workers earn more than unskilled workers; how the supply of workers adjusts to the demand for labour across all professions via wages rates, migration and changes in population; and why prosperity cannot be created by subsidising job training, but rather is created by market forces.

In many ways, Cantillon's contribution to economic thought is equal to, if not greater than, that of Adam Smith. He had real world experience of the ravages of speculation, even if he did profit from such excess. He fully understood the economic and financial carnage that arises from speculation driven by excess money supply. Cantillon laid out economic principles that support a better standard of living, including a focus on savings and productive investment and the role of the entrepreneur in economic growth, and he represented complex economic systems in simple economic models, thus making it easier for the common folk to better understand complex and yet important concepts.

Finally, he fully understood the extraordinary damage that governments and national/central banks can unleash on their citizens because of excess spending on wars and lavish projects, and through manipulation of the money supply.

As the name implies, neoclassical economics evolved from classical economics. Neoclassical economists believe that a consumer's primary concern is to maximise personal satisfaction, and that everyone makes decisions based on fully informed evaluations of utility.[29] Further, neoclassical economics stipulates that a good or service often has value that goes above and beyond its input costs. For example, while classical economics believes that a product's value is derived from the cost of materials and labour, neoclassical practitioners say that consumers have a perceived value of a product that affects its price and demand. Finally, this economic theory states that competition leads to an efficient allocation of resources within an economy. This resource allocation establishes market equilibrium between supply and demand.

According to E. Roy Weintraub, neoclassical economics rests on three assumptions from which neoclassical economists have built a structure to understand the allocation of scarce resources to meet alternative ends. These are that people have rational preferences between outcomes that can be identified and associated with values; that individuals maximise utility and firms maximise profits; and that people act independently based on full and relevant information.[30]

Neoclassical economics dominates microeconomics and, together with Keynesian economics, forms the neoclassical synthesis which dominates mainstream economics today.[31] The neoclassical synthesis was a post-World War II academic movement in economics that worked towards absorbing the macroeconomic thought of John Maynard Keynes into neo-classical economics.[32]

The resultant macroeconomic theories and models are termed neo-Keynesian economics. Mainstream economics is largely dominated by this synthesis, being largely Keynesian in macroeconomics and neoclassical in microeconomics.[33]

Because there is not complete agreement on what is meant by neoclassical economics, the result has been a wide range of neoclassical approaches to various problem areas and domains – ranging from neoclassical theories of labour to neoclassical theories of demographic change.

Neoclassical economics and its modern derivatives have come in for a lot of criticism over the years – rightfully so in my opinion. In fact, not enough. Because, it is these criticisms that strike at the very heart of the problems with modern mainstream economics.

Firstly, neoclassical economics has been criticised for having a normative bias; that is, it does not focus on explaining actual economies but rather on describing a 'utopia' in which Pareto optimality applies.[34] In other words, its proponents are academics who are cloistered in some academic bubble and divorced from reality. Moreover, normative economics talks about economic fairness, or what the outcome of the economy or goals of public policy ought to be.[35]

But fairness to whom? The supplier, the customer, the land-lord, the employer, the employee, the government, or the shareholder? Each is a stakeholder and I am sure each of them would like to see a fair outcome – but with fairness slanted heavily towards themselves rather than others. Besides, the idea of fairness belongs to politics and social policy, not economics.

Another problem of neoclassical economics is that their models are simplistic and oftentimes don't work. Mainstream economists have developed the aggregate demand/aggregate supply (AD/AS) model (Figure 2) to seek to explain the price level and output through the relationship of aggregate demand and aggregate supply in an economy. The AD/AS model is used to illustrate the Keynesian model of the business cycle, and is also used to help estimate the output gap.

Movements of the two curves are used to predict the effects that various exogenous (external) events will have on two variables: real output and the price level.[36] The AD/AS model is one of the most widely used macroeconomic models in the development of both monetary and economic policy, and is often used in conjunction with other economic models.

Figure 2 Aggregate Demand/Aggregate Supply Graph

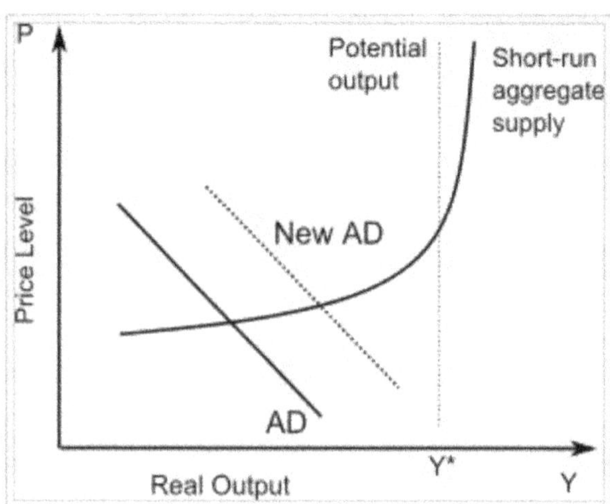

Amazing, isn't it. All the complexities of a modern economy, all the hopes, wishes and aspirations of humanity, all the efforts of millions of farmers, manufacturers, workers, small business owners and everyday people, all depicted in a couple of lines on a two-dimensional graph. It would be scary if it wasn't so serious.

This is not to say that the AD/AS model doesn't have some value, particularly when analysing the dynamics of a specific product or market. It's just that, given economies comprise millions of variables, it loses usefulness at the aggregate, macro-economic level.

Another problem is that neoclassical economics seeks to manage what economists call the output gap – the amount by which actual economic output falls short of its estimated economic potential. Typically, during a recession, actual economic output drops below its potential, which creates a negative output gap. The reverse is true during periods of strong economic growth.

Not surprisingly, use of the AD/AS model and the output gap as policy tools have major limitations. Firstly, according to one of the world's leading mainstream economic bodies, the International Monetary Fund (IMF), 'measuring the output gap is no easy task. Unlike actual output, the level of potential output and, hence, the output gap cannot be observed directly. Potential output and the output gap can only be estimated.'[37]

If the IMF thinks it's difficult, and that its estimates are guesses, then why would filling that gap form one of the primary goals of mainstream economics? It's like shooting at a target in a dark room.

A more fundamental problem, however, is that politicians and policy-makers seek to boost economic growth, and thus reduce the estimated output gap, through policy actions such as low interest rates or increased government expenditure, without fully understanding what is causing the output gap or the ramifications of such meddling. For example, are the problems cyclical, or do they represent long-term structural changes in the economy?

Moreover, constant interference in the economy creates distortions as markets are unable to self-regulate and thus make the necessary adjustments to stabilise the economic system. There is no better example of this than recent actions by central banks to force interest rates lower. Such actions are directly responsible for the massive run-up in asset prices and the concomitant build-up in debt, which will ultimately implode under its own weight. And yet, as we shall see later, it did little to spur growth in the real economy. Despite the obvious limitations of the AD/AS model, this hasn't stopped mainstream economists adopting it as a core macroeconomic tool.

Another problem with neoclassical/Keynesian economics is that it relies heavily on complex mathematical models, such as those used in general equilibrium theory, without sufficient regard to whether these models actually describe the real economy, and whether they work.

Let me make a very bold statement. Given the millions of variables in a modern economy ***nobody***, ***repeat nobody,*** can develop and maintain accurate and dynamic models of a modern economic system. To do so requires perfect knowledge of not only how the economic system works, but also identification and weighting of the different economic variables. It also requires that the structure of an economy remains relatively constant over time.

Of course, this is nonsensical. For example, how do you factor into these models the impact of droughts, floods, famine, wars, revolutions, technological disruption, demographic changes, trade wars, changes in exchange rates, major geo-political events, new legislation, movements in interest rates and financial manias. And even if one could hypothetically develop such a model, the variables and weightings would undoubtedly have changed by the time the model was complete. Mainstream economists acknowledge such failings and seek to get around these modelling problems by simplification – simplifying the economy through aggregation – and by making assumptions.

This creates further problems. Oversimplification means that such models fail to reflect systemic changes that are occurring in the economy. Conversely, too much detail renders them unworkable. In addition, many of the assumptions economists make are simply not valid. For example, people are not always rational, particularly when it comes to financial matters. Otherwise, the world would never experience booms and busts. People's mood changes from minute to minute, day to day, week to week and year to year. Some days they are rational, but at other times they act impulsively and irrationally. If people always acted rationally, you wouldn't have impulse purchases, or people incurring excessive debt. Equally, economists suggest that people act independently based on full and relevant information. How can everybody have access to relevant information always, and even if they did, would they use it? It seems unlikely.

It is little wonder then, that economists get their forecasts wrong, particularly at major economic turning points. But it does beg the question. Why do mainstream economists and policy-makers place so much emphasis on theories and tools that just don't work? Equally, why do mainstream economists arrogantly seek to denigrate other economic schools of thought, for example the Austrian School, which eschew the use of models because these models don't work? Finally, why should anybody take any notice of what mainstream economists say when their underlying theories are so demonstrably flawed? I will cover a range of other flaws in mainstream economic theory and practice later in the book.

As we conclude this chapter, I would like to make several other comments in relation to economics and economists. My criticism is directed primarily towards mainstream economics, particularly proponents of monetarism and Keynesianism/neo-Keynesianism, rather than all economic schools of thought. Austrian school economists, amongst others, have a good track record in predicting economic events and describing how an economy functions.

Mainstream economists have an over-reliance on non-dynamic mathematical models. As a result, they tend to fall into the trap of extrapolating past trends rather than allowing for black swan events, the underlying conditions of which can take years or decades to develop. Although they occur periodically, the exact timing of such events are difficult to predict and yet when they occur, they can wreak havoc on the economy and financial systems. Mainstream economics also fails to look at the interactions between the financial system, asset markets and the real economy. I will also cover this in a lot more detail in later chapters.

I am also more critical of macroeconomics than microeconomics. With macroeconomics, economists study an economy at the macro, or aggregated, level. The problem with too much aggregation, as noted earlier, is that it tends to mask underlying structural changes in an economy, changes which can have major impacts on future economic events. Equally, there are often a multitude of factors affecting the overall economy, factors such as social mood, politics, demographics and technology. As a result, it is often very difficult to determine what impact these factors will have on economic outcomes. In contrast, microeconomics focuses on the behaviour of individuals and firms or on specific industries or products. As a result, economists can undertake far more granular analysis of the factors impacting events at the micro level.

Finally, despite my trenchant criticism of mainstream economics, this brief analysis has also highlighted key features underpinning successful economies: features such as free markets, entrepreneurialism, thrift and private property. Hopefully, after the impending great depression, policy-makers will ignore the prognostications of mainstream economists and move to policies that we know will work.

Part 2
The Development of Modern Economics

Part 2 acts as a segue between economic thought through the ages and economics in the modern era. It also seeks to re-enforce many of the key themes of the book.

These themes are that, firstly, mainstream macroeconomics is not a science, but rather a set of disparate, unproven theories that lag behind developments in the real economy while failing to take heed of the lessons of the past.

Secondly, it looks at the economic damage that runaway inflation and profligate bank lending can do to an economy once the music stops and boom turns to bust.

Thirdly, the book contrasts different approaches to dealing with financial crises. In particular, I highlight the benefits of allowing an economy to adjust to economic shocks on its own, without government intervention. I also demonstrate how government interference and meddling not only prolonged the Great Depression but increased the severity of the depression.

A final theme is to highlight the damage that flawed analysis of the Great Depression by John Maynard Keynes and Milton Friedman has had on mainstream economic theory and subsequent policy prescriptions. Their theories have perpetuated the grand delusion that a select group of self-appointed experts have the knowledge and wisdom to control a natural system as complex as a modern economy, and that we can create massive distortions in an economy without suffering any consequences. It doesn't happen in any other area of life, and it certainly doesn't happen in economics either.

Chapter 4

Creation of the U.S. Federal Reserve

'The role of central banks is to solve problems they create.'

Phil Williams

The nineteenth and early twentieth centuries were a period of extraordinary economic growth and development for the U.S., the likes of which the world has rarely seen. During this time, the U.S. economy expanded twenty-five-fold,[38] the population increased fourteen-fold,[39] while the amount of territory under U.S. control grew from just 13 colonies at the time of independence to 45 states and numerous territories by 1900.[40]

By the end of the nineteenth century, America had surpassed Great Britain as the largest economy in the world, transforming herself from an agriculturally based economy to a mixed economy with a strong manufacturing and services sector. By the beginning of the twentieth century, U.S. per capita income and industrial production were double that of France and Germany, and 50 per cent higher than Britain.[41]

Economic growth was fuelled by many factors including investment in transport infrastructure, especially railroads; innovation and advances in science and technology; migration and strong population growth; advances in skills and education; improved telecommunications; growth in manufacturing; increased trade; urbanisation; growth of the middle class; the development of the large corporation; and the introduction of modern management techniques. The government sector also contributed to economic growth by remaining only a small component of the overall economy, thus putting little burden on the job-creating private sector.

Deflation also played an important part in fuelling economic growth as falling prices, underpinned by infrastructure development and new technology, significantly increased America's competitiveness by increasing efficiency and reducing its overall cost structure. This in turn led to increased demand as products became more affordable to both local and overseas consumers.

Increasing industrialisation also meant that despite a growing labour force, between 1860 to 1890, real wages grew 60 per cent.[42] This demonstrated that with the right conditions, for example strong capital formation and strong productivity growth, the economy, profits, wealth and real wages can all rise together to the benefit of society.

But not everybody prospered. It is estimated that by 1904 for example, one in three people living in cities was close to starving to death.[43] Many worked for subsistence wages and lived in overcrowded, squalid accommodation with poor sanitation, few services and even fewer opportunities to escape the city slums. In contrast, in 1900, the wealthiest 2 per cent of American households owned more than a third of the nation's wealth, while the top 10 per cent owned roughly three-quarters of total wealth.[44]

Despite this stellar growth, during the nineteenth century the U.S economy suffered a series of financial panics and economic depressions. As the real economy and the financial and banking systems began to expand and diversify, the interacting systems became far more complex than anybody could ever hope to understand let alone control. As a result, they became prone to failure and re-adjustment. During this time, the U.S. experienced the Panic of 1819, the Depression of 1839–1843, the Panic of 1873, the Depression of 1893 and the Panic of 1907. While many factors contributed to these downturns, excessive bank lending and speculation proved to be a leading cause of all these financial panics.

Understanding the causes of these crises is important because it was the Panic of 1907 that proved pivotal in the creation of the U.S. Federal Reserve (the Fed) in 1913, undoubtedly the greatest policy failure in U.S. economic history.

In this chapter, I will provide an outline of these panics, with a more detailed overview of the Panic of 1873, the Depression of 1893 and the Panic of 1907, before presenting the curious circumstances surrounding the creation of the Fed.

As we work through this chapter and the remainder of the book, I would ask readers to keep in mind three simple questions. Firstly, why should the banking system be protected from the vagaries of the free enterprise system when companies in non-politically connected industries are allowed to fail? If the answer to this question is that the financial system is too important to fail, then surely, wouldn't it be better to tightly regulate it to ensure it doesn't fail.

Secondly, why should banks that are managed by ethical, honest and prudent managers be forced to compete with and support more reckless operators, who are then bailed out when things go wrong? And finally, how can anybody in a capitalist system support the socialisation of losses onto the taxpayer, while allowing the banking elite to amass fortunes during the good years?

Perhaps the answer to these questions lies in the huge costs of funding wars, political campaigns and running budget deficits to assuage the voting masses. Without the presence of inflation and the ability to create money out of thin air, the political and banking elite would be unable to finance wars, project power and amass fortunes.

Just as banks profit by being able to control the money supply, this is just the price the politicians pay for access to cheap and plentiful funds. This is what a fractional reserve system does. This would not be possible under a hard currency regime as politicians would have to raise taxes to fund wars. And that is far harder than being able to create money out of nothing.

The Panic of 1819 was the first major financial downturn, in peacetime, that America experienced in its short life as an independent nation. While the downturn was triggered by both domestic and international factors, the Panic of 1819 was primarily a financial crisis brought on by lax banking standards, an incompetent central bank – America had one briefly in the early nineteenth century – fraud, and land speculation fuelled by excessive bank lending. This, in turn, led to excessive growth in the money supply, wildly inflated asset prices and a dangerous build-up of debt. Problems in the financial sector were exacerbated by adjustments in the real economy as America and Britain began to adjust to the end of the War of 1812 and Europe started to adjust to the end of the decade-long Napoleonic wars.

Because of the panic and subsequent economic collapse, rural land values fell between 50 and 75 per cent,[45] wiping out thousands of farmers, hundreds of banks and businesses, and increasing unemployment.

While policy-makers passed legislation to ameliorate the worst effects of the downturn on landholders, overall they adopted a hands-off approach to letting the financial system purge itself of its excesses. The legislators of the time understood what modern-day economists and legislators clearly don't. That is, for free markets to work, they must be free to operate, free of intervention from meddling politicians and central bankers, and free to fall when prices get out of line with their true economic value.

America's forefathers had great trust in the people to know what was morally right, far greater than the unprincipled sycophants who masquerade as politicians and bureaucrats today. As a Virginian Congressman wrote in 1820: 'Let the people manage their own affairs...the people of this country understand their own interests and will pursue them to advantage'.[46] Importantly, once the financial system and economy had been cleansed of distortions, economic growth resumed, but from a far sounder base.

The Panic of 1837 was also caused by both domestic and international factors, with the key factors being unsafe and imprudent bank lending, which in turn led to a massive 253 per cent increase in the money supply in just seven years;[47] rampant speculation in real estate, especially in the southern and western regions; and a rapid escalation in state debt, which increased from a modest $26 million in 1830 to $170 million in 1839.[48]

This triggered a spike in inflation, with wholesale prices rising 52 per cent, or almost 19 per cent per annum from 1834 to early 1837,[49] as well as a spike in asset prices. The panic triggered a run on banks as people lost confidence and withdrew their savings. This created a vicious cycle as banks cut back lending and foreclosed on mortgages which in turn led to business failures and increasing unemployment. The resultant crisis triggered a series of rolling recessions and tentative recoveries which lasted until 1843 when sustained growth eventually resumed.

The Panic of 1873 was a financial crisis that triggered an economic downturn in both Europe and America. Like the panics before it, the Panic of 1873 was caused by a combination of international and domestic factors, which included post-Civil War inflation; aggressive and imprudent bank lending, which fuelled widespread speculation, especially in railroads; fraud; and rampant stock market speculation. Due to increased bank lending, the money supply ballooned between 1865 to 1873, growing by a total of 135 per cent, or 16.9 per cent per annum.[50] Unfortunately, this lending boom masked structural weaknesses in the economy.

Most of the investment in railways was funded by debt rather than by a mixture of debt and shareholder funds. Moreover, many of the investments were based on wildly optimistic revenue and profit forecasts, unrealistic cost estimates, cronyism and just plain fraud. For example, Union Pacific – perhaps the worst of the worst – received government subsidies based on the number of miles of track laid. As a result, some lines were purportedly built with a zig-zag configuration just to add a few extra miles.[51] Of course, this lent itself to the third problem: intense lobbying (and corruption) of politicians at all levels of government in return for political favours to railway operators. As Matt Faherty so eloquently put it: 'Lobbying was so rampant that many Congressmen received nicknames based on their railroad of choice.'[52]

The crisis was triggered in September 1873 by the collapse of Jay Cooke & Company, a high-profile company owned by the quintessential insider, railway and banking magnate Jay Cooke. As investors, who had lost fortunes in railroad bonds, sought to withdraw their specie savings (that is, gold), these banks called on their specie deposits from other banks. This started a chain reaction which saw combined bank deposits fall between 1871 and 1873 by more than 20 per cent.[53] It also set off a series of bank failures, which closed the New York Stock Exchange for ten days.[54] The outflow of funds also pushed the reserve ratios for banks down below their mandated 25 per cent, before higher interest rates in the coming months attracted sufficient funds to restore the reserve ratios to more stable levels.[55]

The panic, however, also precipitated a classic free market response which quickly restored financial stability. Since the panic was based in the financial sector and Wall Street, most of the 'panicking' occurred in New York City. The clearing house organised a slush fund in which members could voluntarily deposit specie at interest, which could then be distributed to member banks which needed to keep their balances intact. This was a perfect example of a free market response to a crisis: a voluntary agreement between competitors, in which all banks act in their own self-interest to keep the system alive rather than allowing it to collapse and thereby drag everyone into the abyss.[56] Although 18,000 businesses failed between 1873 and 1875, unemployment peaked at a relatively modest 8.25 per cent.[57]

The movement of interest rates during the panic also provides a wonderful example of the efficacy of free markets in resolving economic problems. In response to the initial panic, between 1872 and October 1873 interest rates shot up from 6 to 9 per cent to 17 per cent.[58] Contrary to what many modern-day economists and central bankers may say, this proved extremely beneficial for the recovery and for the long run health of the financial system in that it attracted scarce resources back into the banking system to restore reserves and put a break on lending to what were clearly poor investments.

Indeed, it would have been poor economics and negligence had policy-makers stepped in to save companies that were poorly managed and had made bad investments. Far better to let these bad apples fall by the wayside and allow remaining funds to be redirected towards companies with competent management, or towards new enterprises, which can drive the next phase of growth. This, in fact, is the essence of capitalism and free enterprise.

Interestingly, the immediate response from some Republicans in Congress was to inflate the money supply. This resulted in the introduction of not less than sixty bills into both houses to increase the money supply by increasing the number of greenbacks in circulation. Fortunately, cooler heads prevailed and 59 of these bills were defeated by the Democrats and their hard money supporters in Congress.[59]

Full kudos must go to President Grant for opposing the monetary lunacy, despite the immediacy of the panic and economic fallout. It would have been far easier to succumb to popular pressure and print money. However, Grant reasoned that while pumping the money supply might help the economy in the short term, in the long run it would destroy the credit-worthiness of the government and financial system through inflation and instability.

Luckily for the American people, the politicians held firm because by 1874, the economy had stabilised. A large infusion of capital into the banking system had allowed reserve ratios at banks to recover to stable levels and interest rates to fall to 6 per cent. Liquidations of weak companies continued for the next several years as the economy cleansed itself of the cancer of financial speculation, malinvestments and downright fraud. By 1874, the economy roared back into life, as GDP increased by over 5 per cent in 1874.[60]

The Panic of 1893 (1893–1897) was part of a world-wide depression and is generally regarded as the most serious depression prior to the Great Depression. In a scene reminiscent of *Groundhog Day*, the downturn was preceded by over-expansion of the banking system, which fuelled speculation and over-investment in railroads. And, as before, many of these investments were financed through bond issues with high interest rates. Concerns over the state of the U.S. economy began to arise in February 1893 with the collapse of the Philadelphia and Reading Railroad.

In April 1893, these concerns were heightened when U.S. Treasury's gold reserves fell below $100 million, setting off a financial panic as investors, fearing that the country would be forced to abandon the gold standard, scrambled to sell off assets and convert them into gold.[61] The panic began in earnest in May 1893, when the National Cordage Company, the most actively traded stock of the time, went into receivership after a failed attempt to corner the market for imported hemp.

Internationally, a financial panic in London combined with falling trade with Europe heightened selling pressure as foreign investors sold American stocks to obtain American funds backed by gold.[62] As the stock market collapsed, banks everywhere began frantically calling in loans, while western and southern banks withdrew substantial deposits from New York banks. This was quickly followed by a string of railroad company and bank failures, which prompted a run on banks, as people lined up waiting to exchange bank notes for gold. Running short of reserves, this forced many banks to suspend specie payments, which further aggravated the financial problems.

Driven by fear, the resulting credit crunch quickly spilled over into the real economy. The downturn hit all areas of the economy including industrial cities, mill towns and rural areas as farmers struggled with high debt levels and falling commodity prices.

During the depression, 500 banks closed, 15,000 businesses failed, and many farms ceased operations. Unlike the previous panics, however, this latest panic had a severe impact on working class people. According to some estimates, total unemployment reached 17–19 per cent of the workforce, with unemployment reaching 25 per cent in New York and 43 per cent in Michigan.[63] Millions of people lost their jobs, their savings and their homes, and were forced out onto the streets. In the bitter winter months, many families starved to death. Soup kitchens opened to help the needy, while some progressive communities established community gardens to help feed the people.[64]

The depression took a severe psychological toll on people from all walks of life. Middle class people still with jobs blamed those who couldn't find work. They also feared violence and anarchy. Meanwhile, many in the lower classes blamed themselves and those in the upper class for their troubles.

The downturn triggered a wave of strikes in 1894 across several industries. The Pullman Strike, one of the more notable strikes of the times, pitted the American Railway Union against the Pullman Company, which manufactured railroad cars, the major railroad companies and the U.S. government. As the strikes turned violent, President Grover Cleveland used troops to end the strike.

The depression also triggered mass people movements as the many itinerants criss-crossed the nation looking for work. One such movement was headed by Ohio businessman Jacob Coxey, a movement that became known as Coxey's Army. Coxey advocated that the government create jobs by undertaking infrastructure projects, funded by the issue of government bonds. Coxey's Army picked up many sympathisers as it headed towards Washington, but it also stirred panic amongst those who feared an insurrection of the unemployed.

Despite the publicity, the march came to nought when Coxey was arrested for trespassing on the Capitol lawn as he tried to read out a prepared speech. An interesting aspect of Coxey's speech bears mentioning. Coxey noted that wages had fallen by one-half in agricultural districts, but where labour is organised, wages had remained static. He also noted, however, that in these areas (with unionised labour), employers had responded by cutting jobs to such an extent that the aggregate of all wages paid had reached starving point.[65]

Perhaps without knowing it, Coxey was highlighting a major problem when people are confronted with severe economic downturns. Understandably, trade unions are strongly opposed to reductions in their members' wages, arguing that they are not prepared to give up their workers' hard-won 'rights and entitlements'. While this is understandable from a union leader's political standing in the union, from an economic point of view, it is often very destructive for their members. The best way for an economy to quickly cleanse itself of excesses and sow the seeds for a healthy recovery is for all factors of production, including wages, to adjust to the new normal. This allows as many workers as possible to keep their jobs, albeit at a lower wage rate, rather than to see mass layoffs. The alternative path is far more pernicious and destructive. If workers hold out in the hope of riding out the downturn, then at best they will retain their jobs while their mates are laid off. At worst, the company goes broke and everybody loses.

By 1897, the economy began to recover and, aided by the Klondike Gold Rush, it grew rapidly over the next decade.

*

The Panic of 1907 was a financial crisis that played out over a three-week period starting in mid-October, when the U.S. stock market fell almost 50 per cent from its peak a year earlier. While the panic began in New York, it quickly fanned out to engulf state and local banks, many of which were forced into bankruptcy. The panic was only resolved through the actions of the financier and philanthropist John Pierpont (J.P.) Morgan, working with the U.S. Government and the New York financial elite to stabilise the financial system.[66]

While the panic took place in a volatile economic environment, it was contained largely to the financial sector.

The Panic of 1907 had its origins in a huge build-up of assets in the financial sector, which fuelled excessive growth in the money supply and a decline in bank reserves. The expansion of credit far outstripped growth in the bank reserves. As a result, between 1865 and 1910, the stock of gold fell from 25.3 per cent (of total note and deposit liabilities) to just 14.2 per cent.[67] Fuelled by this excessive growth in the money supply, between 1896 and early 1906, the Dow Jones Industrial Average (DJIA) trebled before beginning a steady decline.[68]

What sets 1907 apart from earlier panics is that this crisis focused on the trust companies in New York City, rather than the banks. In the early 1900s, trust companies were booming. In the decade before 1907, trust assets grew by 244 per cent, compared to 97 per cent growth in national bank assets and a more modest 82 per cent for state bank assets.[69]

The reasons for this uneven growth were structural in nature. Trusts were traditionally conservative institutions: managing estates, holding securities and taking deposits. As a result, they were subject to far less regulation than their banking counterparts.

This was especially true in terms of reserves. In 1906, for example, New York State instituted a requirement that trusts maintain reserves of 15 per cent of deposits, of which only 5 per cent needed to be kept as currency in the vault. Before this, trusts only needed to maintain what they thought was prudent for their requirements. In contrast, national banks in reserve cities were required to keep a 25 per cent reserve in the form of legal tender or specie.[70]

Sensing an opportunity for expansion, many of the larger trusts in New York City began venturing out into new but riskier areas of business including security underwriting, mortgage lending, direct investment in real estate and call loans (loans made to share investors to buy shares based on the underlying value of the shares themselves). While this growth proved highly profitable, it significantly increased the risk profile of their investment portfolios.

Like bees to a honey pot, many of the major banks found the attraction of controlling trusts too much of a temptation to resist. Many of the major banks took large stakes in the trusts, either by investing directly in trusts via holding companies, or appointing associates as directors. Either way, this gave the financial elite even greater control over the American financial system.

Such relationships were not new to finance or industry at the time, insofar that national banks were generally part of a network of regional banks, while they also established large investments in industrial companies. It made for extremely incestuous and cosy relationships. However, it also exposed the entire system to systemic weakness and contagion should any of the dominoes fall.

With the stock market already in decline, all it needed was a spark to ignite the contagion. Such an event occurred on 16 October 1907, when F. Augustus Heinze's scheme to corner the stock of United Copper Company failed. Although United Copper was only a moderately important firm, the collapse of Heinze's scheme exposed an intricate network of interlocking directorates across banks, brokerage houses, and trust companies in New York City.[71]

Initially, the problems were isolated to several institutions. However, this stability proved short-lived when, on 22 October, crowds turned up at the doors of the Knickerbocker Trust, the third largest trust in New York, demanding a return of their money. As news of the trouble spread, hundreds more depositors queued at the Trust's doors also demanding their money, leading to a fully-fledged bank run. By lunchtime, it was forced to suspend operations. As news of the suspension spread, banks became reluctant to lend any money. Interest rates on loans to stock brokers soared to 70 per cent and, with brokers unable to get money, stock prices fell to levels not seen since 1900.[72]

By this stage, widespread panic was starting to grip the city, and over the next two days, nine New York City banks and trusts failed. The chaos enveloping the City prompted the wealthy financier J.P. Morgan to take charge of the stabilisation effort. Morgan and his associates quickly assessed the books of the Knickerbocker Trust and determined that the Trust was insolvent. As a result, they let it fail[73] but his early intervention was unable to stop the stock market rout, as bankers continued to baulk at making short-term loans to facilitate daily trades.

As conditions continued to deteriorate, Morgan summoned the presidents of all the city's banks to his office for a meeting. He informed them that unless they could raise $25 million within ten minutes, then as many as 50 of the City's brokerage houses would be forced to close. The presidents pledged $23.6 million and the money reached the market just 30 minutes before the market was scheduled to close. The crisis had been averted, at least for now.[74]

Despite these actions, the stock market continued to plummet while bank runs continued apace. This prompted the U.S. Treasury to inject funds into the national banks and for the New York Clearing House to issue loan certificates to banks. This allowed them to retain cash reserves for depositors while allowing banks to continue to settle cash reserves. Morgan was even forced to bail out the City of New York as it was unable to fill a $20 million bond issue.[75]

To preserve precious bank reserves, Morgan set up a small team of trusted advisors to assess the financial viability of struggling banks. Those which were deemed viable were supported by the rest of the banking fraternity. Those considered vulnerable or insolvent were allowed to fail, just as they should in a free market system.

By early November, the worst of the bank runs and failures were over, and confidence slowly started to return to the banking sector. However, the Panic of 1907 set the scene for the creation of the U.S. Federal Reserve banking system.

*

The idea of having a central bank had been a point of contention between politicians since American independence.

Throughout the 1790s, deep divisions began to emerge between those political leaders who favoured a strong centralist government, and those who argued for small government. The divisions were driven by both ideology and self-interest.

The centralists were led by President George Washington and his Treasury Secretary Alexander Hamilton. They argued for a strong centralised Federal government based on a centralised financial system, the centrepiece of which was a national bank that would assume responsibility for the nation's debt and facilitate lending; and a government funded by a system of tariffs and taxes. Hamilton believed that central banking added to the stability of the finance system. Their policies favoured their supporter base, which included big business: the wealthy bankers and industrialists from the northern states.

The opposition group was led by Thomas Jefferson, whose supporter base included the plantation-based economies of the South and small business. Jeffersonians opposed the Federalists for two main reasons. Firstly, they didn't trust the northerners, nor did they wish to subordinate themselves to the wealthy north-eastern business interests. Secondly, Jefferson was a libertarian, who favoured smaller government and the rights of individuals. He distrusted cities, banks and factories and was staunchly opposed to a standing army and navy.

The ongoing conflict between Hamilton and Jefferson led to the creation of a two-party political system: the Federalists led by Hamilton, and the Democratic-Republican Party led by Jefferson. Within a very short space of time, these parties came to dominate the political landscape in each of the states and territories. This debate would continue for much of the nineteenth century and became a central election issue in the 1832 Presidential election which was won by Andrew Jackson on an anti-central bank platform.

In the years leading up to the 1907 panic, there had been renewed discussion over the merits of establishing a U.S. central bank to oversee the regulation of banks and the financial system. In response to the latest crisis, the federal government established the National Monetary Commission, under the control of Senator Nelson Aldrich, to investigate the panic and propose legislation to regulate banks. The House Committee on Banking and Currency also initiated an enquiry into the de facto monopoly of J.P. Morgan and other leading bankers on Wall Street.

While acknowledging the role that Morgan had played in helping to overcome the crisis, the Committee was scathing of the banking industry, finding that officers of J.P. Morgan and Company sat on the Boards of 112 corporations with a market capitalisation of $22.5 billion, representing some 85 per cent of the estimated capitalisation of the New York Stock Exchange.[76] This was an extraordinary concentration of wealth and power in just one man, in just one family.

American policy-makers were also deeply concerned about the number of panics that America had suffered throughout the nineteenth century. They wanted to resolve perceived defects in the prevailing monetary system: namely, an 'inelastic' currency, where the amount of money in circulation was tied to the market value of Treasury securities, seasonal liquidity problems linked to agricultural production, and the disparate nature of reserves which were held in many banks.[77]

As part of his investigations, Aldrich travelled to Europe to study how central banking was handled there. He came away impressed with how the systems worked in Germany and Britain and used them as the basis for design of the new American system.

Aldrich also convened a top-secret meeting of leading bankers at the exclusive Jekyll Island Club off the coast of Georgia to discuss monetary policy, and the establishment of a new regulatory framework for the American banking system. This meeting proved to be one of the most important meetings in modern financial history, for it was here that the most powerful American bankers of the time gathered and set the regulatory framework of the U.S. financial system for the next century.

In addition to Aldrich, the meeting included representatives from the banking behemoths of J.P. Morgan, John D Rockefeller, and a German citizen, Paul Warburg, who represented the interests of the Rothschild banking dynasty in England and France. All told, these folks represented nearly one-quarter of the wealth of the entire world at the time.[78]

The meeting was held in such secrecy that participants travelled in Aldrich's private railcar attached to the back of a southbound train. They were required to arrive separately at a remote railway platform and to use only first names. A couple of participants even adopted the use of code-names, and they never used names in front of the servants. For quite a few years after the meeting, these men even denied that such a meeting had taken place, arguing that they had just been out shooting ducks. In fact, they dismissed an article written by finance writer Bertie Forbes (who later went on to establish the Forbes magazine) about the meeting, claiming it to be preposterous and a mere invention.[79]

So why did the world's most powerful banking interests meet in such secrecy for ten days on an exclusive and remote island resort owned by the wealthiest people in America? Of one thing I can be certain: they weren't there to discuss the latest techniques in yoga and Pilates. But perhaps I do these guys a disservice!

They were there for one, and only one, reason: to further their own commercial interests by stitching up control of the American banking system. This group knew that New York banks were widely distrusted and despised, known in a disparaging way as the 'Money Trust', because of their interlocking directorates and control of the banking system.

They also knew that if the meeting with Aldrich became public, then any legislation emanating from Aldrich's review would immediately be rejected by Congress.

As it was, Aldrich's first bill was rejected by Congress for giving too little control of the banking system to the government and too much power to banking interests. Over the next few years, a subcommittee of the House Banking and Currency Committee worked on reframing the legislation. In the meantime, the banking cartel went into overdrive in rolling out an extremely sophisticated publicity campaign to support the new banking framework. This involved funding grassroot study clubs across the country, printing brochures and sponsoring universities and academics to support their position and extolling the virtues of a central bank. They even went so far as to feign criticism of changes to the legislation that were being proposed by opponents. And, rather than call it a central bank, they covered up its true intent by calling it the Federal Reserve System.

In December 1913, Congress passed the most important bill in U.S. financial history, the U.S. Federal Reserve Act of 1913. This created the U.S. Federal Reserve System, America's central bank. In this one act, Congress bequeathed control of the American banking system and money supply to the wealthiest banking interests in the land. And with no executive oversight. Extraordinary!

So, let's just ponder this for a moment. The financial system is the lifeblood of a modern economy. It touches the lives of every person. It determines how much interest you receive on your savings, how much interest you pay on your mortgage, it controls the money supply, it controls how much credit can be created, which in turn determines bank profits and executive bonuses. And just to re-iterate, all of this under the control of the banking elite.

The Fed is supervised by a Board of Governors. Located in Washington, D.C., the Board is a federal government agency consisting of seven members appointed by the President of the United States and confirmed by the U.S. Senate.[80] The governors are appointed for 14 years, and the terms are staggered, with one expiring every even-numbered year. Once appointed, governors cannot be removed from office for their policy views.

The Act also called for the establishment of up to 12 regional branches to appease the concerns of politicians who wanted to wrest control of the banking system away from New York. Without such a sop, the legislation would have never passed Congress. However, the legislation not only bestowed upon the Federal Reserve Board the power to appoint one third of the members of each of the regional Boards but, more importantly, both the Chairman and Deputy Chairman of these regional banks. This gives Fed-appointed Board members tremendous control over the affairs of the regional Federal Reserve Banks.

Today, the Federal Reserve's responsibilities fall into four general areas:

- conducting the nation's monetary policy by influencing money and credit conditions in the economy in pursuit of full employment and stable prices
- supervising and regulating banks and other important financial institutions to ensure the safety and soundness of the nation's banking and financial system, and to protect the credit rights of consumers
- maintaining the stability of the financial system and containing systemic risk that may arise in financial markets
- providing certain financial services to the U.S. government, U.S. financial institutions, and foreign official institutions,

and playing a major role in operating and overseeing the nation's payment systems.[81]

Over the years, the Fed has come in for strong criticism, including that it is owned by private and/or European banks; most of its profits are distributed to its owning banks; it is not audited; and that it issues the U.S. currency. Some of these criticisms are warranted, others not, and some miss the real issues.

Why are these criticisms worth even addressing? Because the Fed is the world's most powerful financial institution. It controls the U.S. monetary system, which in turn has a profound influence on the world's monetary system. There are billions of dollars of profits to be made by the savvy and well-connected. So, if there is anything remiss with governance or the way the Fed operates, this impacts anybody who has deposits at, or loans from, a bank. That is, everybody! So, let's look at these issues.

It's true that each of the national banks owns shares in the Federal Reserve banks. In fact, they must be members if they want to operate as a bank. However, it is not ownership of the Reserve Banks that determines control of the banking system. Each bank is only allowed one vote, so you can't lock up the voting blocs as you can in ordinary companies. Rather, control occurs through other means such as the ability to appoint people to the U.S. Federal Board and key committees. These appointments, in turn, are controlled through the pervasive and incestuous banking, academic, political and business networks, or through the constant rotation of senior executives from the Fed, to banks, to academia, to government agencies and to corporations.

More influence is peddled at the Hamptons, in board rooms, at the opera, baseball or at universities than worrying about who own the shares. If political donations didn't buy influence and control, banks and other major corporations wouldn't spend hundreds of millions of dollars to buy both side of politics.

If one doubts how incestuous and powerful these networks are, one only needs to cast their mind back to the GFC when Hank Poulson (former Chairman and CEO of Goldman Sachs), as U.S. Secretary of the Treasury, oversaw the bailout of the American banking system. Take oversized bonuses and then get the taxpayer to bail out the very mess your former industry helped create through reckless banking practices. What a great gig if you can get it! So, why didn't the mainstream press and economics fraternity raise any ethical or potential conflict of interest issues?

Some people claim that profits earned by the Fed go to the owning banks. Once again, this is incorrect. The Fed's income comes primarily from the interest earned on government securities acquired through open market operations.[82] Through an agreement between the Fed and the U.S. Treasury, after paying its expenses, and dividends to the shareholding banks (6 per cent per annum on their paid-in capital), the Fed turns the rest of its earnings (approximately 98 per cent) over to the U.S. Treasury. Because of the massive holdings of securities on its balance sheet, Fed profits have soared since the GFC, so much so that it has been remitting close to $100 billion per annum to the U.S. Treasury over the past couple of years.[83]

So, the banks have not been making profits from Fed profits. Bank executives are smart enough to realise that they would quickly lose political support if they killed the golden goose by raking in profits from the Fed's day-to-day operations.

No, there are plenty of profits to be made elsewhere by the well-connected. Politicians win because they get to spend Fed profits. Bank executives win because they get to make supersized profits from the monetary system they control. The only people who get screwed are the common folk.

'Audit the Fed' has also become a popular catch-cry in recent years. This demand is based on the view that the Fed is neither open nor transparent in their activities or how they make their decisions. The Fed counters that they are subject to regular audits. So, the question then becomes: when is an audit not an audit?

The Fed is subject to audits by both government and private sector auditors. And I am sure that the auditors do an excellent job of verifying income statements and balance sheets. Having said that, I am not as convinced that the auditors get to audit the Fed's gold holdings, of which there is widespread conjecture as to whether they still exist in the quantities that they should.

No, the real problem is the lack of transparency over the Fed's decisions and transactions. The U.S. Government Accountability Office (GAO), or 'congressional watchdog', is currently prevented by law from reviewing 'deliberations, decisions, or actions on monetary policy matters', as well as 'discussion or communication among or between members of the Board and officers and employees' related to such deliberations.'[84]

The Fed argues that as they are independent, they shouldn't be subject to political influence. In one sense, they are right. Politicians being politicians, they will always be tempted to reduce interest rates before an election or be reluctant to increase interest rates. However, the Fed's defence is spurious and self-serving.

Firstly, as politicians are democratically elected to serve the interest of the people, they have every right to dabble if they so wish. If they mess up, they will be held accountable at the ballot box. Moreover, we live in a democracy. And in a democracy, people have the right to know how the most important economic system is being managed, how decisions are made and who is benefiting from such decisions. Nobody, especially a banking cartel, should have the right to subvert democratic processes. And yet the Fed, and the banks, do exactly that by not being subject to appropriate review. Which gives you an idea of how powerful the banks are, and how important it is for the banks to control the Fed.

In opposing the push to audit the Fed, Richard Fisher, president of the Federal Reserve Bank of Dallas, stated: 'Who in their right mind would ask Congress – who can't cobble together a fiscal policy – to assume control of monetary policy?' Cleveland Fed President, Loretta Mester, also chimed in, stating: 'They really are about allowing political considerations to influence monetary policy decisions. This would be a tremendous mistake, because it would ultimately lead to poorer economic performance. [85]

Former Fed Governor Ben Bernanke also argues that Congress is not well-suited to make monetary policy decisions itself, because of the technical and time-sensitive nature of those decisions. He says that the Fed needs flexibility to cope with changing economic circumstances and that studies have demonstrated monetary policy achieves better results when central bankers can focus on the longer-term interests of the economy, free of short-term political considerations.[86]

Of course, these arguments are totally bogus and designed to deflect any criticism and oversight, and to protect the banks' control over the financial system. For example, as evidenced by the Great Depression, the dot-com collapse and the GFC, the Fed's performance has been less than stellar. As for Mester's comments, despite the Fed taking a more activist role in monetary policy, the rate of real economic growth in the U.S has been in constant decline since the 1960s. Moreover, her opinions are purely subjective as it would be nigh on impossible to prove her assertions that 'it would lead to poorer economic outcomes'.

There is also a contradiction in Bernanke's arguments about needing flexibility to cope with changing short-term circumstances while focusing on the longer-term interests of the economy. What is the Fed's focus: short-term or long-term? Now the simple answer would be both. But when, and under what circumstances? We don't know, because we don't have access to their deliberations.

It is also arrogant in the extreme to suggest that politicians don't have the necessary technical expertise in relation to monetary matters. Sure, a lot of them don't. But many do. Moreover, as will become evident throughout this book, I don't believe that mainstream economists and central bankers have that expertise either.

As Tennessee politician Davey Crockett said of the banking system after The Panic of 1819: the whole banking system is nothing more than a 'species of swindling on a large scale'. [87] Nothing much has changed since then, and the Fed is front and centre of the greatest swindle of all time.

Finally, given the importance of the financial system to people's well-being, people have a right to know what central banks are doing. For example, how did the Fed fail to foresee the GFC? What was the Fed analysis when Bernanke made the following statements?

a. '*Housing markets are cooling a bit. Our expectation is that the decline in activity or the slowing in activity will be moderate, that house prices will probably continue to rise.*' (Feb 15, 2006)[88]
b. '*We do not expect significant spillovers from the subprime market to the rest of the economy or to the financial system.*' (May 17, 2007)
c. '*The Federal Reserve is not currently forecasting a recession.' (Jan 10, 2008)*[89]

Within months of these statements, the GFC struck, housing prices collapsed, major banks went bankrupt and the world experienced a severe recession which required massive bailouts.

Given modern economists' pre-occupation with economic models, what were these models forecasting when the Fed embarked on the greatest financial experiment in economic history, namely, quantitative easing (QE)? When was the economy going to recover, by how much, and what was the Fed's exit strategy for unwinding QE? Surely, the public has a right to know how accurate their models are so that we can hold the Fed and others to account.

Other questions that need to be asked are: who did they bail out, by how much, what were the terms, who made the decisions, on what basis, and who are they lending to now? And how do they make their interest rate decisions?

These are not inappropriate questions, given what is at stake, particularly given their woeful track record in predicting recessions and financial crises and the amount of money that is at stake. But I suspect one of the reasons the Fed is reluctant to open itself up for review is that it would expose the Fed as the 'emperor with no clothes'. It would also highlight the incestuous nature of the finance industry.

It is also worth noting that non-mainstream economists dismiss the need for a central bank at all. Their arguments that I have outlined below centre on the efficacy of the free enterprise system to cleanse itself of any distortions while drawing into question the very competency of central banks and their staff.

Firstly, they argue that during the 1907 financial panic, the free enterprise system worked as it should have. Powerful vested interests such as J.P. Morgan stepped in to protect their wealth. Moreover, well-run banks which had strong, ethical management, good governance and sound systems fared well in the Panic of 1907. New York had two such banks: National City Bank (the forerunner to City Bank) and Chemical Bank. Both maintained very conservative reserve ratios, that is the ratio of gold and national bank currency to deposits, and conservative loan portfolios. Neither paid interest on deposits (other national banks offered 2 per cent), but they offered something else that had real value before the age of government insurance — security. In time of panic, they would typically increase their deposits as everyday people ran to safety. [90] In contrast, the panic struck primarily those banks which had engaged in reckless behaviour.

Secondly, they point out that central banks have failed in what they were supposed to do – manage the currency and the financial system. Since the Fed was established, America has suffered a series of crises and economic problems including the Great Depression, stagflation of the 1970s, the Savings and Loans Crisis, the dot-com bubble, the GFC and the upcoming great depression of the 2020s. Speculation, poor banking practices and excessive growth in the money supply were primary factors in each of these crises, factors over which the Fed had oversight.

The Fed would also have you believe that it has the best economists in the world and that they are fully capable of managing the economy and engineering favourable business outcomes. They have also raised expectations that they can deliver ongoing economic nirvana. However, if the Fed had been doing its job, it would not have created the massive asset inflation and debt build-up that the U.S. is experiencing, nor would the dot-com bubble and GFC have occurred. That they did is testimony to the incompetence of the Fed.

Having central banks encourages reckless behaviour and actually increases the risk of catastrophic failure in the financial system because banks, especially the large ones, are content in the knowledge that the central bank will bail them out if the economy turns south and they get into difficulty.

One of the key arguments put forward for the creation of central banks focuses on the need to protect depositors from losses incurred through banking failures. This is, of course, a very admirable goal, as everyday mums and dads should be able to trust that their hard-earned savings will be safe. However, the easiest way to achieve this is to ensure that banks and other financial institutions maintain sufficient reserves in gold or equivalents, and that banks behave responsibly. You don't need a banking cartel controlling the banking and monetary systems to achieve this.

Finally, central banking is the very antithesis of capitalism and free markets. Interest rates should be free to find their own level without interference from the banking cartel, and firms should be allowed to fail if they become insolvent.

So, what have we learnt in this chapter? Firstly, despite setbacks including a brutal civil war and multiple financial crises, the U.S economy grew strongly in the nineteenth century due to strong population growth, capital investment and innovation. Despite external impacts, the panics in the nineteenth century occurred largely because of speculation funded by excessive growth in the money supply, fraud, corruption, greed and poor banking practices.

America's founding fathers clearly understood the risks to freedom and prosperity posed by banks and fractional reserve banking. Thomas Jefferson distrusted that banks would ever work in society's interests, while Andrew Jackson argued that it put too much power in the hands of too few private citizens, power that could be used to the detriment of the national government. John Adams regarded paper money beyond specie as theft, while James Madison regarded banking institutions as harmful.[91] They rightfully believed that banks and other financial intermediaries should always be heavily regulated to ensure their lending didn't get out of control.

Thirdly, the economy typically recovered quickly from these panics by allowing market forces to cleanse the economy of weak companies, weak banks and malinvestments.

Fourthly, the presence of central banking is an anathema to free enterprise and capitalism. The economy works best when it is allowed to work unencumbered from outside influence and the finance system is too important to be controlled by the very organisations that it is supposed to regulate.

Finally, sustainable economic growth can only occur when the world returns to 'sound money'.

Chapter 5
The Depression of 1920–21

'The best thing one can do when it's raining is to let it rain.'

Henry Wadsworth Longfellow

The depression of 1920–21 was a sharp, deflationary depression in the U.S. and elsewhere, which lasted 18 months from January 1920 to July 1921. The downturn was longer than most post-World War I recessions, but significantly shorter than the Great Depression, which lasted 132 months.[92]

The 1920–21 Depression is very important from an economic history perspective because it was the last time that authorities let the economy adjust naturally to an economic downturn without external interference through fiscal stimulus or lower interest rates.

In fact, the opposite was true. The government slashed spending while the Fed increased interest rates to allow prices and the economy to adjust to the new post-war environment. The U.S. faced a number of challenges as it sought to transition from a wartime to a peacetime economy. Not only did industry need to retool but the U.S. had to absorb nearly three million armed forces personnel back into the civilian workforce. Inflation had also soared to over 18 per cent per annum[93] in the latter parts of the war while unions had taken advantage of a tight labour market to push their claim for higher wages. The unions had also staged a number of high profile strikes in key industries including iron and steel, the railways and coal.

In short, the economy had developed significant distortions that needed to be cleansed before healthy growth could resume. The government responded by cutting tax rates for all income groups and slashing federal spending from $18.5 billion to just $3.3 billion in 1922. At the same time, the New York Federal Reserve raised its discount rate from 4.75 per cent to a record 7 per cent.[94] As a result, the national debt was cut by one-third.[95] These measures had the effect of taking pressure off the jobs market, easing pressure on consumers and business while slashing at the heart of inflation.

The government also sought to protect farmers and local industries, who were losing their wartime markets as European production came back on line, by imposing tariffs across a broad range of products.

While the tariffs afforded considerable protection to American business, they had very serious side effects, in that higher tariff barriers made it much more difficult for European nations to conduct trade, and therefore to pay off their wartime debts. Unhindered by foreign competition, the tariffs also contributed to the growth of monopolies in the U.S.. Other nations eventually retaliated by raising their own tariffs on U.S.-made goods, leading to a significant reduction in international trade.

The depression was characterised by an extreme drop in consumer prices – the largest year-on-year percentage decline in prices in around 140 years of data – with estimates varying from between 13 per cent to 18 per cent. The fall in wholesale prices was even more severe, falling by 36.8 per cent, the largest drop in prices since the American Revolutionary War. This was worse than any single year during the Great Depression, although adding all the years of the Great Depression together yielded a more severe deflation.[96]

The decline in economic activity was less severe than the fall in prices, with Gross National Product (GNP) falling by between 2.4 per cent and 6.9 per cent. [97] However, unemployment rose sharply, rising from 5.2 per cent to somewhere between 8.7 per cent and 11.7 per cent.[98]

Despite assistance from tariffs, the economic climate was especially bad for business. Industrial production fell sharply. Between May 1920 to July 1921, automobile production declined 60 per cent and total industrial production by 30 per cent. From 1919 to 1922, the rate of business failures tripled, climbing from 37 to 120 failures per every 100,000 businesses. Those businesses fortunate enough to survive experienced a 75 per cent decline in profits.[99] The stock market also reflected the fall in business activity, with the DJIA declining by 47 per cent.[100]

Despite the depth of the deflation and depression, by the late summer of 1921, signs of recovery were clearly visible. By 1922, unemployment had fallen to 6.7 per cent, and 2.4 per cent in 1923.[101]

Economists believe the 1920–21 depression resulted from a surge in the civilian labour force, which increased unemployment; a decline in commodity prices as agricultural production began to recover in Europe; and tighter monetary policy to combat runaway inflation.

Milton Friedman and Anna Schwartz suggest that the depression resulted from an unnecessarily tight monetary policy by the

Fed.[102] This analysis seems disingenuous on several levels. Firstly, with inflation running at nearly 20 per cent, what else was the government to do? Let runaway inflation wreak havoc on consumers and the disadvantaged? Strong action was required to restore price stability, just as former Fed Chairman Paul Volcker did during the late 1970s and early 1980s, when he significantly hiked interest rates to combat runaway inflation.

Their analysis also seems to look at the effect rather than the causes of the inflation. The years preceding 1920 were characterised by a significant increase in the money supply, firstly after reserve requirements had been halved by the 1913 Federal Reserve Act, and then with considerable credit expansion by the banks themselves. [103]

Between 1914 and 1920, total bank deposits more than doubled. The Fed also kept its discount rate (the rate at which it lends directly to banks) low throughout World War I (WWI) and for a brief period thereafter. The Fed only began to tighten monetary policy in late 1919.[104] It seems that it was this artificial credit creation, together with shortages of goods resulting from the war, that set the boom–bust cycle in motion. Once the destructive cycle had started, it was always going to lead to a painful adjustment until excesses had been cleansed from the system.

Moreover, their analysis belongs more to *Alice in Wonderland* than to the real world. What they are suggesting is that an economy can suffer major distortions but that economists can engineer a recovery without any major downsides. If only!

The 1920–21 depression has been an enigma for mainstream economists: firstly, in analysing its causes; and secondly, in trying to understand how the U.S. economy recovered so quickly from the downturn. Had the 1920–21 depression occurred today, the policy response would have been completely different. Big-spending Keynesians would have argued for massive fiscal stimulus and a run-up in debt to bolster aggregate demand, while monetarists would have implored the Fed to reduce interest rates and pump more money into the economy to increase the money supply and create inflation. The government did neither. According to American economist Benjamin Anderson, the U.S. government allowed the economy to readjust on its own:

'[W]e took our losses, we readjusted our financial structure, we endured our depression, and in August 1921 we started up again...The rally in business production and employment that started in August 1921 was soundly based on a drastic cleaning up of credit weakness, a drastic reduction in the costs of production, and on the free play of private enterprise. It was not based on governmental policy designed to make business good.'[105]

The then President, Warren Harding, was equally strident in his views about how to handle an economic downturn:

'We will attempt intelligent and courageous deflation, and strike at government borrowing which enlarges the evil, and we will attack the high cost of government with every energy and facility...We promise that relief which will attend the halting of waste and extravagance, and the renewal of the practice of public economy, not alone because it will relieve tax burdens, but because it will be an example to stimulate thrift and economy in private life.

Let us call to all the people for thrift and economy, for denial and sacrifice if need be, for a nationwide drive against extravagance and luxury, to a recommittal to simplicity of living, to that prudent and normal plan of life which is the health of the republic.'[106]

And the government's plans worked. The economy went through a quick yet painful adjustment but it came out the other side cleansed of struggling companies, and without an overhang of debt.

These people were leaders! They made the tough decisions, they understood that sacrifice was necessary to cleanse the system of structural weaknesses such as inflation and over-extended credit, that insolvent companies needed to be let to fail, and that wage levels needed to reset to realistic levels in order to provide full employment. They also understood the need for people and governments to live within their means.

They understood, either explicitly or implicitly, that economic systems are highly complex natural systems which ebb and flow around a longer-term trend, and that, being a natural system, economies will always self-correct without outside intervention should structural impediments arise, as they invariably will. They understood the basics of economics, which is based on the concept of scarcity, and that the price mechanism always succeeds, if left to work its magic. Concomitant with this, they understood that the less the intervention and distortions, the quicker the recovery.

This philosophy, which will become a recurring theme throughout the remainder of the book, is diametrically opposed to the interventionist policies of modern-day economists, whether they be Keynesians or monetarists, who wrongfully believe that through their policy prescriptions, they can manipulate and control the business cycle and control economic outcomes.

Contrary to the prognostications of these interventionists, what we can say with conviction about the 1920–21 Depression is that the U.S. economy faced major structural problems following the end of WWI and the nation – in fact, the world

– needed to cleanse itself of distortions before it could move towards sustainable growth. Policy-makers took steps to resolve these impediments, the economy went through a deep yet rapid adjustment process and, within a relatively brief period, had moved quickly back to full employment, beginning one of the most prosperous periods in U.S. history.

It is also instructive to compare the American response to the 1920–21 Depression to that of Japan. In 1920, the Japanese government introduced policies designed to prevent deflation by keeping prices artificially high. According to Benjamin Anderson:

'The great banks, the concentrated industries, and the government got together, destroyed the freedom of the markets, arrested the decline in commodity prices, and held the Japanese price level high above the receding world level for seven years. During these years, Japan endured chronic industrial stagnation and at the end, in 1927, she had a banking crisis of such severity that many great branch bank systems went down, as well as many industries. It was a stupid policy. In the effort to avert losses on inventory representing one year's production, Japan lost seven years.'[107]

Sadly, the Japanese failed to learn the lessons of history, as they repeated the same mistakes seven decades later.

Chapter 6
The Roaring Twenties

> *'The Roaring Twenties were the period of that Great American Prosperity which was built on shaky foundations.'*
>
> J. Paul Getty

The 1920s, also known as the Roaring Twenties, was a period of sustained economic growth and major social and political change, a period which transformed the American way of life and established America as the global economic powerhouse of the twentieth century.

The period was characterised by major technological advances, low levels of inflation, high levels of consumer confidence and new attitudes towards consumerism, the introduction of many new products and services, major improvements in productivity and business-friendly governments. It was also a period of rapid credit growth, which not only financed the economic expansion, but fuelled booms in real estate and the stock market.

Despite the 1920–21 Depression and mild recessions in 1924 and 1927, from 1920 to 1929 the U.S. economy grew at the rate of 4.2 per cent per annum, while real GNP per capita grew 2.7 per cent per annum.[108]

Little did the people realise, however, that as a result of runaway credit growth and rampant speculation, particularly towards the backend of the 1920s, it would all come crashing down and end in misery for tens of millions of people in what would become the greatest economic downturn of the twentieth century.

More importantly, there is an eerie parallel between the credit-fuelled boom times of the Roaring Twenties and the credit-fuelled boom times of the late twentieth and early twenty-first centuries, particularly the massive increases in asset prices. The main difference is that now we are starting with unprecedented debt levels and massive budget deficits. But, back to then.

The automotive, petroleum, chemical, electricity, telecommunications, residential construction, entertainment and retail sectors all boomed, transforming the way people lived, worked and played.

Many companies grew larger and their profits soared. This growth created millions of new jobs and increased real wages for many. It was the beginning of consumer heaven when, for the first time, millions of Americans had extra money to spend on a range of new goods.

Internal combustion engines revolutionised transportation, with cars quickly grabbing the lion's share of local and regional transportation, just as railroads had done in the nineteenth century.

Henry Ford changed the face of manufacturing forever when he introduced mass production by way of the moving production line. Mass production proved a boon to the American people, making new products affordable to the middle class. For example, between 1908 and 1925, the price of automobiles fell from $850 to $290. Ford believed that it was better to sell more cars for a small profit, as it meant employing more workers.[109]

The growth in these major industries had a huge flow-on effect as new industries sprang up to support the new products and services. The rapid growth in the number of motor vehicles, for example, spawned the development of gas stations, motels and mechanical repair workshops while promoting the growth of other industries such as tyre manufacturing. New products and technologies also led to unprecedented growth in infrastructure spending, with a huge expansion in roads, the electricity grid and telephone lines. This reduced the isolation felt by rural communities while increasing the transmission of trends and ideas throughout society.

Much of this infrastructure was funded by local governments, who went deeply into debt on the assumption that investment in infrastructure would pay off in the future.[110] The policy-makers were right in one sense, in that it was a good long-term investment. What they didn't reckon on, however, was the Great Depression, which wreaked havoc on their finances in the short-term.

Innovative technology, the continuing shift to electricity and internal combustion fuels, new management techniques and demographic changes led to massive increases in productivity and facilitated a major transformation in American industry. Between 1919 and 1929, labour productivity grew at around 5.4 per cent per annum, while capital productivity grew by 4.2 per cent per annum. This was three to four times greater than productivity increases in the surrounding decades.[111] This increased productivity had very positive economic and social outcomes in that it allowed both wages and profits to rise strongly without stoking inflation.

The greater use of electric power was one of the most crucial factors in improving productivity. In 1900, steam provided 80 per cent of the mechanical drive capacity in manufacturing.

However, by 1920, electricity provided over 50 per cent, and 78 per cent by 1929.[112] Electric utilities with central generating stations using steam turbines greatly lowered the cost of power, with businesses and houses in cities becoming electrified.[113]

The increasing use of electricity had an extraordinarily transformative effect on every facet of American life. It led to the growth of electric street railways; expansion in the production of electrochemicals, for example aluminum and caustic compounds; it facilitated rapid expansion in productivity by allowing factories to operate around the clock; it improved flexibility in the design and layout of factories; and it improved working conditions through improved illumination and ventilation. It was also a key factor behind the growing mechanisation of American industry and consumers benefited greatly from new electrical products such as radios, vacuum cleaners, refrigerators and electric irons.

Declining union membership, improved transportation and advances in technology also helped to improve productivity. For example, the massive increase in the construction of paved roads led to the development of a finishing machine to smooth the surface of cement highways, resulting in a reduction in labour requirement of between 40 and 60 per cent.[114] In the tyre industry, continuing advances in processes and technology, and improvements in quality, meant that between 1910 and 1930, tyre costs per thousand miles of driving fell from $9.39 to $0.65.[115]

With the passage of the Federal Reserve Act, President Wilson appointed Benjamin Strong as Governor of the Federal Reserve Bank of New York. Strong quickly took control of the Federal Reserve System, deciding on Fed policy often without consultation, and even against the wishes of the Federal Reserve Board in Washington.[116]

Under Strong, the Fed pursued an inflationary policy throughout much of the 1920s. For example, Strong cut interest rates in 1924–25 and again in 1927, the latter designed to support a slow-down in the automotive sector, to help struggling farmers suffering chronically depressed agricultural prices, and to prop up the Bank of England by relieving the pressure on sterling and other weak European currencies.[117]

The U.S. also enacted a highly protectionist trade policy, which hampered other countries in trying to sell their goods to the United States. Meanwhile, U.S. banks were encouraged to advance loans to these struggling nations. Hoover believed that even bad loans helped American exports and provided a cheap form of relief and employment.[118]

Despite the loose monetary policy, improved productivity and increased output kept consumer prices in check. As a result, consumer prices remained static for the latter half of the decade, and even fell from 1926 to 1928. All of this worked to increase real wages and improve people's standard of living.

The 1920s were also a period of financial innovation and strong credit growth. Stung by over-zealous bankers and reduced lending during 1920–21, businesses began relying more on retained earnings, and stock and bond issues to raise funds. This increasing self-reliance on funding allowed many companies, which might have otherwise been beholden to banks, to survive the worst of the Great Depression.

The commercial banks responded to these changes by expanding services in other areas including creating personal loan and trust departments, underwriting securities issued by non-financial companies, and offering safe deposit boxes.[119] The intense competition between financial institutions and low interest rates contributed to the credit expansion. This quickly flowed through into the credit-sensitive sectors of the economy: consumer durables, real estate and the stock market. For the first time, hire-purchase arrangements were introduced, allowing consumers to buy expensive products on credit.

Chain stores such as JP Penney started to appear, and catalogue shopping became a popular way of buying goods. Department stores extended generous lines of credit for consumers to purchase their products and used mass radio advertising to attract customers. This was the beginning of the new American culture of consumerism, a culture that continues to define America to this day.

In 1919, General Motors Corporation established a subsidiary to finance sales of its cars. Having demonstrated the advantages of such an arrangement, other producers followed suit, along with a large number of independent finance companies. By 1925, there were more than 1,500 finance companies operating in the U.S. By 1927, nearly two-thirds of new cars in the U.S. were purchased on installment terms.[120]

Increasing consumption also fuelled consumer debt. Between 1920 and 1929, consumer debt as a percentage of personal income doubled to more than 9 per cent.[121]

Savings and Loans institutions (S&Ls) fuelled an orgy of construction across the nation, particularly in the major cities such as Chicago and New York. As a result, mortgage debt, including farm debt, more than tripled between 1919 and 1929.[122] Realtors and developers often sat on the boards of S&Ls, influencing the operation and lending practices of these intermediaries. This lowered lending standards while increasing risk. The growth of auto ownership accelerated the pace and extent of land subdivision and encouraged speculation on city edges and recently converted farmland.[123] Little did people know that the boom was about to come to a grinding halt, leaving the landscape littered with vacant apartment buildings and subdivisions that would remain undeveloped for years to come.[124]

The stock market benefited from low interest rates and easy credit conditions, with the DJIA more than doubling between 1921 and January 1926 from 67 to 157, before topping out on 3 September 1929 at 381 – a 500 per cent increase in under a decade. Leverage also played an important part in the run-up in stocks as individual investors were permitted to purchase shares for 10 per cent down, borrowing from their brokers, who in turn borrowed from the banks. Capital gains of around 30 per cent in 1927 and again in 1928 encouraged the belief that stocks could only go up.[125]

The use of stock pools was also commonplace towards the end of the 1920s. Under these arrangements, groups of speculators pooled their resources to drive up the prices of particular stocks. Once the stock had reached its target price, the speculators then offloaded their holdings, leaving unsophisticated investors holding shares which often collapsed after the speculators dumped their stocks.

As speculation ran rampant in the run-up to the top, turnover of shares surged, so much so that the DJIA increased by over 20 per cent in the first nine months of 1929. In a scene reminiscent of *Back to the Future*, the increase in stocks centered on technology stocks, as investors and speculators rallied around the next new thing. Between 1926 and 1929, an index of the then high-tech stocks (sectors such as communications, electrical equipment and appliances, inorganic chemicals and transportation) rose by over 200 per cent.[126]

Enthusiasm for these stocks ran way ahead of their ability to generate profits. Just like the dot-com boom of the late 1990s, the stock price of the then radio giant RCA rose from just over one to a high of 549 – some 73 times earnings – between 1921 and 1929, even though the company paid no dividends.[127]

The massive expansion in credit also ran well ahead of activity in the real economy. From 1913 to 1929, the ratio of private credit to GDP nearly doubled in the U.S., the UK and Japan. In contrast, the ratio of credit to GDP fell in Germany and was relatively flat in several other European countries.[128]

America was also fortunate to have a series of pro-business governments which adopted free market (laissez-faire) policies, at least as far as Americans were concerned. Government actions, together with market forces, resulted in the concentration of market power in several key industries. The banking sector, for example, benefited greatly from a weakening of anti-trust laws, while American corporations benefited from the imposition of tariffs, which acted to reduce competition from foreign firms.

New technology also increased the concentration of business in the hands of fewer but much larger businesses. Some of this industry concentration came about through vertical integration as firms sought to integrate control over the supply of critical raw materials, while others sought to control the distribution channels for their products.

Industry concentration arose naturally through industrial maturation. The introduction of the assembly line in the automobile industry, for example, gave rise to larger factories and firms which could benefit from economies of scale, improved distribution networks and consumer credit. This resulted in a massive consolidation of power within the sector. Over time, the number of auto firms declined from several thousand to just 44 companies in 1929. Ford and General Motors were the clear leaders, together producing 70 per cent of automobiles. The Great Depression further decimated the industry, so much so that by 1940, only eight American companies still produced cars.[129]

It was a similar story in the tyre industry where between 1921 and 1937, the market share of the five largest firms rose from 50 per cent to 75 per cent.[130]

Between 1925 and 1939, the share of manufacturing assets held by the 100 largest corporations rose from 35 per cent to 42 per cent. Despite the rationale for the increasing reach of the largest firms, the growing size of businesses was erroneously used by some economists as causing the Great Depression.[131]

The 1920s were also an age of dramatic social and political change. For the first time, more Americans lived in cities than on farms. Between 1920 and 1929, the nation's wealth more than doubled, and economic growth swept many Americans into an affluent but unfamiliar 'consumer society'.[132]

The advent of the radio, phonograph records and talking motion pictures revolutionised entertainment. Watching a movie became cheap and accessible, and people swarmed to the new cinemas. By the 1920s, the United States reached its greatest ever output in movies, producing an average of 800 feature films annually.[133] These developments, together with the expansion of the telephone, reduced the tyrannies of distance and brought people together.

The 1920s also brought a feeling of freedom and independence to millions of Americans, particularly the younger generation. Young soldiers returning home, having experienced a different culture and the tragedy of war, wanted to enjoy the pleasures of everyday life.

Cars gave young people the freedom to travel where they wanted, when they wanted. And what many young people wanted to do was dance: the Charleston, the cake walk, the black bottom, the flea hop. Jazz bands played at dance halls like the Savoy in New York City and the Aragon in Chicago; radio stations and phonograph records (100 million of which were sold in 1927 alone) carried tunes to listeners across the nation.[134]

The period was also a golden age for sports, as fans flocked to boxing and baseball to see their sporting heroes. The single greatest sporting hero of the time was the legendary baseballer Babe Ruth. The American public also lauded other heroes including pilot Charles Lindbergh, who became the first person to fly an aircraft non-stop across the Atlantic Ocean.

The era was also one of liberation for a great many women. In 1920, women gained the right to vote, while millions of women moved into the workforce. Young women began to challenge the traditions of their parents and grandparents and express their growing independence by wearing tighter-fitting dresses, drinking alcohol and smoking cigarettes in public. Between 1918 and 1928, cigarette production in the U.S. more than doubled.[135]

Certain sections of society also became somewhat more tolerant during this period of positive social mood. For example, on the stage and in movies, black and white players appeared together for the first time,[136] while it also became possible to go to nightclubs and see white and black people dancing and eating together. Homosexuality also became more visible and somewhat more acceptable in the big cities of London, New York, Paris and Rome.[137]

Despite the increasing wealth, not everybody supported the social changes nor shared the riches. Most women were still poorly paid and were employed in roles such as cleaners, stenographers or waitresses. A great many others worked in the home raising families. The period set off what one historian called the culture wars, pitting city-dwellers against country folk, Protestants against Catholics, blacks against whites, and 'New Women' against advocates of old-fashioned family values.[138] Millions of people in places like Indiana and Illinois joined the Ku Klux Klan. To them, the Klan represented a return to all the 'values' that the fast-paced, city-slicker Roaring Twenties were trampling.[139]

Partly in response to this social backlash against progress, the government introduced prohibition by making it illegal to sell any intoxicating beverages with more than half a per cent alcohol. While this was directed towards asserting some control over what many middle-class folks considered to be unruly migrant masses, all it did was to drive the liquor trade underground and into the hands of gangsters such as the infamous Al Capone. It also had another unintended consequence in that it reduced revenue from alcohol taxes and pushed the onus for tax collection onto the highly unpopular land taxes.

The U.S. also adopted a strong anti-immigration stance, and legislated in 1924 to limit the annual number of immigrants who could be admitted from any country to 2 per cent of the number of people from that country as per the 1890 census. The law was aimed primarily at restricting immigration of Southern and Eastern Europeans, especially Italians and Eastern European Jews, in favour of people from Great Britain and northern Europe.[140] It also severely restricted immigration of Africans and banned outright the immigration of Arabs and Asians. According to the U.S. Department of State Office of the Historian, the purpose of the act was 'to preserve the ideal of American homogeneity'.[141]

While real GNP per capita grew during the twenties, the increasing wealth was not evenly shared. By 1929, 5 per cent of the population held more than one-third of the nation's wealth.[142] Economic growth was also very uneven between industrial sectors, with the economy going through a period of sustained structural adjustment as many traditional industries decayed and were replaced by emerging sectors. Sectors which suffered included the coal industry, which was impacted by oversupply, falling prices and the switch to oil; ship building, which also suffered from falling demand for new ships; cotton, which was subject to competition from new products such as rayon; and railroads, which was subject to increasing competition from automobiles and trucking.

The agricultural sector was particularly hard hit. U.S. farmers had prospered greatly during WWI and responded to higher prices by buying more land and cultivating more marginal farmland. They also increased output by purchasing more machinery, such as tractors and ploughs. The price of farmland rose in response to the increased demand, while the debt of American farmers increased substantially. However, as conditions returned to normal, farmers began to struggle. Between 1920 and 1921, real average net income per farm fell by over 72 per cent and never recovered. The decline in prices, coupled with crippling farm debt, resulted in a rapid increase in farm mortgage foreclosures, which remained high for the remainder of the 1920s.[143] By 1928, half of U.S. farmers were living in poverty. Prices were so low that 600,000 farmers lost their farms in 1924 alone.[144]

The changing fortunes of these declining businesses not only affected the workers but also businesses supplying goods and services to these regions. For example, rural banks that relied on farm loans suffered just as much as the farmers during the early twenties.

These structural changes in the economy were not necessarily good or bad. They just were. Old industries decayed while new industries were born. And while it was difficult for those involved in the decaying industries, the birth of new industries created great opportunities for millions, and substantially increased the standard of living for the majority.

Most black people in the Deep South suffered extreme poverty as they typically worked as labourers or sharecroppers on small farms owned by white landlords. They were also subject to segregation and discrimination in areas such as housing, transport, shopping, health and education. In response, many black people escaped to the northern states to look for work and a better life, only to find themselves living in ghettos in major cities like Chicago and Detroit. The same was true for many uneducated migrants, who ended up working in lower-paid jobs, and people from eastern and southern Europe, who oftentimes suffered prejudice.

By early 1928, the Fed had become deeply concerned about speculation in the stock market and responded by raising the discount rate from 3.5 per cent to 5 per cent between January and July of that year. With nominal consumer prices falling, this put the real discount rate at about 6 per cent. At the same time, the Fed engaged in extensive open market operations to drain reserves from the banking system, further tightening monetary policy.[145] This tightening flowed through into market interest rates with time-money rates rising to 8 per cent, commercial paper rates to 6 per cent, and call rates rising to between 15 and 20 per cent.[146] The process of weaning the economy off five years of rampant money supply growth had begun.

Higher interest rates in the U.S. curtailed capital flows to Europe and South America, forcing other central banks to follow the American lead and increase their own interest rates. This forced a synchronised tightening in global monetary policy. Concerned by rising stock prices, brokers also began raising margin requirements on call loans. By the fall of 1929, margin requirements were the highest in the history of the New York Stock Exchange.[147]

By the second quarter of 1929, it was apparent that economic activity was slowing. The U.S. economy peaked in August and fell into recession in September.[148]

Chapter 7

The Great Depression

'We will not have any more crashes in our time.'
John Maynard Keynes (1927)

'... a serious depression seems improbable; [we expect] recovery of business next spring, with further improvement in the fall.'
Harvard Economic Society (November 10, 1929)

The Great Depression is one of the most studied events in economic history. It is from this analysis that most current mainstream economic theories arose. These theories also gave rise to the dominant role that economists and economic thinking play in today's society: a role, for better or worse, far greater than at any other time in history. The analysis also highlighted a major divergence in thinking between the leading schools of economic thought, for example Keynesianism, monetarism and the Austrian School, one which saw Keynesianism and monetarism emerge triumphant, notwithstanding the glaring deficiencies in both theory and practice in each.

The response from authorities in responding to the economic downturn also represented a marked shift away from policy responses to such events over the previous century. Rather than let market forces help the economy adjust to these shocks and imbalances, the government forcibly intervened to prevent market forces from operating. Propping up wages and prices in the face of structural economic problems and overwhelming deflationary forces, together with other forms of government intervention, would become a hallmark of government policy under both the Hoover and Roosevelt administrations. There seems little doubt that these interventionist policies not only deepened the Depression, but also extended its duration, and the human misery and suffering associated with it.

Chapter 7 is divided into two sections. The first details how the Great Depression began, how government responded and how the depression unfolded. The second part analyses the different theories put forward on the causes of the Great Depression.

How the Great Depression Unfolded

While the U.S. stock market peaked on September 3, 1929, the initial decline was relatively benign. Selling intensified in mid-October and on October 24, 'Black Thursday', the market lost 11 per cent of its value at the opening bell on very heavy volume. The market recovered slightly in the coming days, but with increasing investor concern and more investors facing margin calls, investors decided to exit the market en masse. On October 28, 'Black Monday', the Dow fell a record 38.3 points, or 13 per cent.[149] The Dow lost an additional 12 per cent on 'Black Tuesday', while the volume of stocks traded reached a peak that would not be broken for nearly 40 years.[150] Some stocks actually had no buyers at any price, creating 'air pockets' for these stocks.

The 1929 U.S. stock market crash signified the beginning of the Great Depression, the longest and most severe depression of the twentieth century. It was to have devastating effects in countries rich and poor. Thousands of banks, hundreds of thousands of businesses and millions of farmers ceased operations or became bankrupt.

From 1929–32, U.S. industrial production fell 46 per cent, wholesale prices fell 32 per cent, foreign trade slumped 70 per cent,[151] while unemployment peaked at 25 per cent in early 1933. The DJIA fell nearly 90 per cent before it bottomed in mid-1932.[152]

Newly elected U.S. President Herbert Hoover met with business and labour leaders, telling them that cutting wage rates (the standard response in previous depressions) would be disastrous, because workers wouldn't make enough money to buy the products. According to Hoover, this 'liquidation' of labour would only deepen the depression by reducing their 'purchasing power'. To fulfill Hoover's request that 'the first shock must fall on profits and not on wages',[153] leading industrialists pledged to maintain wage rates, expand construction, and share any reduced work.[154]

The New York Federal Reserve also took prompt and decisive action to ease credit conditions. In addition to lowering interest rates, the New York Fed encouraged banks to borrow freely from the discount window to support brokerage houses which were reeling under the weight of bad debts brought on by the collapsing share market. The New York Fed also bought government securities on its own account to inject reserves into the banking system. In this way, they contained an incipient liquidity crisis and prevented the crash from spreading to money markets.[155]

Even before the onset of the depression, Hoover had bowed to relentless pressure from the farm lobby by establishing the Federal Farm Board (FFB), the purpose of which was to control farm surpluses and boost produce prices. To combat falling prices, it made loans to farmers to keep wheat and cotton off the market, and later started to buy the surpluses and hold the produce in storage. For a while, prices held up and farmers increased production, after which prices fell even more. The surpluses of wheat accumulated to such an extent that the FFB decided to dump wheat stocks abroad, resulting in a drastic fall in market prices. Attempts to maintain the prices of other products such as livestock, cotton and wool also failed.[156]

As economic conditions deteriorated, in what would prove to be a disastrous economic decision, the U.S. government passed the Smoot-Hawley Tariff in June 1930 which raised tariffs on over 20,000 imported goods.[157] The legislation was strongly opposed by leading industrial figures and most economists, who signed a petition protesting the legislation, claiming that the tariffs would turn the recession into a worldwide depression.

They argued that the tariffs would raise the cost of living by 'compelling the consumer to subsidise waste and inefficiency in [domestic] industry'; that the export sector would suffer as they would lose their export markets while increasing the price of imported equipment; other countries would retaliate against the U.S. actions; and finally, Americans with investments abroad would suffer since the tariffs would make it 'more difficult for foreign debtors to pay the interest due them'.[158]

These predictions proved particularly prescient as, almost immediately, foreign countries imposed retaliatory tariffs on U.S. goods. The effect was such that between 1929 and 1933, U.S. imports fell by 66 per cent and exports by 61 per cent.[159] Between 1929 and 1934, world trade fell by 66 per cent.[160]

While external trade was a relatively small component of the overall economy at the time, the trade war brought on by the Smoot-Hawley tariffs hit some sectors such as agriculture, steel, mining and automotive particularly hard. American agriculture, for example, had customarily exported over 20 per cent of its wheat, just over half its cotton and 40 per cent of its tobacco and lard.[161] This trade collapsed. Not only was income decimated, but it also laid waste to capital investment, asset prices and employment.

Not surprisingly, the downturn had severe knock-on effects in the banking system in the affected regions. For example, rural banks in the Midwest and southern states began failing by the thousands. Pittsburgh (steel) saw 11 of its largest banks close in September 1931, while the Detroit banking system (autos) was in complete collapse by early 1933.[162]

Reduced trade also had a major impact on global financial flows, as many countries were unable to acquire dollars to repay their debts. The tariff wars and the subsequent moratorium on debt re-payments created financial crises across America, Europe and a host of nations in South America, leading many countries to abandon the gold standard.[163]

Initially, government and business expenditure held up quite well, spending more in the first half of 1930 than in the corresponding period of the previous year. In contrast, consumers, many of whom had suffered severe losses in the stock market, slashed their expenditures by 10 per cent. In addition, a severe drought ravaged the agricultural heartland of the U.S..[164]

By mid–1930, interest rates had dropped to low levels, but expected deflation and the continuing reluctance of people to borrow meant that consumer spending and investment remained depressed.[165] Prices began to decline, although wages held steady in 1930. By May 1930, automobile sales had fallen to levels below those of 1928. Conditions were worse in farming, logging and mining areas, where commodity prices plunged and unemployment soared.

After the initial liquidity crisis had been contained, monetary policy once again began its contractionary stance. Throughout 1930, officials at the New York Fed repeatedly proposed that the Fed buy government securities on the open market to relieve credit conditions, but they were systematically rebuffed by other members of the Federal Reserve.

The reasons for opposing monetary expansion are instructive. Several felt that much of the investment undertaken in the previous expansion was fundamentally unsound, and the economy could not recover until it was cleansed of malinvestments. Others felt that a monetary expansion would only ignite another round of speculative activity, perhaps even in the stock market. In any event, monetary policy remained contractionary, with the monetary aggregates falling by between 2 per cent and 4 per cent, while real long-term interest rates increased.[166]

The crisis worsened in 1931 as deflation took hold. Production continued to fall drastically, as did prices and foreign trade, while unemployment increased to almost 16 per cent. After stabilising following its initial collapse, the DJIA resumed its fall, falling from 287 to 43 between March 1930 and June 1932 – a fall of 85 per cent.

In early 1931, Hoover introduced a bill providing $25 million in government unemployment relief. The Red Cross opposed the bill, declaring that it would 'to a large extent destroy voluntary giving'. Many private charity organisations, philanthropists, business leaders, social workers and former President Coolidge held similar views, citing the provision of unemployment relief as having a role in creating and perpetuating unemployment in Britain.[167] While this initial attempt at providing relief was unsuccessful, Hoover would be more successful the following year.

In 1931, the government passed legislation* which mandated that prevailing (union) wages be paid by the Federal Government

* The Davis-Bacon Act

for public works projects. Hoover promoted and supported the legislation, as he believed that 'the very essence of great production is high wages...because it depends upon a widening range of consumption only to be obtained from the purchasing power of high real wages...'[168]

Holding firm to Hoover's belief that downward pressure on wages must be resisted at all cost, in early 1932 the government passed further labour laws[†] banning 'yellow-dog' contracts where employees agree not to be a member of a labour union, removed federal courts' authority to issue injunctions against labour disputes, and provided greater ease for workers to organise.[169] This represented a landmark victory for organised labour.

The consequences of these two pieces of legislation, however, had the opposite effect of what was intended. By keeping nominal wages high while prices were falling, real wages continued to rise. With profitability declining, companies were forced to either shutter their doors, reduce employee hours and/or lay off staff, all of which had the effect of increasing unemployment and reducing consumption.

For those lucky enough to keep their jobs and working hours, the Depression improved their standard of living. For the rest, it proved disastrous. Between 1929 and mid–1932, average weekly hours worked fell one-third from over 48 to less than 32 hours per week. In no previous depression had hours worked fallen by more than 10 per cent. Average weekly earnings fell by over 40 per cent, while real weekly earnings fell by over 30 per cent. Sadly, the unemployed suffered the most, with unemployment rising to one quarter of the population, reaching nearly half in particular manufacturing sectors.[170]

† The Norris-Laguardia Act

Much of this unemployment can be directly attributed to Hoover's interventionist policies.

Faced with a Federal deficit ballooning to $2 billion in 1931, Hoover felt that he had to do something to rein in debt. Rather than rein in expenditure, however, he chose to increase taxes. The Revenue Act of 1932 was one of the greatest increases in taxation ever enacted in the United States in peacetime. No group was left unscathed as the government increased sales tax, excise, income tax, company tax and estate tax; increased the price of government services such as postage; and eliminated a range of previous exemptions.

This was the exact opposite of what authorities had done in the 1920–21 Depression and had the effect of reducing the capacity of taxpayers to spend rather than putting money in the hands of consumers. Moreover, it was at complete odds with his measures to keep wages high to maintain consumption. As a result, Federal revenue for 1932 actually declined.

Hoover provided additional stimulus by appropriating funds[‡] for public works such as dams, and the creation of the federal Reconstruction Finance Corporation (RFC). The RFC provided financial support to state and local governments and made loans to banks, railroads, mortgage associations, and other businesses. It had authority to lend up to $2 billion to rescue banks and restore confidence in financial institutions. Unfortunately, $2 billion was not enough to save all the banks, and bank runs continued.[171]

In addition to increased government spending, authorities sought to re-ignite inflation through aggressive monetary policy. From February 1932 to the end of the year, total bank reserves ballooned 30 per cent, which was unprecedented in

‡ The 1932 Emergency Relief and Construction Act

the history of the Fed. As a result, excess reserves held by the Fed increased from 2.4 per cent to 20.3 per cent.[172] Had the banks used these reserves to increase loans, the U.S. money supply would have increased by $8 billion. Instead, the money supply fell by over 5 per cent.[173]

This highlights the impotency of monetary policy in trying to solve a major economic meltdown. Despite the best efforts of authorities to loosen monetary policy and increase demand, people don't necessarily react the way policy-makers theorise when faced with a crisis. People live in the real world, not in the rarified and sheltered kingdom of academia.

Hoover left office in March 1933 at the height of the Depression. Since the peak in 1929, production had fallen by more than one-half and unemployment had hit 25 per cent. The durables goods sector, which included construction, roads, metals, iron and steel, lumber and railroads, sectors which had benefited the most during the boom-times, were also the hardest hit in the downturn.[174]

While non-durable manufacturing production fell 30 per cent, the index of durable manufactures fell 77 per cent. This was also reflected in unemployment in these sectors. Between 1929 and 1933, total employment in the durable goods sectors fell from 10 million to 4 million, while employment in consumer goods, food, farming, textiles, electricity, fuel and so on, fell from 15 million to 13 million.[175]

Of course, these raw statistics mask the real tragedy of the Depression, which was etched in the lives of everyday people as they sought to eke out a meagre living doing whatever they could to survive. President Hoover's name became synonymous with the hardships faced by many. Soup was called 'Hoover Stew', and shantytowns made of cardboard and sheets were called 'Hoovervilles'. One of the largest Hoovervilles was built in 1930 in St Louis. It had its own mayor, churches and social institutions. The shantytown was funded by private donors and existed until 1936.[176] Elsewhere, some 6,000 street vendors walked the streets of New York City in 1930 trying to sell apples for 5 cents each, while breadlines became common place.

The effects of the Depression, particularly for some country folk, were made worse by droughts, which turned farming land into giant dust bowls. In the previous decade, farmers had conducted extensive, deep ploughing of the virgin topsoil of the Great Plains. This had displaced the native, deep-rooted grasses that normally trapped soil and moisture even during periods of drought and high winds. The ecological problems were exacerbated by the rapid mechanisation of farm equipment, which had contributed to farmers' decisions to convert arid grassland into cultivated cropland.[177] The resultant dust bowl forced tens of thousands of families to abandon their farms, with many moving to California and other states, where they found that the Depression had rendered the economy just as bad as the one they had left.

The newly elected Democrat president, Franklin Delano Roosevelt, came to government accusing Hoover of reckless and extravagant spending, for leading the highest spending administration in peace times in America's history, and promising to reduce government expenditure.

Roosevelt called for an immediate and drastic reduction in government expenditures by abolishing useless commissions and offices, saving a quarter of the cost of the Federal Government.[178] He also demanded a balanced budget, low tariffs and a sound currency, while promising to abolish the disastrous policy of prohibition, which had starved the government of much-needed tax revenue.

While he did abolish prohibition, Roosevelt did a backflip on many other policies he had campaigned for as he systematically got rid of laissez-faire capitalism, greatly increased the power of the trade unions, introduced social welfare, and significantly increased the role of government in the economy. In so doing, he prolonged the suffering of the people by extending the Depression, while engaging in class warfare by railing against bosses and tying welfare to recipients to win political support. Indeed, Roosevelt was the socialist's socialist.

The centerpiece of Roosevelt's economic policy was his New Deal, which was a series of programs which were enacted between 1933 and 1938. This focused on what historians refer to as the '3 Rs' – Relief, Recovery and Reform: relief for the unemployed and poor; recovery of the economy to normal levels; and reform of the financial system to prevent a repeat depression.[179]

Almost immediately upon taking office, Roosevelt was confronted with a major banking crisis. Despite constant efforts by the Hoover administration and the Fed to reflate the financial system, the banking system continued to falter. During the 1920s, in a typical year, up to 700 banks failed. Between 1929 and 1933, almost half of the 25,000 banks in the U.S. failed, wreaking havoc on the lives of many who lost their life savings and their livelihoods.[180]

The banks and the public responded to these adverse economic conditions in a rational way. The remaining banks ran down their commercial loans to preserve capital and minimise bad debts. Equally, as the Depression got worse and people feared for their life savings if their bank went under, they began pulling their money out of banks in large numbers. In the latter stages of his presidency, Hoover responded by lambasting the public for their 'traitorous hoarding' and organised an anti-hoarding drive in which he pleaded with the public to stop converting their bank deposits into cash.[181] Despite his pleas, the actions of the banks and the public continued to act as a deflationary counterweight to the inflationary efforts of the Fed and the government.

State governments also responded to the growing insistence of people claiming their rightful, legally owned property, by imposing 'bank holidays', thus permitting the banks to stay in business while delaying the payment of the just claims of their depositors.[182] This would be one of several instances throughout the Depression where desperate governments attacked individuals' property rights and pursued destructive economic policies for the sake of the so-called greater good.

Rather than stem the outflow of funds, however, all these bank holidays did was to increase fear and precipitate an intense scramble by depositors to withdraw their money. To stem the run on banks, in March 1933 Roosevelt took the extraordinary step of shutting all the nation's banks for a week, with many staying closed for much longer. During this time, the Emergency Banking Act was signed into law. It provided for a system of reopening sound banks under Treasury supervision, with federal loans available if needed. The government also passed legislation regulating the securities industry and providing federal insurance of bank deposits.

A month later, Roosevelt further eroded people's property rights when he took advantage of a wartime statute and passed Executive Order 6102, which made it illegal for individuals or corporations in continental U.S. to possess gold coins, bullion and gold certificates. People were required to hand over their gold by May 1, 1933 at an initial price of $20.67 per troy ounce. Those who violated the order were subject to confiscation of their gold and fines of up to $10,000, and/or up to 10 years in prison. The price was subsequently raised in 1934 to $35 per ounce, effectively devaluing the dollar by 40 per cent in order to ignite inflation and jumpstart the economy.

These desperate measures by the government clearly called into focus the efficacy of the Fed, the very organisation that had been set up to oversee stability of the U.S. financial system. The Fed failed then, just as it has since. This is a great example of how desperate politicians and bureaucrats will introduce draconian measures, even if they trample on their citizens' rights, if they believe it is in their own interests to solve problems they created in the first instance.

In a further attempt to strengthen the banking sector, the government passed the Banking Act of 1933, also known as Glass-Steagall. An important motivation for the legislation was the desire to restrict the use of bank credit for speculation, and to direct bank credit into what Senator Glass and others thought to be more productive uses, such as industry, commerce and agriculture.[183]

The Act effectively separated commercial banking from investment banking. Commercial banks, which took in deposits and made loans, were no longer allowed to underwrite or deal in securities, while investment banks, which underwrote and dealt in securities, were no longer allowed to have close connections to commercial banks, such as overlapping directorships or common ownership, nor were they allowed to accept deposits. Other important provisions of Glass-Steagall included the creation of the Federal Deposit Insurance Corporation, the extension of deposit insurance to include state-chartered banks and the creation of the Federal Open Market Committee (FOMC) as part of the Fed.

Despite its lofty intentions to protect the financial system, under intense pressure from the banking elite, key provisions of Glass-Steagall were watered down over the years and the provisions separating commercial banking from investment banking were finally repealed in 1999, just in time for the GFC.

Having survived the banking crisis, Roosevelt set about delivering the first initiatives of his New Deal Plan, which included the National Recovery Act (NRA) and the Agriculture Adjustment Act (AAA).

The goal of the NRA was to eliminate 'cut-throat and destructive competition' by bringing industry, labour and government together to create codes of 'fair competition' and set fair prices – in other words, to establish industry cartels. The legislation was designed to help workers by setting minimum wages and maximum weekly hours, as well as set minimum prices at which products could be sold.[184] The legislation also called for agreements on maintaining employment and production. Anti-trust laws were specifically set aside for this legislation.

In a remarkably short time, the NRA established agreements in almost every major industry in the nation. About 23 million people were employed under the NRA codes. According to some conservative economists, the NRA increased the cost of doing business by 40 per cent,[185] further adding to industry woes in an already tough economic environment.

The NRA was famous for its bureaucracy. Journalist Raymond Clapper reported that between 4,000 and 5,000 business practices were prohibited by NRA orders, which were contained in some 3,000 administrative orders running to over 10 million pages. These were supplemented by what Clapper said were 'innumerable opinions and directions from national, regional and code boards interpreting and enforcing provisions of the act'.[186]

Over 700 industrial codes were created and rigorously enforced by thousands of government code enforcers who could 'enter a man's factory, send him out, line up his employees, subject them to minute interrogation, and take over his books on the instant'. Night work was forbidden. One hapless tailor became famous nationally after he was arrested, convicted and imprisoned by the code police for the crime of pressing a suit for 35 cents rather than the NRA required 40 cents. The NRA was ruled unconstitutional by the U.S. Supreme Court in May 1935.[187]

The purpose of the AAA was to reduce crop surpluses and raise the price of agricultural products by paying farmers subsidies not to plant on part of their land, and to kill excess livestock. The money for these subsidies was generated through an exclusive tax on food-processing companies.

The AAA had mixed results. In 1935, farm income was 50 per cent higher than it was in 1932, which was partly due to farm programs such as the AAA.[188] On the other hand, many people suffered greatly under the legislation. Firstly, people and livestock were starving to death. Farmers slaughtered livestock because feed prices were rising, and they couldn't afford to feed their own animals.[189] The legislation also disproportionately benefited large farmers and food processors, with fewer benefits flowing to small farmers and sharecroppers.[190] Thirdly, reduced production led to increasing unemployment for farm workers. Finally, rising prices for staple products increased the cost of living for everyday people who could ill-afford it. This was yet another example of government policy having unintended consequences.

In 1933–34, the government introduced a number of other relief programs including the Civilian Conservation Corps, which provided unskilled manual labour jobs for the conservation and development of natural resources on government-owned rural lands; the Tennessee Valley Authority, to develop the economy in a region that had been particularly hard hit by the depression; and the Federal Housing Administration, to regulate mortgages and housing conditions.

Herbert Hoover's Reconstruction Finance Corporation (RFC) was greatly expanded by Roosevelt, but this only made capital markets less efficient, thereby prolonging the Depression even further. According to RFC director Jesse Jones, 'The law specified that we should lend only where the borrower could not get the money from others on reasonable terms.' [191] That is, lend only to uncreditworthy borrowers. That makes sense, but only if you are economically illiterate. Guided by this directive, Jones and the RFC redirected billions of dollars in valuable capital to politically connected, but economically questionable, businesses. 'We even loaned money to [the owners of] a drove of reindeer in Alaska,' Jones boasted. The RFC was abolished in the 1955 under a cloud of corruption and scandal. Who would have thought!

The economic impact of the first New Deal Plan was mixed at best. While GDP inched up a touch, driven largely by a partial recovery in personal consumption, unemployment in 1935 remained stubbornly high at 20 per cent, or around 10 million people.[192] The New Deal, however, proved particularly popular with voters, especially amongst traditional Democrats, the white working class, African Americans, labour unions, ethnic minorities, southerners and left-wing intellectuals.

Concerned about limited progress in overcoming the Depression, and with an election looming, Roosevelt launched his Second New Deal Plan, which relied far more heavily on increased Keynesian-style deficit spending as well as initiatives aimed at long-term policy reform. New initiatives included the introduction of government-funded social welfare, further changes to the labour laws and additional infrastructure development programs.

Like its first incarnation, the Second New Deal was attacked by Republicans, conservative Democrats and bankers, amongst others, who argued that it doled out too many federal handouts and smacked of rampant socialism. Such criticism was timely, given the situation in Russia and elsewhere. Not surprisingly, some of the most strident criticism came from the far left, who argued that the New Deal didn't go far enough.

Roosevelt created a federal old-age pension scheme for workers over 65 years of age, funded by a payroll tax on both employers and employees[§]. The scheme also established an unemployment insurance scheme to provide temporary assistance for those out of work, while providing public, maternal and child health services and support for disabled and needy children.

While providing help for the needy, one of the major drawbacks of the scheme was that it was funded by a tax on both workers and employers. This not only increased the cost of employing people, but it also reduced the amount of money employees could spend, both of which worked against economic recovery. According to one econometric study, by 1938, cost increases associated with government-mandated payroll taxes added nearly 1.2 million people to the unemployment queue.[193]

Roosevelt also embarked on additional labour market reforms[¶] aimed at crushing all employer resistance to labour unions by guaranteeing the rights of private sector employees to organise into trade unions, engage in collective bargaining for better wages and conditions, and take collective action, including strike action, if necessary.

These reforms led to a surge in union membership, particularly in the steel and automotive industries, and increasing

---

§ The 1935 Social Security Act

¶ The 1935 National Labour Relations Act, also known as the Wagner Act union militancy through threats, boycotts, strikes, seizures of plants and outright violence. In 1936, for example, the United Auto Workers began a sit-down strike at a GM plant in Flint, Michigan that lasted 44 days and spread to some 150,000 auto workers in 35 cities. By 1937, to the dismay of most corporate leaders, some 8 million workers had joined unions and were loudly demanding their rights.[194] It seems incredible that unions would launch such destructive action when American unemployment still stood at over 14 per cent.[195]

The Works Progress Administration (WPA) was the largest and most ambitious New Deal program, employing millions of unemployed people (mostly unskilled men) to carry out public works projects, including the construction of roads, bridges, parks and public buildings such as schools and hospitals. Support under the WPA was also extended to musicians, artists, writers, actors and directors in large arts, drama, media and literacy projects.[196] Its purpose was to provide one paid job for all families in which the primary breadwinner suffered long-term unemployment.[197] At the time, work relief was preferred over public assistance (the dole), because it maintained self-respect, reinforced the work ethic and kept skills sharp.[198]

Despite being an unmitigated economic failure, Roosevelt's New Deal programs were a resounding political success, as they provided almost unlimited opportunities for political largesse. In 1939, a special U.S. Senate Committee on Campaign Expenditures investigated the programs and found that in many states, workers were required to sign a pledge to vote Democrat and, in some cases, to make campaign contributions as a condition of employment. In some instances, businesses that sold supplies to the government were also required to make campaign contributions to the Democratic Party in return for contracts.[199] In effect, the New Deal was largely a legalised shake-down operation.

Despite popular support amongst workers and minorities, the New Deal was strongly condemned by Republicans and business leaders, who argued that many of the initiatives were counterproductive. The conservative majority on the Supreme Court also ruled that many of the New Deal initiatives such as the NRA and AAA were unconstitutional.

To protect his plans from further meddling by the courts, in 1937 Roosevelt petitioned Congress to alter the make-up of the Supreme Court, alleging that the age of many of the justices was affecting their judgement and ability to work. Roosevelt sought the power to appoint six new judges and replace judges over 70 years of age. In what became widely known as the Court-Packing Scheme, Roosevelt's intentions were obvious to most Americans from the start. He wanted to get rid of conservative judges and stack the court with people more sympathetic to his cause. Not surprisingly, the more he attempted to cover up his plans, the more cynical the public became. In response to Roosevelt's actions, Congress began to vote more conservatively, reducing Roosevelt's ability to pass additional New Deal measures. The scandal took a huge toll on Roosevelt's reputation and marked the beginning of the end of his New Deal program.

By 1936, most economic indicators had returned to the levels of the late 1920s (though unemployment, remained stubbornly high at 14 per cent)[200] and in June 1937, the Roosevelt administration began efforts to scale back the budget deficit by cutting spending and increasing taxation.

In response, the economy experienced a sharp downturn which lasted 13 months. Manufacturing output fell 37 per cent, back to 1934 levels,[201] while production of durable goods fell even faster. Unemployment jumped to 19 per cent, rising from 5 million to more than 12 million in early 1938.[202]

By May 1938, however, the worst of the recession was over as retail sales, employment and industrial production began to improve again.[203] By 1941, America had largely recovered from the Great Depression as wartime expenditures spurred economic activity and structural problems had largely been overcome.

The economic downturn impacted countries in different ways, depending on a range of domestic and international factors. These included the economic structure, reliance on the U.S. for trade and investment, the monetary regime, exchange rate flexibility, the government's response to the downturn, and domestic events in the lead-up to the Great Depression.

Commodity-producing nations such Australia, Canada, South Africa and Chile suffered greatly as falling export demand and commodity prices exerted massive downward pressure on income and wages, exacting a terrible toll on unemployment and business failures, and leading to sporadic bouts of civil unrest. Unemployment reached a record high of 29 per cent in Australia[204] while national income fell by 44 per cent in Canada, the worst of any nation outside of the U.S..[205]

The northern industrial areas of Britain were also particularly hard hit as demand for traditional industrial products collapsed. In 1993, 30 per cent of Glaswegians were unemployed, while in some towns and cities in the northeast, unemployment reached 70 per cent as shipbuilding fell 90 per cent.[206] In contrast, in the less industrialised Midlands and Southern England, the effects were short-lived, and the latter 1930s were relatively prosperous.

Germany was also deeply affected as American loans to rebuild the German economy ceased, while in both the UK and

France, industrial production fell by 23 per cent, wholesale prices by one-third and foreign trade fell by more than half.[207]

In contrast, neither Japan nor China was greatly affected by the Great Depression. China stayed on the silver standard until 1935 after which she moved to a fiat-based currency, which was issued by four Chinese national banks. The Nationalist government also undertook significant reforms to the banking and legal systems as well as building railroads and highways, improving public health facilities, legislating against trafficking in narcotics, and augmenting industrial and agricultural production.[208]

Between 1929 and 1931, the Japanese economy shrank by a modest 8 per cent. Japan responded to the downturn by devaluing her currency and undertaking fiscal stimulus involving deficit spending. The Bank of Japan also undertook measures to counteract potential inflationary pressures. Econometric studies have identified the fiscal stimulus was especially effective in Japan.[209] The currency devaluation also had an immediate effect as Japanese textiles began to displace British products in export markets. By 1933, Japan was out of the Depression as it began to militarise.

The Causes of the Great Depression

The Great Depression is one of the most studied events in economic history. As part of their analysis, economists have pondered several key questions:

1. What caused the Great Depression?
2. Why did this downturn turn into a Depression while other economic downturns were less severe?
3. Why was the Depression so prolonged in the U.S. vis-à-vis other countries, and against previous downturns in the U.S.?

4. What can we learn from the Great Depression to better manage the economy and the business cycle?
5. What, if anything, can we do to avoid another Great Depression?

The startling truth is that the mainstream economic community cannot accurately answer most of these questions. At least with anything that would stand up to the rigours of scientific enquiry.

Now, many of you might ask: why is this such a big deal? Principally because mainstream economists have played an ever-increasing role in advising on the way government and economies operate post-World War II. Politicians, bureaucrats, economists and financial commentators have portrayed economists as being experts in their field, experts who have their bony little fingers set firmly on the economic levers to sail the ship through unchartered waters to a safe haven. Nobody seems to question their conflicting and incomplete theories and opinions. Nor question their obvious failures like the Latin American crisis, the Asian and Russian debt crises, the dot-com bubble and GFC. And knowing no different, fed a continuous stream of propaganda from the government, the banks and the mainstream media, the adoring and/or apathetic public have accepted this narrative.

It is quite extraordinary. Everybody now knows that if you have an economic downturn, then all you need to do is increase government expenditure and reduce interest rates. There is no alternative. This is the way! And even if you don't have an economic crisis, mainstream wisdom is that you must increase government expenditure and maintain low interest rates. We have found economic nirvana. Hallelujah.

But what if this visage was an illusion, a chimera, a deception, a sham, a con, a ruse, where the fawning public found out that mainstream economics is really a hodgepodge of unproven theories, and where many economists don't know the difference between finance and economics. Now that would be truly frightening! Our livelihoods, our prosperity, our physical security and even our psychological health is dependent on a group of people, namely mainstream economists, bureaucrats and politicians, encouraged by the elite, who don't know what they are doing when it comes to economics.

And sadly, all of this arose out of failed analysis surrounding the Great Depression, particularly by Lord Keynes and Milton Friedman. In this section, I will outline the two mainstream economic theories (Keynesian and monetarist), a popular heterodox theory (Austrian school) as well as other useful contributions by Irving Fisher and Hyman Minsky on the causes of the Great Depression. In particular, this discussion will highlight that the Austrian school of economics gives the most complete explanation of the Great Depression.

Hopefully, as we move through this discussion, the reader will ask themselves the crucial question: why have mainstream economists shunned the Austrian school of economics in favour of the deeply flawed analysis by Keynes and Friedman? Perhaps they may come to the same conclusion that I did: because it doesn't suit the interests of the elite.

As noted in Chapter 6, all the pre-conditions for a deflationary depression – excessive debt, sky-high stock prices, rampant speculation and structural imbalances – had been put in place. The only questions left were: What would trigger the downturn? How deep would the depression be? How long would it last? If history was any guide, it should have been a short, sharp downturn of around two years.

Keynesian economics is a macroeconomic theory based on the work of twentieth-century British economist John

Maynard Keynes. Writing in the 1930s, Keynes spearheaded a revolution in economic thinking, challenging the ideas of classical economics that held that a free market economy tends to naturally restore itself to full employment and equilibrium, as long as workers are flexible in their wage demands. He also introduced a number of important economic concepts including the multiplier, the marginal efficiency of capital, the principle of effective demand and liquidity preference.[210] Prior to Keynes, mainstream economic thought posited that the economy existed in a state of general equilibrium with the assumption that if a surplus of goods or services arose, then prices would fall naturally to the point where demand would increase to match supply, and vice versa.

In his magnum opus, *The General Theory of Employment, Interest and Money*, Keynes argued that aggregate demand (total spending in the economy through consumption, investment and government expenditure), not supply, is the key variable that determines the overall level of economic activity and that inadequate aggregate demand could lead to prolonged periods of high unemployment as demand fell short of the potential productive capacity of the economy.[211]

His economic cure for an ailing economy, irrespective of the cause of the ailment, was increased government spending to offset any decline in consumption or investment, even if this meant running budget deficits. This was at odds with the prevailing economic orthodoxy, where balanced budgets were the norm.

Keynes also suggested that:

- aggregate demand is influenced by a host of economic decisions – both public and private – which are sometimes made erratically

- changes in aggregate demand, whether anticipated or unanticipated, have their greatest short-run effect on real output and employment, not on prices
- prices, and especially wages, respond slowly to changes in supply and demand, resulting in periodic shortages and surpluses[212]
- governments should solve problems in the short run rather than waiting for market forces to do it in the long run, because, 'in the long run we are all dead'.[213]

Implicit in Keynes's thinking was that we should manage for short-term benefit without worrying too much about the longer-term consequences.

Based on these premises, Keynes postulated that the level of employment is determined, not by the price of labour as proposed in classical economics, but by aggregate demand, and that in a market-based economy, under-employment and under-investment are likely to be the natural state unless active intervention is undertaken by government.

Central to Keynes's views was that wages are sticky to the downside, particularly in the short-run, as workers focus on nominal rather than real wages. As a result, wage cuts are difficult to effect because of laws and wage contracts. Even classical economists admitted these constraints exist but, unlike Keynes, they advocated abolishing minimum wages, unions and long-term contracts, and increasing labour-market flexibility. Keynes rejected the idea that cutting wages would cure recessions, concluding that it would likely make recessions worse.[214]

In addition to increasing government expenditure, Keynes advocated increasing inflation to reduce real wages while leaving nominal wages unchanged. Of course, this is a pea and thimble trick designed to reduce workers' living standards by reducing real wages through inflation, but Keynes, like modern politicians and economists, believed this was better than telling the truth. Keynes also believed that excess saving, that is saving beyond planned investment, was a serious problem, encouraging recession or even depression. In contrast, classical economists believed that interest rates would fall due to the excess supply of 'loanable funds'. [215] This would rebalance any mismatch between savings and investment by reducing savings and/or increasing investment – without the need for any external intervention.

While Keynesians generally believe in a mixed economy with a predominantly private sector, Keynes argued that active state intervention, including monetary policy actions by the central bank (reducing interest rates) and fiscal policy actions by the government (for example, government investment in infrastructure) was required in order to stabilise output over the business cycle[216] and to reduce the amplitude of the business cycle, which they rank amongst the most important of all economic problems.[217]

Contrary to current practice, Keynes didn't suggest running continual budget deficits. Instead, he suggested counter-cyclical fiscal policies, where deficit spending kicked in when a nation suffers from recession, or when recovery is delayed, and unemployment remains high. He also suggested either increasing taxes or reducing government expenditure to cool the economy in boom times and to prevent inflation.

Economists still argue about what Keynes thought caused high unemployment. Some think he attributed it to wages that take a long time to fall. But Keynes actually wanted wages not to fall, and in fact, advocated that wages be kept stable. A general cut in wages, he argued, would decrease income, consumption, and aggregate demand. This would offset any benefits to output that the lower price of labour might have contributed.[218]

Keynes's economics reflected his political beliefs. Keynes was an ardent supporter of the British Liberal Party, which was a forerunner to the Liberal Democrats. During the nineteenth century, the Liberal Party was broadly in favour of what today would be called classical liberalism: laissez-faire economic policies such as free trade and minimal government interference in the economy. However, in the early twentieth century, the Liberal Party moved its ideology to one of favouring an increased role for the state and greater welfare, in contrast to the more traditional classical liberal focus on self-help, freedom of choice and laissez-faire economics.[219] In other words, Keynes was strongly of the political left.

Given his statist political leanings, it's not surprising that Keynes rejected the fundamental premise of classical economics: that is that economies return to equilibrium through natural market adjustments, in favour of interventionist economic policies and support to maintain wages, irrespective of the economic merit in the efficacy and effectiveness of a more market-based approach in solving systemic economic issues.

Keynes was not the first, and certainly would not be the last, to confuse social policy and politics with economics. While clearly inter-related, they are quite separate disciplines. Confusing the disciplines, chasing short-term pain relief, inhibits efficient and effective market-based outcomes, while leading to waste, additional burdens and unintended consequences, especially over the longer term.

Keynes's work came in for strong criticism almost from the outset, but these criticisms were largely ignored by academic economists and policy-makers at the time. Perhaps the most trenchant critic of Keynes's work came in 1959 from Henry Hazlitt, who gave a chapter-by-chapter dissection of the arguments against Keynes's *General Theory*.

The central flaw in Keynes's thinking, Hazlitt insisted, was his unwillingness to acknowledge that the high unemployment in Great Britain in the 1920s and in the U.S in the 1930s was caused by government intervention, including the empowering of labour unions, that made many prices and wages virtually 'rigid'. Political and special-interest power prevented markets from competitively re-establishing a balance between supply and demand for various goods. Hence, the market was trapped in wage and price distortions that destroyed employment and production opportunities, resulting in the Great Depression.[220]

Hazlitt considered Keynes's inflationary fix crude and dangerous. First, Hazlitt pointed out that Keynes's focus on macroeconomic 'aggregates' concealed the microeconomic relationships amongst a multitude of individual prices and wages across a large range of industry sectors. The price level, wage level, total output, aggregate demand and aggregate supply were all statistical fictions that had no reality in the actual market, or more correctly, a myriad of market places. Thus, the wage level could not be too high relative to the general price level. The extent to which any individual money wage or resource price might have to adjust downwards depended on distinct supply and demand conditions in each individual market.[221] Hazlitt's point highlights why unemployment was higher in some industries and regions than others.

Hazlitt also pointed out that workers and labour unions were very much aware of how rising prices affect the real value of money wages, highlighting how quickly workers ask for pay rises to make up for lost purchasing power.

Hazlitt showed clearly how Keynes was confused about the actual relationships between savings, investment, and the rate of interest. The core of his theory was founded on a bundle of errors and mistakes. This resulted in Keynes's failure to comprehend that saving, investment, and capital formation – not government-stimulated increases in aggregate demand – are the foundations of sustainable employment and rising standards of living.[222]

Hazlitt also took Keynes to task for advocating increasing government control and direction for investment decision-making, questioning where Keynes could find people who were omnipotent, completely informed, rational, balanced, wise and able to rise above any self-interest in order to make appropriate and timely investment decisions and guide the economy back to sustainable health, without leading to further imbalances, wasteful expenditure and runaway debt.

Reflecting on how *The General Theory* had become so well accepted when it had so many obvious flaws, Hazlitt suggested that it appealed to self-interested groups as well as those who wished to overthrow the existing orthodoxy in favour of radical and fashionable ideas about social engineering. Hazlitt also argued that Keynes could dazzle the reader with literary imagery and wit that hid his central logical flaws, suggesting that Keynes used the 'technique of obscure arguments followed by clear and triumphant conclusions'. Whatever the reasons, Hazlitt concluded that the existence of the Keynesian cult is one of the great intellectual scandals of our age.[223]

American economist James M. Buchanan criticised Keynesian economics on the grounds that governments would be unlikely to implement theoretically optimal policies. He also blamed Keynesian economics for what he considered a decline in America's fiscal discipline.[224] Buchanan argued that deficit spending would evolve into a permanent disconnect between spending and revenue, precisely because it brings short-term gains, thus institutionalising irresponsibility in the federal government, the largest and most central institution in our society.[225]

American economist Martin Feldstein argues that the legacy of Keynesian economics – the misdiagnosis of unemployment, the fear of saving, and unjustified government intervention – affected the fundamental ideas of policy-makers. [226] I would go one step further and suggest that it has not only affected the thinking of policy-makers but, together with the introduction of the welfare state by Roosevelt, has tainted the thinking of the broad populace to this day.

American economist Milton Friedman thought that Keynes's political bequest was harmful for two reasons. Firstly, he thought whatever the economic analysis, benevolent dictatorship is likely sooner or later to lead to a totalitarian society. Secondly, he thought Keynes's economic theories appealed to a group far broader than economists primarily because of their link to his political approach.[227]

While Keynesian economics met with some acceptance during the high unemployment era of the 1930s and became the dominant economic ideology in western industrialised countries in the post-World War II era, it fell out of favour during the stagflation of the 1970s as the global economy suffered from simultaneous bouts of high inflation and high unemployment. However, it seems to have made a resurgence following the GFC.

Little of what Keynes advocated survives in modern economic theory. And yet his influence remains strong on two levels. Firstly, his ideas have been endlessly revised and remodeled by academics into a broad range of theories and concepts including neo-Keynesian and post-Keynesian economics – economic theories which form an essential part of current mainstream economic thought.

Despite their incarnation into different forms, many of the basic flaws in Keynesian economics remain. These flaws include reliance on the wisdom of policy-makers and politicians to intervene with the right decisions to resolve economic problems rather than rely on market forces. As a result, there is a tendency to defer difficult decisions, and instead run perpetual budget deficits. Politicians of all hues, but particularly left-leaning politicians, have also exploited Keynes's ideas on government intervention and deficit spending to justify extensive government involvement in the economy as well as their natural tendencies toward profligate spending. This has resulted in high levels of welfare spending and wasted spending on a range of social and ideologically driven projects, all of which takes money out of the hands of those who produce a nation's wealth, while leading to unsustainable levels of ruinous debt.

It is also puerile to focus on aggregate demand rather than understanding that supply and demand are inextricably linked. This is like saying that the left foot is more important than the right foot, that a coin only has one side, that air is more important than water or that you can have yin without yang. Keynes's ideas are not only misguided, but mind-blowingly stupid. As government spending is typically a far smaller component of the economy than the other components, especially consumption, it requires a much larger percentage increase in government expenditure to offset declines in consumption. This means that governments have to run up debt, which eventually needs to be repaid by future generations, or by increasing taxes. Either way reduces consumption, either now or in the future. This focus also assumes that downturns arise from cyclical rather than from structural factors. Failing to address the underlying structural problems just prolongs the downturn.

And yet these economically destructive ideas have been picked up by sympathetic academics, politicians and the mainstream press. For reasons of ignorance, ideology and laziness, they have blindly accepted neo-Keynesian economics without providing any criticism of its obvious shortcomings and flaws, and its role in driving the world into what will undoubtedly become a cataclysmic debt implosion.

*

Monetarism is a macroeconomic theory based largely on the work of the twentieth-century American economist Milton Friedman. Monetarists argue that the Great Depression was caused mainly by a precipitous decline in the money supply which, in turn, was the consequence of poor policy-making by the Fed. Friedman argues that bad monetary policy turned what was a garden-variety recession in an ordinary business cycle into a catastrophe.

According to former Fed Chairman Ben Bernanke, Friedman and co-author Anna Schwartz emphasised at least four major mistakes by U.S. monetary policy-makers.[228] The first error was the tightening of monetary policy in 1928, which they argue was not justified by the macroeconomic environment. They opine that the economy was only just emerging from a downturn, commodity prices were declining sharply, and there was little hint of inflation. Within 12 months of the monetary tightening, the U.S. entered into recession.

The second mistake occurred in September and October 1931, when the Fed raised interest rates after the U.S. dollar came under attack from currency speculators. At the time, most countries adhered to the gold standard. In September 1931, currency speculators attacked the British pound, forcing the Bank of England to abandon the gold standard and allow the pound to float freely, its value determined by market forces.

With the collapse of the pound, currency speculators next turned their attention to the U.S. dollar. In September and October of 1931, global central banks and private investors converted a substantial quantity of dollar assets to gold, reducing the Fed's gold reserves. This attack on the dollar also resulted in a panic in the U.S. banking system. Despite Friedman's criticisms, the Fed's actions in raising interest rates worked, and the attack on the U.S. dollar subsided.

The third policy mistake occurred when the Fed reduced interest rates between April and June 1932, but then reversed course and tightened monetary policy in July 1932, thus undoing any benefit of the lower interest rates. The reason they give for the reversal relates to the philosophy of the Federal Reserve. At the time, some members highlighted the very low nominal interest rates. They argued that lowering interest rates further would delay the inevitable adjustment that was required to purge the economy of the excesses of the 1920s, the so-called liquidationist view.

The fourth policy mistake was the Fed's ongoing neglect of problems in the U.S. banking system, a situation which Friedman and Schwartz believe worsened the downturn. They emphasised the effects of bank failures on the money supply. Because bank deposits are a form of money, the closure of so many banks greatly exacerbated the decline in the money supply. This, together with hoarding of cash, added to the deflationary pressures by depriving the economy of an important source of credit.

Friedman and Schwartz believed that the Fed could have ameliorated the situation by carrying out their assigned role of acting as lender of last resort. This would have entailed being more aggressive in lending cash to banks and engaging in large-scale open market purchases of government bonds from the banks to provide liquidity. According to Friedman and Schwartz, the Fed's actions were the primary cause of the Great Depression: too small and hesitant, and a complete abdication of its responsibilities.

Bernanke concludes by highlighting the need for central banks and other governmental agencies to maintain financial and price stability. As I will discuss at length later, I believe the current Fed, particularly under Greenspan and Bernanke's governorship, has been the major contributor to multiple asset bubbles caused by ultra-loose monetary policy, and that it has been their policies that have laid the groundwork for the looming great depression of the 2020s.

As with Keynesianism, there are several problems with Friedman's theory. The first is Friedman's inability to explain why the U.S. economy rebounded so quickly after the 1920–21 Depression despite the largest collapse in the monetary base in U.S. history,[229] and yet the economy languished for a decade after the 1929 crash despite substantial fiscal stimulus and the actions of the Fed to lower the discount rate.

The second problem is that Friedman's conclusions are speculative in that he merely hypothesises that the downturn might not have been as great, and/or the economy might have recovered more quickly if only the Fed had offset the massive cash withdrawals of the panicked public and kept the overall money supply stable. He offers no evidence as to what might have happened, just speculation, which is hardly a scientific method on which to base what has become one of the mainstays of modern economic theory and practice.

Thirdly, central to their argument is that the decline in the money supply was the primary cause of the decline in prices and output. There is no doubt that the decline in the money supply was part of the great unwinding that occurred during the Great Depression, and indeed it did lead to a decline in output and prices, particularly asset prices. But the reality is that the declining money supply only occurred because asset prices and the economy had been driven up to stratospheric levels by an unsustainable increase in the money supply during the great crack-up boom of the 1920s.

This unwinding reflects one of the great scientific principles, Newton's third law of physics, which states that for every action, there is an equal and opposite reaction. In other words, without the crack-up boom in the 1920s, there would have been nothing to unwind. The problem with Friedman and Schwarz's analysis is that they focus on the outcomes rather than the causes. The reality is that once bubbles are created, there is only one way they can go. Down! Better to prevent a bubble from occurring in the first place, rather than have to deal with its deflation later.

Their analysis is equally flawed in that there were a great many other factors that led to the decline in prices and output, not the least of which was excess capacity that arose in various sectors, for example construction and real estate, as a result of excessive investment due to plentiful credit, as well as structural problems besetting certain industries, particularly agriculture. Their argument also fails to address the fundamental reasons that so many banks failed: their poor management and over-reliance on specific industry sectors which were hit particularly hard, for example steel, automobiles and agriculture.

In suggesting that governments artificially preserve money supply at elevated levels to maintain otherwise insolvent institutions and stop the necessary adjustment process following an unsustainable boom, rather than allow market forces to cleanse the system of weaker institutions and allow the healthier institutions to survive and thrive, is not only contrary to the market-based principles of capitalism, it is also contrary the universal laws of nature that govern all human activity. It might not be fair, nor might we like it, but once excessive imbalances have arisen, there is nothing we can do to prevent these immutable laws of the universe from eventually playing out. Those who suggest they can overcome them, such as politicians and mainstream economists, are snake oil salesmen, pure and simple. Bernanke has been lauded by mainstream economists and the elite as an expert on the Great Depression. It's a pity he majored in depression rather than prosperity. The world would have been a far better place.

*

The Austrian school is an economic school of thought that originated in Vienna during the late nineteenth century with the works of Carl Menger. Other Austrians of note include Ludwig von Mises, Friedrich Hayek and Murray Rothbard. Austrian thinking on how business cycles occur is central to their views on how an economy functions.

Regularly occurring economic booms and busts were first observed from the late eighteenth century and coincided with the start of the Industrial Revolution. The early theorists also observed that booms and busts coincided with changes in banking practices, and their capacity to expand credit and the money supply (first in the form of paper money, and later in the form of demand deposits, which are instantly redeemable in cash at the banks). It was the operations of the commercial banks which held the key to the mysterious recurrent cycles of expansion and contraction.[230]

Austrians view business cycles as the consequence of excessive growth in bank credit (an increase in the money supply), due to an artificially low market rate of interest set by a central bank or fractional reserve banks.[231] Sustained periods of low interest rates and excessive credit creation result in a volatile and unstable imbalance between savings and investment,[232] as well as a misallocation of resources from investment to consumption. Over time, these imbalances and distortions inevitably result in recession as the economy seeks to move back into balance.

According to the theory, the business cycle unfolds in the following way: banks expand credit well beyond their own assets and their clients' funds (deposits). This additional credit lowers the interest rate and stimulates economic activity. Projects (for example, capital investment and mergers and acquisitions) which would have been unviable at higher interest rates now seem profitable. The additional projects also increase the demand for production materials, higher end goods such as machine tools and labour, leading to an increase in the prices of capital, consumption goods and wages as companies compete for the same scarce resources. If the banks curtailed the supply of credit in the initial stages of the boom, the boom would rapidly come to an end. But this seldom occurs.

Instead, as the economy accelerates, people become increasingly optimistic and less risk averse, leading to ever-increasing demand for more credit as the investment boom continues. The credit-driven boom eventually results in widespread malinvestment, overcapacity and an unsustainable debt load.

As social mood turns from positive to negative, the previous boom unwinds as people become more pessimistic, banks tighten lending standards, investment dries up, demand softens, the money supply contracts, and asset and consumer prices fall. Starved of an economy propped up artificially by plentiful amounts of cheap money, companies are forced to lay off staff while others go broke – both of which reduce wages and increase unemployment. The end result is a curative recession, and occasionally a depression if the boom was large enough, as the malinvestments and over-capacity are cleansed from the system and debt is liquidated. At an appropriate juncture, the economy resets at more sustainable and realistic levels, ready for the next phase of healthy growth to begin.

According to Ludwig von Mises: '[T]here is no means of avoiding the final collapse of a boom brought about by credit expansion. The alternative is only whether the crisis should come sooner as a result of the voluntary abandonment of further credit expansion, or later, as a final and total catastrophe of the currency system involved.' [233]

The Austrian explanation of the business cycle is generally rejected by mainstream economists for two key reasons. Firstly, mainstream economists place great emphasis on the need for substantial government intervention in economic affairs, whether that be in the form of interventionist and activist central banks, or in government spending and/or their role in income redistribution between different classes within society. Interventionists, such as Keynes and Friedman, believe that letting market forces play out when the economy is in the contraction phase of the boom–bust cycle is harmful to the economy and society.

Austrian economists believe that the Great Depression illustrates the dangers of government interference in the economy. The economic collapse came as a necessary correction to the artificial boom induced by the Fed's easy money policy in the 1920s. Attempts by the government to remedy the downturn only made matters worse.[234]

Austrian economists also espouse libertarian ideals, individualism and laissez-faire economics, believing implicitly in the ability of the free market to optimise supply and demand, savings and investment, productivity and workers' wages, thereby allowing markets to efficiently and effectively allocate scarce resources and meet consumer needs while increasing the standard of living for the benefit of all citizens. In other words, Austrian economics more closely matches the very essence of economics as enunciated in Chapter 1. They are also highly critical of socialism, arguing that without information provided by market prices, socialism lacks a method to efficiently allocate resources over an extended period of time.

Of course, libertarianism doesn't ensure equal outcomes. According to Rothbard, equality is not the natural order of things, and the crusade to make everyone equal in every respect (except before the law) is certain to have disastrous consequences.[235]

Austrians are also highly suspicious of government as well as the close relationships between big business, big government and big unions. Murray Rothbard, for example, considered the monopoly force of government as the greatest danger to liberty and the long-term well-being of the populace, labelling the State as nothing but a bandit gang writ large – the locus of the most immoral, grasping and unscrupulous individuals in any society.[236] He also cited numerous instances where business elites have co-opted government's monopoly power to influence laws and regulatory policy in order to benefit themselves at the expense of their competitors and the general populace.[237]

Austrians believe that central banking and the fractional reserve fiat currency system are inherently destructive and unethical, tantamount to legalised counterfeiting and financial fraud, and are at the core of financial and many social problems. Instead, they argue for the abolition of central banks, a return to sound money based on gold and a return to 100 per cent reserve backing for commercial banks. And, if this is not achievable, then any bank that becomes insolvent should be allowed to fail and be liquidated.

In keeping with their small government and libertarian ideals, Austrians eschew any kind of military, economic or political intervention in either domestic or foreign affairs.

The second main criticism of Austrian economics is that Austrian theories are typically not presented in mathematical form. Instead, proponents rely mainly on verbal arguments based on what are claimed to be self-evident axioms. Because of this, critics argue that Austrian economics generally lacks scientific rigour, rejects scientific method, rejects the use of empirical data, and that Austrians are excessively averse to the use of mathematics and statistics in economics.[238] The argument that Austrian economics is not based on scientific method is interesting, coming from mainstream economists, given the abject failure of their own theories and economic models.

Austrian economists wear this criticism as a badge of honour rather than as a criticism. They argue that human behaviour is too complex to be studied in a laboratory, let alone be modelled in mathematical formulae, and that humans are not passive and non-adaptive subjects. They also posit that the use of empirical data in and of itself cannot explain anything, which in turn implies that empirical data cannot either confirm or falsify a theory. Essentially, it is impossible to accurately model something as complex as an economic and financial system. Instead their methodology relies on the heavy use of logical deduction and the study of human behaviour.

Despite criticisms of Austrian economics from mainstream economists, Mises and Hayek were two of the few economists who gave warning of a major economic crisis before the crash of 1929.[239] In February 1929, Hayek warned that a coming financial crisis, starting in the stock and credit markets, was an unavoidable consequence of reckless monetary expansion.[240] It was also predominantly Austrian economists who forecast the GFC. The same cannot be said of mainstream economists, few of whom have ever predicted recessions or downturns, either before or even during the early phases of the downturn.

*

In addition to these primary economic theories, other specific theories have been put forward in relation to the cause of the Great Depression.

Perhaps the most famous of these is the debt deflation theory put forward by American economist Irving Fisher. Fisher was America's most renowned economist during the 1920s and was a cheerleader for the Roaring Twenties stock market boom, claiming just prior to the Crash that the stock market had reached 'a permanently high plateau'. Unfortunately, Fisher lost most of his fortune during the Crash and, in the ensuing years, he turned his attention to understanding what had gone wrong.

Fisher argued that two dominant factors led to the Great Depression: over-indebtedness in the first instance, followed by deflation. Fisher tied over-indebtedness to loose credit growth, which fuelled speculation and asset bubbles. He outlined the following nine sequential, interrelated factors that detailed the process of moving from boom to bust.[241]

1. Debt liquidation leads to distress selling
2. Contraction of the money supply as bank loans are paid off (or liquidated)
3. A fall in the level of prices
4. A still greater fall in the net worth of business, precipitating bankruptcies

5. A fall in profits
6. A reduction in output, trade and employment
7. Losses, bankruptcies and unemployment lead to pessimism and further loss of confidence
8. Hoarding of money
9. A fall in nominal interest rates and a rise in deflation-adjusted interest rates.

While eminently logical and a good description of how the deflationary process works in practice, many mainstream economists dismissed Fisher's arguments. For example, Bernanke wrote that: 'Fisher's idea was less influential in academic circles, because of the counterargument that debt-deflation represented no more than a redistribution from one group (debtors) to another (creditors). Absent implausibly large differences in marginal spending propensities...pure redistributions should have no significant macroeconomic effects.'[242] [243]

Bernanke's arguments are clearly nonsense. During debt-deflations brought on by credit-induced booms, nominal and real wealth is destroyed as deflation adjusts over-inflated prices back to more realistic and sustainable levels. Therefore, there is little or nothing to redistribute as the so-called 'wealth' has been destroyed. Moreover, while deflation reduces asset values, the debt remains until it is repaid or liquidated. Which clearly jeopardises the viability of some banks and businesses as their customers go broke.

Additionally, contrary to Bernanke's musings, the destruction of 'wealth' will obviously have significant macroeconomic impacts, at least equal to the level of the distortions created during the boom phase of the business cycle. This will arise for several reasons including the elimination of the so-called 'wealth' effect, where people spend less because they are poorer due to a combination of lower asset prices, more business failures, higher unemployment and increased pessimism as they become concerned about their future and increasingly cautious in their everyday lives.

Bernanke's arguments also threaten the stability of the global financial system in that they have spawned a modern economic orthodoxy that the way to handle debt deflation is reflation: to arbitrarily increase money supply to seek to prevent the adjustment process. This response is dangerous for several reasons.

It allows the distortions to remain in the economy without being cleansed. This can lead to stagnation and sub-par growth, which has been clearly evident since the GFC. Each intervention by monetary authorities also leads to ever-increasing debt which, in turn, leads to a cycle of ever-increasing intervention. Like a drug addict, it requires ever-increasing levels of debt, just to keep the patient stable. It creates moral hazard as financial institutions continue lending, even for marginal projects, confident in the knowledge that they will be bailed out should another crisis arise. Finally, feckless behaviour cannot continue forever, so when the ultimate crash does come, the damage to the global economy and the pain, suffering and social dislocation is magnified.

Bernanke's claim that Fisher's idea was 'less influential in academic circles' smacks of academic arrogance which is hard to justify given the woeful track record of mainstream economists. It also highlights just how out of touch mainstream economists and their theories are to the workings of the real world. That Bernanke is so dismissive of Fisher's explanation says a lot more about Bernanke and other mainstream economists than it does about Fisher's explanation about how debt bubbles deflate.

American economist Hyman Minsky was another who identified debt as a major problem in economic booms and busts. While not talking specifically about the Great Depression,

Minsky sought to provide an understanding and explanation of financial crises, which he attributed to swings in a potentially fragile financial system.

Minsky developed his financial instability hypothesis, which is a model of a capitalist economy that does not rely on exogenous (external) shocks to generate business cycles of varying severity. Rather, he believed that business cycles are endogenous and arise out of (i) the internal dynamics of capitalist economies, and (ii) the system of interventions and regulations that are designed to keep the economy operating within reasonable bounds, that is by governments and central banks.[244] Moreover, this cycle is driven in large part by the accumulation of debt in the private sector.

Minsky broke the process from stability to instability into three phases: hedge, speculative and Ponzi – named after Charles Ponzi, who ran fraudulent investment schemes in the 1920s where he paid returns to the original investors not from investment returns, but from new capital paid into the schemes by new, greedy and gullible investors who were late to the party.

In the hedge phase, the borrower's cash flows cover both interest and principal payments to repay any loans. In this way, the debt is self-liquidating and typifies a properly functioning economy.

The speculative phase kicks in when borrowers resort to interest only loans to fund asset purchases. Borrowers are relying on investment returns to cover the interest and increases in asset price to make a profit. This clearly involves greater risk as the borrowers are speculating on interest rates not going up and asset values increasing, or at least not declining. The longer the boom lasts, the greater the incentive to speculate, and the more speculative borrowers become.

The Ponzi phase, otherwise known as the greater fools phase, represents the final and most speculative phase of the bubble. In this phase, investors are typically highly geared, where cash flows cover neither interest nor principal, and they are relying entirely on rising asset prices to make a profit. As asset prices continue to rise, more and more speculators jump in, forcing asset prices even higher. And then one day, as governments seek to rein in borrowing or for no apparent reason at all, everything stops. Sensing a change in sentiment, investors rush for the exits at the same time, leading to the inevitable crash in asset values. As the carnage continues, banks tighten lending standards, impacting even hedge borrowers, who are unable to secure loans despite the soundness of the underlying investments.

Minsky noted that if hedge financing dominates, the more stable the economy. In contrast, the greater the weight of speculative and Ponzi finance, the greater the likelihood that the economy is a deviation amplifying system, which will become increasingly unstable over time. Paradoxically, he also noted that the longer markets appear stable, the more risky and unstable they become. The false hope of security leads investors and policy-makers into a state of apathy, where they tend to extrapolate stability into the distant future while imbalances are accumulating unhindered.

Minsky's theories have received some support, particularly after the GFC, but once again, despite describing accurately how booms and bust unfold, they have had little influence in mainstream economics, nor have they been incorporated into central bank policies. I can only assume they don't fit the narrative for the elite who benefit the most from runaway credit growth and the associated asset inflation.

Other economists identified additional factors which they believe either caused or contributed to the onset of the Great

Depression. One blamed a so-called productivity shock in the decades leading up to the Depression, which resulted in structural changes to the economy. Another blamed disparities in wealth and income for the Depression, while yet another blamed structural weaknesses in banking.

While there might be a scintilla of truth in some – but not all – of these other theories, none goes anywhere near explaining the complexity of factors that led to the Great Depression. Moreover, once again, they highlight how economic theories come and go within a short period of time.

*

So, what can we learn from these analyses of the underlying causes of the Great Depression and the actions by Hoover and Roosevelt in trying to manage the downturn?

Principally, the Great Depression was a natural consequence of the credit expansion and speculation that occurred in the 1920s. It deepened and was prolonged due to government failure to allow prices and wages to adjust to the new reality, the protectionist policies which led to the collapse of world trade, and the structural problems in banking and agriculture.

The Austrian school's explanation of the causes of the Great Depression is more closely aligned than any other school of economic thought. Austrian economists were the only ones to not only accurately predict the onset of the Depression before it occurred, but stated that the Depression resulted from a bursting of a credit-induced bubble; that higher order sectors, for example, capital goods and assets, would be impacted to a far greater extent than consumer-oriented sectors; and that government interference in the adjustment process prolonged the downturn.

In contrast, Keynes and Friedman's support for interventionist policies were not only misguided but fail to understand the damage that widespread intervention had in allowing the system to self-correct. Roosevelt's extreme interventionism overturned centuries of a culture of stoicism and self-reliance, leading to the culture of handouts, welfare dependency and government intervention in people's everyday lives that pervades western nations today.

Part 3

The Post-war Economy

Between 1960 and 2016 the global economy grew seven-fold from US$14.9 to US$113 trillion.[245] The increase in economic activity was driven by many factors including population growth, together with advances in science and technology, productivity, health and education, management practices, workforce participation and trade liberalisation.

The world also witnessed major changes in the regional composition of economic activity as reflected in the table below.

Table 1 Global GDP by Region – 1960–2016

	1960		2016	
	GDP (US$ Tn) *	World GDP (per cent)	GDP (US$ Tn)	World GDP (per cent)
United States	3,467	23.3	18,244	16.1
Western Europe	4,370	29.3	17,692	15.7

* Converted to 2015 price level with updated 2011 PPPs

China[†]	631	4.2	18,378	16.3
Japan	626	4.2	4,858	4.3
Other	5,816	39	53,840	47.6
Total	14,910	100	113, 012	100

Data Source: The Conference Board[246]

After dominating the global economy in the nineteenth and early twentieth centuries, the U.S. and western Europe lost ground to China, other parts of Asia and Latin America.

This overall growth, however, has masked a host of structural problems, not the least of which has been the huge run-up in debt which has far outstripped the growth in GDP. Between 2000 and 2014, global debt increased from US$87 trillion to US$199 trillion, pushing the global debt to GDP ratio up from 246 per cent to 286 per cent.[247] Since then, it has grown further to hit an all-time high of US$233 trillion in the third quarter of 2017.[248]

The global financial position, however, is far worse than even these figures suggest as they exclude the trillions of dollars of unfunded liabilities that governments around the world have promised their constituents for pensions, healthcare and the like. During the next Great Depression, governments will be forced to walk away from these commitments, leaving many of their constituents impoverished.

Other problems include environmental degradation, the massive waste of scarce resources associated with runaway consumerism and the relentless pursuit of economic growth, burgeoning military expenditure, and the growing incidence of health and societal problems arising from stress associated with modern life.

---

† Alternative rather than official statistics

It is within this context that Part 3 looks at developments in the major economic regions and countries since the end of World War II. Chapter 8 looks at the growth of post-war Japan, with a focus on identifying those factors that contributed to her post-war economic miracle, how excessive credit growth led to an asset boom and a debt crisis in the late 1980s, and how delays in addressing structural issues in the aftermath of the crisis led to Japan's so-called 'Lost Decades'.

Chapter 9 examines China's post-war experience, including describing those factors behind her extraordinary growth. I will also explain how she used mercantilist policies and unfair and illegal practices to exploit the rules-based international trading system for her own advantage, and explain why China should not be trusted.

Chapter 10 examines America's post-war economic experience. The chapter is divided into three sections. The first section shows how America's economy peaked in the 1950s and 60s before the rate of real economic growth slowed over the next five decades. Section 2 details how the elite, through their control of the banking system and use of flawed economic theories, have taken total control of the economy to enrich themselves at the expense of everyday folk. Finally, Section 3 highlights how central banks have not only failed to meet their obligations to deliver price stability and a sound financial system but, through constant interference and meddling, have created the conditions for the next financial crisis. I will also debunk a number of economic myths and 'truisms' perpetuated by mainstream economists and central banks.

Chapter 11 looks at Europe's path to European integration, Europe's post-war economic performance, the GFC and its aftermath. I will also expose the real reasons for Germany's bailout of Greece, before using Iceland and Greece as examples of how to, and how not to, handle a financial crisis.

Chapter 8
The Rise of Japan

'...If you look at mainstream economics there are three things you will not find in a mainstream economic model – Banks, Debt, and Money.'

Steve Keen

At the end of World War II, the Japanese economy lay in ruins and the country faced extraordinary challenges. Her infrastructure, housing and factories had been severely damaged by Allied bombing, while GDP had fallen by 50 per cent since 1939.

And yet, astonishingly, in just four decades, Japan emerged from the ashes to become the second largest economy in the world. From 1950 to 2016, the Japanese economy grew eighteen-fold from US$268 billion* to US$4.86 trillion, while the Japanese standard of living grew twelve-fold, with GDP per capita growing from US$3,207 to US$38,343.[249]

Much of this growth came within the first four decades following the war, with the economy growing by close to 10 per cent per annum in the 1950s and 1960s. By the early 1970s, Japan's rapid rate of economic growth dropped back to a more

* 2015 $US

modest 4–5 per cent per annum as the price of oil soared, labour costs increased, the yen rose and overall demand for Japanese goods weakened.[250] Following the bursting of a debt-fuelled asset bubble in 1989, and despite extraordinary efforts by authorities to stimulate the economy, the Japanese economy entered an extended period of stagnation from which it has yet to fully recover.

The Japanese story is illustrative for several reasons. Firstly, it is a textbook example of how, with a great deal of effort, discipline, self-sacrifice, vision and a clear strategy, nations can grow from poverty to prosperity within a generation. Secondly, it provides an anatomy of a debt-fuelled boom and bust. Thirdly, it demonstrates the ineffectiveness of monetary and fiscal policy in dealing with the aftermath of a bust.

The Japanese post-war economy can be divided into four phases: occupation (1945–1951); economic miracle (1952–mid-1980s); asset bubble (1985–1989); and economic stagnation (1990–present day).

Occupation (1945–1951)

The Japanese economy faced a myriad of problems following her defeat. Food was in such short supply that it was feared that many people would starve to death. Supplies of coal, the main source of energy, temporarily dried up when Korean and Chinese workers, who had been forced to work as slave labour in the coal mines during the war, stopped working.

Japan also had to cope with the millions of soldiers and expatriates returning home as well as those left without jobs as wartime production ceased. It was feared that unemployment would reach 10 million, but this never eventuated. While under-employment remained a severe problem, most people were absorbed into agriculture, coal production and the (informal) services sectors, with people doing whatever they could to survive.

To cope with the collapse in output and high unemployment, the Japanese government resorted to the time-honoured practice of printing money to monetise government deficits while trying to control prices which resulted from the high deficits and money printing. However, all this strategy did was to create triple-digit inflation between 1946 and 1949. Black market inflation was even higher, especially in the initial period. This was the highest inflation that Japan ever experienced, before or after.[251]

In the immediate aftermath of the war, Japan also relied heavily on U.S. aid to provide the necessities of life, while she began the process of rebuilding her shattered economy. In September 1945 General Douglas MacArthur took charge of the Supreme Command of Allied Powers and began the task of rebuilding Japan. The primary goal of the occupation was to transform Japan into a peaceful, democratic nation by disarming and preventing the remilitarisation of the state, dealing with her former colonies, stabilising the economy and introducing political and social reforms. This took place in three phases: punishment and reform; reviving the economy; and concluding a formal peace treaty and alliance. [252]

Phase 1 of the occupation (1945–47) involved dismantling the military and introducing a range of economic reforms designed to boost economic growth while supporting social change. Land reform was one of the earliest reforms, and was seen as important because of the role the wealthy landowners had played in supporting the war effort, as well as their role in continuing a semi-feudal system which hindered the emergence of a true middle class. It involved forcing the large, feudalist landowners to sell their land to small tenant farmers who had previously leased the land.[253]

Allied authorities also introduced a range of business reforms to transform the economy into a free market capitalist system. This included the dissolution of the large Japanese business conglomerates, or *zaibatsu*, together with other reforms designed to outlaw cartels, break up companies that dominated any particular industry and secure market competition and transparency. [254]

Allied authorities also implemented labour market reforms by allowing the Japanese to form labour unions. The proportion of workers belonging to labour unions rose rapidly, from zero in 1945 to nearly 60 per cent in 1948–49.[255] The education system was also reformed by extending compulsory education from six to nine years and political reform also featured strongly in these early initiatives. Some of the more profound political changes included downgrading the emperor's role to that of a figurehead; implementing a democratically elected, bi-cameral parliament; separating power amongst legislative, administrative and judicial branches of government; promoting greater rights and privileges for women; and eliminating all non-defensive armed forces.[256]

The emergence of an economic crisis in Japan and the Chinese civil war, which sparked concerns about the spread of communism in an economically weakened Japan, put the restoration of the Japanese economy at centre stage during the second phase of the occupation. While combatting inflation and implementing tax reform were high on the agenda, the most fundamental problem was the shortage of raw materials required to feed Japanese industry.

The Korean War, perhaps more than any other event during the occupation, proved pivotal in the next phase of economic growth. From 1950 to 1951, trade increased by 34 per cent, while Japanese production increased by 70 per cent, driven in large part by the influx of American military personnel as well as Japan becoming the principal supply depot for UN forces in the region. The war also facilitated a massive increase in foreign currency, which enabled Japanese firms to import much needed raw materials and technology to expand production.[257]

Beginning in 1950, with the political and economic future of Japan firmly established, the third phase of the occupation centered on securing a formal peace treaty to end both the war and the occupation. The final agreement allowed the U.S. to maintain its bases in Okinawa and elsewhere in Japan,[258] thus bringing Japan clearly within the American sphere of influence in the western Pacific.

Japan's Economic Miracle (1952 to mid-1980s)

A number of factors contributed to Japan's economic miracle from the 1950s to the 1980s.

- Japan took advantage of U.S. strategic imperatives during the Cold War by assuming a mercantilist growth strategy. This involved adopting anti-competitive activities by forming cartels and exporting her way to prosperity, while protecting domestic producers from external competition through a series of import barriers including tariffs, quotas and foreign exchange controls. These controls allowed her to maintain an exchange rate at 360 yen to the dollar until 1970, despite running almost continuous trade surpluses. Much of what Japan manufactured was exported, with foreign reserves re-invested in technology, raw materials and energy necessary for further industrial development.

  While Japan benefited greatly from these beggar-thy-neighbour policies, it came at the expense of other signatories to the 1948 General Agreement on Trade and Tariffs (GATT), where countries had committed themselves to reducing tariffs and other trade barriers on a reciprocal and mutually advantageous basis. During the Cold War, Japan could get away with this hardline mercantilist approach as America was more concerned about preventing the advance of communism than a few trade transgressions by her vassal state.

However, by the mid-1980s, Japan came under increasing pressure to liberalise trade. In 1985, she agreed with her trading partners to let the yen appreciate against the U.S. dollar, which led to a doubling of the yen's value within two years. This action and other efforts to restrain exports encouraged Japanese companies to begin moving production overseas.

The continuous trade surpluses generated by her mercantilist policies enabled Japan to become world's largest creditor nation, an extraordinary effort in just a couple of decades.

- Immediately after the war, Japanese officials began the task of planning how to rebuild the shattered Japanese economy. They undertook a detailed audit of the remaining infrastructure, while evaluating proposals for promoting industries and targeting exports on a sector by sector basis. Policy-makers determined that Japan's economic vision should be based on emerging global trends, and that the recovery strategy must be based on heavy industrialisation, technology, skilled labour-intensive industries and trade. Officials also recognised that in the initial stages of recovery, investment was more important than consumption. People would have to endure lower living standards in the short term until economic growth became entrenched. In 1947, they also introduced the priority production system to focus scarce resources on a few strategically important industries such as steel, coal mining, electricity, shipbuilding, and marine and railway transportation.[259]

The Japanese government also continued to develop a series of longer-term plans, adopting policies to allocate resources amongst industrial sectors while seeking to influence the organisation of specific industries.

- Post-war Japan fostered close co-operation between government and big business – the Ministry of International Trade and Industry (MITI) was established in 1949 and given the task of coordinating international trade policy with other groups, including politicians, other government departments and large corporations. A key objective of the ministry was to strengthen the country's industrial base. MITI's approach differed significantly from that which may exist in a centrally directed economy, providing industry with administrative guidance and advice on subjects such as modernisation, technology, investment, domestic and foreign competition as well as protection from import competition, and access to foreign exchange.[260] It also facilitated the rationalisation of firms and industries and stimulated the movement of capital and labour out of declining industries, and/or industries in which Japan did not have a competitive advantage, such as coal and textiles, into promising new industries with high growth potential – first into electronics, steel, petrochemicals, shipbuilding and automobiles, and later into computers, semiconductors, machine tools, precision equipment (notably cameras), telecommunications equipment and consumer goods.[261]

In 1953, the Japanese government reversed the Allied authorities restrictions on cartels by allowing industries to consolidate into a small number of very large corporations. This allowed the remaining companies to maintain higher domestic prices while government tariff policy kept the market closed to foreign products. Through below-cost exports, the Japanese firms were able to drive many of their international competitors out of business.

The reversal of government policy on cartels also saw the emergence of *keiretsu*, which were large companies with interlocking business relationships and shareholdings. Each horizontal *keiretsu* typically included large financial institutions, the largest manufacturing companies, and a large trading company organised around a major bank. Some of the larger *keiretsu* included Mitsui, Mitsubishi, Sumitomo, Fuyo, Dai-ichi Kangyo and Sanwa. The horizontal *keiretsu* helped to provide long-term stability, efficiency, reduced risk and mutual support. The interlocking directorates also prevented hostile takeovers from foreign competitors.

Japanese corporations also developed vertical *keiretsu* which were organised around industry supply chains in automotive, electronics and other industries. They served to coordinate inputs of a great many subcontractors and suppliers as well as the ability to control the distribution and mass marketing of products. The vertical *keiretsu* provided efficient, long-term, reciprocal benefits for a parent company and its suppliers, including coordination of planning and investment, sharing of technology and information, control of quality and delivery, and flexibility throughout the business cycle. Keiretsu used other anti-competitive practices such as using Japanese transport companies, for example ships and aircraft, to transport their goods, thus shutting out foreign competition while costing foreign consumers billions of dollars in additional charges.

The cross-shareholdings provided great stability to major corporations and importantly, instead of being forced to maximise short-term profits, allowed management to invest in plant and equipment, research and development, and in their people to maximise long-term profitability.

The government also enacted controls that allowed her to offer interest rates at lower than potential market rates, thus subsidising economic development by funnelling cheap funds to the larger corporations.[262] Another feature of the close relationships between government, banks and major corporations was 'over-lending'. Owing to a shortage of capital in Japan at the time, major corporations borrowed from their associated banks beyond their capacity to repay, often beyond their net worth. The shortfalls in loans from city banks were made good by loans from the Bank of Japan which, through these practices, exercised complete control over the banking system. This allowed corporations to invest in technology and expand productive capacity, and thus grow their markets and market share.[263]

The government also took direct action in supporting economic development through government investment in infrastructure. As a result, the government rapidly expanded investment in Japanese infrastructure including highways, high-speed railways, subways, ports, airports, dams and telecommunications.

- The Japanese constitution forbids Japanese rearmament and its low military expenditure – around 1 per cent of their GNP – freed up extraordinary amounts of money, which Japan was able divert to productive use, including developing infrastructure and supporting industrial development.[264]
- Japanese people were prodigious savers, with the household savings rate reaching 15 per cent by 1960 and topping 20 per cent in the mid-1970s.[265] The government leveraged this large savings pool to provide low-cost loans to industries favoured for long-term growth.

- Driven by the need for greater productivity and growth, a practice of 'kaizen', the Japanese word for continuous improvement, helped Japanese firms become internationally competitive by improving quality and customer satisfaction, reducing costs, while increasing sales and profits. In the early post-war period, the phrase 'Made in Japan' was often a pejorative term, which referred to the poor-quality or low-end nature of Japanese products such as chinaware. All of this changed in the 1950s, however, when Japanese manufacturers introduced kaizen. In business, kaizen is a management approach that inculcates a company culture that focuses on continuously improving, and standardising all business processes, step by step.

There were other business and management practices supporting Japan's economic development, such as her ability to copy western products, improve on them and then sell them back to the west at lower prices. This approach was enhanced by a strong commitment to research and development, which allowed Japanese companies to excel internationally in their chosen fields. For example, by the late 1970s, Japanese car manufacturers introduced assembly-line robots, which allowed them to mass produce cars with consistently superior quality, little waste and at very competitive prices.

Labour relations also played a major part in Japan's economic miracle. The introduction of trade unions initially led to a period of militancy and strikes, culminating in an acrimonious coal miners' strike in 1960. This gave rise to the development of company-based, rather than industry-wide, unions which, in turn, led to the introduction of lifetime employment with restrictions on dismissing employees, seniority-based promotion and wages, and a commitment to on-the-job training. Any adjustments in labour needs were handled by increasing/shortening the working hours or intra-firm transfers, rather than resorting to layoffs. The improved working conditions and higher wages increased domestic consumption, which fed into a virtuous cycle of economic development underpinned by productivity improvement. However, these practices also put pressure on Japanese companies to continue to grow at any cost, which often meant adopting policies which favoured Japanese workers over foreign workers.[266]

- Ultimately it was the Japanese people who, faced with a devastating defeat in the war (admittedly of their own making), created the Japanese economic miracle. With an extraordinary work ethic, a profound sense of national pride, strict anti-immigration policies, a burning desire to catch up with the west, and a propensity for self-reliance rather than reliance on state welfare, the Japanese people took a long-term view to economic success by selflessly enduring hardship in the form of long working hours and a six-day week, higher domestic prices, and forgoing short-term consumption in favour of investment and long-term growth.

A range of other factors also contributed to Japan's economic miracle. These included the ability for major firms such as Toyota, Nissan, Hitachi and Toshiba to quickly convert from wartime to peacetime production after the end of World War II; the migration of young people from rural areas to the cities seeking new opportunities; access to cheap and reliable energy supplies including oil and coal; a buoyant global economy; access to licensing agreements for a range of new technologies from transistors to steel furnaces; and latecomer advantages which allowed producers to adopt proven technology while avoiding market risks.

While the economic success during this period was laudable, there were some significant downsides. Shielded from market competition and starved of funds, development of many firms in the non-manufacturing sectors lagged behind the larger firms in productivity, wages and other working conditions. Even today, this remains a problem for the Japanese economy as it seeks to undertake structural reforms.

The focus on industrial development also resulted in environmental degradation. For example, water quality deteriorated in lakes, rivers, seas and underground aquifers, while emissions of harmful substances from factories caused very serious human diseases, for example Minamata disease, which are often fatal.[267] Metropolitan and industrial areas also faced significant problems with air pollution, with smoke covering the cities and industrial areas, resulting in an increase in those suffering from asthma.

The consequences of Japan's exponential growth were serious for the U.S.. During the early 1980s, the world was plagued by trade imbalances and slow growth. Between 1980 and 1985, the U.S. dollar had appreciated by about 50 per cent against the currencies of its major trading partners. As a result, the U.S. was running chronic trade deficits to the tune of around 3–3.5 per cent per annum, while the major European nations and Japan were running massive trade surpluses.[268] This put American firms at a serious disadvantage and yet, despite intense lobbying from a range of industry sectors, for ideological reasons the U.S. government initially refused to interfere with the market.

By 1985, however, the corporate campaign had acquired such traction that the U.S. government was forced to act. Faced with the prospect of rising protectionism, in September 1985 representatives from the five largest economies – the U.S., the United Kingdom, West Germany, France and Japan – met at the Plaza Hotel in New York City and, in what became known as the Plaza Accord, agreed to allow their central banks to actively intervene in the foreign currency markets to devalue the U.S. dollar to restore the U.S.'s export competitiveness. Over the next two years, the U.S. dollar depreciated by up to 50 per cent against that of its major trading partners.[269]

The Plaza Accord ultimately proved successful in reducing the U.S. trade deficit with western European nations, but largely failed to fulfil its primary objective of alleviating the trade deficit with Japan, despite Japan accelerating the shift in automotive production to the U.S. and elsewhere. This was due in large part to trade barriers and other structural impediments, which shielded key parts of the Japanese economy from foreign competition.

Asset Bubble (1985–1989)

In the second half of the 1980s, Japan experienced an extraordinary speculative boom in asset prices, a boom that would end in bust – as they inevitably all must – just four years later.

The boom was driven by a range of factors including loose monetary policy, which was designed to cushion the impact of the stronger yen on the economy; excessive loan growth quotas dictated by the Bank of Japan; a government fiscal stimulus package in 1987; taxation and regulations biased towards increasing land prices; inadequate risk management by financial institutions; and overexuberance and overconfidence in Japan's economy. All of this led to a double-digit expansion in debt, excessive borrowing and risk-taking, and aggressive and irrational speculation in stocks and real estate.[270]

The boom was also exacerbated by the Japanese practice known as 'zaitech' or 'financial engineering', in which speculative profits and capital gains were reported as income on corporate financial statements. Zaitech-practising firms obtained low-interest loans and used them to purchase stocks and real estate, which surged in price, helping these firms report blowout earnings, provided asset prices continued to rise. At one point, it is estimated that up to half of Japanese corporate earnings were derived from zaitech.[271]

From 1985 to 1989, Japan's Nikkei stock index tripled to almost 39,000. At its peak in December 1989, Japanese stocks were almost 1.5 times the value of all U.S. equities, and close to 45 per cent of the world's stock market capitalisation. Japanese stocks sold at more than 60 times earnings, almost five times book value and more than 200 times dividends. In contrast, U.S. stocks sold at about 15 times earnings, and London equities at 12 times earnings.[272]

The boom in real estate was even more dramatic, with nationwide land prices rising on average by 50 per cent during the second half of the 1980s.[273] In Tokyo and other metropolitan business districts, the price rises were even more spectacular, with prices in Tokyo's prime neighborhoods rising to levels that made them 350 times more expensive than comparable land in Manhattan, New York. The land underneath the Tokyo Imperial Palace was rumored to have been worth as much as the entire state of California.[274]

By 1990, the total value of Japanese property was estimated at nearly $20 trillion – equal to more than 20 per cent of the entire world's wealth, around double the total value of the world's stock markets, and five times the value of all U.S. property.[275]

The boom sparked all the typical responses of those caught up in a bubble. Speculators threw caution to wind, buying trophy properties including the famous Pebble Beach Golf

Course, the Rockefeller Centre and Columbia Pictures in the U.S., while paying record prices for famous paintings. In Japan, there was a stockbroker on every corner as the stock market became an integral part of Japanese culture. The boom also spilled over into the real economy, leading to excess capacity and overemployment in key sectors including construction and real estate.

Japan's overseas buying spree didn't just stop in America. It also extended to many parts of Australia, including the holiday mecca the Gold Coast, where Japanese interests bought up major hotels, forcing up real estate prices beyond the reach of everyday Australians. I still remember clearly the concerns that many Australians had about the growing wealth of the Japanese and the real fear that they would buy up Australia. Equally, I also have vivid memories of the aftermath of the crash, seeing vacant hotel sites in the heart of the Gold Coast strewn with rubbish and rubble, testimony to what happens when boom turns to bust.

By 1989, Japanese officials had become increasingly concerned with the country's growing asset bubbles and the Bank of Japan decided to tighten monetary policy. Japanese shares peaked in the last days of 1989 before plunging nearly 50 per cent in 1990 and falling to an eventual low of 7,054 in March 2009, 82 per cent below its peak two decades earlier.[276]

This extraordinary fall is testimony to how long asset markets can remain depressed, and is a lesson today's investors could well take heed of.

Japan's imploding stock market bubble also popped the country's real estate bubble, throwing the country into recession and ushering in what became known as the 'Lost Decade'. This would eventually be extended to the Lost Decades as sluggish growth continued into the 21st century.

Economic Stagnation (1990–present day)

Collapsing asset prices left overleveraged Japanese banks and insurance companies saddled with a tidal wave of non-performing loans (NPLs) and bad debts.

Policy-makers responded to the crisis in textbook fashion: slashing interest rates, bailing out financial institutions and allowing banks to delay writing off the debts, turning many into zombie banks. Despite repeated rescue efforts, many of these institutions remained unviable, resulting in a wave of consolidations in the late 1990s.

The government also pumped massive amounts of money into the economy through public works and tax cuts, and running persistent budget deficits which reached 7 per cent of GDP by the turn of the century and a massive 9.5 per cent in 2009.[277] This pushed up the government debt to GDP ratio between 1990 and 2014 from 66 per cent to a mind-blowing 242 per cent,[278] money that will ultimately have to be repaid one way or another by future generations. One day our descendants may well ask: What were these people thinking?

Remarkably, despite massive stimulatory measures undertaken by the authorities, the Japanese economy failed to reach growth rates achieved prior to the asset bubble. This begs the question: why did Japan suffer the so-called Lost Decades when the authorities did everything in the mainstream economists' handbook to stimulate the economy? Surely, if massive stimulus is the answer to handling downturns and any other perceived economic malaise, then Japan's economy should have not only rebounded quickly, but should have been one of the fastest growing economies in the world.

Now some mainstream economists might argue that Japanese authorities didn't go far enough in terms of stimulus. But this is an absurd proposition when not only did the government run up mind-blowing levels of government debt, but the Bank of Japan was a pioneer in experimentation in monetary policy, especially quantitative easing and zero interest rate policies.

It may suggest that the mainstream economists' economics textbook doesn't work, or at least not in all circumstances, or that there were other factors at play which don't form part of the mainstream economic narrative. Or perhaps the decades following the bust were not as 'lost' as some would have you believe.

Having said that, there are couple of things that are unique to Japan that undoubtedly did hinder the recovery. These included Japan's lifetime employment policies that hindered management's ability to lower wages or lay off staff, as well as delays in writing off debts and/or adjusting asset values to the new reality. What this did was to prevent companies from rightsizing their cost structures while preventing zombie banks/organisations from being liquidated and allowing better run companies to flourish.

Japan's asset bubble and subsequent prolonged and sluggish recovery has attracted a great deal of commentary from financial analysts and economists. While some of the analysis has merit in that it touches on elements that impacted the recovery, many of the explanations are quite narrow and focus on mono-causal events. They also lack the integrated and holistic approach offered by the Austrian explanation of the business cycle, nor do they incorporate a true understanding of the human dimensions behind how economies function.

Let's dive in and take a look at some of the evidence. Prominent mainstream economist Paul Krugman acknowledged the existence of a massive asset bubble in the 1980s and argued that Japan's Lost Decade is an example of a liquidity trap, a situation where conventional central bank policies are rendered mute because short-term rates are close to zero.[279] A liquidity trap typically arises when, despite low interest rates, people hoard cash rather than spend.

I would have thought, however, that the creation of a 'liquidity trap' is a natural human response to a cataclysmic economic event, and therefore should come as no surprise to anyone. Hoarding cash seems an eminently sensible course of action when people are scared and uncertain, notwithstanding that it frustrates and renders ineffective efforts by the authorities to kickstart the economy through loose monetary policy. One would have thought that if mainstream economics had any credibility, then its policy prescriptions would take account of the real world vagaries of human emotions and responses, rather than rely on academic theories.

Richard Koo argues that the recession was a balance sheet recession that caused many Japanese companies to become insolvent as their asset values collapsed. Koo believes that monetary policy was ineffective because there was limited demand for funds as firms slashed investment and paid down their debts to restore their financial health. He also believes that it was massive fiscal stimulus that offset the decline in other sectors and enabled Japan to maintain its level of GDP.[280] One element of Koo's argument – that the bust caused many companies to become insolvent – seems eminently logical, because that's exactly what busts do to debt-laden companies.

Scott Sumner argues that Japan's monetary policy was too tight during the Lost Decades and thus prolonged the pain felt by the Japanese economy.[281] This claim is particularly interesting given that the Bank of Japan slashed the discount rate between 1991 and 1995 from 6 per cent to 0.5 per cent and has held it below 1 per cent since then.[282] It's hard to envisage a looser monetary policy. Fumio Hayashi and Edward Prescott argue that Japan's sluggish investment activity and resultant anemic economic performance is due mainly to the low rate of aggregate productivity growth, which in turn was driven by low levels of capital expenditure rather than constrained by a shortage of credit.[283]

Jennifer Amyx suggests that while Japanese policy-makers were well aware of the causes of Japan's economic decline, they were constrained in their actions by institutional inflexibility and the potential short-term harm that such policies would inflict on the Japanese government and people.[284]

Shigeru Otsubo also highlights several uniquely Japanese cultural factors that contributed to the latent recovery by delaying the necessary adjustment processes. These include the Japanese-style system of consensus and co-operation that had served Japan so well in the past but had failed to adjust to a more dynamic international competitive environment. Japan's lifetime labour practices also prevented Japanese firms from undertaking mass lay-offs, notwithstanding the tough economic environment. He also notes that the restoration of a sound financial system by 2002 was a key factor in bringing the economy back to a steady, albeit still weak, growth path.[285]

Analysis of the asset bubble and the so-called Lost Decades raises some key questions, not only in relation to Japan economic performance per se, but also in relation to the broader context of macroeconomic policy and the functioning of economies in general.

First and foremost, how can so many mainstream economists – and there were many more whom I have not quoted – have such differing views on the causes of the Lost Decades? Surely, if there was a common model of how economies work, then the diagnosis of what happened and the solutions to resolving such problems would be both obvious and consistent. The fact that they aren't highlights the obvious shortcomings of current mainstream economic theory and thought, that is, that there is no agreed model of how economies function, just a whole lot of disparate, unproven theories and strongly held opinions. Hardly the stuff a science is made of.

It also seems that many economists simplistically focus on monocausal reasons for economic events. As noted previously, a monetarist will look to monetary causes and solutions for problems, while neo-Keynesians will look to fiscal causes and solutions. However, the reality is quite different. Economies are natural, dynamic and complex systems, which have multiple sub-systems and components interacting all the time. It is nonsensical to focus on just one, or several components to explain the totality of such systems.

Secondly, nearing the peak of the bubble, a 1989 survey of institutional investors showed that most didn't believe that the Nikkei was overvalued.[286] Some argued it was a new era which demonstrated the superiority of Japan's management style. Few saw it for what it really was – a debt-fueled boom, which was sure to crash at some stage as people moved from a feeling of optimism and euphoria to pessimism and fear, as asset prices began to implode.

Ironically, the Bank of Japan had already voiced concern over the massive increase in money supply and the rapid rise in asset prices in the summer of 1986, but failed to act on its concerns.[287]

This raises several issues in relation to booms and busts. Firstly, that our minds allow us to rationalise distortions such as extreme overvaluations in asset markets, even when, by every historical measure, the facts suggest otherwise. This, of course, puts to bed one of the many myths perpetuated by neo-classical economists, that people act rationally in making economic decisions. How can economists suggest that people act rationally when participating in asset booms, when asset prices become unhinged from the underlying economic value of the asset? Paradoxically, understanding that our thinking can become distorted means that such booms and busts will inevitably occur, but with the added complication that the swings will be exacerbated by leverage under fractional reserve banking.

Secondly, were the Lost Decades as 'lost' as they have been portrayed? Mainstream economists and politicians have long portrayed the Lost Decades as a self-inflicted own goal, bought about by insufficient monetary and fiscal responses and by persistent deflation. However, the reality seems to be somewhat different to this narrative.

There is no doubt that the economic growth rate slowed in the aftermath of the collapse in asset prices, averaging between one and 1.5 per cent per annum, compared to 4–5 per cent per annum growth in the preceding two decades.[288] Perhaps the rapid slowing in growth in comparison with previous decades might appear to have been 'lost'. However, there are structural reasons for this slowdown in growth.

Japanese banks were slow to purge themselves of non-performing loans. Faced with failing borrowers and a rise in NPLs, banks initially continued to provide additional loans in the hope that their customers could trade their way out of trouble. All this did, however, was to saddle their customers with even more debt, while reducing bank profitability. It was only when the government and banks became serious about aggressively liquidating NPLs, and the banks were forced to merge, that the financial system started to recover.

The asset bubble also created numerous distortions in the economy, not the least of which was excess capacity in key sectors such as real estate and construction, as well as unrealistic asset price levels. Such excesses had to be unwound before 'normal', healthy growth driven by fundamentals could resume.

Moreover, for the first time, Japanese firms in key industries came under increasing pressure from new, low-cost competitors such as Korea, China and Taiwan. This would have slowed growth, with or without the collapse of the asset bubble.

An extraordinary amount of 'wealth' was also destroyed by the collapse of the asset bubble. Companies and individuals who had geared themselves up for elevated asset prices were wiped out as asset prices reset to more realistic levels, that is the values that were set by the income that the asset could generate. This not only hampered consumption, but it also resulted in a more cautious attitude to spending and saving.

The growth rate in Japanese productivity, a key driver in Japan's economic miracle, also fell substantially across most sectors. For example, total factor productivity in manufacturing grew at an annual rate of 2.3 per cent between 1980–95, compared to 6 per cent between 1955–70. Productivity in non-manufacturing sectors fell from 4.2 per cent to 0.3 per cent during the same time.

Finally, demographic changes played a significant role in slowing economic growth. For example, the total population, which had grown by nearly 50 per cent between 1950 and 1990, peaked in 2015 and has now started to decline. So instead of a rising population supporting growth, a falling population became an economic headwind. At the same time, the median age started to rise, leading to changes in consumption patterns as people in their older years tend to spend less than those in their younger and middle years.

Mainstream economists and commentators also claim that chronic deflation held back economic growth. Once again, the reality is somewhat different. Between 1990 and 2016, changes in the consumer price index (CPI) ranged between -1.4 per cent and 3.3 per cent, with roughly the same number of years of inflation and deflation. Moreover, the actual price index grew from approximately 94.5 in 1990, to 102 in 2000 and 104 in 2016.[289] While not a stellar growth in inflation, one could better describe the period as having stable prices, rather than exhibiting chronic deflation, surely a goal that all policy-makers should aspire to.

Moreover, the CPI had been in steady decline before asset prices collapsed, hitting just 0.4 per cent in 1987 before edging up to 3.3 per cent in 1991.[290] This highlights two things. Firstly, that disinflation had been underway since the CPI peaked at 23 per cent in 1974, so Japan had already achieved consumer price stability prior to the asset price collapse. Secondly, there is an obvious disconnect between movements in asset prices and CPI in the real economy. This is not surprising given that the forces determining inflation in the real economy and asset markets are very different, with asset prices in part being impacted by supply and demand, but more generally by the availability and cost of money, while prices in the real economy are driven largely by supply and demand. This disconnect highlights a fundamental flaw in how central banks currently manage monetary policy. I will cover this in much greater detail when we examine the post-war U.S. economy.

Finally, one can also question how poorly the economy actually performed. While the Japanese economy seems to have been relatively stagnant when measured in nominal terms, from 1994 to 2016, real GDP grew by 23 per cent.[291] Moreover, between 1990 and 2016, GDP per capita grew 22 per cent from US$31,374 to US$38,343. Comparative growth in GDP per capita in other countries was as follows: the U.S. and Germany (43 per cent), United Kingdom (50 per cent), Australia (63 per cent), France (27 per cent) and Italy (8 per cent).[292]

However, is it fair to use 1990 as a base, when Japan had just experienced an asset boom of epic proportions while other countries were at different stages of development? Using 1980 as a base, a completely different picture emerges. From 1980 to 2016, growth in GDP per capita was as follows: Japan (71 per cent), Germany (62 per cent), U.S. (79 per cent), United Kingdom (90 per cent), Australia (94 per cent), France (52 per cent) and Italy (34 per cent).[293]

This analysis allows us to draw a number of conclusions. Firstly, the asset deflation was a direct result of the preceding debt-fuelled, Bank of Japan-induced asset bubble that propelled asset prices far beyond what the fundamentals could support. The economy was always going to suffer as asset prices normalised.

Research by the Bank of Japan also suggests that the effects of a bubble are asymmetrically larger in the bursting period than in the expansion phase. This occurs for several reasons. Firstly, the collapse in asset prices has very adverse effects on the stability of the financial system, due in part to the impact on credit conditions, but also due to its impact on the capital base of financial institutions and the value of the collateral underpinning bank loans. In response, financial institutions become far more risk averse than during the boom period.[294] Collapsing asset values also have a major impact on people's confidence levels, making them far more pessimistic as they come to grips with their falling wealth, and concerns about their future.

The simple conclusion here is: if you don't want a painful economic hangover, don't drink the debt Kool-Aid. Sadly, this is a lesson that politicians, central banks and mainstream economists have difficulty coming to grips with. Perhaps they are slow learners. Or perhaps they have a different agenda to the rest of us. Perhaps both.

The analysis also shows us that the term 'Lost Decades' is misleading in that it suggests that the Japanese standard of living stagnated. This is far from the truth. Not only did the Japanese economy grow in real terms, but the Japanese people continued to enjoy one of the highest standards of living in the world. Using a different base also highlights that growth in Japan's per capita income greatly outperformed other western nations, particularly socialist France and politically dysfunctional Italy.

Although the growth rate did slow from previous periods, it was coming off a high base and had been slowing since the 1980s. Moreover, Japan's economic growth would likely have slowed due to a range of structural factors, factors that are outside the control of governments, and those that have a far greater impact on economic performance over the longer term than monetary or fiscal policy. Japan's recovery was also impeded by delays in cleaning up Japan's corporations and its finance system following the financial crisis.

Thirdly, it puts to bed the myth that Japan's economy stagnated due to persistent deflation. This is not only factually wrong but, as we will see in subsequent chapters, it is also wrong to suggest that economies can only grow with inflation and stagnate or decline when there is deflation.

Finally, there is little evidence that running up huge amounts of debt did much other than to leave future generations with a massive debt to repay, one way or another.

As we close out this discussion on the Lost Decades, it does raise an important question. If the decades were not as 'lost' as many would have you believe, then why characterise them as such?

There are two answers. Firstly, it seems likely politicians had an incentive to portray the Japanese economy in a bad light to justify profligate, often wasteful and yet populist spending.

They had to be seen to be 'doing something', and the profligate spending approach is a far more politically palatable approach then belt-tightening, irrespective of the economic merits and long-term economic damage done by running up enormous amounts of debt.

Secondly, it doesn't fit the post-Keynesian and Monetarist paradigms of how economies actually function. Mainstream economists were hell-bent on creating inflation and it just didn't happen, despite the massive fiscal and monetary stimulus.

Chapter 9

The Rise of China

'The defining moment in American economic history is when Bill Clinton lobbied to get China into the World Trade Organization. It was the worst political and economic mistake in American history in the last 100 years.'

Peter Navarro

At the beginning of the twentieth century, China was in turmoil, with much of the population seeking to overthrow the emperor while key regions were controlled by western imperialist powers.

By the end of the century, China was experiencing a period of extraordinary economic growth that would see her soon become the second largest economy in the world. In the intervening period, she would be invaded by Japan, endure a civil war and a devastating famine, experience a cultural revolution which undermined 4,000 years of cultural development, and suffer the murder of tens of millions of her own citizens in the name of a repugnant and misguided ideology – communism.

Between 1960 and 2000, Chinese GDP grew twenty-fold from US$59 billion* to US$1.2 trillion, before growing nine-fold over the next 15 years to reach US$11 trillion in 2015.

---

* Current US$

And between 1960 and 2016, real GDP per capita grew thirty-six-fold, from US$192† to US$6,900,[295] despite the population doubling from 682 million to nearly 1.4 billion.[296]

China's economic development has been dominated by politics. To provide context for China's miraculous economic miracle, I will provide a brief overview of the three phases: Republic of China (1912–1949); rule by Chairman Mao (1949–1976); and China's economic miracle (1978–present day).

Republic of China (1912–1949)

The Republic of China was established in 1912 following the fall of the Qing Dynasty, putting an end to 4,000 years of imperial rule. At the time, China was still mired in the past. Her economy was largely agricultural, with most of the people living in rural areas, while her social structures, practices and traditions were more medieval than modern.

The Chinese Revolution (1911) was a revolution against many things: foreign imperialism, the Qing monarchy, privilege and inequality, exploitation and corruption, national disunity, and China's military weakness.[297]

From the beginning, the new Republic was beset with internal struggles as regional warlords and revolutionary groups fought for control of the country. In time, this gave rise to the creation of the Chinese Communist Party (CCP), and the Kuomintang (KMT) – the Chinese Nationalist Party.

For the best part of three decades, the CCP and KMT fought a brutal civil war that saw atrocities committed on both sides, as they fought a battle to the death for control of the most populous nation of earth.

---

† Constant US$ (2010)

The Chinese people also suffered immensely at the hands of the cruel and inhumane Japanese occupation forces, who occupied many parts of China from the 1930s.

In the end, the Japanese were defeated and the CCP proved victorious over the nationalists.

Rule by Chairman Mao (1949–1976)

On October 1, 1949, Mao Zedong proclaimed the establishment of the People's Republic of China (PRC). Following his defeat, the nationalist leader, Chiang Kai-shek, and his supporters fled to the island of Taiwan, establishing the Republic of China and proclaiming Taipei its capital.

With a strong and disciplined leadership team in place, Mao wasted little time in implementing his radical agenda. Measures included overhauling the traditional land ownership scheme by confiscating land from affluent landlords and giving it to poor, landless peasants; embracing the Soviet economic model, which was based on state ownership of industry and large collective units in agriculture; eliminating privately owned firms; and centralising political control, government administration and economic planning.

China's changing fortunes had many benefits, particularly for urban populations. Public order and city housing standards improved, life expectancy rose from 36 to 57 years, and urban incomes increased by 40 per cent.[298]

But China's growth wasn't without its problems. Middle-level peasants came to resent many of the rural reforms, while life for urban Chinese became highly regimented, with workplaces organised along socialist principles.

The Great Leap Forward (GLF) (1958–61) was an economic and cultural campaign led by Chairman Mao aimed at rapidly transforming the country from an agrarian economy into an industrialised, socialist state. The central idea of the program was that industrial and agricultural development should occur in parallel.

The GLF is widely regarded as being an unmitigated economic and human disaster that contributed to the deaths of anywhere between 18 and 55 million people.[299] Historian Frank Dikötter asserts that 'coercion, terror, and systematic violence were the foundation of the GLF' and it 'motivated one of the deadliest mass killings of human history'.[300] And the deaths were not just isolated to China. According to genocide scholar Adam Jones, 'no group suffered more than the Tibetans', with perhaps one in five dying between 1959 and 1962.[301]

According to official figures, between 1959 and 1962, GDP fell by 32 per cent[302] as the economy encountered a myriad of problems including a decline in agricultural production, shortages of raw materials, overproduction of inferior-quality goods, deterioration of industrial plants through mismanagement, and exhaustion and demoralisation of the peasantry, intellectuals, and even party officials and government cadres.[303]

The CCP's treatment of their fellow citizens was appalling. Any criticism of the party, or failure to follow directions or meet production targets, was met with brutal punishment including beatings, mutilations, extreme torture or summary execution. Around 6–8 per cent of those who died during the GLF were tortured to death or summarily killed.[304]

Mao was heavily criticised within the Party for the failure of the GLF, forcing him to step down as Chairman of the PRC, though he did retain his position as Chairman of the CCP. He was replaced by the more moderate Liu Shaoqi and Deng Xiaoping, who were given the task of reforming the economy.

The new leadership dismantled many of the policies introduced during the GLF, with decision-making on economic grounds taking prominence over ideological fervour. Their policy agenda included restoring private ownership of plots to farmers, giving production teams greater control over economic planning and production, reducing the size of communes, and transferring unemployed industrial workers to the countryside. The CCP also decentralised its administration by reestablishing its six regional bureaus while taking steps to change the culture within the Party. These initiatives had an immediate effect, as GDP grew by over 60 per cent from 1962 to 1966.[305]

Despite his fall from grace, Mao never went away. And despite the good economic progress, Mao grew increasingly uneasy about what he regarded as the Party's creeping capitalist tendencies and its move away from his beloved revolutionary ideals and ideological roots. Determined to reestablish his brand of communism and restore his personal prestige, Mao resorted to what he knew best: he orchestrated a revolution in which he and his radical clique of fanatics reclaimed the Party leadership while throwing the country into chaos and anarchy.

Liu Shaoqi and future leader Deng Xiaoping were stood aside. Liu was placed under house arrest, and then sent to a detention camp, where he rotted away and died. Deng was slightly more fortunate. He was sent away for a period of re-education, before being sent to work in a factory.

Having wrested control from the moderates, Mao and his radical, murderous supporters embarked on the Cultural Revolution (1966–1976), the stated goal of which was to preserve 'true' Communist ideology in the country by purging remnants of capitalist and traditional elements from Chinese society, and to re-impose Maoist thought as the dominant ideology within the Party.[306]

The movement paralysed China politically, socially and economically. Schools, colleges and universities were shut down and many universities didn't reopen until 1972.[307]

During the Cultural Revolution, nearly 17 million urban youth – people who Mao had used to mount his revolution – were forcibly sent to rural areas, so they could 'develop their talents to the full' through education amongst the rural population.[308] It was only in the late 1970s that these 'young intellectuals', often dubbed China's stolen generation, were finally allowed to return to their home cities.

The Cultural Revolution marked the peak of Mao's rule. With an ageing leadership, the government was wracked by intense infighting as factional leaders fought for future control of the Party. To re-invigorate an economy that had suffered through the turmoil of the Cultural Revolution, Deng Xiaoping, with Mao's blessing, was returned to the senior Party leadership, where he was put in charge of the government, the Party, the military and the economy.

Deng emphatically opposed Party factionalism, and his policies aimed to promote unity as the first step to restoring economic productivity. Much like the post-Great Leap restructuring, Deng streamlined the railway system, steel production, and other key areas of the economy.

On Mao's death in 1976, a large group of party reformers who had become disillusioned with the Cultural Revolution backed the army in arresting the Gang of Four – Mao's four co-conspirators in the Cultural Revolution. Their arrests were met with jubilation and marked the end of another turbulent period in Chinese history.

China's Economic Miracle (1978–present day)

China's rise to become a world power has been nothing short of remarkable. From 1980 to 2011, China's economy grew at the rate of 10 per cent per annum, before falling back to around 7 per cent per annum since then.

China's rapid growth has pulled hundreds of millions of her people out of poverty. Today, the proportion of the Chinese population living below the poverty line of US$1/day has fallen from 64 per cent in 1978 to around 10 per cent.[309] Life expectancy has also risen sharply between 1960 and 2014 from 43.4 to 76 years.[310]

By 2012, China's middle class had reached more than 300 million people.[311] According to the Hurun Report, between 2009 and 2012, the number of U.S. dollar billionaires increased from 130 to 251, giving China the world's second-highest number of billionaires.[312]

Services now account for over 51 per cent of the economy, industry 40 per cent and agriculture just 9 per cent – a far cry from the largely agrarian economy in the past.[313] China is now the world's leading producer of many agricultural and industrial products, including iron and steel, cement, fertilisers, textiles, armaments, consumer products, ships, automobiles and telecommunications equipment. Importantly, as China continues her quest for regional and global hegemony, she is moving into the manufacture of higher end products including aircraft and satellites.

Urbanisation has been a key feature of China's transformation. Between 1980 and 2014, the proportion of the country's population living in urban areas increased from 20 per cent to over 50 per cent. It is estimated that China's urban population will reach one billion by 2030, equivalent to one-eighth of the world's population.[314] As of 2012, there are more than 262 million migrant workers in China, mostly rural migrants seeking work in cities.[315]

China's economic miracle is important for a number of reasons. Firstly, it is a good example of how any nation, even a staunchly communist nation, can achieve prosperity by eschewing centrally planned polices and adopting market-based economic policies. Chinese policy-makers also shunned western mainstream economic theory, pursuing an approach to economic development better suited to China's own political, cultural and social needs.

Secondly, the CCP is a ruthless, authoritarian regime whose leaders will do and say anything, anywhere, to retain power. China will always put China first in everything she does, as the Chinese government does everything in its power to restore China to what her leaders perceive as her rightful, dominant place in the world. Moreover, China will use the same authoritarian measures she uses at home to project power outward.

Equally, it demonstrates how western leaders have been asleep at the wheel, blindly unaware that they were creating a ruthless strategic competitor who plays by its own rules while exploiting the rules-based international trading system by adopting illegal and unfair trade policies to gain unfair economic advantage.

If western nations are to respond successfully to the threats posed by China, their governments must put the needs of their own citizens first over the short-term interests of corporate executives and other vested interest groups who will often be swayed by the lure of Chinese markets, by Chinese influence and corruption, and the illusion of free trade.

Finally, just as Japan found out in the late 1980s, China's recent success doesn't mean that she isn't vulnerable to negative economic forces such as excessive debt, a stressed financial system and malinvestments. The future remains delicately poised.

So let's look at how China rose phoenix-like from the ashes.

In 1978, under the guidance of the new paramount leader, Deng Xiaoping, China embarked on a program of economic and social reforms aimed at transitioning the country from a centrally planned to a market-oriented economy. Aware of the need to tread warily when implementing change, the government adopted a gradualist approach to modernisation. It was only after the government became more confident in its reform programs that controls on private businesses and central government intervention were further relaxed. Deng also coupled economic reform with social reform, jettisoning Mao's class struggle and propaganda campaigns.

Economic reform focused on the Four Modernisations: agriculture, industry, science and technology, and defence.

Deng's first reforms began in agriculture, where he began by decollectivising agriculture and introducing the household-responsibility system, which divided the communes into private plots. Under the new system, peasants could sell any surplus produce above government quotas at market prices. This increased agricultural production by 25 per cent between 1975 and 1985, setting a precedent for privatising other parts of the economy.[316]

Deng also introduced the industrial-responsibility system, which used a similar strategy of privatisation and the dual-price strategy, to promote improvements in state-owned enterprises by holding managers responsible for organisational performance. These reforms were equally successful, increasing productivity while reducing product shortages evident under the Maoist regime. Private businesses were also allowed to operate for the first time since the Communist takeover.

One notable move was the decentralisation of state control to the local level. This gave rise to the development of Township and Village Enterprises (TVEs), which were market-oriented public enterprises under the control of local governments. For a period, TVEs became the most vibrant part of the Chinese economy. Between 1978 and 1996, production by TVEs grew thirty-fold while the number of people employed grew from 28 million to 135 million.[317]

After the mid-1990s, TVEs fell out of favour and were forced to substantially restructure. Despite the decline in the role of TVEs, local and provincial governments continued to play a vital role in China's economic development, as the provinces were given autonomy and responsibility to promote exports and employment.

Deng also established special economic zones along the Chinese coast to attract foreign investment in manufacturing. This proved crucial to economic success as it allowed China not only to leverage its abundance of low-cost labour, but it generated millions of jobs and much needed foreign currency, facilitated the transfer of the latest technology and manufacturing techniques from west to east, and upskilled both management and workers.

Importantly, China permitted foreign investment in selected sectors, for example automobiles, but market access was conditional on the transfer of technology to China, that foreign firms form joint ventures with Chinese State-owned Enterprises (SOEs), and that these firms then integrate Chinese production into their global supply chains.

At the same time, China protected domestic firms from foreign competition by maintaining monopolies in key industries, for example banking, insurance and petroleum, maintaining high tariffs and by banning foreign investment in certain protected industries. It was only when the leadership was confident that Chinese firms could compete with foreign companies, or that they wanted to attract certain technologies and skills, that the government reduced tariffs and opened some industries up for restricted foreign investment.

The reforms continued unabated after Deng's death in 1997 under his hand-picked successors. In 1997–98, large-scale privatisation occurred. Under this scheme, all enterprises, except for a few large monopolies, were liquidated and their assets sold to private investors. This divestment, of course, didn't mean that the Chinese government had taken its hands off the economic levers. The CCP continued to maintain tight controls over key industry sectors, either directly through regulation, or indirectly through party networks.

In 2001, China joined the World Trade Organization (WTO) and over the next few years the government reduced tariffs, trade barriers, and regulations; reformed the banking system; dismantled much of the Mao-era social welfare system; and forced the People's Liberation Army (PLA) to divest itself of military-run businesses.[318] These reforms forced Chinese enterprises to restructure and become more efficient. This resulted in the State sector's share of industrial output falling from 81 per cent to 15 per cent between 1980 and 2005.[319]

Other reforms included a strong focus on education, a gradual reform of the banking system, the re-establishment of stock exchanges as well as efforts to modernise the Chinese legal system.

The conservative Hu-Wen administrations (2002–2012) began to reverse some of Deng's reforms in 2005. This included more egalitarian and populist measures including increasing subsidies and control over the health sector, a halt to privatisation, and adopting a loose monetary policy. This led to an enormous property bubble in which property prices have more than tripled in many cities.[320] The government also provided funds to promote the rise of 'national champions', corporations which could compete with large foreign corporations.[321]

China's growth under her current leader, President Xi Jinping, has continued unabated, albeit at a slightly slower pace. Much of this growth, however, has been accompanied by a huge run-up in house prices and funded by an extraordinary build-up in debt.

There have been many reasons for a China's success. First and foremost, Chinese leadership put China first in every aspect of her development. Like Japan before her, China adopted a beggar-thy-neighbour mercantilist trade policy which focused on protecting domestic industry from the ravages of international competition while driving growth though exports and infrastructure development. This gave China an extraordinary advantage over western nations which adopted freer trade policies, resulting in the transfer of millions of jobs from west to east, while allowing China to develop a world-class industrial base.

I have never understood the west's complicity and passivity in standing idly by while China used these unfair mercantilist policies to grow into an economic powerhouse and emerging military force. It has been clear for years that the mercantilist approach is incompatible with, and vastly more powerful than, the freer trade approach when each are pitted against each other.

I can only put this apathy down to three things: greed, stupidity and arrogance. The greed has emanated from western business leaders' willingness to sell out their countrymen for short-term profits and bonuses by outsourcing jobs to China and other developing nations. Moreover, it seems to be a somewhat short-sighted approach in that corporate leaders have undermined their own middle classes, which will eventually undermine domestic growth and demand, while creating strategic competitors down the track.

The stupidity comes in two forms. Firstly, from economists, academics, corporations, the media, bureaucrats and politicians putting the ideology of free trade over commercial reality. Unquestionably, free trade is the best economic system, provided all nations abide by the rules of fair-play. In practice, however, free trade doesn't exist. All politicians are subject to lobbying by powerful vested interests, and this will always undermine the benefits of free trade. One needs to look no further than the European Union (EU), which was established as a trading bloc to fetter free trade. The same is true for any other nation including Japan and the U.S.. Free trade is only relevant when major powers impose or prescribe it on those small- to middle-ranking nations that don't have the power to resist. The best one can hope for is freer trade.

The second element of stupidity comes in the preparedness of major western nations to willingly give away their intellectual property (IP) and thus their competitive advantage in return for gaining access to the Chinese market. China has only ever been prepared to provide access to the Chinese market when it has been in their own interests to do so, whether it be to create jobs or gain access to specific IP and/or manufacturing techniques.

The failure of western corporations to understand that they were being played for fools is only now starting to dawn on their leaders. But it is now too late; the horse has bolted. China has used western IP to develop world-class corporations in strategic sectors such as automobiles, computing and telecommunications, amongst many other industries. And they will now use this expertise and a large domestic market to successfully compete against their previous benefactors on the global market.

The third factor is American arrogance. It is hard to believe that national agencies such as the CIA would have been blindly unaware of China's regional and international ambitions and that, over time, China would become a strategic competitor that will challenge America's hegemonic hold over regional and global defense and economic affairs. Realistically, China is the only nation that could challenge America in the foreseeable future. It begs the question: did American planners facilitate China's growth so that her industrial/military complex would have a perpetual enemy? Were they asleep at the wheel? Or did they naively favour short-term geo-political appeasement in the hope of integrating post-Mao China into the existing western-led, global free-trade order bound by international law and multilateral institutions over longer-term challenges that such appeasement might bring. Perhaps we will never know, but western powers have created an 800-lb gorilla which will be nigh-on impossible to control or influence moving forward – unless China implodes.

China's high growth rates can also be put down to the low economic base from which she started. Given the poor state of her infrastructure and industry, China benefited greatly during the catch-up phase of development through her low-cost base, plentiful labour and the need for massive amounts of new infrastructure development. China also benefited from its centralised political system, which allowed her to develop long-range plans rather than being trapped in short-term political cycles as happens in the west. Chinese leaders also acknowledged the limitations of central planning as an economic tool, and replaced it with market-based outcomes, especially market-based pricing that reflects product scarcity and consumer needs.

However, rather than rely on the prevailing western economic theory that suggested a big-bang approach to reform and development, China developed her own unique approach to market-based reform. Dubbed 'Socialism with Chinese characteristics', this allowed China to retain control of the reform process while avoiding the problems experienced by the Soviet Union, which saw vast sums of money transferred from state control to well-connected oligarchs, or Latin American countries following the Latin American debt crisis. This allowed her to retain her political system, while maintaining control of the change agenda.

Importantly, China's reform process didn't have a blueprint. While China had broad goals, she followed a gradualist approach to reform, progressing only after experimentation and a review of the previous steps. This had the added advantage of giving the leadership time to gauge the level of support within the Party and the public for proposed changes, while being able to address resistance by those negatively impacted by change. After the disaster of the Cultural Revolution, pragmatism over ideology became paramount in Chinese thinking.

While China moved towards a more market-oriented approach, Chinese officials didn't view the market economy in the same way as western economists, who espouse principles of free trade. Instead, they remained very focused on their key objectives of retaining political power and social stability while gradually raising living standards. As a result, the government was very selective in how and when they opened up the different sectors to competition and investment.[322]

Like Japan before her, China also adopted a long-term approach to economic development, favouring investment, savings and productivity improvements over consumption and welfare. For example, from 1980 to 2015 investment and gross savings averaged around 40 per cent of GDP, nearly double comparable rates in the U.S.[323] while Chinese consumption was about two-thirds of U.S. consumption levels. This investment was channelled into nation-building projects including energy, transportation (roads, ports, railways and airports), telecommunications and dams as well as massive investments in housing, rather than squandered on consumer goods.

China used its large trade surpluses with the U.S. to finance U.S. deficits by purchasing U.S. securities. This allowed Americans to continue buying Chinese products while preventing the yuan from appreciating too strongly against the U.S. dollar.

Much of the Chinese success can also be put down to the Chinese people themselves. Given the right circumstances, the Chinese people are generally extremely hardworking and entrepreneurial, and set great store on the role of family in society.

Education has also played a key role in China's development. By 2010, 94 per cent of the population over age 15 were literate[324] compared to only 20 per cent in 1950.[325] China also placed great importance on tertiary education, particularly in the fields of science, mathematics and engineering. In 2009, China graduated over 10,000 Ph.D. engineers, and as many as 500,000 BSc graduates, more than any other country.[326] China is also the world's second-largest publisher of scientific papers, producing 121,500 in 2010 alone, including 5,200 in leading international scientific journals.[327] How useful many of these papers are is another question, but they are certainly heading in the right direction.

Importantly, Chinese success over the millennia has only ever occurred when she has had a strong central government. Whenever this central control has weakened, China has endured upheaval and decades of bloodshed. For all intents and purposes, the current period could well be described as the Communist Dynasty, or perhaps now the Xi Dynasty. As such, much of China's economic success can be sheeted home to the government's success in maintaining political stability under Communist Party rule. This has been achieved by ruthlessly quashing any dissent while maintaining strict controls over the press, access to information via the Internet and western literature, freedom of assembly and freedom of religion. CCP control has even extended as far as controlling how many children families can have.

Calls by westerners about opening China up to democracy or criticising her appalling human rights record will continue to be ignored by China. China's leadership is focused on two things: China's relentless pursuit of restoring what she believes to be her proper place in world affairs, and retaining power.

In recent times, Chinese authorities have resorted to nationalism rather than ideology as a means of unifying people under Communist Party rule. This was no better exemplified than the successful staging of the 2008 Beijing Olympics, which became a sort of 'coming out' party for China, after decades of being a political and economic backwater.

Not surprisingly, China's impressive growth has not been without its problems. While China's reform has greatly reduced poverty, both income and income inequality have increased. For example, a 2012 study found that the top 1 per cent of the population held more than one-quarter of China's wealth, while 430 million Chinese struggled day-to-day.[328]

At the same time, from 1978 to 2015, the share of national income for the top 10 per cent of China's income earners increased from 27 per cent to 41 per cent, while the share of income of the bottom half of income earners fell from 27 per cent to 15 per cent.[329] Income inequality is even more pronounced between the regions, as economic growth has been centered along the coastal areas and major cities while many in the western regions have missed out.

Economic growth has also highlighted a dark underside to Chinese society: many Chinese people don't have a high regard for laws or the rule of law. In traditional Chinese society, business was based on social relations, so the Chinese consider ethical and moral values more important than laws. The Cultural Revolution also destroyed much of the moral foundation of Chinese society.[330] This disdain for legal niceties has manifested itself in several ways; firstly, through endemic corruption – both at home and abroad; secondly, through state-sponsored theft of IP; and thirdly, through currency manipulation.

Given the leading role that the state plays in Chinese society, it is not surprising that China would be vulnerable to elevated levels of corruption. According to Transparency International, China ranks 79th out of 176 countries, with a score of 40 against a global average of 43.[331]

Although less corrupt than some of its neighbours such as Myanmar, Laos, North Korea, Pakistan and Russia, it is on a par with the likes of Mexico, Columbia, Egypt and Bolivia, none of which are known as bastions of morality. In contrast, it sits well below the rankings of western nations such as the Nordic countries, western European countries, New Zealand, Singapore and the U.S., all of which have strong legal systems and abide by the rule of law.

Corruption has taken many forms including graft, bribery, embezzlement, patronage, nepotism, abuse of power, the sale of state assets at reduced prices, favourable trade deals for associated companies and falsification of statistics. This has been undertaken both for personal gain and political power.

Corruption is believed to reach the highest levels in society. The Chinese People's Liberation Army (PLA), for example, created its own enterprises and engaged in a range of corrupt activities including smuggling and questionable procurement practices. It has also been widely reported that President Xi

Jinping has amassed a private fortune worth well over US$1 billion. Most of the identifiable assets have been acquired by the family of Mr. Xi's elder sister, Qi Qiaoqiao, but obscured beneath assumed names and layers of holding companies.[332]

In 2012, President Xi Jinping used an anti-corruption campaign as a smokescreen to eliminate his political opponents and strengthen his own power base. As of 2016, the campaign had 'netted' over 120 high-ranking officials, including about a dozen high-ranking military officers, several senior executives of SOEs, and five national leaders.[333] In total, more than 100,000 people have been indicted for corruption.[334]

The Chinese government has also actively sponsored the theft of IP and trade secrets from foreign companies to gain access to technology and IP. A 2013 U.S. government enquiry put annual losses through theft of IP at over $300 billion, the loss of millions of jobs and a reduction in U.S. GDP. The enquiry estimated that China was behind between 50 per cent and 80 per cent of the international theft of IP.[335]

The enquiry also noted that in addition to the recent innovation of cyber-theft, China used many old-fashioned means to steal IP: hard-drives stolen by bribed employees; employees temporarily planted in foreign companies to gain access to IP; foreign products reverse engineered and then mass-produced at low cost to compete with the original product; illegal phone taps to steal trade secrets; and digitised products being pirated and sold illegally – the list is endless.

The theft of IP allowed China to quickly acquire the latest technology and IP, thus providing a competitive advantage to compete internationally while shutting international competitors out of the Chinese market.

In addition to straight theft, China and Chinese companies have used a variety of both legal and illegal means to gain competitive advantage. These have included tied foreign aid, soft power, bribery and blackmail, and the purchase of foreign companies to gain access to raw materials, markets and knowledge, and to influence western thought on China's ambitions and interests.

In recent times, China has been particularly aggressive in establishing influence in western universities by funding academics sympathetic to Chinese ambitions as well as language and cultural centres, such as Confucius Institutes.

Resource rich, despotic developing countries such as Pakistan, Iran and African nations have been primary targets to gain access to resources and strategic locations. Two recent examples of China's approach have included lending money to the Seychelles and Sri Lanka for infrastructure projects, knowing that the recipient country will be unable to repay the loans. The next step is taking control of the asset and establishing military bases in these strategic areas.

According to the *New York Times*, from 2000 to 2014 China also suppressed the rise of the renminbi to maintain a competitive advantage for its exports, buying dollars and adding $4 trillion to its foreign reserves over the period. This currency manipulation, together with her mercantilist trade policies and U.S. outsourcing, allowed China to significantly increase her exports to the U.S. at the expense of U.S. jobs.[336]

China's rapid economic development has also led to a range of well-publicised environmental problems including air, water and river pollution, as well as widespread deforestation and soil degradation. Official reports indicate that 20 per cent of China's arable land and one-third of its surface water are polluted, and more than 80 per cent of underground water used by farms, factories and households is too polluted to drink safely or bathe in.[337] The government has recognised these environmental problems and is taking active steps to improve outcomes including large investments in renewable energy and water infrastructure.

But perhaps the greatest problem facing China today lies in her financial system with poor financial governance, weak internal controls and increasing levels of debt. Despite a high savings rate, much of China's infrastructure-led investment boom has been financed by debt. According to McKinsey & Company, between 2000 and mid-2014, total outstanding debt in China increased thirteen-fold from $2.1 trillion to $28.2 trillion. Despite a six-fold increase in nominal GDP, the debt to GDP ratio increased from 121 per cent to 282 per cent. Most of the increase in debt has occurred in the corporate and finance sectors, leaving official government debt at a relatively modest 55 per cent of GDP.[338] Increased debt levels, together with a high reliance of exports, pose significant risks for China should the global economy turn down.

McKinsey has identified three key problems with the growth in China's debt. Firstly, nearly half of the non-financial debt is directly or indirectly related to the real estate and related sectors. Collectively worth as much as $9 trillion, this poses a considerable risk given the rapid run-up in property prices and the size of the construction sector, currently estimated at around 15 per cent of GDP.[339]

Secondly, there has been a rapid rise in the shadow banking sector – entities that engage in non-traditional banking often under the radar of the authorities. Various reports estimate the shadow banking system is worth between US$3–10 trillion,[340] and accounts for 30 per cent of China's outstanding debt. One area of particular concern relates to the sale of wealth management products to unsuspecting depositors in circumstances akin to a Ponzi scheme. The China Insurance Regulatory Commission has recently begun a crackdown on these products, resulting in the arrest of several senior executives on fraud charges. Even if this problem is resolved, other problems in financial governance and greed in the financial system are likely to prove problematical in coming years.

The third problem is the growing debt accumulated in off-balance sheet local-government financing vehicles, which are used to fund infrastructure, social housing and other projects. A 2014 audit of local government finances conducted by the central government found that 40 per cent of local governments rely on land sales to make loan payments, and that 20 per cent of new borrowing is used to repay older loans. Any slowing of the property market would put these entities at risk of default.[341]

Throughout her long history, China has been an elitist, imperialist power, replete with brutal, authoritarian governments, a subservient people and vassal states paying tribute as the price for protection. She has never had any problems in expanding into other regions and subjugating other peoples to her rule. One only needs to look at her illegal annexation and colonisation of Tibet and Xinjiang to see that modern China is no different.

In 2016, China released her latest five-year plan (FYP) with the goal of becoming 'a moderately prosperous society' and doubling GDP per capita by 2020 compared to 2010. The FYP is a continuation of government policy of recent years as it lays out an ambitious agenda to rebalance China's economy, improve the quality of life for its citizens, and address systemic issues such as environmental degradation and industry overcapacity. The FYP also re-enforces the CCP's central role in economic and social development.

China's 13th Five-Year Plan for 2016–2020

The 13th FYP is underpinned by five guiding principles:[342]

1. Innovation – transitioning China from an emphasis on low-end manufacturing and heavy industry towards higher added-value manufacturing. This will involve providing a greater focus on technology, innovation, and research and development, while encouraging entrepreneurialism.

   China's *Made in China 2025 Plan* is integral to its innovation strategy. With the help of huge infusions of state money, the plan targets 10 key sectors for government support including new energy vehicles, information technology, biotechnology, materials and aerospace, amongst others.

   The Chinese government has also demanded that U.S. companies cut the licensing fees that they charge for key patents and has insisted that companies set up joint ventures to do business in China.[343]
2. Coordinated development – improving regional inter-governmental coordination of policies and development to reduce duplication and disparities in development between regions.
3. Green growth – protecting the environment and setting targets and caps for energy use, air quality and reduction of soil and water contamination.
4. Openness – this principle lays out objectives to increase exports and select imports, increase inbound and outbound investment and enhance China's role in global governance. The plan also calls for increased foreign investment in selected industries including aged

care, finance and banking as well as imports of advanced technology and equipment.

'One Belt, One Road' (OBOR) is a key pillar of China's 'openness' policy. Based on the old Silk Road of yesteryear, it involves developing a vast network of railways and ports to establish new maritime and overland trade routes between China and Europe.

Altogether the plan will include more than 60 countries and 4.4 billion people, passing through Asia, Europe, Africa and the Middle East, covering up to 40 per cent of global GDP.

It's expected to cost at least $900 billion, with estimates up to three times that. China has already pledged more than $100 billion and it will be completed in a series of bilateral projects such as the $46 billion China–Pakistan economic corridor, and a $5.2 billion railway that will eventually link Laos, Thailand, Malaysia and Singapore.[344]

The Chinese government said the 'overall vision' is to build a 'road of peace, prosperity, opening up innovation and civilisation' that is open for collaboration with other countries.[345]

OBOR also calls for China to secure access to raw materials necessary for her long-term growth.

5. Inclusive growth – the aim is to provide growth that assists all Chinese people to alleviate poverty, raise living standards and improve access and affordability to essential services including education, health care and social services. This includes extending social security to the entire elderly population, increasing urbanisation, particularly in second, third and fourth-tier cities, as

well as a partial relaxation of the household registration system, which discriminates against rural migrants working in the larger cities.

Under the FYP, China also committed to achieving 'national revival' by 2049, which means restoring her to what she believes is her rightful place as a dominant global power.

People in the west would do well to remember that Chinese leaders have never forgotten their long history, nor the humiliation she suffered at the hands of the imperialist powers in the nineteenth century. China will do everything in her power to restore herself to what she believes is her pre-eminent position in world affairs and to resurrect the golden periods of the Tang and Han dynasties.

Seen in this context, China's regional neighbours and the western world should be deeply concerned at the implications of this five-year plan as it is a continuation of China's highly protectionist, mercantilist trade policies. China will continue to use corrupt, and unfair and illegal means as she seeks to build globally competitive domestic firms to power her exports, while restricting access to her markets and substituting foreign technology and products with local products.

She will also continue to use a mix of Chinese nationalism, both at home and in the large ethnic diaspora abroad, to maintain support for the CCP, while undermining democratic institutions in the west. Equally, she will use her economic strength to bully and coerce western nations and corporations into bowing down to Chinese demands over issues such as Taiwan and Tibet.

Finally, she will use soothing words and rhetoric to try to convince westerners of her peaceful ambitions while using all means to expand regional domination. A current example of China's growing confidence, duplicity and belligerence is her illegal grab for control of a major part of the South China Sea and her subsequent decision to ignore a 2016 ruling by an international court that there is 'no legal basis' for China's expansive claims in the area.[346]

China has also criticised U.S. President Donald Trump's moves to impose tariffs on a range of Chinese imports, saying that such a move would 'seriously hurt the multilateral trading system' under the WTO and it would take legal action.[347] This is an extraordinarily duplicitous statement, given China's flaunting of trade rules through her use of illegal and unfair trade practices over the past 30 years. Such acts of aggression will become more commonplace as her economic power grows.

Finally, while China's recovery from the disaster that was Mao has been nothing short of remarkable, it begs the question, can this continue, given her extreme debt levels and malinvestments, and that her ongoing prosperity is inextricably linked to the global economy?

Chapter 10

Post-war America

'The American Republic will endure until the day Congress discovers that it can bribe the public with the public's money.'

Alexis de Tocqueville

Despite wars, terrorism, oil price shocks, financial crises and the rise of Japan, China and the EU, the U.S. remained the largest economy in the world. Between 1950 and 2016, GDP grew seven-fold from $2.5 trillion to $18.2 trillion, while GDP per person more than trebled from $16,200 to $56,200.[348]

Chapter 10 is divided into three sections: firstly, an overview of the four phases of post-war development: The Golden Age; stagnation of the 1970s; Reaganomics; and slowing economic growth; secondly, an examination of how the elite have used every means at their disposal, including subverting democratic processes and pushing economic theories that favour the rich, to further their own interests at the expense of everyday folk; and finally, the failure of central banks to meet their obligations to deliver price stability and a sound financial system. Their failures have included the use of deeply flawed economic policies, the perpetuation of economic myths and falsehoods that have somehow become ingrained as 'truisms' in everyday economic thought, and the excuses they are now resorting to, to deflect any criticism of their abject policy failures.

Put simply, mainstream economic theory is in tatters and central bankers will be found to have no credibility, other than amongst their sponsors – the elite.

Post-war Economic Development

The Golden Age

The period from the end of World War II to the early 1970s is widely regarded as the 'Golden Age' of American capitalism, a period where the economy grew strongly, unemployment was subdued, and the middle class swelled as productivity and real wages rose. Most social classes shared in the growing prosperity, due in large part to the rise in higher-paid manufacturing jobs and the creation of millions of new jobs.

The boom was driven by many factors, not the least of which was the Baby Boom, a period of increased fertility and positive social mood following two decades of depression and war. It was an exhilarating time as the Baby Boomers flocked to the new suburbs and built vibrant communities. They revelled in an abundance of new consumer products including televisions and an array of household appliances. Construction of the interstate highway system, together with access to plentiful supplies of cheap oil and affordable automobiles, increased mobility and led to the growth of local shopping malls.

Manufacturing expanded to provide new goods while advances in technology greatly expanded productivity and business opportunities. Computing and aviation expanded greatly, providing new opportunities for business and consumer travel. Agriculture also benefited from growing mechanisation and the introduction of new plant breeds.

It was also a period of great social change, as the new generation threw off the shackles of conservatism and revelled in the popular culture driven by an explosion in new forms of music and entertainment. People also marvelled at rapid advances in space exploration, which culminated in the moon landing by Neil Armstrong and Buzz Aldrin in 1969.

The period, however, was not without its challenges, as people feared the possibility of nuclear war, while millions protested America's involvement in the Vietnam War. The American civil rights movement, a mass protest movement against racial segregation and discrimination in the southern United States, also came to national prominence during the 1950s and 1960s.

The Golden Age was shattered by several events that occurred in the early 1970s. These included the partial collapse of the Bretton Woods system, the 1973 oil crisis and the 1973–74 stock market collapse.

In the latter stages of World War II, representatives from the U.S., Britain and their allies met at Bretton Woods in New Hampshire to decide on a set of rules to manage the post-war monetary system. The meetings were motivated by the belief that the inter-war monetary system, which had seen the collapse of the gold standard and the rise of tariffs and discriminatory trade blocs, had failed and that a return to free trade was not only necessary for prosperity, but also for peace.

The Bretton Woods system that emerged resulted in the creation of the IMF and the World Bank. The IMF was given responsibility for overseeing a new system of fixed exchange rates pegged to the U.S. dollar which, in turn, was fixed to the price of gold. It was also to serve as a forum for consultation and co-operation, providing financial assistance to countries experiencing temporary balance of payment problems, and in exceptional circumstances, to provide for adjustments to fixed exchange rates for countries suffering long-term structural problems.[349] The World Bank was responsible for providing loans to aid in the reconstruction of war-torn nations and to provide finance for developing nations. In a sign of their power and disdain for lesser powers, the major powers also agreed that the head of the World Bank would be American, and the head of the IMF would be European. This continues to this day.

Under the Bretton Woods system, countries settled their international balances in dollars, and U.S. dollars could be converted into gold at any time at a fixed exchange rate of $35 per ounce. This committed the U.S. government to backing every U.S. dollar with gold. This placed great responsibility on the U.S. government to maintain confidence in the monetary system by prudently managing its finances and controlling the supply of dollars. Since the U.S. held around three-quarters of the world's official gold reserves, the system seemed secure.[350]

Initially, the Bretton Woods system worked well, as the post-war demand for U.S. goods and services – and dollars – was high. However, as the European and Japanese economies recovered, the U.S. share of global output decreased, as did the need for dollars, making convertibility of dollars to gold more desirable. Ongoing U.S. current account deficits, together with increased military spending and foreign aid, and a small increase in the quantity of gold, resulted in an oversupply of dollars relative to gold.[351]

The Fed stepped into the foreign exchange markets, using currency swaps to defend the U.S. gold stock. International efforts were also made to stem the run on gold. Despite these efforts, U.S. gold reserves dropped year by year as some countries, notably France, insisted on redeeming their dollars for gold at the official rate.

In 1969, the U.S. entered a recession. With inflation on the rise and a run on gold looming, in 1971 President Nixon closed the gold window, meaning that the U.S. would no longer convert dollars into gold, *at any price*. The U.S. dollar was devalued shortly thereafter, as world currencies adjusted to the new system of floating exchange rates. Nixon's decision proved to be one of the most reckless acts of economic vandalism in the twentieth century, as it undermined the Bretton Woods system, and turned the international monetary system into one comprised purely of fiat currency.

While the U.S. dollar was backed by gold, the world suffered no major financial crises. However, any restrictions on governments and central banks to act responsibly were thrown out the window, as governments could now create money and expand credit at will. The massive run-up in debt, chronic trade and budget deficits, financialisation of the global economy, and the series of financial crises over the past four decades can all be traced back to this one momentous decision – the decision to move away from sound money.

Stagnation of the 1970s

The collapse of Bretton Woods, together with rising inflation and the onset of the 1973–75 recession, resulted in the 1973–74 bear market, one of the worst bear markets of the twentieth century. During this time, the DJIA lost over 45 per cent of its value while the British stock market fared even worse, losing 73 per cent of its value.[352]

The next major shock to the global economy came in October 1973, when Arab oil-producing nations imposed an embargo on the sale of oil to the U.S., Great Britain, Canada, Japan and the Netherlands in retaliation to U.S. support for Israel in the Yom Kippur War. By the time the embargo was lifted in March 1974, the price of oil had quadrupled to nearly $12 per barrel.[353]

The embargo had an immediate effect as inflation spiked in many countries, and governments were forced to introduce fuel rationing. Central banks responded by cutting interest rates to encourage growth, deciding that inflation was a secondary concern. Although this was the orthodox macroeconomic prescription at the time, the resulting stagflation (high inflation and high unemployment) surprised economists and central bankers alike, as this didn't accord with the prevailing economic theory – the Phillips Curve – which postulated that there is an inverse relationship between inflation and unemployment. In other words, higher rates of inflation would lower unemployment and vice versa, not increase unemployment. This proved to be yet another failure in a long line of failed economic theories. With Keynesian economics coming under increasing scrutiny, monetarism came to displace Keynesianism as the mainstream economists' theory of choice.

The crisis also led to chronic current account deficits for many oil-importing nations. Oil producers responded by recycling their windfall gains through capital markets to finance these deficits, leading to an unsustainable build-up of debt in many countries, especially in Latin America.

The oil crisis also precipitated the move away from oil-intensive industries, and led many nations to introduce conservation measures, increase oil exploration and develop alternative forms of energy. This was an excellent example of how economies as living, self-regulating systems respond to economic events without the need for government intervention.

But the first oil crisis led to another outcome that would have an enormous impact on the global financial system in the following decades. Under an agreement reached in 1974 between the U.S. and Saudi Arabia, the U.S. agreed to provide military equipment and defense to Saudi Arabia in return for the global oil trade being denominated in U.S. dollars. Saudi Arabia also agreed to re-invest a substantial portion of its oil revenue in U.S. Treasury securities.[354] The agreement once again cemented the U.S. dollar as the de facto global reserve currency, but this time backed by oil rather than gold.

The new Petrodollar system, as it came to be known, had enormous benefits for the U.S. in that it created ongoing demand for U.S. dollars, which allowed the U.S. to fund its ballooning trade and budget deficits in U.S. dollars without putting pressure on the exchange rate or interest rates. In return, it guaranteed the survival of the corrupt and ideologically abhorrent House of Saud. It also meant that the U.S. and the Saudis were joined at the hip, which helps explain the mute reaction from U.S. officials even after the large number of Saudi nationals involved in the 9/11 terrorist attacks became public.

Stagflation continued to grip the nation as inflation and interest rates continued to climb. President Carter responded by deregulating the airlines, railroads and trucking as well as partially deregulating the financial sector. The Fed also hiked interest rates, which peaked at 20 per cent in January 1981, sending the economy into recession. While this tough love proved difficult for many people in the short-run, it broke the back of the inflation cycle, setting the economy up for a decade of growth.

Reaganomics

Ronald Reagan was elected president in 1981, promising a return to the free market ideals that had prevailed before the Great Depression and Roosevelt's New Deal policies. Dubbed Reaganomics, his policies favoured supply-side economics, an economic theory that supports lowering taxes to stimulate savings and investment, while lowering barriers on the production of goods and services. This contrasts with Keynesianism, which focuses on regulating demand.

Reagan's 1981 Program for Economic Recovery had four main objectives: reduce the growth of government spending; reduce federal income and capital gains taxes; reduce government regulation; and reduce inflation by tightening the money supply. He also called for a return to the gold standard and gave support for freer international trade. These policy changes were expected to increase savings and investment, increase economic growth, balance the budget, restore healthy financial markets, and reduce inflation and interest rates.[355]

Reagan's policies are often used to highlight the success of free market economics. However, actual policy achievements belie the rhetoric, demonstrating once again how economic myths, not supported by the facts, can gain traction and go unchallenged.

During Reagan's presidency, the economy grew by over one-third; inflation, unemployment and interest rates all fell; over 20 million jobs were created; the stock market increased substantially (despite the 1987 stock market crash); and between 1983 and 1989, the number of people below the poverty line fell by 3.8 million.[356] These were excellent economic outcomes in anybody's language. But how much of this can be traced back to Reagan's four pillars? Not a lot, if you go by the evidence.

Despite promises to reduce growth in spending, government spending during Reagan's two terms (FY 1981–88) was well above the prevailing rate from 1971 to 2009, while public debt tripled between 1980 and 1988 from $712 billion to $2.05 trillion.[357] Budget deficits were also significantly higher under Reagan than his predecessor. After failing to deliver on his promise 'to get government off our backs', this led Reaganites to fall back on the old political line that 'deficits don't matter'.

Many of Reagan's polices favoured the rich over the lower and middle classes. Changes to the Federal tax system, for example, cut capital gains taxes and reduced marginal tax rates on high-income earners from 70 per cent to around 30 per cent, while shifting the composition of tax receipts towards payroll, social security and new investment taxes.[358] Bracket creep – where wage inflation pushes wage earners into higher tax brackets – also acted as another tax on low-income earners.

And, while overall GDP per capita grew during Reagan's trickle-down policies, income growth slowed for the middle and lower classes (from 2.4 per cent to 1.8 per cent per annum), while rising for the upper class (from 2.2 per cent to 4.8 per cent per annum).[359]

Reagan's track record in trade and deregulation was no better. William Niskanen, a member of Reagan's Council of Economic Advisors, stated that Reagan added more trade barriers than any other administration since Hoover. As a result, between 1980 and 1988 the share of U.S. imports that were subject to some form of trade restraint grew from 12 per cent to 23 per cent.[360] Reagan also railed strongly against the success of Japanese firms, despite Japanese firms providing superior quality, low-cost goods to the American consumer.

Not only did Reagan abandon deregulation started by Jimmy Carter, he increased regulations in some instances. For example, Reagan intensified regulation of the stock market following the 1987 crash. Moreover, instead of ending farm price supports and controls and returning to a free market in agriculture, the administration greatly increased price support, controls and subsidies.[361] This is hardly a ringing endorsement of Reagan's free trade policies or his penchant for deregulation.

Putting aside the feel-good influence of a popular president, factors that did play a role in spurring economic growth following the stagnation of the 1970s included a secular decline in interest rates, a synchronised recovery in the global economy, increased productivity, a boom in science and technology, population growth, favourable demographics and an ebullient social mood that buoyed consumer and investor confidence.

Slowing Growth

The period since the early 1990s recession has been one of profound change in the U.S. economy. It has been characterised by a significant decline in the rate of economic growth, structural changes in the composition of the economy, declining labour productivity, and policies favouring the elite, including the introduction of shareholder value maximisation, increasing globalisation and financialisation of the economy.

During this period, the U.S. also experienced three asset price booms: the dot-com boom, the housing boom and the current stock market boom. All were fuelled by euphoric social mood, greased by plentiful quantities of cheap credit. The earlier booms were also followed by the inevitable bust. The bust of the latter still awaits us.

Unfortunately, the benefits of economic growth have not been shared equally. While the ultra-rich have amassed extraordinary fortunes, the middle class has been pillaged while the poor have remained impoverished. Authorities have also left the economy saddled with historically high debts and deficits, which have sown the seeds for the next Great Depression. I will touch on each of the above changes to the economy in some detail.

Decline in the Rate of Economic Growth

Figure 3 shows average *real* GDP growth, decade by decade, from the 1930s through to 2016. Despite continued economic growth, the underlying trend in the rate of economic growth has been unmistakable – DOWN. And, this is despite, or in part because, of massive fiscal and monetary stimulus by the government and the Fed since the 1990s, and the huge build-up in debt.

Figure 3 highlights that the rate of change in real economic growth peaked in the 1940s. The upturn was driven in large part by several years of extraordinary wartime expenditure, and coming off a low base of growth during the 1930s. The 1950s and 60s were the golden years for American capitalism, boosted by the baby boomers and a period of extreme optimism following the Great Depression and the wartime years. In some years, real year-on-year growth exceeded 8 per cent, and regularly exceeded 5 per cent.[362]

Figure 3 Average Real GDP Growth 1930s–2016

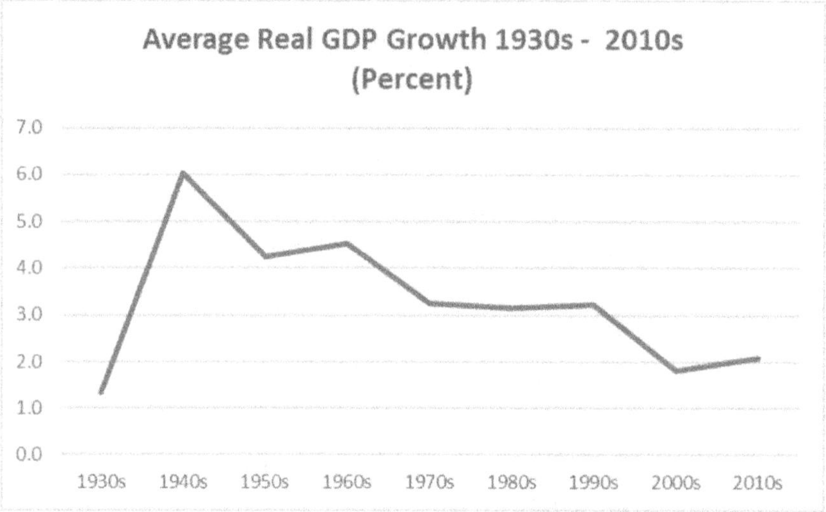

Data Source: Bureau of Economic Analysis

Growth slowed to a more moderate 3 per cent per annum during the stagnation of the 1970s and the Reagan era. Despite a few good years where growth exceeded 5 per cent per annum, the overall growth rate was held back by several recessions, as well as a decline in growth in the good years to between 3 and 4 per cent per annum. Since the turn of the century, economic growth has been anemic at best, with real growth only once exceeding 4 per cent per annum.

Importantly, the decline in the rate of economic growth experienced by the U.S. has also been evidenced in other developed countries, particularly Europe and Japan. So, why has there been this downward trend in the rate of real growth? In broad terms, two key factors drive economic growth: increased productivity, and population and demographics.

Productivity, which measures the ratio of economic outputs to inputs, is the major factor responsible for economic growth, especially growth in per capita income – refer to box below for a breakdown of those factors that drive productivity. Increased productivity is important because it allows businesses and nations to produce more goods using less resources. It can improve living standards for all through better wages and conditions for workers, improved health, greater leisure time, better-quality products at lower prices, better environmental results, and better social outcomes through improved government services. It also improves returns for shareholders, increases competitiveness and is also the key factor that allows an economy to grow without putting upward pressure on prices.

Increased Productivity

Productivity is driven by a number of factors including:

- entrepreneurialism – entrepreneurial spirit, support for entrepreneurs and reward for effort leads to the dynamism and drive needed to power economic progress.
- innovation in technology and know-how, research and development, new products and materials, innovative ways of working and managerial competence.
- competition and a market-based economy, and minimal government involvement and intervention in the economy. Competition promotes productivity through innovation and renewal as well as through the demise of inefficient and outdated firms. In contrast, monopolies and activities that restrict

competition stifle innovation.

- investment in infrastructure, facilities, plant and equipment, people and systems.
- growth of human capital including developing a skilled, flexible, educated and motivated workforce.
- a strong middle class – this not only provides for strong demand, but it also fosters social stability, and upward social and economic mobility.
- sound money and a strong banking sector.
- strong savings and access to finance.
- access to raw materials and natural resources, including water, energy and land.
- a hospitable climate and amenable geography.
- institutional factors including political and social stability, a supportive legal and regulatory framework, freedom of expression and freedom of speech, and a strong, independent and unbiased media.
- freedom of religion and separation of church and state.
- social and cultural factors, including social cohesion, strong family values, self-reliance, a strong work ethic, a strong ethical and moral framework and support for the rule of law.

Changes in population and the demographic profile also affect economic growth by impacting aggregate demand, labour supply, savings and investment, and the cost of welfare and social services.

Demographics is particularly important as demand for products and services changes as people move through the various stages of life, and as people join or leave the workforce.

It is also impacts the proportion of those engaged in the workforce vis-à-vis dependents, such as children and older people. An ageing population tends to put a strain on government services, including medical and welfare costs, while reducing savings as people draw down on their retirement savings. The influence of increased productivity, population growth and demographics reached their peak in the two decades following World War II, but their contribution to growth has progressively faded, particularly since the 1990s.

While many factors supported strong economic growth, other factors have worked to constrain growth. These factors have included structural changes in the economy and its increasing financialisation, with rampant growth in the money supply which has left America with elevated asset prices and swimming in debt. Other factors include falling labour productivity, the gutting of the middle class, a fall in the savings rate, political gridlock, a lack of investment in research and development, and a stagnation in America's education system.

The following looks at several of the more significant factors that have contributed to this worrying slide in U.S. economic performance, particularly since the early 2000s.

Structural Changes in the Composition of the U.S. Economy

Over the past six decades the American economy has undergone major structural changes, which has seen the move to a service-based economy and a significant increase in consumption at the expense of other sectors in the economy.

The growth in consumption from 60 to 70 per cent of GDP since 1960 is important for several reasons. Firstly, the U.S. went from being the world's leading creditor nation to the world's largest debtor nation. Combined with globalisation, this resulted in a surge in imports at the expense of local manufacturing, particularly since the early 2000s, sucking value out of the local economy and exporting American jobs.

Secondly, it was accompanied by a fall in the savings rate and an increase in household debt. Between 1992 and 2017, the personal savings rate fell from 10 per cent to 4 per cent, while the ratio of household debt to GDP increased from 60 per cent to 78 per cent, after topping out at 98 per cent in 2008.[363] What this means is that increased consumption was driven by reduced savings and increased debt. This is hardly a recipe for economic prosperity. It also raises the question of how sustainable this is.

Interestingly, the mainstream media and financial analysts applauded the increasing role of consumption in the economy, notwithstanding how this consumption was funded and the negative impact this was having on long-term economic growth. This just highlights the lack of strategic focus by these groups.

The other major shift in the post-war composition of the U.S. economy came with spending on services almost doubling, largely at the expense of a fall in expenditure on goods. The largest increases in services occurred in housing and utilities, health care, financial services and insurance. In comparison, the proportion of expenditure on goods nearly halved, with most of the relative decline coming from expenditure on basic products such as food and beverages, clothing and footwear.

Changes in the composition of the economy were also reflected in employment. Between 1972 and 2015, employment in the goods-producing sectors of the economy, such as mining, logging, construction and manufacturing fell from 30 per cent of total non-agricultural employment to just 13.8 per cent, with all the decline occurring in the manufacturing sector. Government employment has fallen from 18.2 per cent to 15.5 per cent. In comparison, employment in the services sector has increased from 51.5 per cent to 70.7 per cent, with most of the growth occurring in professional and business services, education, health, leisure and hospitality.[364]

Declining Labour Productivity

The changing make-up of the U.S. economy has had important implications for productivity. Figure 4 shows the percentage change by decade in the rate of growth in labour productivity from the 1950s to 2010s.[365]

Figure 4 U.S. Growth of Labour Productivity 1950s–2010s

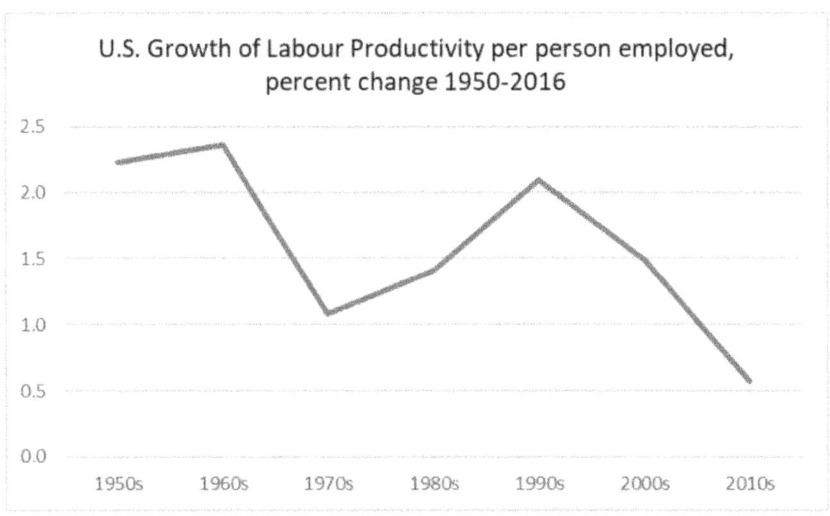

Data Source: The Conference Board

Figure 4 highlights the rapid decline in the rate of growth of labour productivity, particularly since the 1990s. The uptick in the 1980s and 1990s seems to be associated with major advances in technology, particularly IT, which saw labour productivity grow by 3 per cent per annum over several years.

The correlation between the growth in service sector jobs and a slowdown in labour productivity should not really be surprising as the service and government sectors will typically be less productive than the traded goods sector. For example, despite improvements in technology, bureaucrats will continue to shuffle paper, lawyers will continue to clog the courts and chase ambulances, while people will still need to see a doctor or dentist.

The slowdown in the rate of growth in labour productivity re-enforces that prosperity has little to do with government deficits and monetary stimulus, and everything to do with productivity.

How the Elite Hijacked the Economy

Changes to the economy have greatly impacted the lives of millions of American people. The principal impacts have been to transfer wealth from the real sector of the economy to favoured sectors, especially the finance sector, and increase the divide between rich and poor. It also saddled households and businesses with high levels of debt and has increased the fragility of the financial system.

In America, the divide between the haves and have-nots is no better exemplified than the massive increases in the pay of CEOs and those in the finance sector compared to the average worker. When we include salaries, bonuses, stock options and long-term incentives the ratio of CEO-to-worker compensation has increased from twenty-times in 1965 to a peak of nearly 400 times in 2000, to today where it sits somewhere just shy of 300-times. Similarly, between 1979 and 2005, some 58 per cent of the increase in incomes for the top

1 per cent, and 67 per cent of the increase of incomes for the top 0.1 per cent went to executives and those in the finance sector.[366] In 2016, the richest 1 per cent of families controlled a record-high 38.6 per cent of the country's wealth,[367] while the top 10 per cent owned 84 per cent of all stocks.[368]

Those in the bottom and middle classes have not been so fortunate. The American middle class has effectively been gutted through these changes. Between 1990 and 2016, the offshoring of manufacturing plants resulted in the loss of 5 million well-paying manufacturing jobs, or 30 per cent of the manufacturing workforce. These have been replaced by jobs in education and health, and lower-paid jobs in leisure, hospitality and other service sectors.[369] Between the late 1940s and today, the share of labour going to the bottom 90 per cent of income earners has fallen from 42 per cent to 27 per cent. Those who have lost their jobs through outsourcing and other cost-cutting measures have also not fared well, with the average duration of unemployment rising between 1972 and 2016 from 12 to 23 weeks.[370]

In 2015, 43 million people, or 13.5 per cent of the total population, were living below the poverty line. While white people make up 41 per cent of this group, a disproportionate number of Blacks (24 per cent) and Hispanics (21 per cent) are also represented.[371] Given these figures, it is not surprising that in 2017, 42.6 million Americans were receiving food stamps. While this is well below the peak of 47.6 million in 2013, it still means that around one in seven Americans depend on food stamps just to survive.[372] Moreover, the bottom 90 per cent of families now hold just 22.8 per cent of overall wealth, down from about one-third in 1989.[373]

Which begs the question: how have the elite been able to get away with a monumental assault on the lives and finances of everyday workers and the transfer of billions of dollars of wealth to themselves? The answer is simple. The elite own the system.

And they have used every means at their disposal to further their interests. This has ranged from underhand political fixes which have subverted democratic processes, pushing economic theories that favour the rich, control of the Fed and the banking system which has led to financialisation of the economy, and the perpetuation of a range of economic myths and falsehoods that have become so ingrained in everyday economic thought that Goebbels would be proud.

So let's look at a few of the strategies they have used.

Lobbying

In addition to donating hundreds of millions of dollars to political parties and candidates from both sides of the political divide, corporations now spend around $2.6 billion a year on lobbying —more than the $2 billion spent to fund the House and Senate. For every dollar spent on lobbying by labour unions and public-interest groups together, large corporations and their associations spend $34. Of the 100 organisations that spend the most on lobbying, 95 consistently represent business.[374]

In return for this investment, executives get to influence laws impacting their businesses, either by rolling back reforms that may negatively impact their business or pushing for regulations that protect their businesses from competition. A 2014 study by political scientists Martin Gillens and Benjamin Page of Northwestern, for example, showed that over a period of two decades, economic elites and organised interest groups got their favoured policies adopted by Congress and the executive branch about half the time, while legislation to which they were opposed was defeated nearly all the time. In contrast, 'the preferences of the average American appear to have only a miniscule, near zero, statistically non-significant impact on public policy'.[375] They also get to lobby for lower taxes, doling out government contracts and helping to shape public opinion in favour of less government intervention in the economy – unless, of course, it favours their interests. Democracy has failed the American people as politicians have been bought off by the powerful elite.

Corporations have also become adept at minimising tax, shifting profits to low tax jurisdictions and leaving the burden of tax to fall on the low and middle classes. The U.S. political system, particularly at the Federal level, has become so compromised through the influence of powerful vested interests, it has become dysfunctional. People who believe that America is a democracy and that politicians represent the people are delusional. With few exceptions, American politicians represent only three groups: the elite, vested interests and themselves.

Any thought of fiscal responsibility by reining in the massive deficits has gone out the window as the U.S. continues to rack up trillions of dollars of debt. The mainstream media has also been complicit in supporting this orgy of greed. They have elevated executives, talking heads, analysts and fund managers to rock star status, endlessly talking mindless gibberish as they sweat over the latest quarterly results and opine over what the Fed might do. Nowhere is this orgy of deceit more pronounced than the prognostications surrounding the musings of the Fed.

At one stage, the situation became so absurd the media christened former Fed Chairman Alan Greenspan the 'Maestro', supposedly for his ability to manipulate the economic levers to ignite the flames of economic growth. Greenspan took great pride in his 'Fedspeak', characterising his style of miscommunications as 'mumbling with great incoherence'. In one famous incident, he once told a U.S. senator who claimed to have understood what the chairman had just said, that 'in that case, I must have misspoken'.[376] Sadly, the only thing that Greenspan and his successors have done is stoke the flames of multiple asset bubbles, fuelled by unlimited quantities of cheap money.

Corporations and special interest groups have also used a variety of means to push information supportive of their interests. Google, for example, has allegedly cultivated financial relationships with professors at universities across the country by financing hundreds of research papers to defend against regulatory challenges to its market dominance. These grants have ranged from between $5,000 to $400,000.[377] If you value your health, never get between an academic and a research grant.

In another example, a real estate lobby group in Australia threatened to withhold all advertising from a local newspaper after a journalist wrote an article talking of a property bubble, unless the newspaper wrote an article talking up the property market. The newspaper naturally caved in. Mind you, Australia is in the midst of a massive housing bubble brought on by, you guessed it, an unlimited supply of cheap credit, but never let truth get in the way of greater profits.

Of course, corporations aren't the only ones to use such tactics. Environmental activists have also invested heavily in think-tanks and positioned themselves in government bodies to support their causes, while George Soros has used his Open Society Foundation to push his globalist, left-wing political agenda.

But perhaps no one group has been more complicit in

aiding and abetting the widespread redistribution of wealth and the failure to identify and address the fall in the rate of economic growth than the economics 'profession' – a word I use very loosely. It has been mainstream economists who have provided the theoretical concepts and frameworks which have provided the justification for policy-makers and the elite to pursue their agendas. The problem, however, is that not only do most of these frameworks not work for the benefit of all, but they are fundamentally flawed in their design.

The fact that economists would promote such theories should not be surprising, however, given that so many economists are employed in the finance sector, in academia, in government and with industry groups – all major beneficiaries of their economic theories.

Economic Concepts that have Favoured the Elite

Economists are continually coming up with economic theories and concepts on how the world works, and how they can purportedly improve people's lives. While some of these seem conceptually sound, oftentimes they either fail in practice or are usurped to favour the elite. Two of the more prominent economic theories that have favoured the elite in recent times have been shareholder value maximisation and globalisation. Let's look at each in turn.

The introduction of shareholder value maximisation (SVM) has been one of the most pernicious factors affecting economic growth and the distribution of wealth. It is pure greed writ large.

The concept of SVM was first mooted by Milton Friedman in the early 1960s, who argued that a company had no 'social responsibility' to the public or society. Instead, he argued that there is only one responsibility of business – to use its resources and engage in activities designed to increase profits for the benefit of the business owners, so long as it stays within the law. He went further by suggesting that in a free society, the exercise of social responsibility by businesses is a 'fundamentally subversive doctrine'.[378] Strong words indeed from one of the doyens of modern mainstream economics.

SVM gained momentum in the 1980s and was given further impetus in 1990 when academics suggested that large salaries were insufficient to maximise executive performance. Instead, they argued that the most effective way to motivate executives was to align executive compensation, in the form of money and stock ownership, to increases in shareholder value, particularly share prices.[379] This led to a fundamental re-alignment in executive remuneration, heavily weighted towards bonuses in the form of stock options. These changes had profound effects on the way companies are run.

Unconstrained by any thought of ethics or the greater good, executives with short-term tenures focused almost exclusively on short-term performance to boost share prices and maximise their own wealth. Investing in apprenticeships, staff training, research and development and long-term growth strategies fell out of favour. Slashing costs, financial engineering, stock buybacks, corporate restructuring, and mergers and acquisitions funded by increasing debt took precedence over long-term investment.

This gave rise to the 'wham, bam, thank-you-mam' transactional style of management, where executives took no prisoners and were beholden to nobody except analysts and the financial media, hedge funds, banks and mutual funds, all of whom were under the same set of financial pressures to perform. In 2015, for example, share repurchases (US$520 billion) and dividends (US$365 billion) totalled US$885 billion, compared to net income of US$847 billion – corporate executives spent more on dividends and share buybacks than they earned in income. Since 1985, overall distributions to shareholders (dividends plus buybacks) have ranged between 80 and 90 per cent of adjusted net corporate income, leaving just 10 to 20 per cent of profits available for investment in R&D and capital investment.[380]

Corporate raiders have also been complicit in this short-term approach to business. Funded by unlimited amounts of cheap finance and incentivised by the potential for massive profits, corporate raiders and hedge fund operators took over companies, slashed payrolls and other costs, loaded the company up with debt, and then floated the company on the stock market, so mum and dad investors could 'share' in the remaining spoils – which were next to nil after the corporate vultures had picked the bones clean.

While corporate raiders and the financial media have lauded the role that these corporate vultures play in releasing 'value from so-called underperforming companies', I have yet to be convinced about the long-term economic benefits of stripping companies of their assets and then saddling them with high levels of debt. Sure, the elite argue that it 'unlocks value' from otherwise moribund companies with 'lazy' balance sheets. But the only people benefiting from these activities are corporate insiders, hedge funds, corporate raiders and banks. Certainly not those who lose their jobs through the corporate restructuring that invariably accompanies such activities.

Moreover, I also remain to be convinced about how much value these activities contribute to a company's share price, particularly over the long term. While there have been some standout examples – Microsoft, Apple, Amazon and Berkshire

Hathaway – where management has played a pivotal role in the company's success, I would put that down to entrepreneurialism rather than SVM. These companies would have been successful with or without SVM.

For the more run-of-the-mill type companies, however, it seems that plentiful cheap credit has been a major contributing factor in a rising tide of across-the-board share price growth. It remains to be seen how well SVM works when credit dries up and share prices collapse in the next financial crisis. I suggest it might go the way of the dodo.

Moreover, it is little wonder that with short-term profits and huge incentives as the primary driver for politicians, financiers and corporate executives that basic social mores have declined so precipitously.

Is it really good enough for corporations to export polluting industries to developing countries, disrupt the social fabric of small towns or accept sweat-shop conditions for the workers making goods for western markets, just for the transitory pursuit of dollars? For many in the elite, I suspect the answer is a resounding yes! But for ordinary folk, I suspect not.

At a broader level, I believe one needs to occasionally step back and ask some basic questions like: Is unfettered greed and the relentless pursuit of money and prestige what life is all about? Or are things like family and community more important? Given our lives are so short, and we can't take our money and reputation with us, I think economists and the elite need to get a better perspective on what is really important in life.

Globalisation refers to movement of goods, services, capital, people, technology, information, ideas, knowledge and culture around the world. Of course, it is not a new phenomenon. People have been exploring new lands and interacting with different cultures throughout the millennia. What is new, however, is the scope, speed and level of interaction and economic integration that has occurred in the post-war era.

Economic globalisation comprises the globalisation of production, finance, markets, technology, organisational regimes, institutions, corporations and labour.[381] Three factors have been pivotal in increasing globalisation: technology, policy and institutions.

Over the centuries, technology has been a major factor in facilitating global expansion. For example, in earlier times, it was the advent of more advanced sailing ships and new navigational aids. Today, it is no different as new forms of transport and handling (for example, shipping, jet aircraft, trucks and containerisation), telecommunications (such as the Internet and mobile devices) and information technology (such as laptops and advanced computer systems) have lowered the cost of transport and made doing business over vast distances far easier.

Keen to avoid the calamitous effects of protectionism during the Great Depression, western policy-makers also embarked on a series of market-based reforms designed to increase competition and support the free flow of goods and capital around the world.

These reforms began immediately after World War II with the launch of the General Agreement on Tariffs and Trade (GATT), the purpose of which was to promote international trade by reducing or eliminating trade barriers such as tariffs or quotas. Other reforms included the establishment of the European common market, the opening up of the Chinese economy, the collapse of the Soviet Union, the Uruguay round of multi-lateral trade negotiations, the launch of the European monetary union and the establishment of the World Trade

Organization (WTO) in 1995.

World trade responded positively to these initiatives, with trade in goods between 1960 and 2016 growing from 19 per cent to 42 per cent of global GDP.[382] Finance and labour also became global commodities, as lenders, investors and workers sought out the best returns.

Multi-national corporations have thrived in this environment, outsourcing manufacturing and other operations to developing countries to take advantage of cheap labour, and less stringent environmental and safety laws. They have also exploited every available avenue, including tax havens and transfer pricing, to minimise taxes.

Globalisation has had many benefits. It has drastically increased the living standards of tens of millions of people living in developing nations; facilitated the plentiful supply of quality goods and services at low prices; and provided workers with opportunities to travel and work in different countries.

But it has also come at a cost. Millions of western workers' jobs have been outsourced to lower cost countries, many permanently. The damage hasn't been isolated to workers in the west. Some companies have exploited workers in developing countries and taken advantage of lax environmental standards to establish operations. Millions of people from developing countries have also been shut out of markets in developed nations through protectionism imposed by western nations. Perhaps it is not surprising that many people have become disillusioned with globalisation and loss of national sovereignty, and are starting to hanker for the return of a simpler lifestyle and the good ole days.

Financialisation of the Economy

Thomas Jefferson once wrote: '… banking establishments are more dangerous than standing armies; & that the principle of spending money to be paid by posterity, under the name of funding, is but swindling futurity on a large scale.'[383]

Henry Ford commented: 'It is well enough that people of the nation do not understand our banking and monetary system, for if they did, I believe there would be a revolution before tomorrow morning.'[384]

Charlie Munger, vice chairman of investment firm Berkshire Hathaway, also observed: 'I do not think you can trust bankers to control themselves. They are like heroin addicts.'[385]

Jefferson, Ford and Munger clearly didn't trust bankers. And with good reason. The finance sector has been no less destructive to the wealth and prosperity of modern-day folk than it has been over the centuries, as a wave of financialisation has swept the economic landscape since the 1980s.

So, what do we mean by financialisation? 'Financialisation refers to the increasing importance of financial markets, financial motives, financial institutions, and financial elites in the operation of the economy and its governing institutions, both at the national and international level.'[386] Its defining features include a massive rise in the level of debt, and a concomitant rise in the size of the finance sector relative to the rest of the economy.

For centuries, banks have played a key role in the growth of the economy, providing safe storage for people's money and acting as an intermediary between savers and borrowers. For the most part, bankers have acted responsibly, assessing risk while protecting their depositors' funds. However, from time to time, bankers get caught up in the euphoria that accompanies speculative manias. This was no more evident than the bank runs in the nineteenth century and the aftermath of the intense speculation that accompanied the Roaring Twenties. Authorities acted responsibly in the aftermath of the Great Depression by imposing tight restrictions on the banking sector.

Banking is a simple business. The business model is to make money from other people's money. The more money they lend, the more profit they make, the richer they become. Hence, bankers are incentivised to lend as much money as they can, even to people who will struggle to repay their loans. Moreover, their job is made far easier under a fractional reserve banking system because there are virtually no limits on the amount of money banks can lend. As a result, bankers will always be compromised in their chase for profits, especially when coupled with SVM, and for that reason alone, they can't be trusted to act responsibly.

Since the 1980s, banks have increasingly taken advantage of deregulation to rapidly expand their services, their balance sheets and their profits. Banks have also embraced technology and innovation to develop a series of exotic new products such as derivatives and collateralised debt obligations (CDOs), all designed to increase leverage, lend more, and in some instances, to fraudulently pass off the risk to third parties. And yet, when faced with problems of their own making, executives of the major banks have been able to rely on governments and central banks to bail them out. Heads I win, tails you lose. What an extraordinary scam!

So, how successful have bank executives been in their pursuit of ever greater profits and wealth? Financialisation of the economy has paid handsomely for those working in finance. Between 1965 and 2015, the ratio of finance sector profits to total corporate domestic profits more than doubled, from 12 per cent to 27.3 per cent. And this, despite employment in the finance sector remaining static at around 6 per cent of total employment.[387]

Financialisation has also richly rewarded the elite, who have a high proportion of their wealth tied up in the stock market. Figure 5 shows the ratio of capitalisation of the U.S. stock market to GDP from 1975 to 2017.[388] This highlights that the total value of U.S. stocks has risen 375 per cent, or nearly four times faster than economic growth, all on the back of increasing debt. Moreover, capitalisation of the U.S. stock market is back at extreme levels seen just before the GFC and dot-com crash. And we know how that ended.

Figure 5 Capitalisation of the U.S. Stock Market to GDP 1975–2017

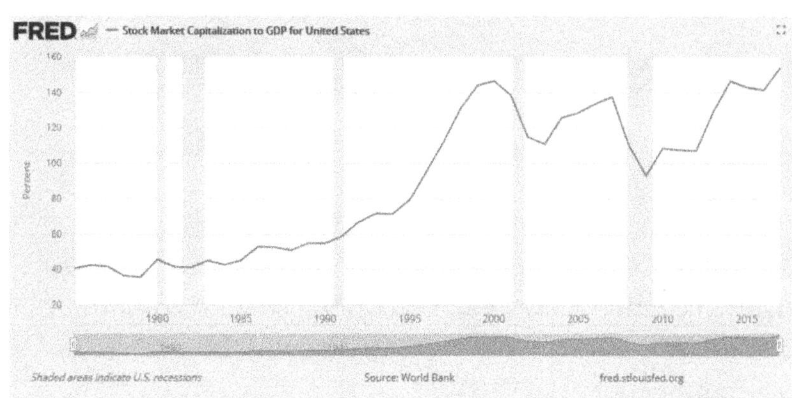

Source: FRED: Federal Reserve Bank of St Louis

At the same time, financialisation and globalisation have turned tens of millions of everyday people into financial serfs, living week to week just to pay their loans to the rentier class.

Figure 6 shows household debt from 1945 to 2018. During this period, total household debt grew from $29 billion to $15.2 trillion. In the 35 years between 1945 and 1980, household debt grew $1.4 trillion. However, since 1980 household debt has ballooned by nearly $14 trillion.[389]

Moreover, despite significant deleveraging in recent years, household debt has just exceeded debt levels just prior to the GFC.

Figure 6 U.S. Household Debt 1945–2018

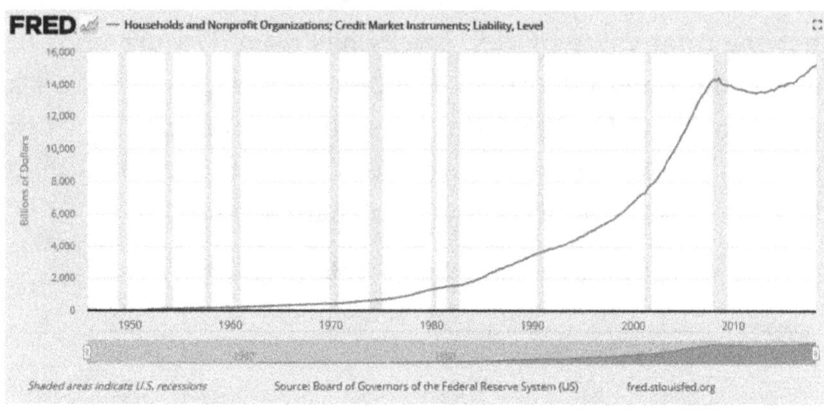

Source: FRED: Federal Reserve Bank of St Louis

While mortgage debt remains the largest component of household debt at around 65 per cent, in a little over a decade the value of student loans has risen threefold to nearly $1.5 trillion, and now represents around 10 per cent of all household debt.[390]

Higher education in the U.S. is a rort. While mortgage holders can walk away from their mortgages through jingle mail, discharging student loans through bankruptcy is almost impossible under current U.S. law.[391] This allows university administrators to reward themselves handsomely with excessive salaries while charging exorbitant fees for university courses and locking students into loans that are almost impossible to avoid.

No wonder defaults on student loans are rising. Between 2003 and 2017, the number of student loans 90+ days in arrears has increased from 6 per cent to over 11 per cent.[392] Moreover, according to the non-profit Institute for College Access and Success, there are a record 8.5 million federal student loan borrowers who are in default as of June 30, 2017.[393] The only way for this rort to be stopped is for people to be able to declare bankruptcy on student loans, just like any other product.

And while household debt service payments as a per cent of disposable personal income have fallen between 2007 and 2017 from a high of 13.2 per cent to 10.3 per cent, this reflects historically low interest rates.[394] As interest rates continue to rise, this will rapidly increase the burden of debt repayments on households in any future downturn.

Financialisation, together with rampant government spending, has also left the economy saddled with historical levels of debt. Figure 7 (over page) shows the ratio of total U.S. debt to GDP from 1947 to 2017.[395] This graph shows the massive growth in total debt since 1980, with the ratio at 350 per cent now exceeding the peak of 300 per cent reached during the Great Depression.

No sector has been spared increasing debt. Not surprisingly, total debt in the finance sector showed the strongest growth, growing four-fold from 20 per cent to 80 per cent of GDP between 1980 and 2017, after peaking at 120 per cent in 2008. Household and business debt have also grown strongly since the 1950s, while Federal Government debt has turned up sharply since the GFC.

Central Banking has Failed

The rising prominence of central banking in modern-day life has been the most treacherous development in modern economics.

Figure 7 Total U.S. Debt as a Per Cent of GDP

Total U.S. Debt as a % of GDP
1947 - 2017

Data Source: FRED: Federal Reserve Bank of St Louis

People can ignore wayward economic theories. However, they cannot avoid the intrusion that interventionist central banks and their dangerous policies have had on the lives of everyday folk.

Central bankers know nothing about the importance of sound money, and have learnt nothing of the history of financial crises, nor the dangers of fractional reserve banking. Their approach to managing inflation by targeting consumer price inflation is deeply flawed: firstly, because central banks don't control consumer prices; and secondly, because their approach focuses on the symptoms rather than the causes of inflation, namely excessive growth in the money supply. They also know little about what stimulates economic growth. As a result, mainstream economists have failed to halt the inexorable decline in the rate of economic growth, despite massive monetary and fiscal stimulus.

However, wanting to create the illusion that they know what they are doing, they have invented a whole array of new policies: policies like inflation targeting, quantitative easing and zero interest rates, policies which not only don't work, but have created cataclysmic fractures in the world's financial system. At the same time, they have created the myth that they can control economic outcomes while creating other myths including that they control interest rates and that deflation is an anathema to economic growth.

But central banks haven't been alone in this epic failure. Their failures have laid bare the failures of modern mainstream economic theory, while governments have also resorted to underhand political fixes to deceive the public. And, as it has become more obvious that their policies don't work, central bankers have doubled down by blaming other factors for their failures.

But let's be clear. Their policies have been instrumental in the financialisation of the economy which has led to the transfer of billions of dollars of wealth from everyday folk to the elite. Moreover, constant interference in the economy and financial system have not only created the boom–bust cycles of the past three decades, but they have created the conditions for the next financial crisis.

If they were alive today, J.P. Morgan and his co-conspirators would look back in pride that the creation of the Fed did exactly what they wanted: delivered control of the global financial system to the elite.

Central Banks' Approach to Price Stability is Deeply Flawed

One of the primary goals of central banks is to maintain price stability. Why are stable prices so important? Consider an economy with no inflation. The prices we see today will be the same tomorrow, next week, next year and the year after. This allows people to make choices without having to worry about the impact of volatile price movements on their decisions. People don't need to bring purchases forward as they might if they believe prices are going to be more expensive in a few months or a few years' time. Equally, they don't need to delay purchases if they think prices will fall.

As a result, economists rightfully argue that low inflation is consistent with economic growth and a stable economy. Inflation has several drawbacks. By its very nature, inflation reduces the purchasing power of money over time. You can buy less for the same amount of money. Inflation also tends to discourage investment and long-term economic growth by creating uncertainty amongst both consumers and businesses. Stable prices give firms greater certainty when making investment decisions as they can better estimate projected returns.

Inflation, particularly high inflation, tends to lead to booms and busts. If left unchecked, inflation can quickly spiral out of control as people come to expect ever-increasing prices. Eventually, prices reach such extreme levels that the economy collapses under its own weight. This is no better evidenced than in Zimbabwe and the Weimar Republic.

Inflation can also make an economy uncompetitive. If prices are rising in one country faster than in other countries, exports become uncompetitive while making imports more competitive against locally made goods. If the country has an open economy, the economy will adjust by seeing their currencies fall. This makes imports more expensive while making exports more competitive. However, if the country is unable to devalue its currency, such as those peripheral countries in the Euro-zone, this can lead to higher trade deficits, lower economic growth, lower wages and higher unemployment.

Another drawback is that inflation impacts stakeholder groups in different ways: some negatively and others positively. It is particularly harsh on those people on fixed incomes, such as pensioners and workers, many of whom suffer a reduction in their standard of living as pensions or wages are unable to keep pace with increases in prices. It is also very difficult for savers, who are forced to sit idly by and watch the purchasing power of their hard-won savings erode over time. This problem is exacerbated if inflation is high and interest rates low.

In contrast, borrowers tend to be big winners from inflation. Borrowers benefit because they can pay off their loans with money which has less value. Take, for example, somebody who borrows $100,000 to buy a house. As the debt stays the same, while their wages are rising through inflation, they have more money to pay down the loan more quickly.

Governments also benefit in several ways. Firstly, as wages increase, workers are forced into higher income tax brackets, which increases the government's tax take. Moreover, as sales taxes are calculated as a percentage of the sales price, sales tax receipts also grow as prices rise. Secondly, welfare payments and government wages generally don't keep pace with inflation. As a result, governments benefit by having increased revenue and lower real wages and expenses. Finally, as governments are typically borrowers, they also benefit as they can pay down their debts with money which has less value than when the debts were incurred.

Deflation, or falling prices, has the opposite effect. It tends to benefit low-income earners, those on fixed incomes and savers while punishing governments and debtors. This is because it increases the purchasing power of money. Thus, the poorer members of society and savers can buy more for every dollar of income. Conversely, governments' tax take stagnates while borrowers find it more difficult to repay debt.

This gives governments and borrowers a strong incentive to promote inflation over deflation, and it goes a long way to explaining why governments eschew deflation and support inflation targeting.

Central banks – Current Approach to Inflation Targeting

Central banks introduced inflation targeting as a key weapon in their fight against inflation. Inflation targeting is a relatively new phenomenon, having been adopted by central banks in New Zealand, Canada, Sweden, the UK and Australia in the early 1990s. The U.S. and the ECB were latecomers to setting specific inflation targets, with the U.S. setting the specific target of 2 per cent as recently as 2012. Most central banks regard price stability as restricting consumer price inflation to 2 per cent per annum over the medium term. Others use a target range of between 2 and 3 per cent to allow for short-term fluctuations in prices.

Common measures for consumer price inflation include the Consumer Price Index (CPI), and the core Personal Consumption Expenditure (PCE) index. Core PCE excludes so-called volatile items such as food and fuel from the calculation of inflation to supposedly provide a more stable measure of the underlying rate of movements in consumer prices. However, no matter which target, or whatever measure, the current approach to inflation targeting and monetary policy by central banks is deeply flawed.

Conventional economic wisdom is that inflation rises during periods of economic growth as demand outstrips the supply of goods and services, forcing prices to rise, while inflation falls during periods of economic weakness.

Central banks seek to influence the CPI by moving interest rates up or down to either reduce or increase demand. Changes in interest rates, however, are a crude monetary tool, in that they don't discriminate between the impact of interest rate changes on diverse groups within society, different economic sectors, or between the prices of assets and goods and services.

Moreover, there are a myriad of factors that can impact the prices of goods and services, almost all of which are outside the control of central banks. These include the level of market competition, outsourcing, globalisation, technology and digital disruption, innovation, changing consumer preferences, taxes, government regulations, politics, geo-politics and even the weather. Combined, these factors have a far greater impact on prices than central banks ever will.

Let's look at a simple example to highlight the point.

Figure 8 (over page) shows three different views of the CPI from 1947 to 2017: the CPI for all items for urban consumers, the CPI for medical care and the CPI for rent on the primary residence. The graph highlights that the cost of medical care (top line in 2017) has risen thirty-six-fold since 1947, compared to around twelve-fold for both general CPI and rent (bottom lines). It also shows the wide divergences in the indexes since 1985.

It would seem to me that central banks have as much control over the cost of medical care as people have over death and taxes. The same holds true for the price of many other products such as oil, farm produce, food and beverages, clothing and footwear, education, entertainment, computers, telecommunications and so on. Prices of these products are driven by conditions in their own markets, not by the actions of central banks.

Figure 8 Consumer Price Index: All Items, Medical Care and Rent 1947–2017

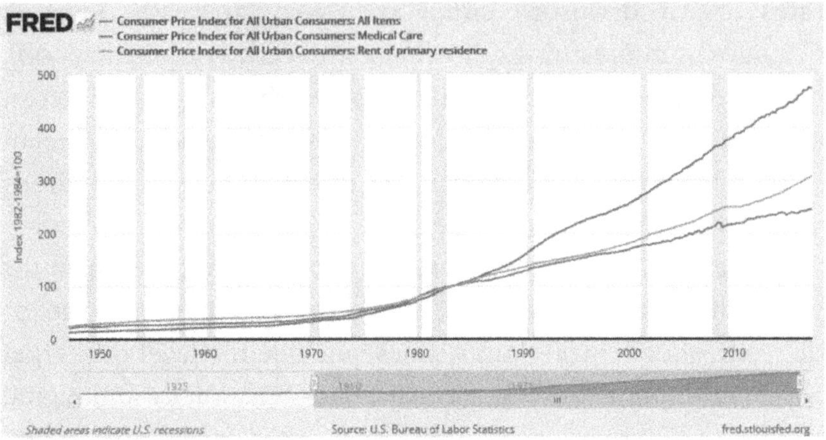

Source: Federal Reserve Bank of St Louis

Which begs the question: why would central banks seek control over something that they can barely *influence*? It seems to relate to their flawed Keynesian view of the world, which reduces most economic factors down to aggregate demand.

Inflation targeting also raises several other questions.

Firstly, why use CPI? While the CPI is a relatively broad measure, one of its key failings is that it only measures one type of inflation – prices paid by consumers for a basket of goods and services. However, it doesn't measure other types of inflation such as producer price inflation, wage inflation, commodity inflation, currency inflation and particularly asset price inflation. While some of these other types of inflation feed into consumer inflation, the relationships can be somewhat obtuse and the causes quite unrelated.

And why is 2 per cent the ideal rate, rather than zero, which would represent true price stability? According to the Fed, a 2 per cent inflation rate is 'best aligned with its congressionally mandated goals of price stability and full employment. Over time, a higher inflation rate would reduce the public's ability to make accurate longer-term economic and financial decisions. On the other hand, a lower inflation rate would be associated with an elevated probability of falling into deflation, which means prices and perhaps wages, on average, are falling – a phenomenon associated with very weak economic conditions. Having at least a small level of inflation makes it less likely that the economy will experience harmful deflation if economic conditions weaken.'[396] In other words, it's a Goldilocks target: not too hot, not too cold, just right.

Other reasons put forward by economists is that it serves as an anchor point for private-sector inflation expectations; it does not materially distort economic decisions in the community; it allows for the inevitable uncertainties that are involved in forecasting, and lags in the effects of monetary policy on the economy; and it allows a role for monetary policy in dampening the fluctuations in output over the course of the cycle.

Of course, there is a fundamental problem with the Fed's explanation right up front: that 'deflation is a phenomenon associated with very weak economic conditions'. Later in this chapter, I will demonstrate that deflation is not always associated with very weak economic conditions. In fact, I will demonstrate that the U.S. economy has performed exceptionally well during periods of deflation. But where deflation can become a problem is under a fractional reserve banking system when debt spirals out of control. This then sets the economy up for serious bouts of asset and debt deflation, which becomes almost inevitable under a fractional reserve banking system.

Another problem is that it is quite unclear from this explanation what price stability means. Once again, are we talking about consumer prices, commodity prices, wages, asset prices or all of the above? If all of the above, then targeting CPI is flawed – it is too narrow, insofar that runaway asset price inflation has been at the heart of almost all financial panics throughout history. Using a 2 per cent increase in CPI as the inflation target is equally problematical. Using 2 per cent rather than zero means that, over time, the compound effect of even small annual price increases significantly reduces a currency's purchasing power. For example, at an inflation rate of 2 per cent per annum, the price of a $100 basket of goods would double over 35 years; at 3 per cent per annum, it doubles in just 23 years. In other words, the purchasing power of money falls persistently over time. Tough if you are on struggle street. It would be far better if this drawback could be negated by keeping money sound and prices stable – if inflation remained at zero.

Admittedly, if wages are increasing at the same rate as inflation, then purchasing power can be maintained. However, as noted earlier, inflation impacts different groups in different ways – some positively, some negatively. Wages typically lag inflation, so wage-earners are always playing catch-up and it is typically the poorest in our society who are the most negatively affected.

In addition, as the CPI is an index, its value can be, and in fact has been, manipulated by politicians. I will cover later in this chapter: some of the lengths politicians have gone to, to change the calculations of the CPI and how this has cheated American taxpayers, particularly the less well-off in society.

Inflation is a Monetary Phenomenon

Milton Friedman, the famed monetarist, once remarked: 'Inflation is always and everywhere a monetary phenomenon in the sense that it is and can be produced only by a more rapid increase in the quantity of money than in output.'[397]

In this regard, Friedman was correct. The true definition of inflation is 'an increase in the volume (supply) of money and credit relative to the supply of available goods and services'.[398] Equally, deflation is defined as a decline in the supply of money and credit relative to the supply of available goods and services.

Other types of inflation such as consumer price inflation, wage inflation and asset inflation are basically by-products that result from this true cause of inflation. The example in the box demonstrates that inflation is a monetary phenomenon.

Inflation is a Monetary Phenomenon

It's probably easiest if we use a simple example to demonstrate how inflation is purely a monetary phenomenon. Let's take a group of people living in an isolated community. They are self-sufficient, they use dollars and the money supply has historically grown at the same rate as changes in the supply of goods and services. Under such a scenario, overall wages and prices remain stable over the years and people's standard of living improves in line with increases in productivity and/or their own effort.

Should consumer preferences or the supply of goods change for one reason or another, for example drought, then relative prices of specific goods and services will move up or down to reflect market conditions until balance has been restored. However, the overall level of inflation will remain stable because the money supply has moved in line with output.

Let's look at another scenario where mainstream economists convince politicians that they can improve their voter's standard of living and government coffers by doubling the money supply. While there are a few sceptics who believe you can't get something for nothing, the politicians are convinced. Academics write papers supporting the central bankers' theories, while the mainstream press is enlisted to help convince the public. Over the next few weeks, the money supply begins to increase rapidly, and this eventually flows through into wages. Some people feel much wealthier and rush out to spend their newfound wealth. The problem is that the supply of goods and services hasn't increased in line with increases in the money supply. This causes people to bid up the prices of goods, services and asset prices, thus creating a vicious cycle of inflation.

Those on low wages and fixed incomes suffer greatly, since their incomes can't keep pace with the price increases on basic goods and services. The wealthy benefit greatly because they spend less of their income on basic products and have their wealth tied up in rising asset prices.

As difficulties begin to emerge, central bankers get their economist friends to write economic papers explaining how good things are, and that the community would be even better off if they doubled down and doubled the money supply yet again. Once again, the politicians and mainstream media quickly come on board. They rarely mix with the poor and middle class in any event, receiving positive feedback from their wealthy donors and benefactors, whom they socialise with at the club and the opera. Over time, central bankers continue to encourage increases in the money supply, leading to runaway inflation, until the system implodes in on itself.

The above definition of inflation has two components. The first relates to the supply of money and credit. The second relates to the supply of available goods and services. Let's look at each of these components in turn.

Economists use a range of measures to measure money supply. Not all of them are widely used and the classifications can vary by country. Money is typically divided into two categories: narrow money and broad money. Narrow money (typically indicated by M0 and M1) includes coins and notes in circulation and other money equivalents that are easily convertible into cash. Broader money includes M1 plus short-term deposits in banks and 24-hour money market funds (M2) and longer-term deposits in banks and money market funds (M3 and M4).

Credit refers to debt funding provided by banks and other financial institutions to the private non-financial sector in the form of loans and securities. It includes loans to consumers (mortgages, personal loans, credit cards, auto loans, student loans and so on) and business.

Under a fractional reserve banking system, there is virtually no limit to the amount of money and credit that can be created by the banks. It is this feature of fractional reserve banking that creates the booms and busts as credit expands and then implodes under the weight of bad loans and malinvestments.

The reference to money and credit has become increasingly complex in recent years due to financial innovation. Credit was historically provided by banks and nonbank financial institutions such as savings and loans associations, credit unions, insurance companies and general financiers. However, financial innovation has given rise to the growth of a range of new lenders, including what is commonly called the 'shadow banking system'. This is a collection of investment banks, hedge funds and other non-bank financial institutions that replicate some of the activities of regulated banks, but operate outside of the traditional regulatory environment. This makes tracking their activities and the overall size of the credit market more difficult and can also increase overall financial market risk.

Figure 9 shows the U.S. money supply (as measured by M2 plus total credit to the private non-financial sector) and nominal GDP from 1959 to 2017. The most striking feature of this graph is the rapid increase in the money supply from around 1980 compared to the growth in GDP.

Figure 9 U.S. Money Supply and Nominal GDP 1959–2017

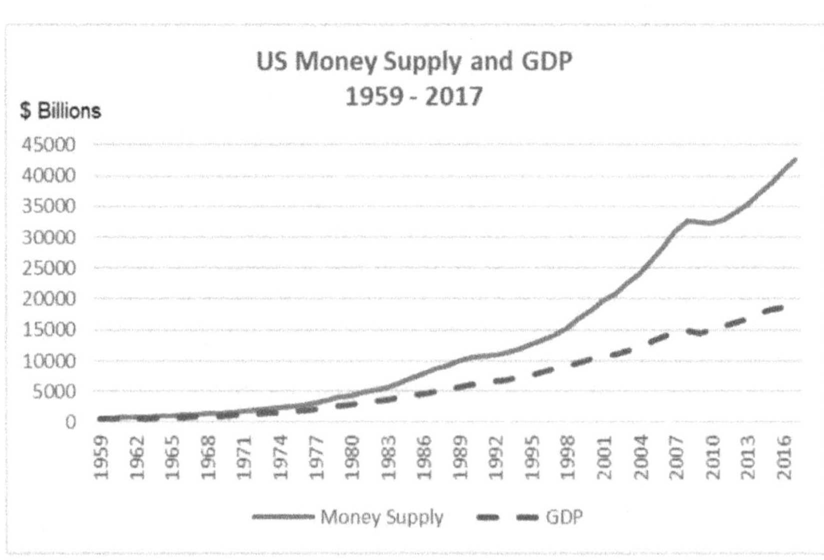

Data Source: Federal Reserve Bank of St Louis

While both measures moved in lockstep from 1959 to 1980, growth in the money supply accelerated after 1980, and then accelerated at an even faster rate during the 1990s and 2000s. Not surprisingly, this came at a time when the Fed, under the leadership of Alan Greenspan and his successors, Ben Bernanke and Janet Yellen, took an activist role in monetary policy and dramatically increased the money supply.

Table 2 shows the percentage increase in the U.S. money supply, GDP and CPI for the periods 1959–2017 and 1980–2017. The data shows the extraordinary growth in true inflation, as measured by the growth in money supply, compared to GDP and the CPI.

Table 2 Increase in the U.S. Money Supply, GDP and CPI – 1959–2017

	1959 – 2017 (Per cent)	**1980 – 2017 (Per cent)**
Money Supply	6,344	980
GDP	3,713	682
CPI	836	295

Data Source: Federal Reserve Bank of St Louis

From 1959 to 2017, growth in the money supply was almost double the growth in nominal GDP, and over seven times the increase in the CPI. Despite starting from a higher base, the increase in money supply was no less impressive for the period from 1980 to 2017, growing one and a half times economic growth, and over three times faster than consumer price inflation.

What this highlights is that the real rate of inflation, as measured by the increase in the money supply, has been far greater than central banks have acknowledged, or perhaps even understood. It also highlights that the Fed has failed in its mandate to maintain price stability when using the true definition of inflation. More importantly, by dropping interest rates to record low levels, central banks have actually increased true inflation and created the asset bubbles of recent years.

We noted earlier the conventional economic wisdom that inflation rises during periods of economic growth, and that central banks seek to influence the CPI by reducing interest rates to increase demand, and vice versa. So what has been the recent experience in relation to the relationships between GDP, interest rates and inflation? Not as good as central bankers would have you believe, if the evidence of the past three decades is anything to go by.

With interest rates trending down to record lows, one would have expected the rate of economic growth to have picked up. This didn't happen. Figure 3 shows that the rate of growth in real GDP has been steadily falling since the 1940s, with a sharp fall in the rate of growth since the 1990s. But this shouldn't have happened with interest rates falling.

Equally, despite record low interest rates and the massive increase in the money supply, consumer price inflation should have picked up rather than fallen. This also shouldn't have happened. Figure 10 (over page) shows the annual percentage change in the U.S. CPI (for all items) from 1960 to 2017.

Three features on the graph stand out: firstly, the high inflation during the 1970s, which was driven in large part by the oil crisis and military expenditure associated with the Vietnam War; secondly, the sharp decline in inflation during the recessions in the early 1980s following a hike in interest rates to combat runaway inflation; and finally, the three decades of disinflation that started in the 1990s.

The disinflation has been driven by structural forces rather than by the actions of central banks. In fact, it seems sheer

Figure 10 Per cent Annual Change in U.S. CPI 1960–2017

Source: Federal Reserve Bank of St Louis

coincidence that the disinflation became evident at the same time as banks introduced inflation targeting. The important changes were globalisation and the rise of the global corporation; excess manufacturing capacity, especially in China; technology and digital disruption; structural changes in the workforce, including falling union membership; and a relatively peaceful global environment.

So, what can we make of all of this? Principally, that growth in the money supply is not directly related to strength in the real economy, it is not directly related to the CPI, and it has not fuelled increases in the rate of real economic growth. Instead, it has led directly to the financialisation of the economy, a phenomenon which has enriched the elite, particularly bankers, at the expense of mainstream Americans.

More importantly, this firmly suggests that the very foundations upon which modern monetary policy and central banking are based are fundamentally flawed.

Asset Inflation – A New Macroeconomic Model

So, if the massive increase in the money supply didn't result in increasing consumer inflation and robust economic growth, then where did the money go?

The simple answer is that increases in the money supply have fuelled speculation and growth in asset markets leading to the bubbles and busts in real estate, the stock market, art and other asset markets.

To understand how this occurred, I have developed a new model of the global macroeconomic system. Figure 11 highlights that the macroeconomic system consists of three distinct components: the real economy, the financial system and asset markets.

Figure 11 Global Macroeconomic System

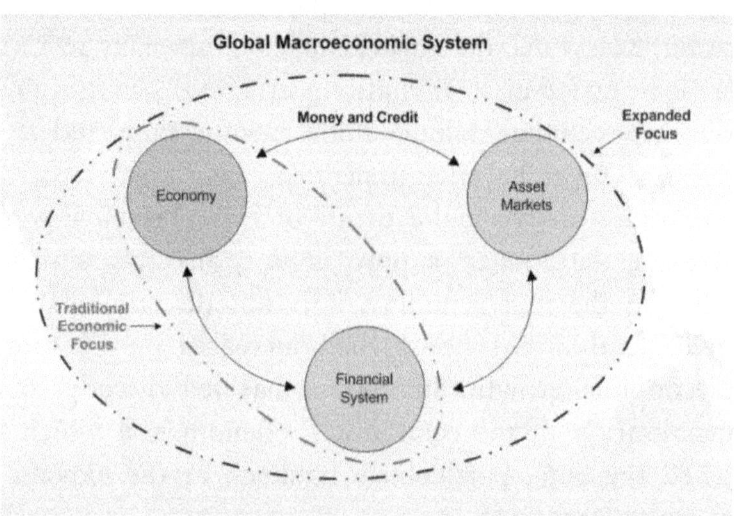

The real economy, as we noted in Figure 1, consists of households, firms and government. The purpose of the real economy is to facilitate the production and consumption of goods and services between the different stakeholders in an efficient and effective manner. The real economy consists primarily of the product and resources markets.

The financial system consists of banks, insurance companies, pension and mutual funds, and other non-bank financial institutions. The main purpose of the financial system is to facilitate the exchange of funds between lenders, investors and borrowers. Another key role is to protect depositors' funds from loss. Financial markets consist primarily of money markets, capital markets and foreign exchange markets.

An asset is something of value that an entity – a person, a firm or a government – owns, or has use of and benefits from. Assets include any number of items ranging from property, shares, cash, precious metals, and financial instruments such as bonds to collectibles such as art, clocks, motor vehicles and fine wines. In commerce, people would generally expect to derive an income stream from the use of assets, but in other contexts, particularly during manias, they may hold them for speculative purposes. Others may also hold assets as a store of value.

In the context of my model, an asset market is a market in which established assets are traded.

It's worth noting that when assets are created, for example when a new building is built, the value of that construction is included in measurements for the real economy – in GDP. Once it has been created, any subsequent trade takes place in the asset market. There is also some cross-over between bonds created in the financial systems and traded in asset markets. For the purposes of this model, such nuances are largely irrelevant.

The three main components of the macroeconomic model are all inter-related and financed by the flow of money and credit between the different sectors. There are a number of reasons for segmenting the economy into the three components. Firstly, it challenges assertions that asset markets behave in the same manner as the real economy. Secondly, it undermines the very basis of how central banks define price stability and their subsequent approach to inflation targeting and monetary policy. It recognises the impact that boom and busts in asset markets can have on the real economy and also that the cost and availability of credit affects asset markets to a far greater extent than activity in the real economy. Finally, it highlights the impact that central banks' current approach to monetary policy has on different stakeholder groups.

Let's look at each of these points in turn. Historically, the focus of macroeconomic theory has been on the real economy. This is not surprising given that macroeconomics grew out of the field of microeconomics, whose primary focus is on supply and demand in the product and resources markets.

One of the key principles of microeconomics is that, given free markets, demand for goods and services tends to fall when prices rise, and rise when prices fall. This is evident, for example, when we look at the changes in consumer behaviour when the price of petrol rises and falls. When prices rise, people either reduce their driving, move to more fuel-efficient vehicles and/or seek alternative modes of transport to offset the additional costs for fuel. When prices fall, they tend to drive more and move back to their gas-guzzlers. The same is true for most products and services where prices are elastic.

Another principle in mainstream economic theory is that people behave rationally when they make economic decisions.

These economic principles, however, often do not apply when we are dealing with asset markets. In periods of intense speculation, the opposite occurs – demand rises when prices rise, and demand falls when prices fall. This was no more evident than in the dot-com boom, the housing boom and the current share market boom. This is because people are driven more by emotions such as fear and greed than by rational behaviour, particularly in volatile and emotionally charged markets. In buoyant asset markets, people focus on capital gains rather than securing an income stream. Similarly, when prices are falling, people panic and get out at any cost before the market sinks further.

Segmenting the economy into three components challenges central banks' current approach to inflation targeting.

As noted earlier, central banks define price stability as maintaining consumer price inflation at around 2 to 3 per cent per annum. But the CPI only applies to the prices of consumer goods and services in the real economy. Therefore, it excludes movements in asset prices, markets where prices are often far more volatile than in the real economy.

How can central banks claim to have price stability when asset prices rise or fall sharply in line with asset booms and busts? Unless of course, central banks are controlled by the banks, which benefit the most from runaway growth in the money supply. Surely, price stability should include price stability in prices for goods and services, and assets. And the best way to do that is ensure that we have sound money – where the money supply grows in line with economic output.

Separating asset markets from the real economy also highlights the impact movements in asset prices can have on the real economy, and vice versa. One of the primary mechanisms for this is via the wealth effect, which recognises the impact increasing or falling wealth has on the real economy. Economists recognise the impact that rising asset prices have on spending. This was no more in evidence than in the recent housing boom, when people were encouraged by banks and real estate agents to use the increased 'value' in their properties to borrow and spend more.

The reverse is obviously equally true. Falling asset prices exacerbate problems in the real economy through bankruptcies and defaults of people, corporations and financial institutions. It also recognises that asset price inflation can be equally debilitating for everyday folk as consumer price inflation. For example, runaway inflation in house prices not only pushes up rents, but it also makes it very difficult for young people to enter the housing market. It also pushes up the size of mortgages, creating financial serfs out of everyday people.

Segmenting the economy as per Figure 11 also recognises the variable impact that the cost and availability of credit has on different sectors of the economy. For example, asset prices, and demand for durable goods such as cars and white goods, are particularly sensitive to conditions in financial markets, while consumption of staple goods such as food is less affected.

Given most of the elite's wealth is tied up in property and financial assets, they have benefited far more from asset price inflation than ordinary citizens. As a result, access to plentiful low-cost credit has been a veritable money-making machine for corporate insiders, bankers and the wealthy. The greater the amount of money and credit created, the greater the profits for the elite. No wonder that the Fed has excluded asset prices from their deliberations in setting interest rates. Doing so would kill the golden goose that banks and their benefactors have relied on for their own growth and prosperity.

Figures 5 and 12 highlight the extent to which the elite have benefited from rising asset prices and from excluding asset prices from inflation targeting. As you will recall, Figure 5 showed that the total value of U.S. stocks grew 375 per cent, or nearly four times faster than economic growth between 1975 to 2015.[399] It is the same for house prices. Figure 12 shows the S&P/Case Shiller U.S. National Home Price Index from 1975 to 2017.[400] The graph highlights that U.S. house prices are now the highest in the past 40 years, even higher than the peak just prior to the GFC.

Figure 12 S&P/Case Shiller U.S. National Home Price Index 1975–2017

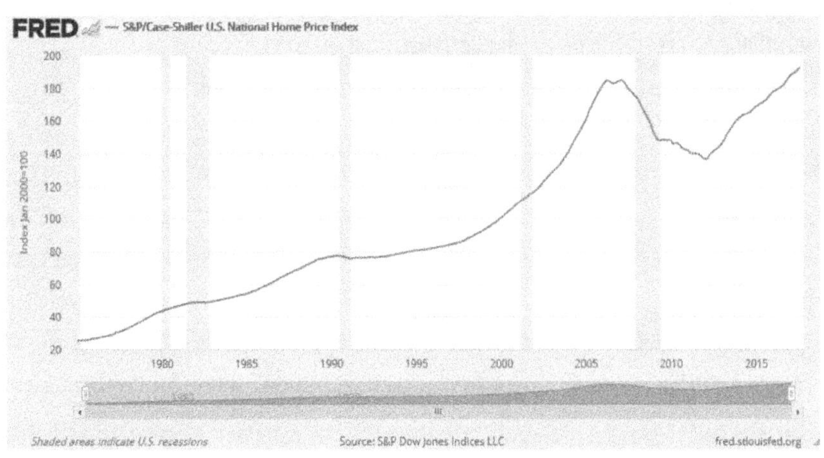

Source: Federal Reserve Bank of St. Louis

The acceleration in the both of these indexes shows a remarkable correlation with the increase in the money supply as depicted in Figure 9 (Money Supply and GDP). However, it is at odds with the disinflation in the real economy that occurred during the same period.

This highlights that the Fed's failure to include asset prices in their economic models and inflation targeting has not only had serious drawbacks for the economy in terms of booms and busts but has clearly favoured the rich over the poor. More importantly, however, central bank policies have created the biggest inflationary spiral in history, an event that will unwind into perhaps the greatest depression the world has experienced, namely the Great Depression of the 2020s.

This also raises another important question: if mainstream economists have been found to be so wrong on fundamental issues such as how to define inflation and deliver price stability, then where else could they be wrong? Over the years we have been bombarded with messages from mainstream economists and the mainstream media about key economic matters. Some of these revolve around central banking, while others centre on general economic matters.

As a result of this constant messaging, everybody now knows that central banks have absolute control over the economy, are staffed by the best minds, they can control economic outcomes and that central banks control interest rates. We also know that deflation is bad for the economy and that economic growth will pick up once inflation returns. And we also know that share prices always go up and free trade exists. These messages have been pushed for so long and by so many commentators that they have become truisms. No doubt about it. Everybody knows that these are true.

But what would happen if we found that these weren't true at all, but rather myths. Wouldn't it once again bring into question the efficacy of mainstream economics and credibility of mainstream economists?

Well, I will leave you to make up your minds, but hopefully the evidence I provide will suggest that many, if not all, of these truisms are not truisms, but myths and falsehoods.

*

Over the past three decades, central banks have positioned themselves, with the help of the elite, as being omnipotent. They are portrayed as being masters of the economic universe, wise beyond belief, able to collect and analyse huge amounts of data, run powerful economic models and make prescient and timely decisions that deliver never-ending prosperity. If you believe the rhetoric, central bankers have become so powerful they have tamed the business cycle.

Aggregate demand has been central to mainstream economic thinking since Keynes began theorising, especially with mainstream economists' fixation on trying to control aggregate demand to manage the output gap. Control of aggregate demand is one of the cornerstones of neo-Keynesian and monetarist thinking. Therefore, failure of governments and central banks to control aggregate demand would undermine the very basis of mainstream economic theory.

Governments seek to influence aggregate demand through changes in government spending and other policy measures. Central banks seek to influence aggregate demand by movements in interest rates.

So, have central banks tamed the business cycle and created the conditions to deliver never-ending prosperity?

I believe that central banks have far less, if any, meaningful control over aggregate demand (which I use as a proxy for economic activity) than many believe. This is because it is people who make their own economic decisions, based on the prevailing social mood and their own particular circumstances, rather than by what authorities say or do. In other words, it is individuals who control economic activity, not governments or central banks, particularly over the medium to long term.

Moreover, not only are central banks not able to control economic outcomes, but their constant meddling has created massive economic distortions which have resulted in the boom and busts while sowing the seeds for the next Great Depression. So, let's look at the evidence. Two key factors drive aggregate demand: firstly, people's willingness to spend, and secondly, their capacity to spend.

Economic systems are complex, natural, self-regulating, living systems that are driven by the thoughts, behaviours and actions of people. In other words, people are at the heart of economic systems. If authorities are to control, or at least influence, economic outcomes, then they must make human behaviour and emotions front and centre of their policy responses. Otherwise, their policy actions are unlikely to yield the desired outcomes.

Economists have long understood the linkages between psychology and economic activity and have sought to integrate psychology into their economic theories. This has led to new fields of study such as behavioural economics, which studies the effects of psychological, social and emotional factors on the economic decisions of individuals and institutions. These studies seek to understand how people make economic decisions, how they assess risk and how this translates into activity on financial markets and in the real economy.

Over the years, these studies have given rise to various economic theories such as the theory of rational expectations, and the efficient-market hypothesis (EMH). The theory of rational expectations states that people make informed choices based on their rational outlook, available information and past experiences. The EMH is an investment theory which assumes that people make investment decisions based on rational expectations using all available information. The implication is that asset prices fully reflect all available information, meaning that it would be theoretically impossible for stocks to 'beat the market' because they always trade at their fair value. In other words, investors would be unable to purchase undervalued stocks or sell stocks for inflated prices.

Of course, this is nonsense. If the EMH were true, then legendary investors like Warren Buffett would never have amassed a fortune by buying good companies at below market prices. Nor would speculative bubbles ever arise, because people would be buying assets based on analysis and an assessment of fair value, rather than emotion.

People are complex beings whose moods continuously change: minute to minute, hour to hour, day to day, week to week, year to year. At times, we can behave rationally. At other times, we can behave impulsively, emotionally and irrationally. If people didn't behave this way, companies wouldn't spend so much money on marketing trying to appeal to people's emotions, and people wouldn't get caught up in the euphoria of manias and speculative booms.

However, there is certainly truth to the idea that people tend to extrapolate past and current experiences into the future. In fact, this is a common failing amongst forecasters and planners, including economists, who often look at the past 12 months and project this experience into the future. It is also a common failing amongst those 'buy and hold' investors who assume that their stocks will keep on performing as they have in the past, or speculators who, in good times, assume that prices will only ever keep on rising.

The application of human behaviour to finance and economics is currently the focus of a new field of study called socionomics. Socionomic theory postulates that human behaviour is influenced by ongoing changes in social mood. Social mood is defined as a shared mental state amongst humans that arises from social interaction. Social mood predisposes individuals in the group towards common emotions, beliefs and actions.[401] According to socionomics, social mood waxes and wanes positively and negatively over time.

Positive mood gives rise to periods of optimism, confidence, openness, good health, inclusiveness, innovation and economic growth. Positive social mood tends to be associated with a host of positive social phenomena such as rising stock prices, re-election of incumbent politicians, tolerance, peace, deregulation, democracy, the popularity of happy movies and pop music, brighter colours and shorter skirts. Taken to extremes, it can also lead to recklessness and speculative manias.

In contrast, negative social mood leads to pessimism, fear, gloom, distrust, cynicism, introspection, isolation, divisiveness, ill-health and exclusiveness. Periods of negative social mood tend to be associated with recessions, falling stock prices, increasing regulation, rejection of political incumbents, darker music, horror movies, the popularity of darker colours and longer skirts, intolerance, civil unrest, repression, persecution, authoritarianism and war.

Social mood is best measured by changes in the stock market, with increases in stock prices being associated with periods of positive social mood, and vice versa. The Great Depression is an example of negative social mood while the Roaring Twenties and the dot-com boom are examples of strong positive social mood.

Several features set socionomics apart from other theories of social interaction. Firstly, socionomics turns causality on its head by suggesting that social mood drives social events and economic outcomes. Therefore, it is positive social mood (optimism) that drives markets higher, not higher markets creating positive social mood – although I am sure there are feedback loops.

Secondly, social mood is endogenous and unconscious - – social mood is driven internally within people rather than by external events. As a result, this tends to drive herding as people unconsciously follow the herd, much like lemmings over a cliff. This herding instinct is no better exemplified than by trends in fashion, music and politics as things fall in and out of favour in an almost mesmerising manner.

Thirdly, social mood is not linear, but moves in fractals – similar patterns that recur at different degrees. Fractal patterns are commonly found in nature, for example snowflakes and leaves, but also in human activities such as art and music.

Socionomics argues that the stock market also moves in fractals in line with constant changes in social mood. Thus, movements in the stock market at lesser degrees, such as hourly or daily stock movements, exhibit similar patterns at higher degrees, such as weeks, months, years, decades and even centuries. Such a phenomenon should not be surprising, if social mood ebbs and flows as socionomics suggests.

Fourthly, socionomics suggests that most people within any society are sub-consciously subject to the same forces of social mood at the same time. An inference from this is that the actions of politicians, bureaucrats, bankers, business people and consumers within a particular society will be subject to the same underlying trends in social mood. And, at times, this might well spillover simultaneously to multiple nations.

Herding

Herding helps to explain why manias and depressions occur at regular intervals. Since the 1980s, the western world has experienced a series of speculative bubbles in asset prices, driven by extreme optimism and positive social mood. Each of these bubbles exhibit some common traits:

- a willingness by people to borrow large sums of money, oftentimes well beyond their capacity to repay debts from their incomes.
- a willingness by banks to lend substantial amounts of money to pretty much anybody with a pulse, irrespective of the potential risks and capacity to repay loans based on normal levels of income.
- a determination by vested interests, such as real estate agents, stock brokers and the mainstream media, to stoke the flames of euphoria through whatever means possible.
- justification by 'experts' that we have reached a 'new era' of everlasting economic well-being, naturally brought about by learned political and economic leadership.
- a reluctance by central banks to 'lean against the wind' to slow the mania.
- an increased level of risk-taking and wrong-doing by unscrupulous operators, coupled with a reluctance by regulators to undertake investigations and commence prosecutions until after the bubble has burst.

Herding should not be controversial, in that many species engage in herding to survive. Just look at the way fish, buffalo and wildebeest herd to give individual animals the greatest chance for survival. As animals, human beings could well exhibit herding instincts to maximise their own chances of survival.

The practical application of socionomics on economic policy is profound. If social mood does in fact drive human behaviour, then this makes it nigh-on impossible for authorities to control consumer and business behavior. No amount of cajoling by politicians and central bankers can make consumers open up their wallets and spend when they lack confidence and are afraid of the future. This goes a long way to explaining why people responded to the GFC the way they did: by increasing savings and cutting back spending, which was in stark contrast to what authorities wanted.

It also explains why central bankers are reluctant to take the punch bowl away when the party is in full swing. Rather than being the dispassionate, clinical decision-makers that they would have us to believe, central bankers are subject to the same trends in social mood as the rest of us. All the more reason why central banks shouldn't exist.

Socionomics is a relatively new theory and therefore, like all theories, needs to be treated with caution until further work is done to either prove, disprove and/or modify it. However, the theory to date looks promising.

Having looked at our willingness to spend, the second factor influencing aggregate demand is our *capacity* to spend. This, in turn, is influenced by two factors: macroeconomic forces and individual circumstances.

At the macro level, people's capacity to spend is influenced by the general state of the economy, and by social and geopolitical factors. At the individual and family level, our capacity to spend is influenced by factors including age, marital status, health, education, skills, wages, employment status and employment prospects, taxes, savings, interest rates, access to credit, debt servicing and level of indebtedness.

Importantly, people's capacity and propensity to spend changes as they move through the various stages of life. For example, a young married couple's needs will vary quite considerably from those of retirees, many of whom are often forced to curtail their spending as they lose a regular income stream and run down their retirement savings. Ageing populations will clearly act as a major drag on economic growth in coming decades, irrespective of the desires or actions of politicians and central banks.

The hollowing of America's middle class through outsourcing and offshoring has also greatly impacted consumers' ability to spend. Many consumers have resorted to increasing debt or running down their savings to maintain their standard of living. Over the medium term, however, this is a zero-sum game as debts pile up and consumers are forced to either restrict their spending to pay down debt or default.

The above suggests that people's willingness and capacity to spend are far more important factors than interest rates in determining aggregate demand. It also highlights why western economies have suffered lower growth in recent decades, despite massive amounts of fiscal and monetary stimulus.

*

Another question which is fundamentally important to the application of monetary policy is: do central banks control interest rates? The evidence suggests that they don't have anywhere near the level of control that they profess. Figure 13 (over page) shows the yield on 10-year U.S. Treasury Bonds from 1954 to 2018.[402] The yield on 10-year bonds is important for several reasons. Firstly, it is widely used by corporations and financial institutions as the benchmark for pricing debt securities such as mortgage rates and commercial loans. Banks add a margin above the benchmark rate to cover their costs and generate profits.

Figure 13 Rates on 10-year U.S. Treasury Bonds 1954–2018

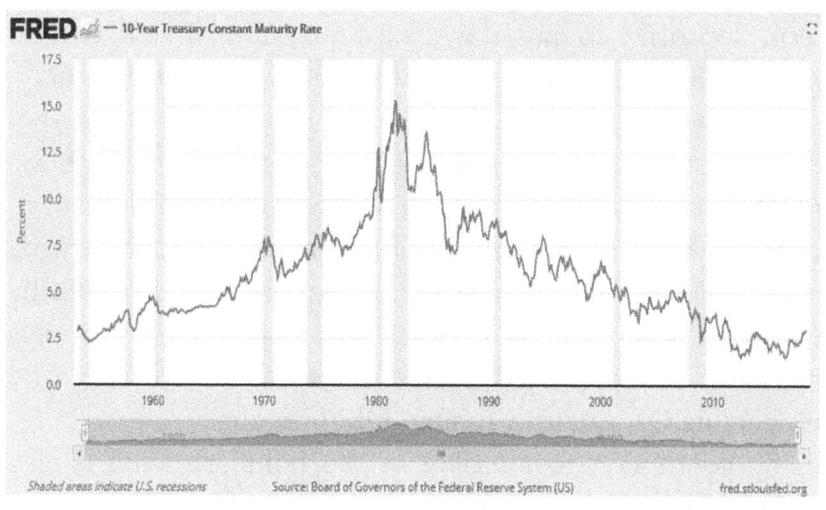

Source: Federal Reserve Bank of St Louis

Secondly, because they are heavily traded, the yield better reflects longer-term economic sentiment than many shorter-term notes and bonds. In addition, because the market is so large, the yield on 10-year bonds is set by market participants rather than by government or central banks. The bond market is generally seen as a very good barometer of the bond market's view of the health of the economy.

In contrast, the Fed has traditionally sought to influence interest rates by setting the overnight cash rates (Federal Funds Rate) for loans between depository institutions (banks and credit unions) on their reserve funds, and then conducting open market operations to maintain the overnight rate at the target rate. If the Fed believes the economy is slowing, it will reduce the overnight cash rate to stimulate demand. Conversely, if it thinks the economy is growing too quickly, it will increase the Funds rate to slow activity.

Since the GFC, the Fed has changed its approach to monetary policy by greatly expanding its purchases of longer-term securities to put downward pressure on longer-term interest rates to support economic activity and job creation.

Whether this works remains to be seen, but I am very doubtful for several reasons. The first problem is that the bond market is so large that the Fed would find it difficult to continue the open-ended purchase of bonds without blowing the whole financial system up, despite its theoretically unlimited ability to create money out of thin air. I think this has been acknowledged by the Fed's decision to stop and unwind its Quantitative Easing (QE) program.

By continuing to interfere in the bond markets, it also creates distortions in finance markets by eliminating market discipline, discouraging governments to undertake structural reforms and by creating distortions in asset markets as valuations become increasingly divorced from fundamentals.

Even if the Fed did undertake prolonged bond buying, it would eventually be faced with the need to unwind its position. It could do this in several ways. It could sell the bonds back into the market, which would put upward pressure on interest rates, which in a heavily indebted environment would prove problematical. It could maintain the size of its bond holdings by rolling over the bonds as they mature. This would be neutral to ongoing monetary policy. Or in the case of bond defaults, it could write the debt off its balance sheet. Of course, there are practical limits to the extent of losses central banks could suffer through widescale defaults or through open-ended QE. Moreover, if taken to extremes, ongoing QE would eventually lead to government spending spiralling out of control, market participants losing faith in the financial system, or both. This would eventually lead to higher real interest rates and possibly an implosion in the financial system.

Figure 13 is interesting for several reasons. It highlights that interest rates on 10-year bonds bottomed at around 2.5 per cent some 70 years ago, before climbing to a high of 15 per cent in 1981, and then falling to a low of 1.5 per cent in 2016. This suggests that interest rates move in long-term cycles rather than by the short-term machinations of central banks.

It also shows that since the Fed was created in 1913, the U.S. economy has experienced one and a half interest rate cycles, during which the U.S. has experienced the highest peak in interest rates in nearly 230 years, a Great Depression and multiple financial crises.[403] So much for the Fed's mandate for price stability and financial management.

Also curiously, GDP expanded at its fastest rate in the two decades following the end of World War II. And yet this was at a time when long-term interest rates tripled from 2.5 per cent to 7.5 per cent. In contrast, between 1990 and 2016, interest rates have fallen by more than 80 per cent from 9 per cent to 1.5 per cent, while the rate of growth in real GDP has been slowing.

This contradicts a fundamental tenet of modern economic orthodoxy: namely, that high interest rates stifle real economic growth; and that low interest rates stimulate growth. This would help explain why the real economy has responded lethargically, despite repeated attempts by central banks to boost the economy by lowering interest rates. Perhaps the real reason why the economy has not responded to frenetic central bank actions is because it is driven by structural forces that are outside the control of governments and monetary authorities.

The cyclical nature of interest rates is further highlighted in Figure 14 (over page), which shows long-term U.S. interest rates (30-year bonds where available) from 1790 to 2011. This graph shows four clear cycles over the period. The first cycle lasted 34 years from 1790 to 1824; the second lasted 76 years from 1824 to 1900; the third lasted 46 years from 1900 to 1946; and the fourth cycle lasted 70 years, from 1946 to 2016.

Figure 14 highlights several features associated with the long-term nature of interest rates. Firstly, the cyclical nature of long-term interest rates began well before the creation of the Fed and has continued unabated since its creation.

Secondly, the rhythmic nature of interest rates has occurred under both gold-backed and fiat monetary systems. However, the highest spike in interest rates over the past 230 years occurred after Nixon severed U.S. dollar links with the Gold Standard and inflation ran rampant during the 1970s. This suggests that market participants reacted to the risk associated with rampant inflation by demanding higher interest rates.

Figure 14 Long-term U.S. Interest Rates 1790–2011

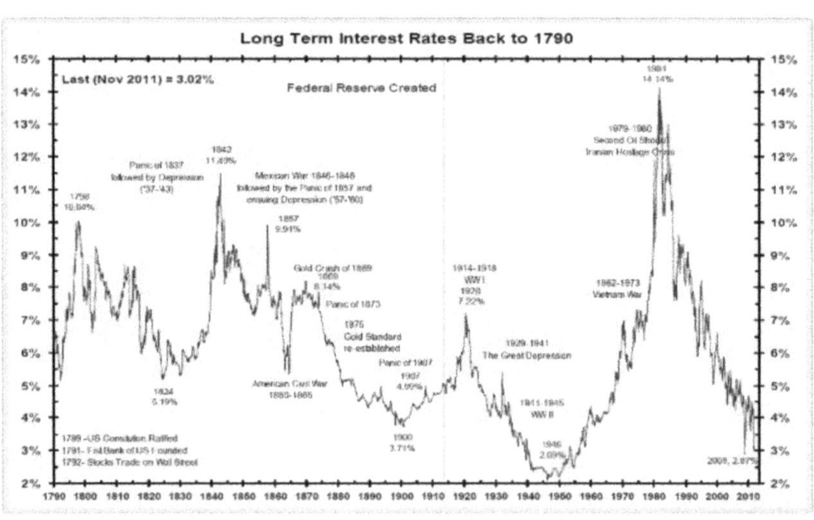

Source: Bianco Research LLC [404]

Thirdly, the peaks and troughs don't seem to align with major geo-political events such as wars. For example, interest rates peaked during WWI, but bottomed during WWII.

Finally, recent movements in yields suggest that the interest rates have bottomed and have started an inexorable rise over the next long-term cycle. For example, the 30-year bond rate climbed to 3.4 per cent in October 2018 after hitting a cyclical low of 2.11 per cent in July 2016.[405] This breakout above the previous high of 3.2 per cent achieved in May 2018 would suggest that the 30-year bull market in bonds is over, and that the next bear market in bonds is underway. And all of this despite central banks' efforts to keep interest rates as low as possible to supposedly ignite growth.

Recent movements in yields in 10-year Treasury bonds also support the trend change in 30-year bonds.

Each of the above observations suggests that interest rates move in a long-term cyclical pattern irrespective of world events. It also suggests that the forces driving interest rates are far stronger than the actions of governments and monetary authorities. Therefore, the actions of monetary authorities are unlikely to have a material on interest rates, particularly over the longer term. Finally, it highlights that low interest rates are not necessary for sustainable real economic growth.

If true, then this undermines the 'truism' that central banks control interest rates and that low interest rates are essential for strong economic growth.

*

Do share markets always go up?

If you listen to the continual babble from financial commentators, there is never a good time not to own shares.

Figure 15 S&P 500 Index 1870–2018

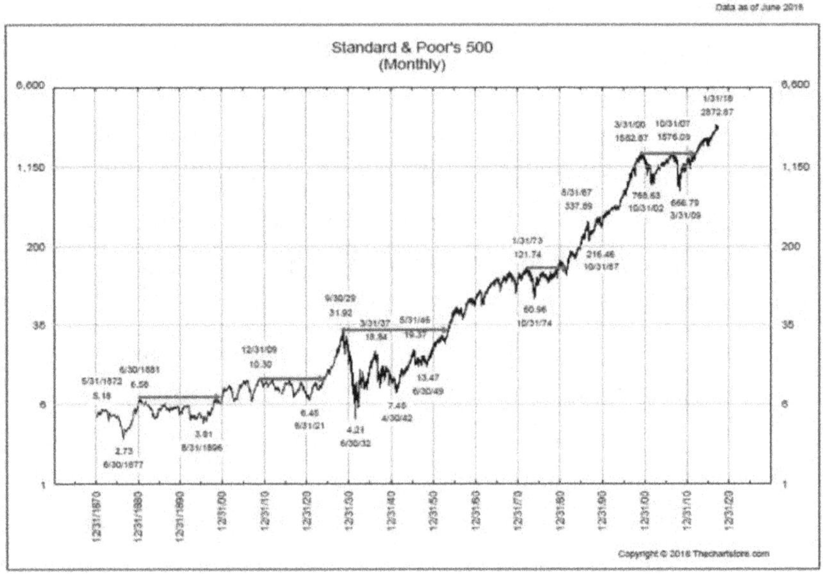

Source: www.thechartstore.com

Of course, we know this is not true, but what is the reality, especially since so many people will be relying on their investments to fund their impending retirement?

Figure 15 shows the Standard & Poor's 500 stock market index in log scale from 1870 to 2018.

Several features stand out on the chart. Firstly, share markets don't move in a linear fashion, but rather ebb and flow over long periods of time. While the trend in the stock market has generally been up, there have been long periods where the stock market has been flat or falling. Moreover, after a stock market crash, the time to exceed the previous peak can take anywhere from nine to 25 years, with an average of over 16 years.

Moreover, the cumulative time spent below a previous top has been 82 years, or 55 per cent of the total time between 1870 and 2018. This suggests that people buying near the top can wait a very long time before even recouping their investment, let alone making a return on investment. The losses from stock market collapses have ranged from 37 per cent to 87 per cent, with an average loss of 55 per cent from peak to trough.

A comparison of long-term interest rates (Figure 14) and stock prices shows that there has generally, though not always, been an inverse relationship between interest rates and share prices. For example, 30-year bond yields peaked in 1920, triggering the powerful run-up in stocks in the Roaring Twenties. Equally, after peaking in 1981, the massive decline in interest rates has been accompanied by a 37-year bull market in stocks, with the S&P500 growing more than twenty-three-fold over this period. This compares to just a six-fold increase in the index in the 84 years from 1870 to 1954. Conversely, rising interest rates from 1900 led to 20 years of stagnation in stock prices.

If these relationships hold true, then the expected increase in long-term interest rates could well usher in a protracted and deep bear market in stocks, leaving millions of baby-boomers facing retirement with an incredibly bleak future.

*

Now would be an appropriate time to challenge another central tenant of modern economic orthodoxy: that moderate inflation is good for the economy and deflation is bad for the economy.

As we noted earlier, one of the primary reasons central banks have set inflation targets between 2 and 3 per cent is that 'a lower inflation rate would be associated with an elevated probability of falling into deflation, which means prices and perhaps wages, on average, are falling — *a phenomenon associated with very weak economic conditions*. Having at least a small level of inflation makes it less likely that the economy will experience harmful deflation if economic conditions weaken.'[406]

It seems strange that central banks would be concerned about cheaper prices. For example, I have never yet met a consumer who complains when the price of petrol falls by 50 cents a litre, the price of laptops falls by a half, car dealers provide 0 per cent finance plus three years' free servicing, airlines and hotels drop their prices or retailers put on their Xmas sales. In fact, quite the opposite. People race out to take advantage of these deals because they know that lower prices improve their standard of living by allowing their hard-earned dollars to go further. In fact, according to economic theory, cheaper prices should increase demand, not reduce it.

So, why do central banks worry about deflation, and are their fears warranted? The answer to the second part of the question is: yes, and no. Just as there are many forms of inflation, there are also many forms of deflation: consumer price deflation, wage deflation, currency deflation, asset price deflation, debt deflation, and so on. There are also many of causes of consumer price deflation including innovation and technology, geo-politics, reduced taxes, globalisation, outsourcing, increasing competition, the weather and peace.

Deflation can be divided into two categories: good deflation and not-so-good deflation. Good deflation is often associated with supply side changes; that is, with those factors which reduce input costs such as raw materials, production and distribution costs. Economists generally equate not-so-good deflation with weak economic conditions due to weakness in aggregate demand. Part of this fear has to do with concerns that wages are often sticky to the downside, meaning that if prices are falling and wages aren't falling as fast, this can put pressure on company profits, which in turn can lead to firms laying off workers.

This has led them to the simplistic conclusion that moderate inflation is necessary for growth, and that deflation must be avoided at all costs. Some of these concerns also arise from analysis of the Great Depression, which mainstream economists cite as a failure of government policy to boost government expenditure in light of falling private consumption, and a failure by monetary authorities to increase the money supply.

As we know, there were a great many factors that led to, and prolonged, the Great Depression, including the 1920s asset boom and government policy aimed at maintaining nominal wages despite falling asset and consumer prices. Prices were simply reverting to more sustainable levels following a debt-induced bubble.

The mainstream economists also point to Japan's alleged 'Lost Decades', in which Japan has experienced low growth despite repeated attempts by the government and the central bank to boost growth. If fiscal and monetary stimulus work as they suggest, then Japan should have the highest growth rate in the world! It has not been through lack of effort by the government and central bank that economic growth hasn't returned to earlier levels. Instead, what it shows is that this type of stimulus doesn't work and Japan's slow growth has more to do with structural factors than monetary and fiscal stimulus. The recovery was further impeded by Japan delaying cleansing the system of underperforming companies and loans.

Moreover, this focus on the Great Depression and the more recent Japanese experience overlooks a wealth of other data which suggests that economies can grow equally well, if not better, with deflation than with moderate inflation.

American economist A. Gary Shilling has written extensively about inflation/deflation and collected statistics for the U.S. going back to the middle of the eighteenth century. Between 1749 and 2008, Shilling calculated that average prices increased by 1.3 per cent per annum. He also showed that prices have fallen an average of 1.2 per cent per annum during the 168 years of peace and risen by an average of 5.9 per cent during the 91 years of war.[407]

These figures should not be surprising given that wars typically involve a significant increase in military spending, which puts pressure on scarce resources and disrupts supply, as resources are diverted to wartime use and productive capacity is destroyed. In contrast, during peacetime, people can just get on living their lives and improving their standard of living while firms focus on innovation, lifting productivity and making money.

A look at specific time periods tells a similar story. From 1869 to 1916, a period of nearly 50 years, nominal GNP grew 650 per cent, while average annualised wholesale prices fell by 0.74 per cent. Equally, from 1919 to 1940, despite the economic collapse associated with the Great Depression, GNP grew 18 per cent, while average prices fell 2.3 per cent.[408]

Looking at somewhat shorter periods, from 1922 to 1929, GDP grew 42 per cent, or around 6 per cent per annum, while the CPI increased by only 1.7 per cent over the seven years.[409] In effect, the U.S. had genuine price stability. And this, despite the significant increase in the money supply during the same period. CPI was kept in check by productivity improvements, which put downward pressure on prices. Between 1950 to 1959, GDP grew 74 per cent, while CPI grew 23 per cent. And again, from 1960 to 1969, GDP grew 88 per cent, while CPI grew 25 per cent.

This evidence contradicts central banks' argument that inflation is essential for growth, and that deflation must be avoided at all costs. Instead, the evidence demonstrates that economies can experience robust growth, either with deflation or mild inflation. It also supports my contention that mild deflation, rather than inflation, is the natural order of things in a healthy and vibrant economy with sound money.

Asset price deflation, however, is a very different proposition. Falling asset prices are a natural consequence of asset price bubbles which, driven by excessive debt, become unhinged from the value of the underlying asset. Just as rising asset prices spur economic growth, debt deflation almost invariably drags economic growth down. And, just as in physics, the damage caused by the debt deflation is directly proportional to the debt inflation. As central bankers and the world are just about to find out, there is no escaping these natural laws.

Importantly, the above findings are supported by researchers at the prestigious Bank of International Settlements (BIS) – the central bankers' central bank – who undertook extensive analysis of the links between inflation/deflation and economic output. Their study looked at data that spanned 140 years, from 1870 to 2013, and covers up to 38 economies. It also examined data under different monetary regimes.[410]

Their findings, published in 2015, contradicted the main premise underlying central banks' current approach to monetary policy – that consumer price deflation is associated with weak economic conditions.

BIS found that the link between deflation and growth does not suggest a clear negative relationship as deflations have coincided with both positive and negative growth rates, with the Great Depression being the most obvious negative relationship. In fact, in the postwar era, BIS found that the growth rate has actually been higher during deflation years, at 3.2 per cent versus 2.7 per cent.

They also found that there is a very strong association between asset price deflation and lower economic output. Asset price deflation erodes wealth and collateral values and so undermines demand and output.

The researchers note that one problem in assessing the costs of consumer price deflation is that they often coincide with periods of asset price deflation. It is possible, therefore, to mistakenly attribute to the former the costs induced by the latter. In other words, the underlying cause of the economic decline is asset price deflation, while the symptom is consumer price deflation.

BIS also found that it is misleading to draw inferences about the costs of deflation from the Great Depression, as it was an archetypal event. The episode was an outlier in terms of output losses. And the losses could well have been associated with other causes, such as falls in asset prices and bank failures rather than consumer price deflation. This is a key finding because many mainstream economic theories are based on analysis of the Great Depression by Keynes and Friedman. If the Great Depression is an anomaly, which I believe it is, then policy based on analysis of the Great Depression is equally flawed.

BIS also found that there is a strong and consistent correlation between both property and equity price deflation and lower economic growth. This should not be surprising as asset price deflation leads to declines in aggregate net wealth – people go broke and become poorer. These findings suggest that monetary policy should first and foremost be directed at preventing credit-fuelled asset booms.

Finally, BIS suggested that if a financial crisis does arise, then once the financial system has been stabilised, authorities should focus on addressing the nexus of debt and poor asset quality head-on, rather than relying on aggressive and prolonged loose monetary policy. This is completely at odds with what global central banks have done. I think the evidence strongly refutes central bank arguments that deflation is bad for the economy, and that we need inflation to stimulate economic growth. Just another myth in a long line of mainstream economics mythology.

But it does beg the question: if the evidence is such that mainstream economics' fixation with deflation is wrong, then why would central banks perpetuate such a myth?

One explanation might be that central bankers suffer from groupthink. Not surprisingly, university economics courses are dominated by mainstream economic theories. Alternative schools of economic thought are either excluded or included as electives. It therefore stands to reason that if economists are being taught the same thing – even if these theories are wrong – then graduates from these courses will be equally deluded. This is particularly so when leading lights such as Ben Bernanke are so wedded to their messiahs of economic thought, such as Friedman, while being totally dismissive of alternative theories. So much for the pursuit of excellence in academia.

Equally, is some ambitious young economics graduate who wants a career in central banking or the finance sector going to raise doubts about mainstream economic theory? That's a career-limiting move right there.

Another explanation is that asset inflation is critical to the ongoing profitability of the finance sector. As we've mentioned previously, increasing bank profitability – and therefore increased bank executive bonuses – is inextricably linked to increases in the money supply and the concomitant asset price inflation. Without ongoing inflation, bank executive bonuses decline. It's a huge incentive for executives to pull out all stops to protect their multi-million dollar bonuses by perpetuating the myth.

Governments also benefit, at least in the medium term, from asset price inflation in several ways. Firstly, some of their taxes are based on rising asset prices, particularly property taxes. Secondly, asset inflation generally gives rise to increased economic activity – but once again, only in the short run. Far better then, to goose the economy for short-term gain and hope the subsequent collapse falls on somebody else's watch.

There is perhaps another, less likely explanation. When central bankers talk about their fears of deflation, they are more worried about asset and debt deflation than consumer price deflation. And well they might be. Asset and debt deflation are devastating to an economy and people's lives. Perhaps these bankers are happy to mislead the public by confusing consumer price inflation and asset price inflation, knowing full well that the mainstream press and banks will never know the difference, nor challenge them on their dishonesty. Whether this alternative is true, I don't know. I am perhaps looking for any explanation for how mainstream economists can be so wrong.

*

What about free trade? Does it exist? The world is only too aware of the damage that protectionism can wreak on global trade. This is no better evidenced than when America increased tariffs at the start of the Great Depression, which led to retaliatory action and a dramatic fall in global trade. Free trade is very important for global prosperity, and economists are right to push the mantra of free trade – provided it exists.

The problem, however, is that it doesn't exist. Many nations practise neither free nor fair trade. Whether it be farmers in Japan, Europe or the U.S., or big pharmaceutical companies, politicians are being constantly lobbied by powerful vested interests to protect their industries from competition. And many governments have succumbed to this pressure, protecting local industries through a variety of means including tariffs, quotas, foreign exchange controls, subsidies, administrative roadblocks and regulations such as health, safety and environmental controls. In fact, the EU was developed as a trading bloc to hinder free trade with the outside world, while as we have seen, China has used mercantilism and illegal means to gain unfair advantage in trade with western countries.

So, how much has this illusion of free trade cost the American people in recent times?

Between 2000 and 2017, the U.S. ran a cumulative trade deficit of $9.9 trillion, or 3.8 per cent of cumulative GDP.[411] This is an extraordinary figure when one notes that the rate of real economic growth has averaged around 2 per cent per annum over the same period. This is nearly $10 trillion of wealth that has been sucked out of the U.S. economy.

So, who have been the major beneficiaries of this American largesse? According to the U.S. Census Bureau, over the same period, the U.S. ran a cumulative trade deficit of $800 billion with Canada, $900 billion with Germany, $1 trillion with Mexico, $1.3 trillion with OPEC and Japan, $2.2 trillion with Europe and a staggering $4.4 trillion with China.[412]

Those are huge numbers of American jobs and a massive amount of wealth exiting America while enriching the lives of foreigners. And yet, the elite don't care. They make exorbitant profits and bonuses irrespective of whether goods are produced at home or abroad, while the average American suffers in silence.

One has to question how successive U.S. presidents – Clinton, G.W. Bush and Obama – and Congress could have systematically sold out their own people to a myth. They have been weak and failed to stand up for everyday Americans. No wonder that the political outsider Donald Trump has been right to debunk the myth of free trade and call out the hypocrisy of the elite – people who preach the mantra of free trade while hiding behind the veil of protectionism.

No wonder that we have also seen the shrill calls from Chinese and European leaders who cry foul that Trump is breaking down the so-called rules-based international trading system of the past 30 years. Of course they are crying foul, because they have been found out and exposed as the rank hypocrites that they are. Their growing prosperity has been built at the expense of everyday Americans.

Of course, it would be wrong to blame America's trade woes totally on Europe or China. Other factors such as SVM, globalisation, financialisation, falling education standards, dysfunctional politics, increasing debt and increasing consumption in the U.S. have also contributed greatly to her problems.

Trump was faced with a very difficult decision. Do nothing and allow America to continue to export her wealth, continue to see her middle class gutted and continue to subsidise the growth of the authoritarian China as she continues to become an increasingly dangerous military and economic strategic competitor. Undoubtedly, this would have been the easiest option, particularly in the short-run. But it would also have been the worse option over the medium to longer term.

Another option would have been to try to negotiate freer trade. Of course, this would never have been an option because Europe and China would have delayed talks for so long that America would have continued to bleed jobs and wealth for years on end.

So, Trump was right to call this out this hypocrisy. Moreover, if China and Europe were really interested in free trade, they would start to dismantle their trade barriers and move towards free trade. However, this is an unlikely scenario as it would reduce the benefits they receive by their unfair trade. In the end, this will undoubtedly end very badly for the global economy and will exacerbate the looming depression, as China and Europe push back.

Of course, Trump will be blamed – the world needs a scapegoat. But the reality is that the factors leading up to the looming next Great Depression – massive debt and economic distortions – have been brewing for decades. Unfortunately for him, Trump will be the one caught holding the baby.

The previous discussion obviously leads into the next question: if mainstream economists and central bankers are prepared to mislead the public, either through flawed theories or malevolence, then what else are authorities prepared to do?

*

I am not quite sure if you are like me, but from time to time I get the feeling that politicians don't always tell the truth. On the 'truth-ometer', the degree of honesty might range from little white lies to straight-out porkies.* We also know that politicians will resort to desperate, often draconian, measures in times of crisis, irrespective of how it affects their constituents.

Let's look at one example of how changes to the calculation of the CPI cost American taxpayers hundreds of billions of dollars. It is also instructive to look at how politicians, in cahoots with mainstream economists and the mainstream media, go about deceiving ordinary folk in getting their policy changes through.

Politicians identify a problem they want to fix. Initially, they float an idea or problem with their friends in the mainstream media, and then co-opt compliant academics, labelled in the media as 'experts', to prosecute the case. Armed with irrefutable evidence from these experts, the public are duped and the new policy is enacted.

Let's take the CPI. It was originally designed to help businesses, individuals and the government understand the impact of inflation on their activities. For many years, the CPI worked reasonably well for these purposes.

However, in the early 1990s, press reports began to emerge that the CPI was significantly overstating inflation. The reports argued that if the inflation rate could be reduced, then increases in government entitlements such as social security could be held in check, thus helping to bring the budget deficit under control. While bringing government expenditure under control is a worthwhile economic objective, it should not be done by deceiving the public.

The government enlisted the support of prominent mainstream economists Michael Boskin, then chief economist to the first Bush Administration, and Alan Greenspan, Chairman

---

* Rhyming cockney slang for outright lies

of the Fed, to prosecute their case. Their first attempt didn't quite work out as expected, leading to a political furore that killed consideration of Congressionally mandated changes in the CPI. As a result, President Clinton was forced to use Plan B, where the Bureau of Labor Statistics (BLS) quietly stepped forward and began surreptitiously changing the system.

They did this by making several adjustments to the way the CPI is calculated. Historically, the CPI was calculated by measuring changes in prices of a fixed basket of goods and services typically consumed by the average household. This provided a consistent way to track price changes over time. It is also the method still used by many other nations to measure CPI.

However, the Clinton administration made several changes to the way the index was calculated. The first change related to the way the CPI took account of relative changes in the prices of similar goods. Say, for example, that the price of steak moves up at a faster rate than chicken. Economists argued that people would switch to the cheaper product or to a lower-quality product like hamburger mince. Because of this theoretical substitution, the government changed the relative weighting of the two products to reduce the weighting of the product whose price was rising and substituting the prices of the lower-priced goods.

The government also changed the method of calculating the index from an arithmetic to a geometric weighting of products in the basket. The effect of these changes was that it automatically gave a lower weighting to CPI components that were rising in price, and a higher weighting to those items dropping in price.

The government also introduced what they call a hedonic quality adjustment to take account of changes in the quality of goods and services. This adjustment is particularly relevant for those goods which are impacted by rapid developments in technology, such as computers and consumer electronics. Let's use the example of a computer manufacturer which releases a new laptop at the same price as the previous version, but with superior features. Here, the government calculates the so-called benefits associated with the improved features and treats this as a cost reduction when calculating the CPI, notwithstanding that the consumer has paid the same price as the previous version and may or may not use the additional features.

In recent years, economists and their friends in the media have also sought to exclude changes to prices of basic goods and services such as food and fuel when referring to the CPI – the so-called core rate of inflation. Their stated rationale is that changes to such basic items can be volatile due to changes in the weather or seasonal movements. However, this ignores the fact that these are the prices paid by everyday people for everyday items. If fuel prices rise, the cost of living rises. Playing down changes in these prices might be theoretically OK – although I doubt that – but real people don't live in the economic world of fantasy and theory. They live in the real world. And excluding such real-world factors understates the real impact of inflation on the lives of the vulnerable.

Inflation is also removed from nominal economic growth to calculate real GDP. Understating inflation overstates real economic growth, something politicians from all sides benefit from.

Price indexes are used for a large variety of purposes. Therefore, understating the real inflation rate can have profound impacts. For example, price escalators based on the CPI are used in a multitude of commercial contracts including rent adjustments, and by governments in determining adjustments to welfare payments. Therefore, any changes in the way the indexes are calculated can have significant impacts on commerce and people's lives. This is no small matter.

American economist John Williams suggests that changes made in the CPI methodology during the Clinton, Carter and Reagan administrations have reduced current social security payments by roughly half from where they would have otherwise been.[413]

Not surprisingly, the BLS and mainstream economists dispute Williams' analysis. While they acknowledge that calculation of the CPI has problems, they disagree with his analysis, which they believe overstates the degree to which the CPI understates the actual level of inflation. While the truth probably lies somewhere in between, I believe governments and their bureaucrats have a strong incentive to understate the level of inflation, firstly, to reduce their welfare payments, and secondly, to overstate real economic growth.

*

It was former U.S. Treasury Secretary Timothy Geithner who once said: '*Most financial crises were caused by a mix of stupidity, greed, recklessness, risk-taking and hope.*'[414] What he didn't allude to, but perhaps should have, is that his comments apply equally to the role that central bankers played in the run-up to the GFC as it did to banks. His comments could also be extended to central banks' policies post the GFC.

On October 19, 2007, stock markets around the world crashed, ushering in the beginning of the GFC. Ben Bernanke responded on October 31, stating: '*It is not the responsibility of the Federal Reserve – nor would it be appropriate – to protect lenders and investors from the consequences of their financial decisions.'*[415] At the same time President George W. Bush stated: *'The government's got a role to play, but it is limited. A federal bailout of lenders would only encourage a recurrence of the problem.'*[416]

Within days of these statements, the Fed, in conjunction with other central banks, embarked on the greatest financial experiment in world history. This involved bailing out numerous financial institutions – protecting lenders and investors of the consequences of their financial decisions, while implementing Quantitative Easing (QE) and a Zero Interest Rate Policy (ZIRP).

QE is an unconventional form of monetary policy where a central bank creates new money electronically, out of thin air, to buy financial assets like government bonds and even shares. QE and ZIRP aim to stimulate economic growth by encouraging consumption and investment, and returning inflation to target.

Of course, when QE and ZIRP were launched, central banks failed to announce that these measures were experimental, that they had not been successfully tried before, and that they had no exit plan on how and when they would be unwound. That would have given the game away. Instead, these measures were launched in a state of sheer panic. But at least terms like QE and ZIRP sounded exotic enough to suggest central bankers knew what they were doing. The sad reality is that QE and ZIRP have not only failed to ignite economic growth but created massive distortions in the world's financial system.

Moreover, only the well-connected were bailed out. Ordinary Americans were thrown to the wolves and left to fend for themselves. But that's the way the elite designed the Federal Reserve system.

In total, the six central banks that embarked on QE – the Fed, the European Central Bank (ECB), the Bank of Japan, the Bank of England (BoE) and the Swiss and Swedish central banks – now hold more than $15 trillion in assets, more than four times the pre-crisis level. Of this, more than $9 trillion is government bonds, which represents 20 per cent of total outstanding debt owed by the governments.[417] And this excludes possibly countless trillions more in implicit guarantees to save the financial system.

Not surprisingly, central bankers have been lauded by their adoring fans in the mainstream media and Wall Street for their decisive actions. Some commentators even went so far as to say that Ben Bernanke saved the global economy, while the great man himself *humbly* admitted that the threat of a second Great Depression was very real, and that it was only averted by his prompt and decisive actions.[418]

What Bernanke and his fellow travellers failed to admit, however, is the role their misguided policies played in creating the GFC. The scene for financial crises had been laid decades earlier by Nixon, when he took the U.S. off the gold standard, and by Alan Greenspan, through his loose money policies, his sanguine views on asset bubbles and his bailouts.

Greenspan had strenuously argued that rather than try and pop asset bubbles, authorities should focus on cleaning up the mess after they burst. He based this argument on his belief that it was difficult to judge when asset prices deviated from fundamental value and increasing interest rates might not quell speculation. He asserted that monetary authorities had the tools to keep the harmful effects of a bursting bubble at a manageable level, provided they respond in a timely fashion, and that trying to pop the bubble might do more harm to the real economy.[419]

Greenspan's claims are, of course, disingenuous at best. There is sufficient data available to track asset values over time and to understand when asset values might be becoming extended. Equally, history has shown time and again that the larger the bubble, the greater the collapse. As for Greenspan's claims that one can '*keep the harmful effects of a bursting bubble at a manageable level*', presumably he is talking about minimising the harmful effects on those banks which own, and are bailed out by, the Fed. Not those millions of common folk who lost their houses and jobs as a result of the failed Fed policies.

Money is subject to the same market forces as any other commodity. The higher the demand relative to supply, the higher the price (interest rates). The lower the demand, the lower the price. The combination of ultra-low interest rates and massive liquidity have done enormous damage to the economy by eviscerating price discovery in credit markets, triggering an orgy of speculation and turning global financial markets into casinos.

Market-determined interest rates are essential to the efficient and effective functioning of economic systems in that they regulate the flow of funds between savers and borrowers, and between various sectors of the economy. By seeking to interfere in the free functioning of money and credit markets, central banks have created distortions in savings and investments by not allowing interest rates to find their natural level. It is ridiculous for politicians, central bankers and economists to suggest that central bankers are better able to determine interest rates than market forces. Central banking is more akin to communism than capitalism.

Moreover, given money's vital role in the economy, the ramifications caused by the distortions their meddling creates can be disastrous as evidenced by the fall-out from the dot-com bubble and the GFC. By seeking to keep interest rates at ultra-low levels for so long, they have once again encouraged businesses and consumers to load up on debt. This has clearly had the effect of allowing speculators to bid asset prices up to extreme levels. And we know from history how this story ends.

With interest rates so low, central banks have also forced people to take greater risks just to earn a modest return on investment, while imposing financial repression on millions of retirees who have suffered because of extremely low interest rates on their retirement savings. In March 2018, total savings deposits in the U.S. totalled $9.1 trillion.[420] Assuming interest rates are 1 per cent below where they might otherwise have been – and this is conservative – this equates to $91 billion that savers have foregone due to QE. Surely it is not the role of central banks to punish savers and pensioners for the benefit of bankers and debtors. Nor is it the role of central banks to force investors into riskier investments just to earn a modest return on investment.

Of course, debtors, especially governments, have benefited handsomely from this financial repression by reducing the amount of interest paid on their debts. U.S. federal government debt currently stands at $17 trillion. At 1 per cent interest, this equates to a saving of $170 billion per annum in interest payments. Can you imagine the impact on government finances if interest rates rise by a modest 3 per cent? That's $510 billion in additional interest payments at a time when the economy will be crippled.

Make no mistake. These failed policies will come back to haunt those who have racked up trillions of dollars in debt as interest rates begin to rise. By bailing out the banks, central banks have also created moral hazard – banks are no longer concerned about managing risk because they know the Fed will bail them out. The major banks have become so confident of future bailouts that they have coined the phrase 'too big to fail', flagging that they will be systemically too big to let fail in the next financial crisis. And yet, the amazing thing is that the Fed and Congress have done virtually nothing to contain this systemic risk. Surely, if a bank is too big to fail, then it should be split up or downsized so its failure doesn't cause systemic risk. And surely, this is the role of the Fed and the government. Unless of course, they are controlled by the elite.

I was one of the few analysts globally to publicly predict the GFC and to declare at the time QE started that QE, or 'counterfeiting money', wouldn't restore prosperity. Admittedly, while asset markets have rebounded strongly since the GFC, much of this growth has been driven by increasing debt, meaning that the world is poised for another financial calamity as asset markets roll over and debt implodes.

Not surprisingly, there has been overwhelming support for QE and ZIRP/NIRP, especially amongst politicians, mainstream economists, institutions such as the IMF, the mainstream media and financial commentators, analysts, corporate executives and banks. In seeking to defend its policy of QE, in 2012 the Bank of England (BoE) acknowledged that it is the elite that have benefited the most from QE: 'By pushing up a range of asset prices, asset purchases have boosted the value of households' financial wealth held outside pension funds, although holdings are heavily skewed, with the top 5 per cent of households holding 40 per cent of these assets.' [421]

This statement is interesting in that it seems to acknowledge that QE was aimed at boosting asset prices as well as stimulating economic growth, but central banks don't include asset prices in their inflation targeting. This is very convenient for the elite, who are the major beneficiaries of such central bank largesse. The BoE also stated that QE has lowered borrowing costs which has acted to stimulate spending while noting that most people in the UK would have been worse off without QE, including savers and pensioners. Of course, this is mere conjecture on several counts.

Firstly, savers and pensioners have been amongst the hardest hit due to ultra-low interest rates. Secondly, young people trying to enter the housing market have been severely disadvantaged by increasing house prices, while others have been saddled with huge mortgages pushed up by ever-increasing house prices. Thirdly, returns on annuity pension funds have also been negatively affected by low interest rates. Fourthly, QE has in no way contributed to supporting sustainable growth by encouraging structural changes within the economy. Finally, low interest rates have encouraged governments, corporations and households to increase debt to unsustainable levels. So, while QE and ZIRP might have staved off a depression in 2008, all it has done is kick the can down the road to some future time. When the bust inevitably comes, savers and pensioners once again will be crushed.

But there is a glimmer of hope. Since late-2017, a minority of policy-makers and commentators have begun to question the effectiveness of the program and become increasingly concerned about another financial crisis. For example, Klaas Knot, the head of the Dutch central bank, warned that while the market currently seems resilient, the picture of low volatility and the over-valuation in a range of investments resembles the period just prior to the GFC.[422]

Wolfgang Schäuble, the outgoing German finance minister, also cautioned that there was a risk of new bubbles forming because of the trillions of dollars that central banks had pumped into the financial markets through their bond-buying programs. On this count, Schäuble is wrong. The bubbles have already formed. All we are waiting for is for them of burst.

Even Janet Yellen, the former head of the Fed, warned there was a risk that persistently easy monetary policy could eventually lead to increased leverage and adverse developments.[423] In Yellen's case, however, this statement comes just after she opined that the banking system is 'very much stronger' due to Fed supervision and higher capital levels, and because of this, another financial crisis is unlikely 'in our lifetime'.[424] Her comment that 'easy monetary policy could eventually lead to increased leverage' is also amazing given the massive run-up in debt since QE began. Given debt is already at record levels, I just wonder what Yellen night regard as 'increased leverage'?

St. Louis Fed economist Stephen Williamson also chimed in by observing that there's little to indicate that the QE program that expanded the balance sheet worked as it was intended. Williamson went on to say that with respect to QE, there are good reasons to be sceptical that it works as advertised, and some economists have made a good case that QE is actually detrimental.[425] Even Alan Greenspan partially acknowledged failure when he said that the bond-buying program was ultimately a mixed bag. He said that purchases of securities did lift asset prices and lower borrowing costs. But it didn't do much for the real economy. He also said that effective demand is dead in the water and the effort to boost it via bond buying had not worked. Boosting asset prices, however, had been a 'terrific success'.[426]

Greenspan's comments are interesting for several reasons. Firstly, it acknowledges the tenuous relationship between loose monetary policy and demand in the real economy. In other words, it undermines the whole basis of monetary policy that lower interest rates increase demand. It is also difficult to understand why the Fed would regard boosting asset prices to bubble proportions as a 'terrific success', unless central banks are rooting for the elite. Moreover, the wealth effect might be positive on a rising tide, but it is devastating when the tide goes out, as it inevitably will.

Sadly, recognition of these problems is too late. Policy-makers should have acted to address structural problems and extreme debt levels after the GFC. Instead, through their misguided actions, central banks have continued to create extraordinary asset bubbles in real estate, bonds and share markets. Sadly, there is only one way this will end – with the Great Depression of the 2020s.

*

While some central bankers have belatedly started to raise concerns about their approach to monetary policy, especially inflation targeting and QE, most policy-makers and financial commentators seem bewildered and confused that their policies haven't worked as expected, while others have started to cast the blame elsewhere for their policy failures.

Let me be very clear. These belated acknowledgements of failure and suggestions for future policy frameworks highlight that central bankers still just don't get it. The New York Fed, for example, has implicitly acknowledged problems with the

Fed's use of the CPI to target inflation by developing a new measure of inflation: the Underlying Inflation Gauge (UIG). The UIG comes in two forms: the 'prices-only' UIG, which is based on 223 disaggregated price series in the CPI and is comparable to a 'core' inflation measure; and the 'full data set' UIG, which incorporates all the data of the 'prices-only' UIG plus 123 macroeconomic and financial variables.[427]

The broader measure includes other data sets such as producer prices, real variables such as employment and supplier deliveries, labour measures such as unemployment rates and average weeks worked, financial indicators such as the prices of oil, gold, exchange rates and stock indexes and money measures.

In a further acknowledgement the Fed's policy framework is deeply flawed, Ben Bernanke has put forward a radical proposal for a new monetary framework which involves central banks targeting the level of prices over the economic cycle, rather than the annual growth in prices. What he is proposing is that if inflation falls below the price target, central banks would make up inflation shortfalls by keeping rates lower for even longer on the promise that inflation would overshoot by the cumulative amount of the undershoot. The framework is intended to keep bond rates low and ultimately raise inflation expectations.[428]

Not to be outdone, the Reserve Bank of Australia (RBA) has also stepped in to ponder why its policies aren't working. The deputy governor of the RBA stated that one of the key reasons the RBA is having problems with its inflation targeting is because key statistics for output and inflation are not released until four months after the end of the quarter. In case of inflation, releasing the information earlier would help identify changes in the trend sooner.[429]

The RBA is also perplexed as to why wage growth is so static, despite low unemployment. Amazingly, it lays the blame partly on business and its 'laser-like focus on containing costs', which has seen workers lose out.[430] They also suggest that the Phillips Curve might have flattened. This same RBA official also stated that people shouldn't see monetary policy as the only game in town and that the cult of central bank independence has placed pressure on central banks to do more.[431]

The RBA's comments and attempt to deflect criticism are deeply troubling for several reasons. Firstly, it suggests that it does not understand the real cause of inflation – excessive growth in the money supply, relative to the supply of goods and services. Nor has it come to terms with the fact that it doesn't control CPI. Thus, getting data more quickly for something that it does not control is strange, especially when it is supposed to be managing inflation over the medium term.

Secondly, for economists to criticise business for trying to keep costs under control is bizarre in the extreme. Surely it is management's role to remain competitive and keep costs under control. This highlights just how far out of touch these people are. The comments also imply that the RBA still believes in the Phillips Curve – that there is an inverse relationship between inflation and unemployment. As noted previously, the Phillips curve was discredited with the stagnation of the 1970s.

Elsewhere, as the ECB's failure with monetary stimulus to generate robust economic growth has become increasingly obvious, ECB President Mario Draghi has also started to cast the blame elsewhere. In a statement made in 2016, Draghi warned that monetary policy alone cannot end the EU's economic malady. Instead he called on governments to undertake measures to improve productivity, including labour market reforms.[432] He also suggested that Germany embark on a round of deficit-funded investment spending.

Of course, central bankers were happy to ride in on their charges to save the world from a catastrophe of their own making and promise that they could return the economy to prosperity, but when their flawed theories haven't worked, they are looking to deflect criticism.

As we move into the next downturn, we can be assured that central banks will resort to ever more desperate measures while looking to deflect blame for their own policy failures even further afield.

As we conclude this discussion, I will leave you with the following thought: how could so many so-called 'experts' have got it so terribly wrong, and yet they were never called out for their obvious failures? They either don't know what they are doing, the elite are clearly in control – or both.

Chapter 11
Post-war Europe

'Bureaucracies are like parasites. They start off as small isolated colonies but once they become established, they multiply forever, feeding off and eventually subsuming the host.'

Phil Williams

By the end of World War II, much of Europe had been devastated. Cities lay in ruin, key infrastructure had been destroyed, and most merchant shipping had been sunk. The region's economies had been devastated while millions were living in refugee camps on aid from the United Nations Relief Fund. Food shortages were particularly severe, especially in the harsh winter of 1946–47, and many were expected to die.

Over the next seven decades, Europe emerged phoenix-like to become one of the pre-eminent global economic powers. From 1950 to 2016, real GDP grew seven-fold, while living standards improved dramatically, with GDP per capita growing five-fold to US$38,567.[433] Europe's post-war development was dominated by efforts to integrate national economies under the control of supranational bodies such as the EU, boost economic growth and reduce the possibility of war.

As we trace through post-war developments, readers will note that many of the key themes discussed in earlier chapters were also evident in post-war Europe. These include multiple examples of how, given a chance, politicians and bureaucrats will continually seek to expand their powers to encroach on the lives of everyday citizens and how politicians will resort to devious means to meet their own ends. Also similarly, it shows how politics not only intersects with economics, but can have a major negative impact on economic outcomes and people's living standards. The discussion will continue to expose the fundamental flaws in mainstream economic theory as well as economic myths. Finally, I will expose the truth behind the Greek bailouts while using the experiences of Iceland and Greece following the GFC to demonstrate the best way to respond to a financial crisis – and clearly how not to respond to a financial crisis.

The European post-war economy can be divided into three phases: the Marshall Plan (1948–1952); integration and growth (1952–2007); and the GFC and ongoing stagnation (2007–present day). The discussion will focus primarily on the 28 nations currently comprising the EU, together with Switzerland and Norway.

The Marshall Plan (1948–1952)

In 1947, European economies were still operating at well below their pre-war levels and showing few signs of growth. Agricultural production was 83 per cent of 1938 levels, industrial production was 88 per cent, and exports only 59 per cent.[434] In line with the post-war agreements, the UK and the U.S. had pursued a rigorous policy of demilitarisation and de-industrialisation in German-occupied territory. This included partially dismantling her heavy industry and putting the main coal-producing regions under international control.

However, by July 1947, two things happened to change American thinking. Firstly, American policy-makers realised that economic recovery in Europe could not progress without the reconstruction of the German industrial base and that an 'orderly, prosperous Europe requires the economic contributions of a stable and productive Germany'.[435] Secondly, the strength of Moscow-controlled communist parties in France and Italy began to worry Washington.[436]

In early 1948, in response to these concerns and in line with America's new policy of containment, Congress signed off on a substantial foreign aid package to support the reconstruction of European economies. Known as the Marshall Plan, U.S. goals were to rebuild war-devastated regions, remove trade barriers and regulations, modernise industry, encourage an increase in productivity and prevent the spread of communism.[437] It was also hoped that increased economic prosperity would provide vital support for political stability in the region. The Marshall Plan was also expected to provide a financial benefit to American producers by opening up additional export markets and growing the global economy.

In the early planning phases of the proposed plan, the Americans had held lengthy discussions with their Russian counterparts about participating in the program. Some eastern bloc countries, notably Poland and Czechoslovakia, had shown strong interest in participating in the scheme.

In the end, the Soviets rejected the initiative for several reasons, none of which had anything to do with the good of the Russian people, but everything to do with the ambitions of its political elite. Understandably, the Soviet leader, Joseph Stalin, had no interest in helping the Germans in any way, particularly in helping them rebuild their economy. Apart from the recent carnage that Germany had inflicted on the

Russian people, Stalin had set his mind on subsuming the whole of Germany into the Soviet sphere of influence. Helping the Germans resurrect their economy would have run counter to his broader objectives.

Stalin was also concerned about some of the conditions attached to the scheme. Firstly, to be eligible for aid, recipients would have to undergo a detailed audit of their financial position, a situation Stalin found unacceptable. Equally, credit would only be extended based on economic co-operation between European nations. This would have given the west a certain level of control over the Soviet economy, a situation which was clearly incompatible with the authoritarian Soviet regime and Stalin's desire for self-sufficiency.

In rejecting the program, the Soviets mounted an all-out attack against the Marshall Plan. Not only did they portray the scheme as an attempt by the ruling American elites to enslave the weakened capitalist countries of Europe, they argued that the 'bosses of Wall Street' were taking the place of Germany, Italy and Japan. The Soviets now portrayed the world as splitting into two camps: the imperialist and antidemocratic camp (America) and the anti-imperialist and democratic camp (Soviet Union).[438]

As an aside, I feel Stalin didn't fully understand the meaning of 'democracy', just as Americans today seem to have misplaced the definition of the term. Authoritarian control by ruthless dictators (Russia and China) or control of politicians by the self-serving elite (America) doesn't equate to democracy, no matter how you dress it up.

In more practical terms, the Soviets demanded that the French and Italian communist parties maximise efforts to sabotage implementation of the Plan, while also ensuring that Poland and Czechoslovakia didn't participate in the scheme.

The Americans countered Soviet moves by arguing that the Soviet stance was another indication that the Soviets wanted to isolate Eastern Europe and enforce authoritarian rule.

Starting in 1948, the Marshall Plan ran for four years. During this period, the U.S. provided over $12 billion (approximately $120 billion in 2016 dollars) in aid to western Europe.[439] Funds were generally distributed to beneficiaries on a per capita basis, although slightly more went to America's wartime allies.

The Marshall Plan had several benefits. It provided much needed financial support, particularly in providing hard currencies that European countries lacked at the time. It also supported economic growth. By 1952, the economic output of all Marshall Plan participants was at least 35 per cent higher than in 1938,[440] and over the next two decades Western Europe enjoyed unprecedented economic growth and prosperity. Growth in the European economy also stimulated the American economy by providing a market for American products.

The Marshall Plan was also one of the first elements of European integration, in that it erased trade barriers and established institutions to coordinate the economy on a continental level.[441] Finally, the Marshall Plan reduced the power and influence of communist parties in Western Europe.

In response to the Marshall Plan, the Soviets launched their own aid plan, known as the Molotov Plan. This plan, which took the form of a series of bilateral trade agreements, was designed to support economic development in eastern bloc nations while reorienting the eastern economies away from the west and towards the Soviet sphere of influence. The Soviet plan proved less successful than its western counterpart, particularly when measured by economic growth in the two regions.

European Integration and Growth (1952–2007)

The history of post-war Europe has been dominated by the relentless drive to integrate the nations of Europe. Initially, the motives behind integration were well-intentioned. It was to be used as a means of escaping centuries of war and conquest, and supporting economic development. Integration was also initially designed to be narrow in scope, being restricted to a handful of nations and focused primarily on trade.

However, over time these motives came to be increasingly subverted as ambitious and self-serving bureaucrats and politicians seized every opportunity to assume greater powers for themselves while imposing greater control over people's lives. Germany and France also increasingly flexed their economic muscle as they sought to dominate all aspects of European life. The process European politicians and bureaucrats followed to expand their power makes for an interesting case study. Let's call it 'takeover by stealth'.

It starts out with a well-intentioned initiative with a limited number of participants and a limited scope. However, not happy with their limited powers, ambitious operatives look at other areas for expansion. This may take the form of increasing the number of participants or expanding the areas which they wish to regulate and control. Of course, with a bureaucracy and power structure already in place, those in control naturally ensure that they remain in control after the takeover but with greatly expanded power and influence.

Takeover by stealth gives centralists the time and resources to garner support amongst the elite while systematically isolating and crushing any opposition. By the time people have woken up to what has happened, the takeover is largely complete.

It could also be compared to the fable of the boiling frog, which says that if you suddenly put a frog into boiling water, it will realise it is in danger and jump out. But if you put a frog into cool water and heat the water up gradually, the frog may stay in the water until it is boiled alive. What the fable is suggesting is that if change comes quickly, then people will take a stand against the erosion of their rights. However, if the change is introduced incrementally, then people have time to adjust to the changes and tend to more easily adapt, particularly if such changes are supported by a well-orchestrated media campaign. So let's look at how European integration and expansion actually played out.

The idea of the peaceful integration of Europe had been raised as far back as the early nineteenth century. In 1818, Tsar Alexander of Russia suggested a kind of permanent European union and even proposed the maintenance of international military forces to provide support to member states against aggression.[442]

The subject was picked up again after WWI, when Richard von Coudenhove-Kalergi wrote the Pan-Europa manifesto in 1923.[443] His ideas influenced others such as Aristide Briand, who served 11 terms as Prime Minister of France, and Winston Churchill, the British wartime Prime Minister. While Churchill initially didn't see Britain as being part of the United States of Europe – it still was head of the British Commonwealth of Nations – he believed that France and Germany must take the lead, together with Britain, the U.S. and Russia, in forging a new Europe.[444]

The first steps towards integration came with the creation of the European Coal and Steel Community (ECSC), which was formally established in 1951. Its founding members were France, West Germany, Italy and the three Benelux countries: Belgium, the Netherlands and Luxembourg.

The ECSC was first proposed by French foreign minister Robert Schuman in 1950. The purpose of Schuman's plan was to establish a new economic and political framework by making war not only unthinkable, but materially impossible. This was to be achieved by creating the world's first supranational body – an international organisation with power and influence that would transcend national boundaries or governments – to take control of production of coal and steel and establish a common market. The ultimate objective was the creation of a 'United States of Europe'.[445]

The ECSC consisted of four bodies:

- a High Authority with a principal role to ensure that the treaty's objectives were met and that the common market functioned smoothly.
- the Common Assembly, which comprised 78 representatives, typically national MPs nominated by their respective governments. The Assembly exercised supervisory powers over the High Authority.
- the Special Council of Ministers, which was composed of representatives of national governments. The Council's primary roles included harmonising the work of the High Authority and that of national governments, which were still responsible for the state's general economic policies, and issuing opinions on certain areas of work of the High Authority.
- The Court of Justice, which was to ensure compliance with ECSC law, along with the interpretation and application of the Treaty.[446]

These four bodies provided the foundation for today's European Commission, the European Parliament, the Council of the European Union and the European Court of Justice.

The ECSC had mixed results. By 1954, the agency had removed nearly all barriers to trade between its members in coal, coke, steel, pig iron, and scrap iron. As a result, trade in these commodities rose dramatically.[447] The High Authority also provided finance to help modernise factories, improve output and reduce costs, while costs were further reduced by the abolition of tariffs at borders.[448] The Authority also played a key role in transitioning workers impacted by increased global competition to other sectors.

In contrast, the ECSC had little effect on coal and steel production, which was influenced more by global trends than local efforts. In addition, companies were able to easily get around rules designed to control cartels and regulate mergers, leading to incidents of price fixing.

The next step in the march towards integration came in 1957 with the creation of the European Economic Community (EEC) and the European Atomic Energy Community (Euratom). The aim of the EEC, also known as the Common Market, was to bring about further economic integration amongst its six founding members, including a common market and customs union, while Euratom was established to promote co-operation in the development of nuclear power. The EEC, established as a trade bloc, facilitating trade amongst its members while imposing restrictions on companies wishing to compete with European firms, became the most important of these bodies and quickly expanded its powers.

Discussions over agricultural protection proved a major stumbling block to further integration and the expansion of free trade. At the time, member states intervened extensively in their agricultural sectors. This included regulating what was produced, at what prices produce would be sold, and even how farming was organised. Some members, particularly France, and all farming organisations, wanted to maintain strong state intervention in agriculture. Then French President, Charles de Gaulle, was also deeply opposed to supranationalism, and feared other members challenging France over its agricultural policies.[449]

Negotiations over development of the Common Agricultural Policy (CAP) proved difficult. The result is often explained as a political compromise between France and Germany: German industry gained access to the French market. In exchange, Germany helped to pay for France's farmers.[450] In the end, the CAP became an integrated system of measures that worked to maintain commodity prices at target levels. It did this by applying import levies and quotas to restrict imports, through direct intervention in the market to buy surplus production, and by subsidising production through the payment of direct subsidies to farmers.

Since its introduction, the CAP has undergone substantial reforms which have moved it from a production-oriented policy towards a system which consists of direct subsidy payments and support for sustainable rural development.

CAP has been strongly criticised since its inception. While some of the concerns have been addressed through recent reforms, other criticisms remain. The most striking of these is that it is anti-competitive, and that it is designed to protect a small, but radical and vocal, constituency at the expense of foreign producers and the vast majority of European consumers. For example, while agriculture makes up less than 2 per cent of European GDP, the Institute of Economic Affairs estimates that CAP has pushed up food prices on average by 17 per cent across Europe. That's a huge impost to pay for a protected minority. And while the CAP budget has shrunk from 71 per cent of the total EEC budget in 1984, it still represents a sizeable 38 per cent of the total budget.

The CAP also favours those countries in the EU that have larger agricultural sectors, notably France and Spain, over other countries such as the Netherlands and the UK, which are more highly urbanised. This unashamed protectionism undermines the credibility of any European politicians who preach the mantra of free trade and demand that others, such as the U.S. Trump Administration, play by international trade rules.

The next phase of integration came in 1967 when the ECSC and Euratom combined with the EEC to form the European Communities. The 1960s also saw the first attempt at expansion, when Denmark, Ireland, Norway and the UK applied to join the Communities. However, President de Gaulle vetoed the move, believing British membership was a Trojan Horse for U.S. influence in Europe. Denmark, Ireland, Norway and the UK were admitted in the early 1970s after de Gaulle left office, while Norwegians rejected membership in a referendum. Portugal, Spain and Greece joined in the 1980s, while East Germany joined in 1990 following German reunification.[451]

Austria, Finland and Sweden all joined in the 1990s. However, the largest influx of new members occurred in 2004, when ten countries, including many former eastern bloc countries such as Poland, Estonia and Hungary joined. Romania and Bulgaria joined in 2007, while Croatia was the last country admitted in 2013.[452]

In 1993, the EU superseded the European Community following ratification of the Maastricht Treaty. The treaty ushered in far-reaching economic reforms through the creation of the European Economic and Monetary Union (EMU) and the creation of the three pillars of the EU. This treaty, together with the Schengen agreements, was designed to facilitate the free movement of goods, services, capital and people throughout Europe's internal market.

The primary purpose of the EMU was to support further economic integration while introducing rules to encourage member states to adopt sound economic policies. Under the treaty, members were required to maintain inflation at no more than 1.5 percentage points higher than the average of the three best performing (lowest inflation) member states, limit government debt to 60 per cent of GDP, and keep annual budget deficits below 3 per cent of GDP.

When it suited their own purpose, politicians from leading countries paid lip service to the need for fiscal discipline. For example, despite the edict to keep budget deficits under control, several countries, including Germany, France, and most notably Greece, broke this rule, casting serious doubts on the ability of the euro area to maintain discipline. While handing over certain powers to the EU, member states retained control over their national budgets, tax policies, and labour and capital markets.

The EMU also led to the establishment of a common currency (the Euro) and the European Central Bank (ECB), which is responsible for all monetary policy in the eurozone. The ECB sets a common interest rate for all eurozone members and aims to maintain inflation rates below, but close to, 2 per cent over the medium term.

The EMU and the common currency had several benefits. These included lower transaction costs and greater discipline amongst members which were restricted in spending or devaluing their currency to get out of economic difficulty. However, it also brought with it a number of structural problems which became apparent during the GFC. I will cover this in greater detail shortly.

The Maastricht Treaty also created the three pillars. This involved rolling Euratom, the ECSC and the EEC into the EC, while creating several other bodies covering justice and home affairs, policing and judicial co-operation and security. These were further streamlined in the Lisbon Treaty when they were consolidated into one body, the EU.

To make it easier for people to travel amongst EU countries, the EU also adopted the Schengen arrangements. These arrangements abolished internal borders and harmonised visa requirements, enabling passport-free movement across most of the bloc. While these new arrangements had benefits, they also had major downsides including the mass migration of people from poorer countries to the wealthier nations. This not only created social problems but led to locals losing their jobs and putting downward pressure on wages.

The Treaty of Lisbon came into force in 2009. Its aim was to simplify and streamline the institutions that govern the EU, and make the EU more democratic, more transparent and more efficient.

Prominent changes included the move from unanimity to qualified majority voting in at least 45 policy areas in the Council of Ministers; an increase in the legislative power of the European Parliament forming a bicameral legislature alongside the Council of Ministers; new powers for the European Commission and European Parliament; and a consolidated legal personality for the EU.[453]

The Treaty also made the Union's bill of rights, the Charter of Fundamental Rights, legally binding. For the first time, the Treaty also gave member states the explicit legal right to leave the EU and the procedure to do so. This would subsequently pave the way for Britain's decision to leave the EU less than a decade later.

Political power and representation have changed considerably since European integration began. For example, in 1979, the first European Parliamentary elections were held across all nine-member states to elect 410 Members of

European Parliament (MEPs). Seats were allocated to the states according to population, and in some cases were divided into constituencies, but members sat according to political groups. Socialist parties working together under the Europe-wide Confederation of Socialist Parties won the most seats, followed by a combined Christian Democrat/European People's Parties, the Conservative European Democrats and the communists.[454]

The Treaty of Lisbon also made two major changes to the political structure of the EU. Firstly, it reduced the number of MEPs from 785 to 751, while redistributing voting weights between member states using a degressively proportional system – smaller states are allocated more seats than they would otherwise be allowed – in proportion to their population. Despite these changes, the top six nations have 56 per cent of MEPs, led by Germany (12.8 per cent), France (9.9 per cent), the UK (9.7 per cent) and Italy (9.7 per cent). In contrast, the ten smallest nations have just 12 per cent of MEPs.

Secondly, the treaty also changed the role of national parliaments by granting them prior scrutiny of legislative proposals and the opportunity to comment before the Council and Parliament can take a position. However, it removed the right of national vetoes in several areas including fighting climate change, energy security and emergency aid. Unanimity was still required in the areas of tax, foreign policy, defence and social security.[455]

Despite the creation of the EU, member countries have also retained membership of traditional regional groupings which work alongside the EU protocols. These include the Visegrád Group (the Czech Republic, Hungary, Poland and Slovakia), the Nordic Council (Denmark, Finland, Iceland, Norway and Sweden), the Baltic Assembly (Baltic republics of Estonia,

Latvia and Lithuania) and the Benelux Union. These groups encourage co-operation with one another on energy, economic, political and cultural issues. The presence of these groups could become critical should the EU break apart, as I fully expect in the coming Depression.

Economic Performance

By all rights, Europe should have had one of the best performing economies in the world. It had a large consumer base, plentiful resources and its industry was protected from the worst of competition through an array of protectionist measures. So how did it fare?

The top five European nations (Germany, France, the UK, Italy and Spain) dominate the European economy, representing 65 per cent of total output in 2016, compared to just 11 per cent from the smallest 16 nations.[456]

Between 1980 and 2016, Cyprus, Ireland, Luxembourg and Malta had the fastest growing economies, all more than trebling in size, while Bulgaria, Croatia, Greece, Hungary, Latvia and Romania lagged the rest of Europe.

At almost $100,000 per person per annum, Luxembourg had the highest per capita income in Europe. Austria, Denmark, Germany, Ireland, the Netherlands, Norway, Sweden and Switzerland all had per capita income greater than $46,000 per annum. In contrast, people from the former eastern bloc countries such as Bulgaria, Croatia, Hungary, Latvia, Poland and Romania dominated the poorest people in the EU. Greeks also fared poorly, with per capita income falling by nearly 30 per cent since the GFC.

I noted earlier that between 1950 and 2016, Europe's real GDP grew from US$3 trillion to US$20.4 trillion. However, this impressive performance has masked a deeply disturbing trend in economic growth. Figure 16 shows the average rate of change in real GDP by decade from the 1950s to 2016. After peaking at 5 per cent in the 1960s, the rate of growth in real GDP has been in inexorable decline. Since 1980, annual real economic growth in EU countries has exceeded 3.5 per cent just three times, with the highest growth rate topping out at 3.9 per cent in 2000. And yet despite, or perhaps because of, record amounts of fiscal and monetary stimulus, economic growth reached 2 per cent just twice since 2010. Very poor economic performance indeed, especially since the ECB took it upon itself to guide Europe towards prosperity!

Figure 16 Europe: Average Real GDP Growth 1950s–2016

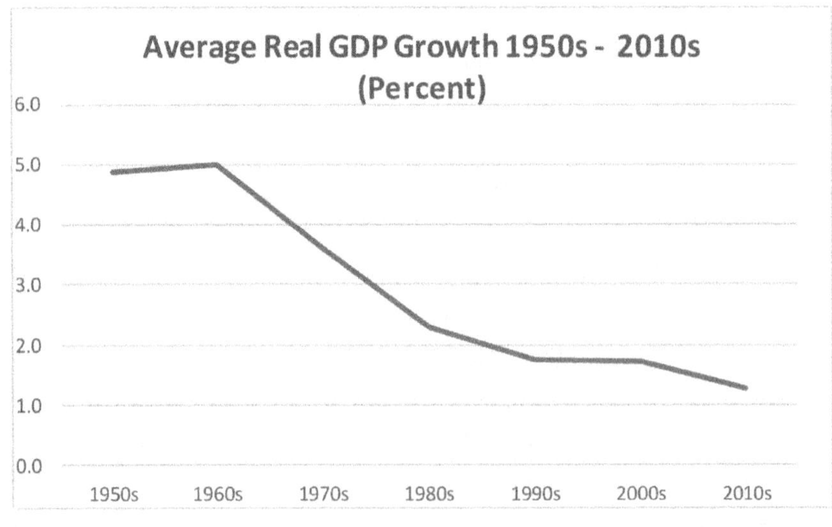

Data Source: The Conference Board[457]

Interestingly, the graph for European growth is eerily similar to the graph for the U.S. economy, suggesting that common factors might have been at play.

Figure 17 shows the average rate of change in total labour productivity by decade from the 1950s to 2016.*

Figure 17 Europe: Average Change in Total Labour Productivity 1950s–2016

Average Change in Total Labour Productivity 1950s - 2010s (Percent)

6.0
5.0
4.0
3.0
2.0
1.0
0.0

1950s 1960s 1970s 1980s 1990s 2000s 2010s

Data Source: The Conference Board[458]

After peaking at 5 per cent in the 1960s, labour productivity has been in constant decline. Importantly, the decline in labour productivity mirrors the decline in GDP, suggesting two things: firstly, that there is a strong correlation between economic growth and growth in labour productivity (as one would expect); and secondly, there seems to be little correlation between economic growth, budget deficits, monetary stimulus and low interest rates, as mainstream economists would have us believe. This then raises the obvious question: why do politicians, economists, and central banks persist with their

* Note: data for some of the smaller nations is unavailable from 1950–1980. The absence of this data, however, is unlikely to impact the analysis in any material way.

policies when they clearly don't work? And why do financial commentators drink the same Kool-Aid?

There seem to be several reasons why growth in labour productivity has slowed so precipitously. Firstly, the European economy has experienced similar structural changes to that of the U.S., particularly the move towards a service-based economy.

Secondly, Europe has very strong labour laws which cover areas such as individual labour rights, rights to information, consultation and participation at work and rights to job security, as well as a raft of regulations covering workplace health and safety and anti-discrimination. These severely restrict a company's ability to lay off staff or restructure businesses in line with market changes.

Thirdly, there has been a general fall in the level of investment since the 1980s. As we know, investment in critical infrastructure, plant and equipment and the like is critical to building the productive capacity in an economy. And yet, while investment as a percentage of GDP has remained relatively stable in a number of countries, it has fallen in some countries by two-thirds or more.

Finally, public spending on social welfare – health, old age, labour market programs, unemployment benefits and social housing – has risen significantly since the 1920s, but especially since the mid-1960s. In the mid-1930s, spending on social welfare averaged around 2.5 per cent of GDP. By the 1960s this had grown to between 10 and 15 per cent. Since then, expenditure on social welfare has exploded, with spending ranging from anywhere between 20 per cent (Switzerland) to between 28–31 per cent (Germany, Greece, Sweden, Denmark, Italy and France).[459] While such spending might well have positive social benefits, spending on social welfare acts as a drain on the productive capacity of the economy.

Let's turn our attention to the economic performance of those countries which have recently joined the EU. One would have thought that one of the primary reasons for wanting to join the EU would be to increase economic growth. It is clear, however, that joining the EU has proven anything but the economic nirvana that many people might have wished for. Rather, the rate of economic growth has fallen in *every* country, in some instances by up to two-thirds, since these countries joined the EU, robbing their citizens of billions of dollars in economic output.

Table 3 shows the average rate of economic growth for 13 nations that have joined the EU since 2000. The table shows the year joined, together with the average rate of economic growth in the 10 years immediately preceding the year joined, together with the average rate of economic growth for the 10 years following the year of joining. It also shows which countries are in the eurozone.

Table 3 Rate of Economic Growth for New EU Nations

Country	Year Joined	1994–2003 (Per cent)†	2004–2013 (Per cent)	In the eurozone
Cyprus	2004	4.2	1.3	Yes
Czech Republic	2004	2.6	2.4	No
Estonia	2004	5.9	3.0	Yes
Finland	2004	4.0	1.2	Yes
Hungary	2004	3.2	1.1	No
Latvia	2004	4.9	3.2	Yes
Lithuania	2004	4.3	3.7	Yes
Malta	2004	4.4	2.3	Yes

† **Data for Bulgaria and Romania show economic growth from 1997–2006 and 2007–2016 respectively**

Poland	2004	4.5	4.0	No
Slovak Republic	2004	4.4	4.2	Yes
Slovenia	2004	4.4	1.5	Yes
Bulgaria	2007	3.7	1.9	No
Romania	2007	3.2	2.4	No

Data Source: The Conference Board[460]

While it is difficult to identify specific reasons for these declines, some of the more obvious explanations include the adoption of a common currency, excessive regulations, declining labour productivity, the GFC and sluggish growth in the rest of the EU.

Which begs the question. Why would any of these countries want to stay in the EU or the eurozone, particularly if the EU continues to whittle away economic and political sovereignty?

GFC and Economic Stagnation

The GFC quickly plunged the European economy into a deep recession. Between 2008 and 2009, real GDP in Europe fell by $830 billion, or 4.3 per cent. The crisis hit some countries more than others. Economic output, for example, fell by over 14 per cent in the Baltic states; 8 per cent in Finland and Slovenia; and 7 per cent in Croatia, Hungary and Portugal. In contrast, Belgium, Norway and Switzerland suffered only a 2 per cent decline, while Poland's economy actually grew by 3 per cent.[461]

The recession also took an extraordinary toll on people. Unemployment soared, reaching a peak of 26.3 million people, or 12 per cent of the workforce in 2013. Greece and Spain were especially hard hit, with unemployment peaking at a staggering 27.5 per cent in Greece and 26.1 per cent in Spain.[462]

Young people suffered greatly. In 2015, more than half of 15–24 year-olds were unemployed in Greece and Spain, while youth unemployment also reached extremes in Croatia (45 per cent), Italy (43 per cent), Cyprus and Portugal (35 per cent), and Slovakia (30 per cent).[463] In 2015, youth unemployment still remained above 20 per cent in many other countries including Belgium, Bulgaria, Ireland, France, Poland, Romania, Finland and Sweden.

In contrast, youth unemployment in Germany peaked in 2009 at 11.6 per cent before falling to 7 per cent in 2016.[464] Clearly, it pays when you control the eurozone and can export your way to prosperity at the expense of the peripheral nations!

It is hard, however, to understand why youth unemployment remained so high in these laggard nations. It suggests that either wages for young people were too high for their level of skills and experience, that labour laws are too rigid, that cultural norms and welfare systems encourage sloth, or that the education and training system is failing them. Whatever the reason, this will have very serious social, political and economic ramifications moving forward, particularly as we head into the next downturn. For the long-term benefit of these nations, it would have been far more important to get the next generation into the workforce rather than create an underclass, which will ultimately undermine society. Unfortunately, economic, social and political foolishness seems to have prevented the necessary adjustments from taking place.

The GFC also triggered the European debt crisis when several eurozone member states (Greece, Portugal, Ireland, Spain and Cyprus), together with Iceland, were unable to repay or refinance government debt or bail out over-indebted banks. The specific causes of the debt crisis varied. In some countries, the crisis originated in the banking sector. In other instances, the problems were far more deep-seated and structural in nature.

The ECB responded to the crisis by providing liquidity to the financial system and providing backstop facilities to governments. As time progressed, the ECB also sought to stimulate growth and inflation by adopting a negative interest rate policy (NIRP) and implementing QE.

With interest rates already at very low levels, in 2014, the ECB lowered the interest rate on its deposit rate – the interest rate banks receive for funds parked overnight at the central bank – to -0.10 per cent. It was subsequently lowered to -0.20 per cent and -0.30 per cent, and then in March 2016 to -0.40 per cent, where it has remained.[465] In effect, banks were paying the ECB to keep their funds with the ECB.

In making the announcement, the ECB stated that not only would there be no direct impact on people's savings, but the ECB's interest rate decisions will benefit savers because they support growth and thus create demand. It also stated that a central bank's core business is making it more or less attractive for households and businesses to save or borrow, but this is not done in the spirit of punishment or reward.

Initially, the ECB restricted its purchases of bonds to sovereign nations. However, when this started to distort financial markets, the ECB extended its bond-buying program to corporate bonds. From March 2015 to March 2016, net purchases of public and private sector securities averaged €60 billion per month. This was subsequently increased to €80 billion per month when growth and inflation failed to respond to QE as hoped. By September 2017, ECB bond holdings totaled €2 trillion.[466]

Of course, the outcomes from QE and NIRP have been the exact opposite of what the ECB promised. NIRP and QE have not only failed to stimulate the economy, they have had unintended consequences. Firstly, despite statements to the contrary, their policies have actually punished savers as interest rates have remained at ultra-low levels for many years. Secondly, they have disrupted the normal functioning of financial markets, forcing people to chase higher-risk investments such as junk bonds, just to earn a modest return on investment. Insurance companies are particularly vulnerable because many companies have historically offered what now look like very high levels of guaranteed returns over very long periods. A 2014 study in Germany found that some insurers need to earn a yield of more than 5 per cent to meet guarantees to their policy holders. This is looking increasingly difficult when 10-year German government bonds yield less than one-quarter of 1 per cent.[467] ECB actions also supported the relentless run-up in debt, thus adding to financial instability rather than reducing it.

ECB actions have also not been without detractors. German economists and bankers have been particularly scathing of ECB policies, claiming that the stimulus is not just unnecessary but potentially damaging to the eurozone. The BIS has also been critical of ECB policies, particularly NIRP. They state that the policy could have serious consequences for the financial sector, claiming that the viability of banks' business models as financial intermediaries may be brought into question. They also note that some mortgage interest rates in Switzerland, which also runs a NIRP, have actually increased rather than fallen.

The EU also responded to the crisis by creating the European Financial Stability Facility (EFSF) and the European Financial Stabilisation Mechanism (EFSM). Each of these facilities was aimed at preserving financial stability in Europe by providing financial assistance to members suffering financial difficulty. The EFSF and the EFSM raised funds on the open markets with guarantees provided by euro members. The EFSF was authorised to borrow up to €440 billion and the EFSM up to €60 billion.

These were subsequently replaced by the European Stability Mechanism (ESM), which was established in September 2012 as a permanent firewall for the eurozone. Its aim is to safeguard and provide instant access to financial assistance programs for member states of the eurozone in financial difficulty. It has a maximum lending capacity of €500 billion.[468]

The European debt crisis is interesting for many reasons, but none more so than the way the crisis unfolded in Greece and Iceland. Their experiences highlight that there is definitely a right way and a wrong way to tackle a financial crisis should one arise. Unfortunately, current mainstream economic theory and practice is predicated on the wrong way.

Iceland did many things that mainstream economists suggest it shouldn't have done in handling the crisis. It let its old banks fail, leaving bond-holders, shareholders and even foreign depositors to wear the losses; it took control of financial institutions and made domestic deposits in the banks priority claims; it implemented austerity measures; it introduced capital controls; and it punished business leaders who had committed criminal acts in the lead-up to the crisis. But most importantly, it let its currency devalue – although, to be honest, it had no real say in this as foreigners were going to do this anyway. After a short sharp correction, the system had been cleansed of malinvestments, people had learnt the lesson of speculation, excessive debts and too large a financial system, and the economy was set on the path to growth.

The European debt crisis also revealed how important a nation's culture and ethical framework is in terms of economic outcomes, and also how its people react when they are confronted with adversity. In contrast to Iceland, Greece is a socialist welfare state, which has shown that it is not prepared to take the steps necessary to solve its problems. But it is not only Greece's fault. By admitting Greece and other peripheral nations into the eurozone, and then keeping them there, Germany, the IMF and the EU prevented the automatic economic stabilisers from kicking in. Had Greece been able to devalue her currency, her people would not necessarily have had to endure the suffering and deep psychological pain associated with the prolonged depression. This is not to say her people wouldn't have suffered, but the transition wouldn't have been prolonged for decades.

Moreover, the reality is that, despite the bailouts, debt write-downs and attempts at austerity, Greece's economy is still as structurally impaired now as it was at the beginning of the crisis, perhaps more so, because her government debt is still unsustainable. The best thing for the Greek people would be for her to default, leave the eurozone and go back onto the drachma. At least then, Greeks would be in control of their own destiny. The debt crisis also exposes the real motivations for Germany's bailout of Greece: motivations which were not at all driven by altruistic intentions towards the Greek people, but rather driven by blatant self-interest and the German government's desperate need to bail out German banks which were heavily exposed to European debt. Moreover, once the crisis had passed, German authorities were willingly prepared to throw the Greek people, and anybody else for that matter, to the proverbial wolves.

The debt crisis illustrates how people should be sceptical about comments made by those in authority or with a vested interest in specific outcomes. Throughout the GFC and its aftermath, there were numerous examples of people in very senior positions making statements which proved to be not only misleading but totally incorrect. The general assumption that people working within bureaucracies know what they are doing is also false. This conclusion comes after many years working with bureaucrats and politicians. This is not to say that people are nice or not nice. It has more to do with the stultifying nature of bureaucracies. Moreover, if things go wrong, expect obfuscation or a cover-up.

I have made some bold claims, so let's look at the evidence.

Turning our attention firstly to Greece. The simple fact is this: Greece should never have joined the eurozone, and should have exited at the first opportunity. She suffered from major structural weaknesses, and once she joined she lost all control over her currency, and therefore the ability for her economy to more easily adjust to economic shocks by allowing the currency to depreciate.

On one level, Greece's economic problems arose from an amazing degree of dishonesty, incompetence and mismanagement by Greek politicians and officials and the actions of militant trade unions. Its collapse highlighted all the problems associated with a socialist welfare state. On another level, however, Greece's problems arose through structural problems brought about by adopting the Euro as her currency.

Greece's economic nightmare was inevitable. What was not inevitable, however, was the collective punishment that the western powers, particularly Germany and the IMF, mercilessly inflicted on the Greek people to save European banks, particularly German banks, from contagion and bankruptcy, and to keep the eurozone and EU intact. According to the BIS, by December 2009, German banks had amassed claims of $704 billion on Greece, Ireland, Italy, Portugal and Spain, much more than the German banks' aggregate capital.[469] In other words, they had made some terrible banking decisions and lent more than they could afford.

While western nations have sanctimoniously criticised Greece for running up such large levels of debt, what they have been less forthright about is acknowledging the failure of not only the banks which lent with gay abandon, but also by the gross failure of regulatory authorities, especially the ECB, in allowing banks to run up such large debts to unreliable borrowers.

Greece is a highly corrupt nation. According to Transparency International's Corruption Perception Index, Greece scored 36/ 100, ranking it as the most corrupt country in the EU.[470] For years, Greek governments had bought votes by agreeing to overly generous pensions and benefits to civil servants and retirees. The statutory retirement age for men ranged from 45 to 65 years, with almost 75 per cent of Greek pensioners retiring before the age of 61. Estimates put spending on pensions at 17 per cent of the country's GDP. This was not only amongst the highest in the EU, but it also required very large state subsidies.[471]

Politicians also used civil services and other public-sector agencies to exchange political favours for votes and influence. Tertiary students were given free education, lodging and books. Greece was generous to those with large families, and there were inbuilt systems of local protectionism to guard against competition.[472] Elsewhere, the government favoured the business elites with tax-free status, while some state employees were paid salaries without actually having to turn up for work. This had major repercussions throughout the greater economy insofar that it undermined professionalism, integrity and morale for both public and private sector employees.

The pervasive influence of vested interests and the country's business and political elites also negatively impacted Greece's economy. In 2015, profits as a share of business income in Greece totalled 46 per cent, compared to Italy (42 per cent), France (41 per cent), Germany (39 per cent), the U.S. (35 per cent), and the UK (32 per cent). Insiders received subsidies and contracts, and outsiders found it hard to break in. According to the World Bank, Greece is one of the hardest places in Europe to start a business. The result is that competition for market share is weak and there are few firms with new ideas.[473]

Tax evasion rivalled drinking ouzo and retsina, eating, dancing and smashing plates as the premier national pastime for the Greek people. Estimates suggest that the government collected less than half of the revenues due in 2012.[474] Data for 2012 indicated that the Greek 'black economy' or 'underground economy', from which little or no tax was collected, represented a full 24 per cent of GDP.[475] In 2015, estimates put the amount of evaded taxes stored in Swiss banks at around €80 billion.[476]

Militant trade unions also fought hard to prevent the government from reining in benefits, mobilising workers, staging rallies and mounting significant political pressure to stop any reforms. In the end, however, their actions proved counterproductive as they helped saddle the nation with debt and contributed to making the economy uncompetitive. This is a classic example of how vested interests use their power at the expense of others in society, only to see these benefits destroyed when market forces work their magic to restore equilibrium.

Greece also falsified key economic data to gain entry to the eurozone. Member states were required to meet strict criteria prior to joining which included keeping the budget deficit below 3 per cent of GDP, having a government debt ratio below 60 per cent of GDP, maintaining low inflation, and having interest rates close to the EU average. The Greek government, however, employed the services of leading Wall Street investment bank Goldman Sachs to hide its debts. This was achieved through cross currency swaps, where billions worth of Greek debts and loans were converted into yen and dollars at a fictitious exchange rate, thus hiding the true extent of Greek loans.[477]

Greece also suffered from problems associated with unreliable government data. Previously published data was continually revised, making it impossible to predict GDP growth, deficits and debt. The extent of the data problems became evident during the 2010 bailout, when the government forecast of debt increased substantially following the GFC. For example, the government forecast public debt to hit 120 per cent of GDP during 2010.[478] The actual figure, after the debt crisis, the 2010 bailout, and the GDP contraction, ended up being closer to 150 per cent.[479]

Greece's economy was uncompetitive from the time she entered the eurozone. While Greece has great natural beauty and a revered history, much of the country is mountainous, and only about 30 per cent of land can be cultivated. Her labour productivity (per person employed) ranks in the bottom three in western Europe, more than 25 per cent below the average. These problems were exacerbated as unit labour costs in peripheral countries in western Europe, such as Greece, increased at a faster rate than labour costs in the core countries such as Germany, further eroding Greece's competitiveness.[480]

Another contributing factor to the debt crisis was the failure by financial markets to properly price Greek debt. After joining the eurozone, interest rates on Greek and German government debt were essentially the same for the next seven years. The fact the euro was Greece's currency never meant Greece was as good a financial risk as Germany. Yet once the Greek government could borrow as cheaply as the German government, it did so while spending with gay abandon.[481]

Between 1999 and 2008-09, excessive spending increased both the Greek budget and trade deficits from below 5 per cent to 15 per cent of GDP.[482] These deficits were funded directly by debt. Between 1980, when Greece joined the EEC, and 2007, the government debt-to-GDP ratio grew five-fold from a modest 21 per cent to 103 per cent.[483]

The Greek debt crisis started in 2009 and was triggered by the GFC and revelations that previous data on government debt and deficits had been understated by the Greek government.[484] This led to a crisis of confidence which saw interest rates on 10-year government bonds soar to 30 per cent in 2012.[485] This prompted the ECB, the Eurogroup and the IMF (the Troika) to bail out the Greek government.

The first bailout occurred in 2010 when the IMF and eurozone countries agreed to lend Greece €110 billion over three years in return for Greece implementing a series of draconian austerity measures.[486] Credit rating agencies immediately downgraded Greek government bonds to junk status, while the Greek people responded with anger by mounting protests, riots and national strikes.

The austerity program consisted of tax increases, spending cuts, government reforms and the sale of government-owned assets. According to the program, Greece had to undertake a fiscal adjustment of more than nine points of GDP between 2010 and 2012[487], 'a record fiscal consolidation by OECD‡ standards'.[488] Between 2009 and 2014, the actual change (improvement) in structural primary balance was 16.1 points of GDP for Greece, compared to 8.5 for Portugal, 7.3 for Spain, 7.2 for Ireland, and 5.6 for Cyprus.[489]

Such a rapid fiscal adjustment, combined with the inability of Greece to depreciate her currency had a catastrophic impact on the Greek economy, including a major decline in GDP and a blowout in government debt. Incredibly, the impact of such a large fiscal adjustment on the Greek economy had been underestimated by the IMF, apparently due to a calculation error.[490] Indeed, this calculation error and

‡ Organisation for Economic Co-operation and Development

the associated austerity measures magnified the debt problem by severely depressing GDP and thus making the debt unsustainable. With Greece's economy languishing in depression, in 2011 the Troika agreed to a second bailout package. This included additional loans as well as a settlement with banks, which reluctantly agreed to write-off 50 per cent of Greek debt.[491]

Come 2015, and with the economy still flailing, European and Greek officials began negotiations for a third bailout package. Not surprisingly, anger at the ongoing depression and austerity measures created a political firestorm in Greece, which forced the government to take the issue to the people. In July 2015, a large majority voted to reject the bailout terms, causing global stock indexes to tumble, a run on Greek banks and the imposition of capital controls limiting the amount of money people could withdraw from banks.

Despite the overwhelming vote against further austerity measures, the Greek parliament agreed to a slightly modified third bailout package. In return for further bailout funds, Greece agreed to increase taxes, implement tighter controls over the collection of VAT, and reduce spending further. Unfortunately, Greece never had a genuine commitment to economic reform, so her economy remains uncompetitive.

The debt crisis had devastating impacts on Greece's economy and her people. Between 2008 and 2013, economic activity fell by more than 25 per cent, unemployment soared to 25 per cent, and GDP per capita fell by 24 per cent.[492] By February 2012, it was reported that 20,000 Greeks had been made homeless during the preceding year, and that 20 per cent of shops in the historic city centre of Athens were empty.[493] By 2015, the OECD reported that nearly 20 per cent of Greek people lacked funds to meet daily food expenses.[494]

The massive increase in taxes had the opposite effect of what was intended, decreasing rather than increasing revenue. Those who could avoid tax, did so, sometimes by relocating their operations overseas. Those that couldn't, suffered. Tax debts in Greece totalled 90 per cent of annual tax revenue, the worst figure in all industrialised nations.[495]

The re-adjustment process fell disproportionately onto the less well-off in society. By 2014, an estimated 44 per cent of Greeks were living below the poverty line.[496] One researcher found that the poorest households faced tax increases of 337 per cent,[497] far above the tax increases incurred by the wealthy.

When the IMF initiated the first Greece bailout, the then IMF chief Dominique Strauss-Kahn said that Greek people should not fear that IMF intervention would worsen Greek's economic crisis. Rather, he said, the IMF was there to help, and that the Greek people should think of the IMF as a 'co-operative organisation' where the countries of the world work together to help those in trouble by providing resources and advice on behalf of the international community.[498]

Sadly, he totally misled the Greek people and once again proved that one should never trust politicians, or those international bodies run by the elite, for the elite. What the Greek government should have done was default, return to the drachma and allow the Greek currency to devalue. While causing distress in the short term, it would have given Greeks control of their own economy and their own destiny, rather than giving control to Germany and European bureaucrats.

The devastating fall in economic activity worsened the debt crisis, sending the ratio of government debt to GDP soaring from 120 per cent to 180 per cent,[499] and forcing the government to default on a $1.7 billion IMF payment in 2015. The deterioration in debt also forced the IMF to reluctantly admit in July 2015 that the 'debt dynamics' of Greece were unsustainable due to its already high debt level and policy actions taken since the crisis began.[500]

In other words, the IMF admitted that the draconian austerity measures that the Troika had imposed on Greece had made the situation far worse for the Greek people than it might have otherwise been. Moreover, the IMF's actions highlighted the gross incompetence and ethically questionable behaviour of those working within the bureaucratic behemoth.

In a damning critique of the IMF's bailouts of Greece, Portugal and Ireland, a study by the IMF's own Independent Evaluation Office, which answers solely to the board of executive directors, found that the IMF's top staff misled their own board in making a series of calamitous misjudgments on Greece which failed to grasp an elemental concept of currency theory. They became euphoric cheerleaders for the euro project, all the time ignoring warning signs of impending crisis.[501] In an astonishing admission, the report also said its own investigators were unable to obtain key records such as who made decisions or what information was available or penetrate the activities of secretive 'ad-hoc task forces'.

The report said the whole approach to the eurozone was characterised by 'groupthink' and intellectual capture. They had no fallback plans on how to tackle a systemic crisis in the eurozone – or how to deal with the politics of a multinational currency union – because they had ruled out any possibility that it could happen.

The IMF also persistently played down the risks posed by ballooning current account deficits and the flood of capital pouring into the eurozone periphery and neglected the danger of a 'sudden stop' in capital flows. The report noted that at its core, the IMF displayed a failure to grasp the elemental point that currency unions with no treasury or political union to back them up are inherently vulnerable to debt crises. States facing such a shock no longer have sovereign tools to defend themselves. Devaluation risk is switched to bankruptcy risk. Not surprisingly, non-European members of the IMF were also highly critical of the European-centric nature of the IMF.

If ordinary Greek (and Portuguese, Spanish and Italian) people were the main losers from the debt crisis, who were the winners? The answer is simple: the European banks; the core countries, especially Germany; and European bureaucrats.

As part of the bailout efforts, Greek debt was shifted from the European banks directly to the Troika, and indirectly to European taxpayers. The figures are staggering. Figure 18 shows the movement in external Greek debt – owed mostly to private banks and bondholders – between 2009 and 2014. This highlights that between 2009 and 2014, Greek debt owed to French, German, Dutch, Portuguese and Italian banks and other private lenders fell from €140 billion to around €36 billion. French banks were particularly aggressive in offloading Greek debt.

Figure 18 Banks Bail on Greek Debt

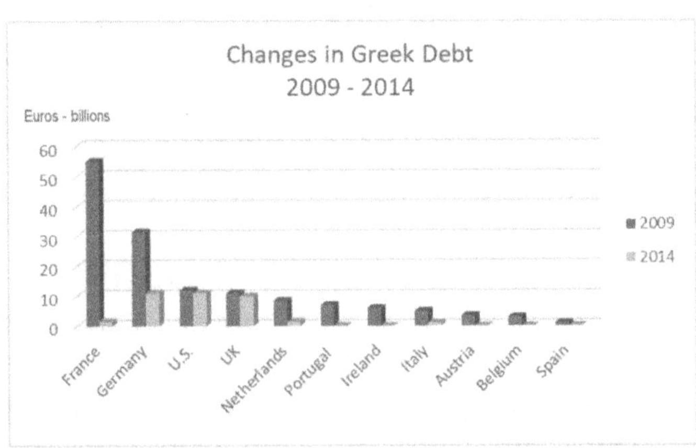

Data Source: David Stockman[502]

Figure 19 shows government exposure to Greek debt in early 2015. The largest individual contributors to the bailout funds were Germany, France, Italy and Spain, with roughly €260 billion of the €320 billion debt.[503] The IMF was owed €32 billion and the ECB €20 billion. Foreign banks had little Greek debt.[504]

Figure 19 Government Exposure to Greek Debt 2015

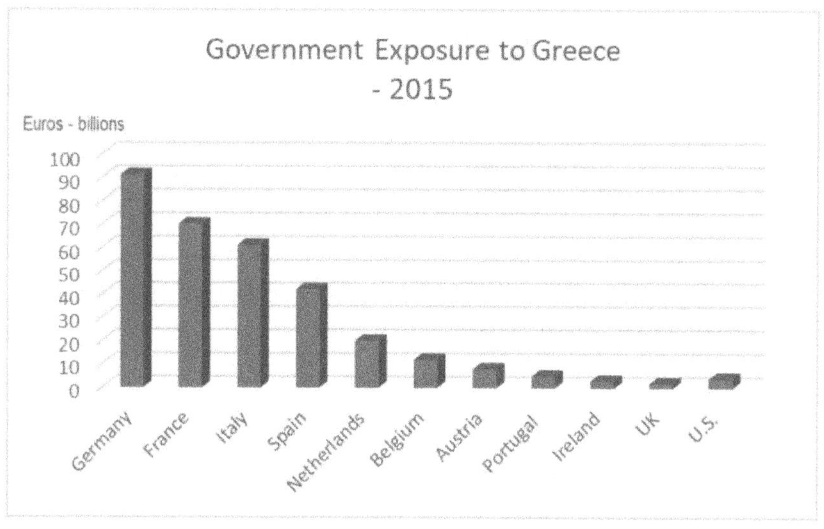

Data Source: David Stockman[505]

Actions by the Troika to bailout European banks by transferring debt from banks to taxpayers was not only scandalous, but undemocratic. When I studied economics, I never undertook a course called 'Bailout 101'. What I did study, however, was creative destruction, which is a fundamental feature of capitalism. Why should banks, with their highly paid executives, not be subject to the laws of economics? Either they are too important to the economy to fail, in which they should be either be nationalised, broken up or highly regulated, or they should be allowed to fail, with all the attendant consequences.

The more extraordinary problem is that France, Spain and Italy are economic cot-cases. All three countries suffer from high debt, high unemployment, bloated bureaucracies and antiquated labour laws. Should Greece default, the chances of these countries being able to carry such losses is unlikely. Importantly, the money the IMF loaned Greece was also in gross violation of its own credit standards and long-standing rules. Conveniently, European countries controlled about one-third of the fund's voting rights.[506]

Despite's Europe's power, the fact is that all IMF members, including economic powerhouses such as Peru, Costa Rica and Senegal, might need to cover the losses if Greece defaults. Can you imagine the political uproar if Greece defaulted on its debts? Of course, Germany would never allow this to happen as her international reputation would be trashed, but it would be fun to watch.

The debt crisis also highlighted the gross ineptitude of regulatory bodies, which allowed European banks to incur such high levels of debt. In hindsight, this should not be surprising given the nature of bureaucracies. It is, of course, a quaint irony that France hasn't run a budget surplus for over 40 years, and yet a former French Finance Minister is currently head of the IMF.

Germany has been the major beneficiary of the EU and eurozone. Between 2000 and 2015, Germany's current account swung from a deficit of 1.7 per cent of GDP to a surplus of 8.6 per cent.[507] Put another way, Germany's trade surplus in 2016 was $300 billion, the world's largest. There were several reasons for this massive surplus, including a decades-long accord between companies and unions which allowed companies to invest without unions holding companies to ransom. Germany exercised wage restraint to keep export industries competitive and was assisted by a stable political system, moderate consumption and strong savings. Its cohesive society also demonstrated a strong work ethic. However, Germany's surpluses have also come at the expense of countries like Italy, Greece and Spain, which have run persistent deficits – factors which eventually led to the crisis.[508]

Without a common currency, such persistent imbalances would typically self-adjust by allowing Germany's currency to appreciate and the currencies of those countries with chronic deficits to depreciate. Importantly, such adjustments would occur over time, rather than having the need for the inevitable crisis. It is no wonder, then, that Germany and the IMF argued so strongly for the euro and why, immediately following the GFC, they fought so stridently to keep Greece in the eurozone. Greece's exit could well have triggered a stampede for the exits by countries such as Italy, Spain and Portugal, thus threatening Germany's trade surplus.

Interestingly, leading European officials have recently changed their attitude towards Greece staying in the eurozone. Prior to shifting the debt from European banks onto European and global taxpayers, keeping Greece and other peripheral nations in the eurozone was critical to core Europe's own survival. With the risk now mitigated, the Greek people have become dispensable.

In late 2014, Michael Fuchs, a senior member of German Chancellor Angela Merkel's party said: 'The times where we had to rescue Greece are over. There is no potential for political blackmail anymore. Greece is no longer of systemic importance for the euro.' Other German commentators suggested that unless the country can leave the eurozone and restore competitiveness through currency devaluation, further cuts in debt will be required.[509]

In other words, the bailout was never about Greece. It was always about protecting German interests. Moreover, these statements are explicit acknowledgement of the failure of the eurozone experiment by including peripheral nations like Greece, Spain, Portugal and even Italy in the common currency. Using terms like 'there is no potential for political blackmail anymore' is clearly designed to cast blame onto the Greek people. Yes, the Greek people are their own worst enemies. But surely prudent bankers should have known this and taken such matters into consideration. Moreover, such a statement obfuscates the structural problems within the EU and eurozone as well as the role poor financial oversight and banking played in the run up to the crisis. It also hides Germany's real reason for supporting the Greek bailout – to protect German banks. Sadly, the ECB and governments have learnt little from the GFC as the world hurtles lemming-like into the next financial crisis.

If the Greek crisis was an example of how not to handle a financial crisis – other than if you are a German government trying to protect your own banks – Iceland provides an excellent example of how to properly handle a financial crisis.

The Icelandic financial crisis was a major economic and political event that was caused by the failure of the three largest privately owned banks in Iceland. It resulted in an economic recession (2008–2010) where the economy contracted 8 per cent and employment fell by 6 per cent,[510] and accompanied by a surge in social and political unrest. Relative to the size of its economy, Iceland's banking collapse was the largest experienced by any country in economic history.[511]

The cause of the Icelandic financial crisis is fairly straightforward. After Iceland deregulated its banks in 2001, Iceland 'went from being an Artic backwater that specialised in fishing and aluminum smelting to an Artic backwater that specialised in global finance'.[512] Iceland's three biggest banks grew to ten times the size of the economy by offering foreigners, particularly British and Dutch citizens, higher interest rates than they could get at home. They then used this money to go on an overseas spending spree, paying over the top for foreign real estate and companies, even soccer teams. Of course, the warning signs of Iceland's impending doom were clear well before the collapse, but only if you were prepared to ignore the hyper-optimism that drives booms, and look at the facts, which was that Iceland's banking model was broken.

Coming from a small domestic market, Iceland's banks financed their expansion with loans on the interbank lending market, in particular short-term loans, and deposits from foreigners. As they were about to find out, using short-term financing for long-term loans is never a good practice. Households also took on large amounts of debt, equivalent to 213 per cent of disposable income, which fuelled inflation.[513] Inflation was exacerbated by actions of the Central Bank of Iceland (CBI), which effectively printed money on demand.

With inflation running at 14 per cent per annum,[514] the CBI held interest rates at 15.5 per cent.[515] However, with interest rates in the UK at 5.5 per cent, and just 4 per cent in the eurozone, this encouraged overseas investors to hold deposits in Icelandic króna. This not only led to the overvaluation of the króna, but also led to a massive increase in the domestic money supply. In the 12 months to September 2008, the Icelandic money supply (M3) grew 56.5 per cent, compared with GDP growth of 5 per cent.[516] By the second quarter of 2007, Iceland's external debt stood at seven times GDP.[517] Iceland was effectively sitting on a financial volcano. All it needed was for the right conditions to trigger the eruption.

Throughout 2008, Icelandic banks found it increasingly difficult to roll over debt. With confidence in Iceland's financial system waning, between January to September 2008, the Icelandic króna fell by 35 per cent against the euro.[518] As rumours of growing problems with her banks started to swell, depositors began withdrawing their savings from foreign subsidiaries of the major Icelandic banks. Then, in early October 2008, private interbank credit facilities to Icelandic banks were shut down. With her major banks failing, Iceland was on the brink of collapse. The size of the problem put it beyond the capacity of the CBI to act as lender of last resort, and the government was forced to act. However, because the combined size of banks had grown so large, the government didn't have the means to save the banks.

As a result, they were forced to place the banks into receivership, resulting in losses for their shareholders and foreign creditors. To avoid a credit crunch, the failed banks were then restructured into a new and an old bank. The new state-owned banks took over the domestic activities and were recapitalised by government with a capital ratio of 16 per cent of all assets. The international businesses remained with the old banks for winding up.[519] The rescue operations of the central bank, along with the restructuring and recapitalisation of the banks, increased the public debt ratio by about 20 percentage points of GDP.

To stabilise the financial system, the government enacted a range of other measures. These included declaring that all 'domestic deposits' in Icelandic banks would be guaranteed, imposing strict capital controls – restrictions to control movements of capital to and from Iceland – to stabilise the value of the Icelandic króna, and securing a US$5.1 billion sovereign debt package from the IMF and Nordic countries to fund the budget deficit and restoration of the banking system. The international bailout support program led by IMF officially ended in 2011, while capital controls were lifted in 2017.[520]

Outside Iceland, nearly 350,000 retail depositors in the UK and Netherlands that held accounts in the 'Icesave' branch of *Landsbanki*, one of the big three Icelandic banks, lost a total of €6.7 billion of savings. Depositors' funds were eventually made good by the British and Dutch governments.[521]

A statement by a senior member of the CBI that the government did not intend to 'pay the debts of the banks that have been a little heedless', and that foreign creditors would 'unfortunately only get 5–15 per cent of their claims',[522] led to a diplomatic stoush between Iceland and its allies, particularly Britain.

The UK government responded to the loss of depositors' savings by using provisions of Britain's anti-terrorism legislation to freeze Icelandic assets in the UK. It also announced that the UK government would foot the bill to compensate fully the funds held by the estimated 300,000 UK depositors, and that it would launch legal action against Iceland to recover the money.[523]

The British, Dutch and Icelandic governments sought to reach agreement on reimbursing depositors, but these agreements were twice rejected by the Icelandic people in two referendums. The matter was subsequently referred to the Court of Justice of the European Free Trade Association States (EFTA Court), but in a shock decision – at least to the Brits – in 2013 the court cleared Iceland of all charges, meaning that Iceland was freed from the disputed obligation for deposit guarantees worth €4 billion, plus accrued interest to UK and the Netherlands.[524]

The Icelandic stock market fell by more than 90 per cent during the crisis, weighed down by the collapse of the three major banks, which together represented 73 per cent of the value of the stock market index. The value of other equities varied from +8 per cent to -15 per cent.[525]

In the aftermath of the crisis, the government, working with the IMF, took steps to ward off future crises by strengthening regulatory oversight of banks and curbing foreign currency loans. The authorities also sought to tamp down the oversize presence of banks in the economy by encouraging growth in tourism, fisheries, tech start-ups and renewable energy.[526] In late 2008, the government also established a Special Prosecutor's Office to investigate suspected criminal conduct leading up to, in connection with and in the wake of the banking crisis. While some former business leaders were acquitted, many were found guilty and sentenced to jail for a range of crimes including insider trading, market manipulation, tax non-compliance, major breach of trust and fraud.[527]

By 2011, the Icelandic economy had turned the corner. With the cheap króna, tourism had exploded and become Iceland's biggest industry, overtaking fishing and banking. With the number of visitors approaching 2 million a year, tourism revenue topped $3 billion in 2015, a third of the country's export earnings. Tourism is also the single biggest employer, accounting for a tenth of all jobs.[528]

Importantly, by letting the banks fail rather than take on their debts, the Icelandic government was not left with a crippling debt overhang, as other countries had been. After climbing between 2007 and 2011 from a modest 41 per cent to a high of 113 per cent, the government debt to GDP ratio has continued to fall to 87 per cent in 2015.[529]

Moreover, between 2011 and 2016 economic growth averaged 3 per cent per annum, the unemployment rate fell to a near-record low of 2.6 per cent, while workers enjoyed double-digit wage increases.[530]

So ends the tale of two countries – Greece and Iceland.

Part 4

The Great Depression of the 2020s

Chapter 12

The World Economy at a Tipping Point

'Today, there are three kinds of people: the have's, the have-not's, and the have-not-paid-for-what-they-have's.'
Earl Wilson

Throughout this book, I have established unambiguously the historical link between financial crises and runaway inflation, reckless banking and debt-fuelled asset booms. Without exception, these debt-fuelled asset booms have ended with immense human pain and suffering as financial markets and the economy implode as they seek to rid themselves of malinvestments, imbalances and excessive debt.

All of which raises a fundamental question. With all their resources and the plethora of economic PhDs at their disposal, how could the mainstream economics 'profession' and central banks not only fail to understand the lessons of history, but implement policies which have created the pre-conditions for the forthcoming Great Depression of the 2020s?

Is it because of mainstream economists are not particularly smart and have little real-world experience? Are leading economic thinkers arrogant in the extreme, and actually believe that they have tamed the business cycle and can deliver economic nirvana? Do they really believe debt and deficits don't matter and can continue to grow forever without any adverse consequences? Do they have such faith that in an age of fractional reserve banking and fiat currencies, central banks can continue to bail out reckless governments and banks? Is it because of groupthink? Is it because mainstream economists don't know the difference between finance and economics, or because they confuse economics with other disciplines? Is it because mainstream economists and central banks are captives of the elite? Or is it all of the above?

This chapter will examine key factors that have brought the global economy to the cusp of a disaster equal to, if not greater than the Great Depression, together with factors that will impact the global economy throughout the 21st century. These factors include increased debt levels, extremes in asset markets – property, equities and bonds – population, demographics and the accompanying pension timebomb, and complacency.

*

After the GFC, it was widely expected that the world's economies would deleverage. Instead, debt has increased to unprecedented levels, leaving the world's financial system teetering on the brink of disaster. According to McKinsey & Company, between 2007 and 2014 global debt increased by $57 trillion, or 41 per cent, to $199 trillion, greatly outstripping growth in GDP. As a result, the total debt to GDP ratio increased from 269 per cent to a record 286 per cent.[531]

Figure 20 Global Total Debt by Type

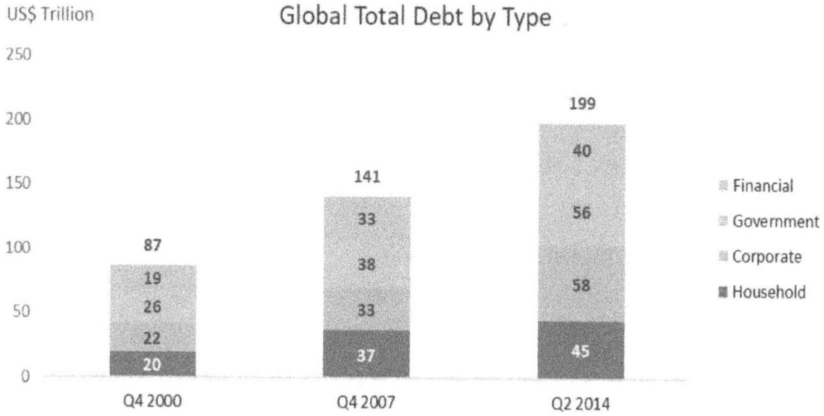

Data Source: McKinsey Global Institute

Much of this increase occurred in the government sector under the weight of massive fiscal stimulus. By mid-2014, nine countries had total debt to GDP ratios above 300 per cent: Japan, Ireland, Singapore, Spain, Greece, Belgium, Portugal, Denmark and the Netherlands, while another 13 more had debt ratios above 200 per cent.[532] Since then, the race to financial Armageddon has continued unabated. By mid-2017, global debt had risen to a further record of $233 trillion, putting the global debt to GDP ratio at around 318 per cent.[533]

Increasing debt levels raise some key questions moving forward. Firstly, how much higher can debt levels go before they become unsustainable and implode? Can they ever be repaid without far higher inflation? Will modern politics ever allow countries to enact policies to cut government spending and reduce debt? What impact will falling debt levels have on future economic growth, and will we need another financial collapse and massive defaults to do the job for us?

The answers to these questions depend on the type of debt, who owes the debt and the strength of the underlying economy.

An economy's ability to reduce debt depends on a range of factors including population, economic growth, budget deficits, interest rates, inflation, the structure of the economy, exchange rates and last but certainly not least, the political leadership required to make the tough economic decisions.

Unfortunately, with an economy addicted to ever-increasing levels of debt, the prognosis to stop debt rising further, let alone pay down debt, is not good. In fact, it is very bad. The rate of real economic growth has been falling for decades, interest rates have bottomed and are moving up, budget deficits are going in the wrong direction, we have an ageing population in the west and we have a dearth of real political leadership.

Central banks have been desperately trying to kickstart consumer price inflation and economic growth to pay down the debt their policies created. Unfortunately, they are only now finding out that their misguided policies not only don't work, but they can never control economic outcomes. Western economies are now stuck in the grip of a low-growth, low-inflation environment, which will soon be overwhelmed by an avalanche of deflation.

Governments have also been continuing to run large budget deficits. There are several reasons for this. Firstly, they have taken the advice of Keynesian economists, whose mantra seems to be that to spend beyond your means is to deliver prosperity. Secondly, politicians lack the moral fortitude of our forebears to lead and argue the case on how to live within your means and deliver prosperity. Politicians, supported by a compliant media, have also hidden behind the façade of mainstream economic theory and runaway asset prices to cover up their own inadequacies which tend towards placating the general public, a group who have been raised on an ever-increasing diet of public welfare and consumerism, and who are now unable, or unprepared, to live within their means and to go without.

Growth in government debt has also made a mockery of the conflicting advice given by economists on how to handle a debt crisis. In the aftermath of the GFC, mainstream economists encouraged G20 governments to undertake fiscal stimulus to kickstart their economies. In contrast, the IMF requires highly indebted nations to implement austerity measures to reduce debt. So, what is it: stimulus or austerity? While one could legitimately argue that it depends, it seems to be stimulus and bailouts if you are a major power, but austerity if you are a small nation that owes money to western banks. Moreover, surely it is more prudent to prevent debt levels from reaching unsustainable levels before being forced to take draconian measures to reduce debt.

The debt growth also makes a mockery of claims by socialist leaders in the west that austerity has been harmful to their constituents. For example, after the 2017 UK election Bloomberg ran this headline: '*U.K. Labour Party Leader Jeremy Corbyn said that politics has changed, and that people have had enough of austerity.*' This is an amazing and grossly irresponsible statement given the increase in debt. In most instances, austerity never began! However, it does highlight the extraordinary lack of insight by political leaders into how economies function and how wealth is created.

The simple fact is this: industry creates wealth while governments destroy wealth and redistribute other people's money. Since the GFC, the ratio of household debt to income has declined significantly in only five countries – the U.S., the UK, Ireland, Spain and Germany. In other countries, the ratio of household debt to income is higher than in the U.S. and the UK at the peak of the credit bubble.

In Australia, for example, household debt as a proportion of disposable income reached 194 per cent in 2017, compared to 70 per cent in 1990.[534] Moreover, between 2004 and 2016, growth in Australian household debt far exceeded growth in income and assets, with average household debt increasing by 83 per cent in real terms, compared to a 49 per cent increase in asset prices and a 38 per cent increase in gross income.[535]

The Australian position, however, is even more precarious than these figures suggest. According to the RBA, around 30 per cent of all mortgage debt will be subject to reset from interest-only loans to principal and interest loans over the next four years. This will push up monthly repayments by as much as 40 per cent, putting house prices and already stretched households under enormous pressure.[536]

The poor state of many of Europe's banks poses another risk to the stability of the financial system, especially as many of them hold significant amounts of sovereign debt on their books. As we know from the GFC, this creates a potentially dangerous solvency problem in times of economic crisis as debt problems are transmitted from the government to the banks and back again, creating a potentially self-re-enforcing death spiral.[537]

The risk for bank solvency is exacerbated by the size of non-performing loans (NPLs) in some European countries. For example, as at December 2016, the ratio of NPLs to GDP stood at 40 per cent for Cyprus and Greece, 20 per cent for Slovenia and 15 per cent for Italy and Slovenia. Any future financial crisis would quickly put Europe's banking system at risk.

*

Central bank stimulus measures since the GFC have greatly increased financial risks by encouraging risky lending, elevating asset prices and by forcing people into increasingly risky investments to chase yield.

Figure 12 showed that U.S. house prices are at their highest level in over 40 years and are now higher than prior to the GFC. The same is true for equities. Figure 21 shows the total value of all listed shares on global stock markets as a percentage of global GDP between 1975 and 2015. The index has now surpassed the peaks prior to the GFC and the 1987 stock market crash, highlighting the impact that financialisation of the global economy has had on stock prices.[538]

Figure 21 Stock Market Capitalisation to Global GDP 1975–2015

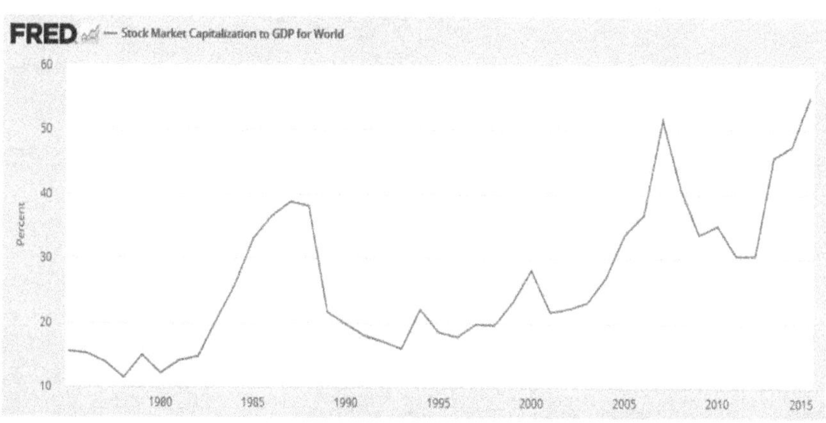

Source: Federal Reserve Bank of St Louis

Figure 22 (over page) shows the Shiller CAPE Price Earnings (PE) Ratio from 1881 to 2017.[539] PE ratios are one of the most widely used measures to assess whether a stock, or the stock market, is under or overvalued. It compares the latest reported earnings and current market prices. Robert Shiller's CAPE PE ratio is based on average inflation-adjusted

Figure 22 Shiller CAPE PE Ratio 1881-2017

Source: http://www.multpl.com/

earnings from the previous 10 years. Figure 22 highlights that the current U.S. S&P 500 index is at extreme levels, above the level of the stock market before the 1929 and 1987 stock market crashes, and only second to the peak reached during the dot-com mania. All prior periods of excessive values ended in either depression, crisis or recession.

Not surprisingly, the record-breaking run-up in U.S. stocks has been associated with a huge increase in margin debt, which ballooned to an all-time high of $666 billion in January 2018. Importantly, post GFC, the growth in margin debt has far outpaced the growth in the stock indexes, significantly increasing the risk of loss should the market turn down.[540] Central banks' low interest rate and QE policies have also forced investors such as pension funds into high-risk investments just to earn modest rates of return.

Only recently have institutions begun to question the wisdom of these policies. In a statement that could well be in the running for the 2017 Captain Obvious Award, in October 2017 the IMF warned that the increasing use of exotic financial products tied to equity volatility by investors such as pension funds is creating unknown risks that could result in a severe shock to financial markets.[541] Wasn't the use of exotic financial products one of the primary causes of the GFC? If so, why haven't they been banned rather than allowed to flourish? And why hasn't the IMF worked with governments to reduce the considerable risks posed by the huge amount of outstanding derivatives?

The IMF also opined that the combination of low volatility and low interest rates had facilitated the use of leverage to increase returns, and that a sustained increase in volatility could trigger a sell-off in the assets underlying these products, amplifying the shock to markets.

I have four responses for Captain Obvious. Firstly, it was central bank policy to keep interest rates at low levels for sustained periods to jumpstart the economy, policies that were supported by the IMF. It failed! Secondly, surely central banks and governments, with their army of PhDs, would have thought through the ramifications of their policies, including unintended consequences, before embarking on the greatest financial experiment in history. No credible organisation would embark on such policies without working through the escape plan. It seems obvious that policy-makers were so convinced that low interest rates and money printing would work, that they didn't even consider how they would exit QE and ultra-low interest rates. What folly, what stupidity, what arrogance!

Thirdly, increased risk-taking by investors has been obvious for the past 25 years. Ultra-low volatility is a relatively recent phenomenon and suggests that markets are approaching a peak. Finally, why has it been only recently that the IMF has started to voice concerns? Perhaps, because as a bureaucracy, they are now trying to protect any semblance of a shattered reputation that they may have. It won't work. Incompetence has been exposed for all to see.

*

The prospect of unwinding the greatest monetary experiment in history that is QE, NIRP and ZIRP has many senior executives and policy-makers deeply concerned. In 2017, Jamie Dimon, Chairman of JPMorgan Chase & Co. suggested that the unwinding of central bank bond-buying programs is an unprecedented challenge that may be more disruptive than people think.

Dimon said: 'We've never had QE like this before, we've never had unwinding [of the Fed's balance sheet] like this before. Obviously, that should say something to you about the risk that might mean, because we've never lived with it before.' And this: 'We act like we know exactly how it's going to happen and we don't.'[542]

This is damning stuff. Dimon is the consummate insider, a person whose company has benefited significantly from the Fed's largesse. Surely, his connections at the Fed should have thought through the ramifications of such an experiment. That such an insider would publicly countenance that the Fed doesn't know what is going to happen is an absolute indictment of Fed competence.

Central banks are also clearly worried, if not petrified, by what they have done and how they unwind this experiment. Tentative steps by the Fed to wind back QE resulted in a market temper tantrum in 2016. Equally, the European market has become so dependent on massive QE stimulus that Mario Draghi has found it difficult even to announce the end of the ECB's bond-buying program for fear of a market implosion.

As we know, 10-year U.S. Treasury Bonds peaked in October 1981 before a 30-year bull market saw the yield bottom at 1.4 per cent in July 2016. Since then, the yield on 10-year bonds has more than doubled to 2.9 per cent, and any breakout above 3.2 per cent would suggest that the bull market in bonds is over and a bear market is underway. A bear market in interest rates would be catastrophic for the highly indebted global economy.

Any increase in interest rates would send governments and consumers into cardiac arrest as the cost of additional interest payments skyrocket. For example, with U.S. federal government debt currently standing at around $20 trillion and rising quickly, a modest increase in interest rates of 2 per cent would increase the government's interest repayments by $400 billion per annum. Just the increase in debt repayments alone would amount to 10 per cent of the U.S. federal government expenditure. This would not only place intense pressure on existing budget deficits but make it impossible for governments to handle any deterioration in budgets in the face of a recession.

The burden of increased debt repayments would also drain money away from the real economy, putting pressure on highly leveraged governments, corporations and households, while slowing economic growth. For example, with total global debt sitting at around $230 trillion, an increase in interest rates of just 1 per cent would increase interest payments by $2.3 trillion per annum. It would also put significant downward pressure on asset values and prices in general, leading to a vicious downward spiral as bankruptcies soar and banks tighten lending as they seek to minimise risk and protect their balance sheets.

Finally, bond holders would suffer massive capital losses as interest rates rise. This is because bond yields move inversely to bond prices. This would be especially problematical for organisations such as insurance companies, mutual and pension funds that are typically large holders of bonds. A bear market in bonds would likely turn into a stampede as bond holders race for the exits to avoid further capital losses. Under such a scenario, interest rates would likely rise far quicker and far higher than anybody currently thinks possible.

*

Right now, millions of people are at work believing they can retire and that their pensions will be secure. Little do they know that a crisis in pension funds is looming, and it is unlikely pension funds will be able to meet their obligations. The pensions timebomb has arisen because pension obligations have risen far faster than the resources set aside to fund them. And shifting demographics, insufficient contributions and increasingly lower returns are only making the funding shortfall worse.

A 2017 report by the Hoover Institution found that as of 2015, unfunded liabilities of U.S. state and local government pensions total $3.85 trillion. However, only $1.38 trillion, or less than half that amount, is recognised by state and local governments. The rest is 'hidden debt'.[543]

The report also noted that while state and local governments claimed they ran balanced budgets, in 2015 the shortfall in funding pensions was $167 billion. This deficit equals 18.2 per cent of all state and local government revenue, suggesting that state and local government budgets are far from balanced when pension costs are included. It also found that of 649 U.S. pension systems, average investment returns were only 2.87 per cent, compared to an average discount rate of 7.36 per cent – that is, the rate of return needed to fund obligations. And the problem is only going to get worse as most state and local governments continue to understate their pension costs and liabilities, using the assumption that their assets will achieve annual returns of 7 to 8 per cent, while ignoring the enormous risks that pension funds have taken in this low interest rate environment to boost returns.

The problem is not isolated to government pensions. A study by Wells Fargo Securities in 2016 found that big American corporate pension schemes are facing their worst deficit in 15 years, with enough money to cover just 76 per cent of the estimated $2.1 trillion in liabilities. Despite pouring almost $500 billion into their funds since 2009, the deficit in 2016 was estimated to be around $500 billion.[544]

The future of these corporate schemes is made worse because they've been piling into longer-term bonds to avoid the volatile swings of stocks. Between 2008 and 2016, bond allocations have increased from 29 per cent to about 42 per cent.[545] However, as interest rates start to rise, this leaves fund managers with a major dilemma. Do they sell existing holdings and lock in losses? Do they liquidate their positions to buy more bonds? Or do they increase contributions?

The choices are dire. Provided many of these funds don't go bankrupt in the meantime, governments and corporations will be forced to either increase contributions, raise taxes, reduce pay-outs or vary times that people can access their funds. Whichever way, economic growth will be reduced, and many retirees can look forward to an impoverished retirement.

Unfortunately, the U.S. is just a mirror image of the deep-seated problems in other jurisdictions throughout the world.

*

So far, the analysis in this chapter highlights problems that already exist. However, emerging trends in population and demographics will have a significant impact on the global economy now and in the coming decades.

The United Nations (UN) has developed extensive population databases for each country and region. The data from 1950 to 2015 are based on estimates of actual population, while projections from 2016 to 2100 have been developed using different scenarios. The data presented here is based on the medium variant scenario.

Figure 23 shows estimates of world population by region from 1950 to 2100. Between 1950 and 2015, the global population tripled from 2.5 to 7.4 billion people. By 2100, it is expected to grow by a further 50 per cent to reach 11.2 billion people.[546] The most obvious features of the graph are the strong rise in Africa's population and the mid-century peaking in Asia's population. What is less obvious is the projected 12 per cent decline in Europe's population between 2015 and 2100 from 740 to 650 million.

Figure 23 World Population 1950–2100

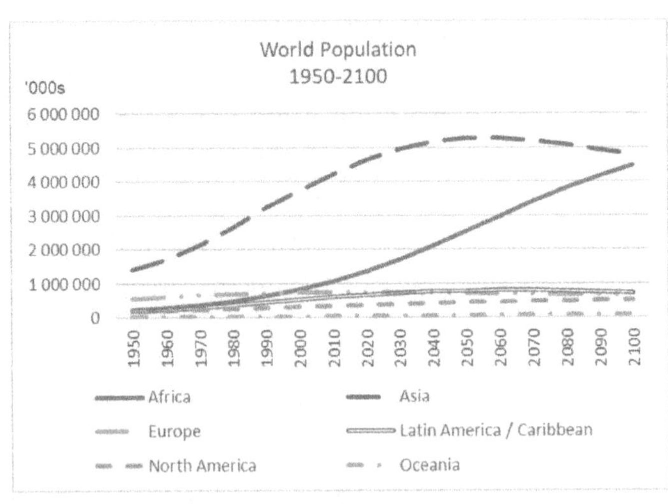

Data Source: United Nations

Asia's population is expected to peak at 5.3 billion in 2060, before tapering off to 4.8 billion in 2100. China's population will peak at around 1.4 billion and India's at 1.7 billion before tapering off to 1 billion and 1.5 billion respectively. Pakistan, Bangladesh, Iraq and the Philippines are also expected to grow strongly. In contrast, Japan's population peaked in 2009 at 128.6 million and is expected to fall steadily to 85 million by 2100.

Between 2015 and 2100, Africa's population is expected to nearly quadruple in size to 4.5 billion people. This represents a staggering growth of 38.5 million people each and every year. East and West Africa are both expected to quadruple in size to 1.6 billion, with most of the growth occurring in Ethiopia, Tanzania, Kenya and Mozambique (East Africa), and Côte d'Ivoire, Niger, Nigeria and Mali (West Africa). Middle Africa is projected to grow five-fold from 150 million to 750 million, with Angola and the Democratic Republic of the Congo growing strongly. Northern and Southern Africa are also forecast to grow, but at a more subdued pace.

Europe's population is expected to peak around 2022, before starting a steady decline over the rest of the century. Eastern and Southern Europe are expected to suffer the greatest losses, with Moldova's population projected to fall by 50 per cent, and Bulgaria, Poland, Romania, Latvia, Albania, Croatia and Serbia all losing 40 per cent. In contrast, the population is expected to grow by between 20 and 50 per cent in Norway, Sweden, the UK, Ireland and Switzerland by 2100.

Canada and the U.S. are expected to grow 40 per cent by the end of the century while Central America is expected to grow by around 30 per cent.

(Interested readers can find a table showing a more detailed breakdown in global population by region from 1950 to 2100 on my website: www.philipwilliamsauthor.com).

Figure 24 shows estimates of the dependency ratio for the major regions from 1950 to 2100. The dependency ratio measures the number of dependents (children aged between zero to 14, and people over the age of 64) compared to those deemed to be of working age (people aged 15 to 64). The higher the ratio, the greater the perceived burden for those of working age in supporting a young or ageing population.

Figure 24 Dependency Ratio 1950–2100

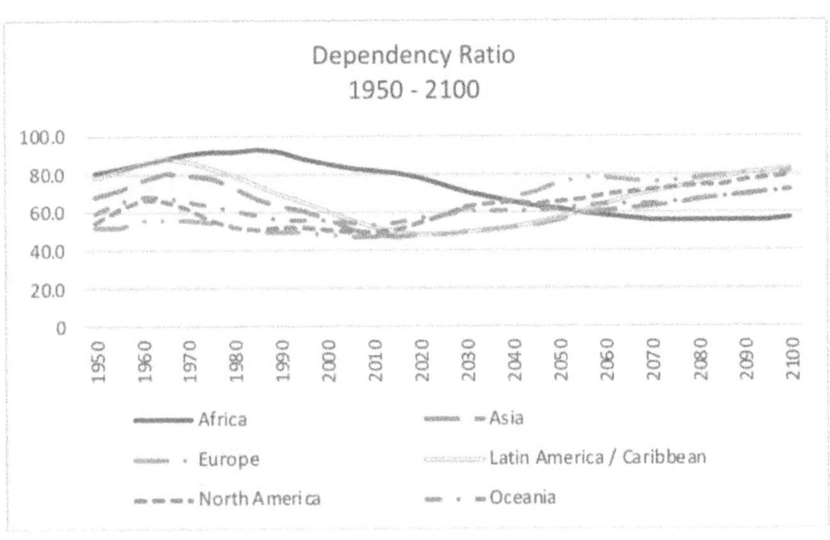

Data Source: United Nations [547]

In most regions the dependency ratio has been falling steadily since the 1960s. This has contributed significantly to economic growth due to a growing workforce as well as demographics favourable to both consumption and investment.

However, with the ratio having now bottomed in many regions, it is expected to climb for the remainder of the century. Africa is the only exception, with a very favorable demographic profile forecast for most of the 21st century.

The ageing population will begin to affect western nations progressively over the next two decades, with maximum impact in Europe around 2060 and other regions sometime later. Country by country analysis suggests that the dependency ratio could get as high as 90 per cent, meaning that there are only 10 per cent of working age people compared to 90 per cent of nonworking age. Clearly the economic system would collapse well before then, but it does highlight the enormous challenges – economic, social, political and military – that lie ahead.

So, what does this discussion on population and demographics mean for the global outlook in coming decades?

Firstly, the forward-looking figures are only estimates. There are many factors that could impact the growth projections including war, famine, disease and fertility rates, so they are what is projected to happen, not what will happen. If they do occur, such a large increase in population growth in Africa could herald in one of the greatest booms in economic history or be an unmitigated disaster. Success will depend on good governance, a reduction in corruption and violence, good education, strong institutions, religious harmony and the cessation of inter-tribal rivalry, factors that have been largely absent throughout Africa's history.

The increase in population, particularly in Africa and India, will also place great strain on resources, both physical, such as water, food, energy, land and infrastructure, and in services, such as sanitation and waste management, law enforcement, defence, education and health. Consequences for the environment and pollution are similarly profound. If mankind is responsible for global warming, as some would have you believe, then such a large increase in population could well have a devastating impact on the climate. It also raises the fundamental question of the carrying capacity of planet Earth.

I am doubtful that Africa can grow as the UN suggests. I doubt whether these nations can handle such a massive population. Rather, I believe it will usher in a continuation of the widescale suffering brought about by famine, war, disease, poverty and social conflict.

An increasing African population, coupled with a declining European population, could also lead to one of the largest mass migrations in human history, putting a huge strain on European resources and society, and potentially destroying centuries of European culture and traditions. This would pose extraordinary problems for European people trying to integrate millions of poorly educated people with vastly different cultures into an already burdened and rapidly ageing society. The social and economic impact on local communities could be catastrophic.

When coupled with the financial headwinds discussed earlier, this declining population and deteriorating demographics could well usher in an economic calamity which could well see living standards fall across the board for all but a few of the well-off.

For people with insufficient means, life will be tough. Many will quickly go through what little is left of their meagre savings. Many will lose their homes and be forced onto the streets, into sub-standard accommodation or forced to move in with family. People will be required to stay in the workforce longer, either through necessity or by governments increasing the retirement age. But the jobs on offer, or that older people can physically undertake, will be limited and pay little. As people begin to retire, they will draw down their savings, reversing the up thrust in global asset markets in recent decades. This will exacerbate the financial problems.

Consumption will plateau or fall as older people reduce spending, either through necessity or through reduced needs.

The psychological pressures on the once-proud baby boomers who have lived the dream will also exact a terrible toll, potentially leading to increased substance abuse, violence and suicides. An ageing population will put a massive strain on government services, particularly in areas such as health, pensions, welfare payments, infrastructure and housing, at a time when heavily indebted nations can least afford it. Charities will respond by increasing their support in place of diminishing government support.

An ageing population is also likely to lead to a shortfall in skills, particularly in those sectors required to look after the elderly, and also in those jobs requiring manual labour. Those of working age could also well object to being forced to look after a large ageing population, raising resentment and increasing social tension. This will be particularly the case in societies that don't value extended family relationships.

Some sections of society may well also respond to these problems by mounting the call for forced euthanasia. Ethically, this would be an abhorrent development. However, it could well be the only way some members in society see in managing declining economic and social conditions.

Government revenues will also come under immense pressure as the economy stagnates or declines. Governments will respond by seeking to raise taxes, which will reduce demand by working-age consumers; and by cutting back on services, which will reduce retirees' standard of living. Governments will also be forced to prioritise services between different stakeholder groups, pitting one group of society against another. Funds available to maintain infrastructure will be constrained, leading to a further deterioration in roads, rail, electricity, water and sewerage, schools and hospitals.

Spending on defence and law and order will also suffer as funds are diverted elsewhere. This is likely to expose western nations to increased threats from abroad, from homegrown terrorists as well as from petty thugs and thieves looking to take advantage of a deteriorating situation. The reduced policing will lead to more widespread ghettos and no-go zones in those areas inhabited by minorities and disaffected community groups. People could well be forced away from cities and into remote communities for protection and a better lifestyle.

While this paints a gloomy outlook, governments and citizens do have options to alleviate some of the worst impacts. The onslaught of the demographic decline will occur gradually, so people have time to plan and adjust. Governments, for example, could encourage people to have larger families, and also encourage migration of younger, educated people who will assimilate into their community. People can also work to protect themselves by ensuring their savings and pensions are invested in safe institutions. Finally, while changes in population and demographics will not trigger the impending depression, they will exacerbate the social, political and economic impacts, and make the recovery more difficult.

*

Despite record amounts of debt, surging asset markets and potential problems associated with unwinding central banks' bond-buying programs, investors seem remarkably sanguine about economic risks.

The VIX measures market expectations of near term volatility (as conveyed by stock index option prices) in the stock market. Figure 25 shows that in late 2017 the VIX recorded its lowest level in 30 years, even lower than it was immediately before the GFC and the dot-com crash.

It subsequently ticked up in early 2018 following a mild sell-off on Wall Street, but has subsequently fallen back to near historically low levels (data as at July 2018).

Figure 25 CBOE Volatility Index (VIX) 1990–2018

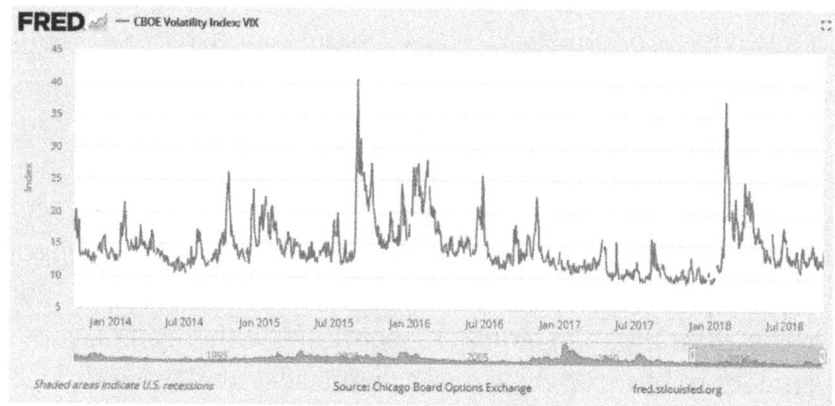

Source: Federal Reserve Bank of St Louis

Other measures which suggest complacency abounds are that pension and mutual fund managers are holding record low levels of cash; there are four times as many bulls as bears; margin debt is at record levels; while the spread between junk bonds and government bonds is also near historically low levels. Perhaps one reason investors are so confident is that they believe that, should another financial crisis arise, central banks will once again step in and bail out the major banks. Others also believe that with a fiat currency, major central banks have the ability to continuously create money out of thin air.

Central bankers are also optimistic. At the annual meetings of the IMF and World Bank in October 2017, the

IMF bumped up its global forecasts for economic growth. Central bankers also seized on the opportunity to ready investors for tighter money as they predicted economic expansion will finally ignite inflation. Federal Reserve Chair Janet Yellen said her 'best guess' was that prices would accelerate soon, a sentiment shared by other central bankers.[548] In a splendid example of doublespeak however, despite her 'best guess', Yellen also acknowledged that there are reasons to worry slow inflation will persist. At least we know why economists have two hands – on the one hand this, on the other hand that.

The Bank of Japan governor also said he would maintain his massive stimulus program aimed at igniting inflation – even though it hasn't worked for the past 25 years. And Draghi said that although there were some signs that wages were finally increasing, he hedged, saying, 'we're still not there', meaning 'I'm going to continue with my crazy experiment to blow up the world's financial system, even though it's been a proven failure'.

Before looking at how a global depression may play out, it is also worthwhile noting that since U.S. President Trump was elected, stock markets have boomed and the U.S. economy, boosted by massive tax cuts, has also grown strongly. It is also worthwhile noting that historically, a stock market collapse has preceded a decline in economic activity, for example dot-com and GFC, often by up to nine months.

So, despite strong current economic growth, the underlying fundamentals are still bad and asset prices remain stretched.

Chapter 13

How the Depression May Play Out: Four Scenarios

> *'The way you create deflation is you create an asset bubble.'*
>
> Stanley Druckenmiller

While there is no knowing what will trigger the next financial crisis, there is no doubt one is coming. There is also no doubt that the next crisis will cost millions of jobs, bankrupt hundreds of thousands of businesses, lead to the loss of people's life savings, their houses and their families, and create untold misery and suffering. And given we live in a highly connected world, there is also no doubt that the crisis will spread globally.

The only question is how it will play out? Will we muddle through like we did after the GFC, or will we experience something far worse? Given that nobody can accurately predict the future, I have developed four high-level scenarios on how the next financial crisis may play out. These are:

1. Muddle through
2. Hyper-inflationary depression
3. Short sharp depression
4. Prolonged deflationary depression.

Each scenario is based on the following core set of events. A random event triggers a financial crisis. It could well be that China begins to rein in her debt, which causes its property market to fall; the economy enters a recession; debt problems in emerging markets and/or Italy rattle investors; Brexit unravels; cracks in the EU emerge; trade tensions escalate; oil supply is disrupted, causing oil prices to surge; a major conflict arises, for example the Middle East; the U.S. experiences a political crisis; fears of inflation emerge; interest rate rises intensify; a major bank or corporation collapses; or the stock market tumbles for no apparent reason.

Whatever the cause, pessimism spills over into stock markets, precipitating a major sell-off in global stocks, which is exacerbated as margin debt is called in and automatic trading systems generate sell orders. After the initial rout, stock markets stage a partial recovery before resuming their slide. The next leg down is where the real damage is done as relentless selling pressure emerges. Panic soon spills over to the banking system, and inter-bank lending dries up. The banks respond by calling in loans and tightening lending. The speed of the collapse causes fear and panic, re-enforcing the rout.

How authorities respond to the slump determines how the crisis plays out.

Scenario 1: Muddle Through

Scenario 1 could equally have been called 'Kick the can down the road' in that it envisages a re-run of the GFC – rather than addressing the massive debt and other structural problems, authorities continue their massive stimulus programs in the hope that they can eventually reflate the economy and pay down the debt with devalued money.

Under this scenario, falling stock prices lead to a loss of confidence in both the economy and financial markets. Central banks respond quickly by providing liquidity to the banking system and bailing out any large banks and other major corporations that get into trouble. Governments also initiate an array of stimulus measures to stabilise the system and kickstart the economy. The IMF and EU also work quickly to negotiate rescue packages to prop up ailing governments in Europe and elsewhere.

After several years of deep recession, stability is eventually restored, stock markets bottom before recovering. Central banks and governments continue with their stimulus measures to boost economic growth, but burdened by structural problems and massive debt, economic growth remains anaemic at best. Yet again, authorities have been able to stave off an economic catastrophe, kicking the can down the road until the next time.

Scenario 2: Hyper-inflationary Depression

The Hyper-Inflationary Depression mirrors the events of the Weimar Republic, which experienced a period of hyper-inflation in the early 1920s. It led to the collapse of the German financial system, precipitated the rise of Adolf Hitler and eventually led to World War II.

Under scenario 2, the world experiences a severe economic depression which lasts for a number of years. However, as the world fails to respond to the stimulus, central banks become ever more desperate and ratchet up their monetary stimulus. The money printing becomes so large that hyper-inflation takes hold. As asset and consumer price inflation intensifies, money becomes worthless, obliterating people's savings and resulting in untold human misery. This eventually leads to the collapse of the world financial system and the end of the U.S dollar as the reserve currency. Governments are forced to return to sound money, such as the gold standard, in order to restore stability.

Scenario 3: Short Sharp Depression

This scenario mirrors the actions of policy-makers during the 1920–21 and Icelandic depressions where authorities took a light-touch approach to the unfolding crisis by allowing the financial and economic systems to adjust naturally to their new lower levels until they were cleansed of malinvestments, structural problems, and weak banks and corporations.

It results in a deep, sharp depression of between two to three years where unemployment soars, stock markets fall precipitously while nominal prices, wages and industrial activity all fall significantly. Unfortunately, this is the price to pay for economic mismanagement. While the human suffering is intense, it is not as prolonged as in scenario 4. Moreover, once cleansed of struggling companies and poor investments, and without an overhang of debt, the economy should be well-placed to begin a sustained recovery. As this approach is diametrically opposed to the policies recommended by mainstream economists and central banks, as depicted in the other three scenarios, it is the most unlikely scenario, other than in isolated instances.

Under this scenario, bail-ins and bailouts are not countenanced. As the financial crisis unfolds, larger, insolvent banks are placed into receivership and restructured into 'old' and 'new' banks. Bad and doubtful debts are left with the old bank, resulting in total losses for their shareholders and bondholders. The new bank is nationalised, recapitalised and takes over viable loans as well as the domestic operations of the failed banks, thus keeping the economy ticking over. Governments guarantee all domestic deposits to protect the savings of households and business and prevent bank runs. Interest rates rise as the remaining banks seek to rationalise credit while attracting deposits and rebuilding their deposit base.

The IMF provides sovereign debt packages to struggling nations to help stabilise their banking system. Currencies are allowed to depreciate while capital controls are implemented to facilitate orderly management of the currency. Unfortunately, this is not available for members of the eurozone, which makes the necessary adjustments to their economies far more difficult.

Businesses are allowed to fail, leading to a strong rise in unemployment and as a result, both consumption and investment fall significantly, leading to a large decline in nominal GDP. As consumer prices and wages fall substantially, asset prices fall in line with the collapse in the money supply. Share prices could well fall by up to 80 to 90 per cent, while the nominal prices of property, goods and wages all fall by between 30 to 40 per cent.

Governments encourage the private sector to grow and ease pressure on consumers and business by slashing expenditure to the core, returning the budget to surplus and paying down debt. Government waste, subsidies and handouts are eliminated, government payrolls and welfare are slashed, controls on minimum wages are abolished while business red tape and regulations are also cut. In all, there is a focus on returning the economy and society to one based on thrift, high savings and investment, strong entrepreneurialism, a strong work ethic, minimal welfare, small government and sound money.

Finally, governments restructure the financial system to eliminate future systemic risk, while the legal system kicks in, prosecuting those accused of committing unlawful actions associated with the crisis.

While this scenario has proven time and again to provide the best economic and social outcomes in the shortest possible time, it is also the least likely scenario as it is highly unlikely that policy-makers will implement it. Society no longer respects the values that made western nations great – thrift, self-sacrifice, entrepreneurialism and a spirit to serve others and our nations before ourselves. Policy-makers have become convinced that they must 'do something', notwithstanding that this is the worst outcome for the people, both in the short- and the long-run.

Interest groups will also fight strenuously to retain their 'rights'. Banks will fight to the death to be bailed out while retaining control of the financial system. Subsidised industries will fight hard to retain their subsidies, unions will die in the ditches to maintain nominal wages, social justice warriors will fight to maintain welfare, while activist socialists will launch a massive campaign as they fight to undermine the capitalist system.

All the while, Rome burns while everyday folk suffer.

It will take a catastrophic depression for banks to lose monopolistic control over the financial system, for the welfare mentality to be destroyed and for political leaders to discard their misguided economic policies before sanity prevails. Hence scenarios 2 and 4.

Scenario 4: Prolonged Deflationary Depression

The Prolonged Deflationary Depression scenario is a re-run of the Great Depression, as governments adopt policies like Roosevelt's New Deal policies, which act to deepen and prolong the economic downturn. Given the structural problems that exist today, and a failure to let the adjustment process take its course, the Great Depression of the 2020s could well last five to 10 years or more and inflict untold suffering on tens of millions of everyday people. Given the massive levels of debt, a deflationary depression of epic intensity is the most likely scenario for the coming depression.

Central banks will respond quickly to the initial crisis by providing liquidity to the banking system and bailing out any large banks and other major corporations that appear vulnerable. Governments will also step in with measures to stabilise the financial system and to stimulate economic growth. So far, it's a pretty standard response. We've been through similar episodes recently with the dot-com crash and the GFC and while things were difficult for a time, we came through these downturns relatively unscathed.

However, for some reason, this time is different. The standard response doesn't work as expected. Social mood continues to plummet and markets continue to fall. Governments and central banks are overwhelmed by the sheer scale of leverage and debt. Structural fault-lines in the economy and the rotten core of the financial system are laid bare for all to see.

The financial system will take some massive hits, forcing the large-scale closure of banks. Declining asset prices put financial institutions under immense pressure, exposing fraud, excessive leverage and poor lending practices. Banks will respond by calling in loans, increasing interest rates to cover risk and by restricting lending. Weaker banks, including some of the largest institutions, will face collapse and need to be bailed out at huge cost. Others will merge with larger banks at pennies in the dollar. But many smaller banks will fail and counter-party defaults on derivatives will also cause enormous damage to the financial system.

Bank failures and falling confidence will lead to a precipitous fall in the money supply as debt implodes, ushering in a massive debt deflation, bringing with it falling asset prices, commodity prices and the prices of goods and services.

With a collapsing stock market, stocks will plumb new depths, falling to levels not seen in the past 30 years. By the time this is all over, the DJIA could well have fallen by 80 to 90 per cent to below 5,000. Property prices could also collapse by as much as 40 to 50 per cent, forcing millions of people out of their homes and onto the streets.

Despite massive monetary stimulus, interest rates will continue to rise in line with their long-term trend, leading to a full-blown crisis in bonds as major institutions, including central banks, experience enormous capital losses on their bond-holdings. These capital losses will lead to further selling, exacerbating the rise in interest rates which, in turn, increases debt servicing costs, putting pressure on households, businesses and governments, while reducing consumption and investment. Credit will also become difficult to obtain, even for the most credit-worthy customers. Driven by fear and self-interest, governments, central banks and the elite will become increasingly desperate, imposing ever more draconian authoritarian measures, as the crisis persists.

Restrictions will be imposed on the amount of money that depositors can withdraw from their own bank accounts. Bail-ins, where creditors and depositors, rather than taxpayers, take a loss on their holdings will be enacted to rescue financial institutions on the brink of failure while depositors are forced to swap deposits for bank shares. Other forms of money will also be banned, with governments confiscating gold and prohibiting the use of crypto-currencies and central banks will also expand the types of securities they purchase to include lower-rated government and corporate bonds as well as equities.

Of course, few will see the irony that these measures are a direct result of the failure of governments and central banks to ensure proper governance of the financial system.

While these measures are bad enough, the most draconian measure still awaits us. As the crisis continues to unfold, and despite the obvious security risks, we will hear increasing demands from prominent economists of the need to eliminate cash and move to a cashless (electronic) society. Harvard economist Kenneth Rogoff has stated that cash should be banned, arguing that central banks could impose negative interest rates more easily. Consummate insider Lawrence Summers, a former economic adviser to President Obama and ex-Treasury Secretary, points to research showing that corruption is aided by paper currency in larger denominations, such as Uncle Sam's $100 bill and the 500-euro bill.[549]

The move away from cash is already underway. Several countries including India have already banned high denominations notes, claiming it is part of the drive against drugs, corruption and money laundering. JPMorgan Chase has also taken the plunge, allegedly banning the storage of 'any cash or coins' in its safety deposit boxes, while restricting borrowers from using cash to make payments on credit cards, mortgages, equity lines, and auto loans.[550] This is extraordinary, given that cash and coins are still legal tender.

But these proposals are not about drugs, corruption or money laundering. If it was, then governments would have banned lobbyists and political donations, and regulated illicit drug use long ago.

No! Eliminating cash and moving to controlled electronic transactions is about controlling how people spend their money. Banning cash allows central banks to impose their economic nirvana of negative interest rates. This not only makes future bank runs impossible but, by imposing high negative interest rates, it would force people to reduce their savings and spend their money – whether they wanted to or not – in some misguided policy about aggregate demand. It also gives governments the means to confiscate people's hard-earned savings as they deem fit.

And to what end? Eliminating cash is unlikely to work. Unemployed people don't have money while those who do would probably prefer to incur the penalty of negative interest rates rather than spend money for something they don't want.

Eliminating cash would also be an outrageous attack on freedom, and the final step towards authoritarian rule, robbing people of their savings and handing their money over to the banking cartel. Any move to eliminate cash must be resisted at all cost.

The spill-over to the real economy will be far greater than occurred during the GFC. At the depths of the depression, GDP will drop by 30 to 40 per cent while global trade falls sharply as a global trade war erupts. Commodity prices collapse, with oil likely to fall to around $10 per barrel. The ensuing fallout may look something like the following picture.

Pessimism amongst consumers and business will escalate, leading to a rapid decline in prices and profits, while pushing bankruptcies, unemployment and deficits to extreme levels. Despite falling prices, governments and trade unions resist calls for lower wages, exacerbating an already worsening employment situation. Unemployment will reach 30 to 40 per cent, and much higher in some areas. It will be particularly high in areas that benefited most from the boom, for example real estate, finance, construction and technology. But no areas are left unscathed. The services sector will also be hard hit as people are unable to afford their cable TV, their social media, their latest IT gadget, their holidays and, as they rail against consumerism, the closure of tens of thousands of stores and thousands of shopping malls becomes inevitable.

Higher education will be particularly hard hit, as endowment income plunges and defaults on student loans surge. Many institutions will fail while others slash fees and staff and reduce course offerings to core disciplines such as medicine, engineering and science. Declining tax revenues and increasing costs put government budgets under enormous pressure, forcing budget deficits higher, while sending many local and state governments to the wall. With their finances in turmoil, governments will be forced to cut back on services, with a disproportionate impact on the elderly and the poor. Suicide rates and drug use will surge as people struggle to cope. Massive losses on bonds could also well see the Fed fail.

Desperate for money, governments will impose a range of new taxes while looking to confiscate money from the wealthy. Falling asset prices force private and public pension plans to walk away from their obligations, creating massive hardship for those reliant on these schemes.

With trillions of dollars of wealth destroyed, the elite's wealth will be buffeted by precipitous falls in asset prices, but the resultant decline in inequality will be of little comfort to those without jobs, without money and without hope. As society fractures along a range of fault-lines including race, ideology, the environment, employment and social status, massive demonstrations will be held to demand that the government 'do something' to stop the suffering. They lead to little.

Violence escalates as extremist movements become popular. Gangs roam free and some areas become no-go zones. Authorities are periodically forced to impose martial law to restore law and order. Homelessness surges, creating suburban slums and increasing violence. Residents in well-to-do areas employ armed guards to protect their families and property. Others establish communities of like-minded people in rural areas.

Socialists look to exploit the depression by blaming the failure of capitalism for people's woes. Little do they realise that the depression was not caused by a failure of capitalism, but by the hijacking of capitalism by the elite for their own purposes. Society also becomes more conservative. Political correctness and identity politics fall out of favour as people focus on their own survival rather than pursuing radical ideologies and a leftist agenda. Environmentalists will be pilloried as the fear of global warming evaporates. Many turn to religion for spiritual support while others join sects. Illegal immigrants and minorities are targeted as intolerance grows and people fight for survival. Thousands are killed while hundreds of thousands are deported. Separatist movements gain popularity and some states, for example California, could split into smaller states, while others look to secede. Anti-government sentiment grows while new political parties emerge. Government corruption also grows as desperate politicians seek to win elections by buying votes.

However, despite the prevailing pessimism and harsh economic times, some people will prosper by buying good businesses and property at fire-sale prices. People's resilience also shines through as many turn to community gardens and community support to get by. Acts of kindness will abound as religious groups and charities step in to fill the void left by the withdrawal of government services. These groups will provide food and amenities such as very basic accommodation to large groups of people.

*

And where is Europe in all this? It will be at the epicentre of this looming economic and financial tsunami. Europe's fragile banking system will finally be exposed, weighed down by tens of billions of euros of non-performing loans and insolvent banks which have been propped up for years.

The ECB will respond by ratcheting up its QE, but to no avail, as it is swamped by the sheer magnitude of the debt problem and declining confidence. The financial crisis will quickly spill over to the real economy, ushering in a tidal wave of fear and panic. Nations on the European periphery who are in the eurozone will be particularly hard hit as they are unable to devalue their currencies to restore competitiveness.

The IMF and other bodies will be forced to provide rescue packages to debt-laden nations, but these offer only light relief. People will rail against austerity measures, adding to further unrest.

High youth unemployment will fuel resentment towards the elite, escalating social tensions and ushering in riots, strikes and civil disobedience. Some countries will impose martial law to quell civil uprisings. Unions will strike to protect wages and conditions, but all this does is send unemployment soaring as companies are forced to shutter their doors or cut back staff. Already saddled with high debts, governments will be forced to cut back services, increase taxes and dramatically scale back pensions, adding to people's woes.

Some of the highly indebted nations within Europe, such as Greece, Spain, Italy and Portugal, default, leading to further chaos in the banking system. Greece finally sees sense and either leaves, or is booted from the eurozone, causing chaos as she returns to the drachma. Other nations quickly follow suit, leading to the end of the euro and the eurozone. This will add to the chaos in currency and financial markets, and in the real economy.

The ECB, the European Commission and Germany will rightfully come in for harsh criticism, while Germans grow tired of supporting the rest of Europe. It will lead to the scaling back or abolition of the ECB as nations re-establish their own central banks. This leaves the ECB left holding trillions of European bonds. Left with no mandate and no authority, many nations default on these bonds.

The result will be that Europe splinters as nationalism takes hold, bringing an end to the great European experiment. Many former eastern bloc nations will turn away from the west and restore ties with Russia. Some European nations will also retain their informal alliances such as the Visegrád Group, the Nordic Council and the Baltic Assembly. Countries such as Italy, Spain and Belgium will fracture as calls for succession grow stronger. Catalonia, northern Italy and Flanders will break away while even parts of Germany seek autonomy and independence. Scotland could also look to secede from the UK.

The negative social mood will ramp up tensions between nationals and immigrants, leading to violent clashes and increasing calls to repatriate migrants. This prompts more terrorist attacks. As the depression continues, hundreds of thousands of Muslims and African migrants will be expelled and forcibly repatriated from Germany, Sweden, Belgium, France, Italy and Greece.

In some predominantly Muslim areas, especially in Belgium and the UK, sharia law emerges as policing and the legal system fail to cope. Turkey will respond to the unrest by becoming more aggressive in her attempts to recreate the Ottoman Empire and to support Muslims living in Europe. Her aggression will see Turkey kicked out of NATO.

Regional tensions between historical enemies will also re-emerge, increasing the likelihood of regional clashes. Likely flashpoints include Greece and Turkey, Russia and Georgia, and the Ukraine. Sectarian tensions will also remain high in the Middle East. With collapsing oil revenues, tensions within Saudi Arabia reach boiling point, threatening the rule of the House of Saud. Elsewhere, rivalry between Sunni and Shia Muslims continues unabated.

*

Canada and Australia will suffer severe economic downturns as commodity prices collapse and their housing markets implode. Since the GFC, both countries have experienced a housing bubble of epic proportions, driven largely on the back of rising household debt which reached record levels. As their export revenue collapses and asset prices implode, both will experience a downturn as deep as the 1890 Depression. Stock markets could well fall by 70 to 80 per cent while house prices fall by 40 to 50 per cent.

There seems to be a perception that because of China's incredible rise in economic power and her centralised government that somehow China would be spared the worst of any global economic downturn. However, this will not be born out. Since the GFC, China has accumulated an extraordinary level of debt, particularly in the shadow-banking system, meaning that rising interest rates place enormous pressure on all sectors of the economy. The financial system and the local government sector are particularly vulnerable to any downturn.

China's export-oriented industries will also suffer terribly as the trade wars escalate. Like Japan before her, Chinese firms will resort to selling down their overseas assets and repatriating the money to shore up their finances. This puts further pressure on asset prices in western countries. The depression will expose massive problems in governance as well widespread corruption and mismanagement.

But it will have its greatest impact on everyday Chinese, as they see trillions of dollars of wealth destroyed as the debt bubble implodes, bringing down both the stock market and house prices. This will create extraordinary unrest right across the country. Any dissent however, will be met with brutal repression as President Xi Jinping uses every means at his disposal to maintain law and order.

*

So what will bring an end to the global depression?

It is difficult to say. But it is quite likely that the depression will end at different times in different regions. It is also likely that, given her economic, political and social problems, Europe will suffer the most from the global depression. On a more general level, global economies only begin to stabilise as malinvestments and debt are wrung from the system, and prices and wages fall to more sustainable levels.

As people look back on this tragedy, they will be haunted by a simple question: How could this have been allowed to happen? And the simple answer is this: It shouldn't have.

If only policy-makers had pursued sensible economic policies which focus on true laissez-faire economics rather than continually meddling in the economy.

If only they had eschewed the foolishness of mainstream economics based on the flawed foundations of Keynesianism and monetarism, the world would not have continued to run up huge debts.

If only governments had pursued policies of sound money, the world would not have created massive asset bubbles.

If only the world had not given control of its financial system to the elite, we would not have created the greatest financial bubble in history.

If only we had learnt the lessons of history.

If only.

Part 5

The Future is in All our Hands

Chapter 14
How to Restore Prosperity

'We discussed politics, but we also talked about the importance of hard work, personal responsibility, living within your means, keeping your word. These lessons stay with you throughout your life.'

Bob Ehrlich

We have spoken at length about the causes of the Great Depression of the 2020s: the use of fiat currencies; the failure of mainstream macroeconomic theory; government policies which have corrupted capitalism; corporate greed and control of the world's economic and financial systems by the elite.

Now that we know what doesn't work, let's turn our attention to what we can do to restore prosperity. First and foremost: we must wrest back control of the financial system from the elite. Next, we need to return to sound money. We then need to return to laissez-faire economics. And finally, we need to implement measures designed to increase productivity.

Not to put too fine a point on it, despite the glaring failures of mainstream economic theory, challenging the orthodoxy of mainstream economists and central banks, and wresting back control of the financial system from the elite will be extremely tough.

The first and most obvious problem is that we are dealing with very powerful vested interests – the banking cartel, central banks, international institutions, media companies, the economics 'profession', corporate executives, financial commentators, lawyers, real estate developers and politicians – many of whom have grown fabulously wealthy under the existing system of monetary inflation and bailouts. They will not easily relinquish control of the banking system or the economy.

Mainstream economists have also built their reputations and careers on theories which have proven to be wrong. Some of these people work in prestigious universities. Many others work in the finance sector or the media. To change their opinions would be an admission of failure, something they will not willingly do. They will do everything in their power to deflect and ignore criticism, while using their positions to espouse their latest theory in the hope of remaining relevant. There may be the odd mea culpa from mainstream economists, acknowledging that while they made some mistakes, they have learnt from them. Let's move on, they will say. This will allow them to transition from the old to the new but remain in control. Unfortunately, as we have noted with Ben Bernanke and the New York Fed's latest musings on inflation targeting, the new will be the old – just dressed differently. The fact remains: the new theories remain fundamentally flawed. It also goes without saying that they will go into minutiae to undermine alternative points of view, or just arrogantly reject new ideas with bland one liners. Politicians from all sides of politics have also built their policies around these flawed economic theories.

Perhaps the easiest way to challenge these groups is to ask some basic questions.

- Why did you not predict the GFC or the Great Depression of the 2020s?

- Why didn't massive monetary and fiscal stimulus restore sustainable and robust economic growth?
- Why did you adopt the same policies that caused the dot-com bubble and the GFC and think you would get a different outcome?
- Why have you learned nothing from history about the damage caused by credit-fuelled asset bubbles?

After that, the real work begins.

There are four steps involved in delivering transformational change.

Firstly, we need to create the need for change. We need to create the burning platform where the desire for change far outweighs the fear of change. There are two ways to initiate transformational change: vision-led and discovery-led.

Vision-led change occurs when a leader paints a vision of the future that people can buy into. A good example is when President Kennedy galvanised a nation by announcing that America would put a man on the moon within the decade. Discovery-led change is triggered by use of facts or adversity to mount the case for change. The anti-smoking campaign is an excellent example of discovery-led change where doctors used the adverse effects of smoking to prosecute the case for change.

Given the level of control that the elite have over global economic and financial systems, it seems likely that it will require a financial crisis of epic proportions to create that burning platform, to give people the resolve to wrest control of the financial system from the elite, and to discredit mainstream economic theory. We can't waste this opportunity.

The second step in change involves developing a vision for the future. In this case the vision could be that of a society which has a financial system independent of the elite, an economy with sustainable growth and where people live a simpler and more meaningful life and their effort is rewarded.

All change involves uncertainty. People will often resist change, even if their current circumstances aren't particularly good. For change to be effective, people need to be able to confidently take that leap of faith into the future. The third step in the change process involves painting picture of what life will be like in the new environment. People need to be able to see how they fit in. What will their life be like? What jobs might they have? Will they be able to afford a home? If there is a glimmer of hope, most people will follow.

The final step in transformational change involves defining how we will achieve our vision – what do we need to do to move from where we are now to where we want to get to?

Surprisingly, the steps to deliver sustainable prosperity are not that difficult. First and foremost, we need to return to sound money. Sound money means that there are automatic constraints over the rate of growth of the money supply so that the money supply grows in line with growth in the real economy. The creation of the Fed, Nixon's decision to leave the gold standard and the rise of activist central banks have been leading factors in destroying sound money. These factors gave rise to the emergence of fiat currencies and unconstrained credit growth which has led to runaway inflation. They have also led directly to the financialisation of the global economy. Lender of last resort facilities have also encouraged financial instability by allowing banks to take extraordinary risks, safe in the knowledge that if they run into trouble, they will be bailed out.

Returning to sound money means reversing each of these decisions. We need to eliminate fiat currencies and return to either the gold standard or some other mechanism such as Special Drawing Rights, which are outside the control and influence of politicians and banks. It also means ending fractional reserve banking and a return to 100 per cent bank reserves.

It means eliminating central banks so they can't bail out their mates or manipulate interest rates. Leaving central banks in place would provide an opportunity for the banking sector to incrementally expand their powers so that, over time, we would end up where we currently are. We need to remove that possibility.

And it means eliminating artificial currency blocs so that nations retain control over their own currencies and their own destinies.

So, what are the benefits of sound money?

Sound money means a return to the sound banking practices of the 1950s and 60s. It means that money is still available, but it is lent for productive rather than speculative purposes, and that money is lent to people who can afford to repay the loans. It means that interest rates reflect market conditions and also reflect the balance between savings and investment, rather than being manipulated by the elite. It means reversing financialisation of the economy, which means the banks and the finance sector become a much smaller component of the overall economy. It will put an end to the boom–bust cycle of the recent years that has had such a devastating impact on people's lives.

It means an end to the rampant asset inflation that has made houses unaffordable for young people, turned people into financial serfs as they drown under the weight of huge loans and created the inequality in income and wealth that pervades society. It means that universities will need to offer courses that have some meaningful purpose and people can afford, rather than locking students into a lifetime of debt servitude on courses of little value.

Returning to sound money allows society to take back control of the financial sector from the elite.

The next step in restoring sustainable growth is to return to laissez-faire economics. Markets are complex, adaptive systems that change over time to reflect fluctuations in demand, consumer preferences, changes in technology, the supply of goods and so on. They must be allowed to adapt without interference from governments, unions or corporations. Failure to do so creates distortions and malinvestments, while preventing the economy from ridding itself of any imbalances that may arise from time to time.

This will mean allowing markets to function properly. To do this, it means banning lobbying and political donations; allowing banks and other major corporations to fail, no matter their size; encouraging competition, while eliminating anything that stifles competition; focusing on free trade rather than countenancing mercantilism; and accepting that, from time to time, there may be market failures.

And it will also mean discarding monetarism and neo-Keynesian economics to the dustbin of history.

The final step in restoring prosperity will be to focus on those factors that increase productivity. We covered these extensively earlier in the book. But just to recap. This will include encouraging and rewarding entrepreneurialism and innovation, fostering capital investment, developing human potential, and supporting a strong private sector and savings ethos. It will also require a focus on social and cultural factors, including social cohesion and encouraging a strong, vibrant middle class. While we must minimise the role of government, we will need strong institutions, including a supportive legal and regulatory framework.

But most importantly, it will require ordinary people to unite, to rise up and right the wrongs, and challenge the elite. That is our challenge.

I hope this book might be a starting point in beginning the change process.

Glossary

- Bill of exchange is a written order used primarily in international trade that binds one party to pay a fixed sum of money to another party on demand or at a predetermined date. They are similar to cheques and promissory notes and can be drawn by individuals or banks. The difference between a promissory note and a bill of exchange is that the latter are generally transferable by endorsements and can bind one party to pay a third party that was not involved in its creation
- Capital refers to both tangible and non-tangible items such as:
    - Capital stock – those items that are used in the production of goods and services such as factories, commercial buildings, shops, computers, tools, plant and machinery, and infrastructure such as roads, dams and railways.
    - Financial stock – this includes the amount of money invested in organisations. It includes the owner's capital

such as the money invested by sole traders, shareholders and governments as well as money provided by financiers.

  - Working capital – this is the money that is tied up as goods and services are produced and sold, for example work in progress, finished goods stock and debtors.
  - Intellectual capital – this is closely linked to human capital and covers things such as trademarks, formulae, music, computer programs and the like.

- Consumer Price Index (CPI) is a measure of changes over time in retail prices of a basket of goods and services representative of consumption expenditure by resident households.
- Consumption consists of expenditure by consumers on household goods and services, including spending on everyday items such as food, clothing, rent, telecommunications, entertainment and transport as well as spending on durable goods such as motor vehicles and household equipment, for example whitegoods.
- Credit is defined as a contractual agreement in which a borrower receives something of value now and agrees to repay the lender at some later date.[551] There are many types of credit including mortgages, business loans, car loans, student loans and credit card loans. The term credit is inextricably linked with the term debt.
- A credit default swap (CDS) is a financial swap arrangement where the seller of the CDS will compensate the buyer in the event of a debt default (by the debtor) or some other credit event. The buyer of the CDS pays a fee to the seller and, in exchange, may expect to receive a payoff if the asset defaults.
- Durable goods are goods that yields value over time rather than being completely consumed in one use. Examples

include motor vehicles, whitegoods, plant and equipment and buildings.

- Employee income is the total remuneration in cash or kind, payable to an employee in return for work done by the employee. Employee income includes actual wages paid, any social contributions (e.g. superannuation payments), penalty payments, supplementary allowances and commissions, tips and gratuities.
- Entrepreneurs are those individuals who combine the other factors of production to produce new innovative products and services or new ways of producing existing goods and services.
- Exports refer to the sale of goods and services from one country to another. It includes exports of goods, services and capital.
- Fiat money (or fiat currency) is not backed by anything of intrinsic value, for example precious metals, or pigs.
- Feudalism can be regarded as a set of reciprocal legal and military obligations amongst the warrior nobility revolving around the three key concepts of lords, vassals and fiefs.[552] A lord was a noble who owned land, a vassal was a person who was granted land by a lord, and the land was known as a fief.
- Finance sector comprises banks, credit unions and other non-bank intermediaries. While separate from the real economy, the financial system is integral to the proper functioning of the real economy system as it acts to consolidate savings from other sectors while providing money and credit to the real economy.
- Foreign sector includes transactions carried out with other nations.
- Fractional reserve system is a monetary system where the total amount of money in circulation is backed by less than the equivalent value in gold.

- Government expenditure includes both consumption and investment spending by local, state and federal governments, and government enterprises on goods and services.
- Gross Domestic Product (GDP) is the broadest quantitative measure of a nation's total economic activity. It represents the monetary value of all goods and services produced within a nation's geographic borders over a specified period of time. There are two sides to calculating GDP: expenditure (demand) and income (supply), or more colloquially, supply and demand. The expenditure, or demand, side of an economy consists of final expenditure on all goods and services. It is calculated as:
    - Consumption + Government Expenditure + Investment + Net Exports (Exports – Imports).

      The income, or supply, view of an economy looks at income earned by key sectors of an economy. It is calculated as:
    - Employee Income + Gross Operating Surplus + Gross Mixed Income + Net Taxes

GDP can be presented in different ways including real GDP, nominal GDP and GDP per capita.

- GDP per capita (that is per person) is calculated by dividing a nation's GDP by its total population.
- Gross National Product (GNP) is equal to GDP plus any income earned by residents from overseas investments minus income earned within the domestic economy by overseas residents.
- Gross operating surplus is the income from production of corporate enterprises.
- Imports refer to the purchase of goods and services from one country to another. It includes imports of goods, services and capital.

- Investment expenditure includes spending on tangible assets such as dwellings, factories, railways, aircraft, machinery and equipment, as well as on intangible assets such as computer software, mineral exploration and entertainment, literary and artistic originals.
- Land includes not only the physical land but also the mineral resources under the ground. It also extends to include rivers and oceans and the creatures that live within the rivers and oceans.
- Labour, also known as human capital, covers all human activity ranging from the effort expended in subsistence living, manual labour used to produce goods and services to the intellectual labour provided by professionals such as architects, scientists, engineers, accountants, computer programmers, doctors and nurses to deliver their services.
- Macroeconomics is the branch of economics that studies the behaviour and performance of an economy as a whole. It focuses on the aggregate changes in the economy such as unemployment, growth rate, gross domestic product and inflation.
- Margin debt refers to borrowing from a brokerage firm (through a margin account) to purchase shares. The underlying shares act as security for the loan.
- Microeconomics is the study of individuals, households and firms' behaviour in decision making and allocation of resources.[553]
- Mixed income denotes the income from production of unincorporated enterprises.
- Money is defined as any object or record that is generally accepted as payment for goods and services and repayment of debts. Money is broader than just the notes and coins,

as it includes currency and near-money, such as credit, as well as banking and checking accounts.

- Net exports are the value of a country's total exports less the value of total imports. Net exports make a positive contribution to a nation's wealth while net imports generally detract from a nation's wealth, as money pours out of the domestic economy to pay for imported goods and services.
- Net taxes refer to taxes payable on goods and services less any subsidies on production and imports.
- Nominal GDP reflects GDP in current-day dollars i.e. not adjusted for inflation or deflation.
- Non-durable items are goods that are immediately consumed in one use or ones that have a short lifespan. Examples include food, fuel, cosmetics and footwear.
- 100 per cent gold standard exists when all the money in circulation can be exchanged for an equivalent amount of gold.
- Open-market operations are activities undertaken by central banks to provide liquidity and stimulate the economy i.e. central banks purchase short-term government debt from financial institutions.
- Output gap is an economic measure of the difference between the actual output of an economy and its potential output. Potential output is the maximum amount of goods and services an economy can turn out when it is most efficient – that is, at full capacity.
- Promissory note is a financial instrument that contains a written promise by one party (issuer) to pay another party (payee) a specific sum of money, either on demand or at a specified future date.
- Real GDP is an inflation-adjusted measure that reflects the value of all goods and services produced by an economy

in a given year, expressed in base-year prices. It is often referred to as constant dollar GDP. Real GDP gives a more realistic assessment of growth over time.

- Savings represents that portion of disposable income that is not spent on consumption of goods and services.
- Specie represents money in the form of coins (typically gold or silver) rather than notes.

Notes

I would like to acknowledge the use of Wikipedia as a general source of information on a range of topics throughout this book. This has been supplemented by a significant range of other information sources.

Part 1

1. Richard Lipsey, Gordon Sparks and Peter Steiner (1973), *Economics*, Harper & Row, Publishers, Inc pp 8–10
2. The Alchemists: Three Central Bankers and a World on Fire - Neil Irwin - Google Books
3. https://en.wikipedia.org/wiki/History_of_money
4. https://dailyreckoning.com/the-fall-of-the-roman-denarius/
5. www.cato.org/pubs/journal/cjv14n2-7.html
6. Bernardi, A. (1970:49) "The Economic Problems of the Roman Empire at the Time of Its Decline"
7. http://content.time.com/time/specials/packages/article/0,28804,1877351_1877350_1877322,00.html
8. https://mises.org/library/krugmans-call-housing-bubble
9. https://www.britannica.com/topic/Financial-Crisis-of-2008-The-1484264

10 https://www.britannica.com/topic/Financial-Crisis-of-2008-The-1484264
11 https://www.britannica.com/topic/Financial-Crisis-of-2008-The-1484264
12 https://www.britannica.com/topic/Financial-Crisis-of-2008-The-1484264
13 https://thinkprogress.org/wall-street-banks-earned-billions-in-profits-off-7-7-trillion-in-secret-fed-loans-made-during-the-893833d1b65a/
14 https://www.britannica.com/topic/Financial-Crisis-of-2008-The-1484264
15 https://www.afse.fr/global/gene/link.php?news_link=2015123312_AdvertSEP2.pdf&fg=1
16 https://mises.org/library/aristotle-private-property-and-money
17 www.worldhistoryonline.org/middle-ages-history/difference - between feudalism-manorialism
18 Philip Daileader, 'Feudalism', The High Middle Ages, Course No. 869, The Teaching Company, ISBN 1-56585-827-1
19 https://en.wikipedia.org/wiki/Middle_Ages
20 http://en.wikipedia.org/wiki/Great_Divergence
21 http://www.slideserve.com/aizza/physiocrats-and-mercantilism-1371651
22 http://mises.org/daily/4701 - Sir Josiah Child: False Friend of Freedom Mises Daily: Friday, October 29, 2010 by Murray N. Rothbard
23 http://mises.org/daily/4701 - Sir Josiah Child: False Friend of Freedom Mises Daily: Friday, October 29, 2010 by Murray N. Rothbard
24 ses.org/daily/4701 - Sir Josiah Child: False Friend of Freedom Mises Daily: Friday, October 29, 2010 by Murray N. Rothbard
25 https://www.britannica.com/topic/physiocrat
26 www.ggdc.net/maddison/historical_statistics/horizontal-file_03-2007.xls
27 http://www.newworldencyclopedia.org/entry/Classical_economics
28 https://mises.org/library/richard-cantillon-founding-father-modern-economics
29 https://www.investopedia.com/terms/n/neoclassical.asp
30 E. Roy Weintraub. (2007). "Neoclassical Economics". The Concise Encyclopedia of Economics. Retrieved September 26, 2010, from http://www.econlib.org/library/Enc1/NeoclassicalEconomics.html
31 Clark, B. (1998). *Principles of political economy: A comparative approach*. Westport, Connecticut: Praeger.
32 Fonseca, Gonçalo L. "Neo-Keynesian Synthesis". www.hetwebsite.net. The History Of Economic Thought Website. Retrieved 7 May 2017

33 Clark, B. (1998). *Political-economy: A comparative approach*. Westport, CT: Preage
34 Alfred S. Eichner and J. A. Kregel (1975) "An Essay on Post-Keynesian Theory: A New Paradigm in Economics", Journal of Economic Literature, V. 13, N. 4 (Dec.): pp 1293–314
35 Paul A. Samuelson and William D. Nordhaus (2004). Economics, 18th ed., pp 5–6 & [end] Glossary of Terms, "Normative vs. positive economics."
36 https://en.wikipedia.org/wiki/AD%E2%80%93AS_model
37 http://www.imf.org/external/pubs/ft/fandd/2013/09/basics.htm

Part 2

38 www.ggdc.net/maddison/historical_statistics/horizontal-file_03-2007.xls
39 http://www.u-s-history.com/pages/h986.html
40 https://www.quora.com/How-many-states-had-formed-in-the-year-1900-and-which-ones
41 Paul Kennedy, *The Rise and Fall of the Great Powers* (1987) p 243
42 Timothy D. Tregarthen Libby Rittenberg (1999). Macroeconomics (2nd ed) Worth Publishers p 177
43 http://www.loc.gov/teachers/classroommaterials/presentationsandactivities/presentations/timeline/progress/cities/
44 Tindall, George Brown and Shi, David E. (2012). *America: A Narrative History (Brief Ninth Edition) (Vol. 2)*. W. W. Norton & Company. ISBN 0393912671 p 589
45 http://en.wikipedia.org/wiki/Panic_of_1819
46 http://mises.org/library/1819-americas-first-housing-bubble
47 http://wiki.mises.org/wiki/Panic_of_1837
48 http://wiki.mises.org/wiki/Panic_of_1837
49 http://wiki.mises.org/wiki/Panic_of_1837
50 http://wiki.mises.org/wiki/Panic_of_1873
51 http://www2.gcc.edu/dept/econ/ASSC/Papers2013/ASSC2013-FahertyMatt.pdf
52 http://www2.gcc.edu/dept/econ/ASSC/Papers2013/ASSC2013-FahertyMatt.pdf
53 McCartney, E. Ray. Crisis of 1873. Minneapolis, Minn.: Burgess Pub. Co., 1935. p 88
54 Charles Poor Kindleberger, *Historical Economics: Art or Science?* Berkeley, CA: University of California Press, 1990; p 321
55 http://www2.gcc.edu/dept/econ/ASSC/Papers2013/ASSC2013-FahertyMatt.pdf

56 http://www2.gcc.edu/dept/econ/ASSC/Papers2013/ASSC2013-FahertyMatt.pdf
57 Lord Keynes (2012-01-26). "Social Democracy for the 21st Century: A Post Keynesian Perspective: US Unemployment, 1869–1899". Socialdemocracy21stcentury.blogspot.com. Retrieved 2013-12-08
58 McCartney, E. Ray. *Crisis of 1873*. Minneapolis, Minn.: Burgess Pub. Co., 1935. p136
59 http://www2.gcc.edu/dept/econ/ASSC/Papers2013/ASSC2013-FahertyMatt.pdf
60 http://www2.gcc.edu/dept/econ/ASSC/Papers2013/ASSC2013-FahertyMatt.pdf
61 http://www.encyclopedia.com/history/united-states-and-canada/us-history/panic-1893
62 Whitten, David O. "EH.Net Encyclopedia: Depression of 1893". eh.net. Retrieved 2009-04-20
63 http://en.wikipedia.org/wiki/Panic_of_1893
64 Parshall, Gerald. "The Great Panic Of '93." U.S. News & World Report 113.17 (1992): 70. Academic Search Complete. Web. 26 Feb. 2013
65 http://projects.vassar.edu/1896/depression.html
66 https://en.wikipedia.org/wiki/Panic_of_1907
67 http://wiki.mises.org/wiki/Panic_of_1907
68 https://en.wikipedia.org/wiki/Closing_milestones_of_the_Dow_Jones_Industrial_Average#The_Century_Turnover_Bull_Market_.281896.E2.80.931906.29
69 Moen, Jon; Tallman, Ellis (1992), "The Bank Panic of 1907: The Role of the Trust Companies", *The Journal of Economic History* 52 (3): 611–30, doi:10.1017/S0022050700011414
70 https://www.frbatlanta.org/-/media/documents/filelegacydocs/ern390tallman.pdf
71 https://www.frbatlanta.org/-/media/documents/filelegacydocs/ern390tallman.pdf
72 https://www.frbatlanta.org/-/media/documents/filelegacydocs/ern390tallman.pdf
73 https://www.frbatlanta.org/-/media/documents/filelegacydocs/ern390tallman.pdf
74 http://en.wikipedia.org/wiki/Panic_of_1907
75 https://www.frbatlanta.org/-/media/documents/filelegacydocs/ern390tallman.pdf
76 Bruner, Robert F.; Carr, Sean D. (2007), *The Panic of 1907: Lessons Learned from the Market's Perfect Storm*, Hoboken, New Jersey: John Wiley & Sons, ISBN 978-0-470-15263-8

77 http://www.let.rug.nl/usa/essays/general/a-brief-history-of-central-banking/two-remaining-major-defects.php
78 http://www.bigeye.com/griffin.htm
79 http://www.whale.to/b/m_ch_1.html
80 https://www.federalreserve.gov/aboutthefed/officialtitle-preamble.htm
81 https://www.federalreserve.gov/faqs/about_12594.htm
82 https://www.federalreserve.gov/faqs/about_12799.htm
83 http://www.latimes.com/business/la-fi-federal-reserve-profit-20160111-story.html
84 https://www.brookings.edu/blog/ben-bernanke/2016/01/11/audit-the-fed-is-not-about-auditing-the-fed/
85 http://thehill.com/policy/finance/231822-fed-fires-back
86 https://www.brookings.edu/blog/ben-bernanke/2016/01/11/audit-the-fed-is-not-about-auditing-the-fed/
87 https://www.theglobalist.com/panic-of-1819-the-first-major-u-s-depression/
88 https://www.businessinsider.com.au/bernanke-quotes-2010-12#zJVg5RTZXhpChEv2.99
89 https://www.businessinsider.com.au/bernanke-quotes-2010-12#YM5qlhhIbe9ZrdOX.99
90 https://mises.org/library/defense-bank-failures
91 http://mises.org/library/panic-1819
92 US Business Cycle Expansions and Contractions, National Bureau of Economic Research. Retrieved on September 22, 2008
93 https://inflationdata.com/articles/inflation-consumer-price-index-decade-commentary/inflation-cpi-consumer-price-index-1913-1919/
94 https://fee.org/articles/the-depression-youve-never-heard-of-1920-1921/
95 https://mises.org/library/forgotten-depression-1920
96 Vernon, J. R. (July 1991). "The 1920–21 Deflation: The Role of Aggregate Supply". Economic Inquiry. Western Economic Association International. 29 (3): 572–580. doi:10.1111/j.1465-7295.1991.tb00847.x
97 Christina Duckworth Romer (1988). "World War I and the postwar depression; A reinterpretation based on alternative estimates of GNP". Journal of Monetary Economics. 22 (1): 91–115. doi:10.1016/0304-3932(88)90171-7
98 Romer, Christina (1986). "Spurious Volatility in Historical Unemployment Data" (PDF). The Journal of Political Economy. 91: 1–37. doi:10.1086/261361
99 Anthony Patrick O'Brien (1997). "Depression of 1920–1921". In David Glasner, Thomas F. Cooley. *Business cycles and depressions: an encyclopedia*. New York: Garland Publishing. pp 151–153

100 "Dow Historical Timeline". Dow Jones Industrial Average
101 https://mises.org/library/forgotten-depression-1920
102 Romer, Christina (1989). "Does Monetary Policy Matter? A New Test in the Spirit of Friedman and Schwartz". NBER Macroeconomics Annual. 4: 121–170. doi:10.2307/3584969. JSTOR 3584969 – via JSTOR
103 https://mises.org/library/forgotten-depression-1920
104 https://mises.org/library/forgotten-depression-1920
105 https://mises.org/library/forgotten-depression-1920
106 https://mises.org/library/forgotten-depression-1920
107 Benjamin M. Anderson, Economics and the Public Welfare: A Financial and Economic History of the United States, 1914–1946 (Indianapolis: Liberty Press, 1979 [1949]), pp 88–89, 90
108 https://eh.net/encyclopedia/the-u-s-economy-in-the-1920s/
109 http://www.bbc.co.uk/schools/gcsebitesize/history/tch_wjec/usa19101929/2riseandfall1.shtml
110 https://en.wikipedia.org/wiki/Roaring_Twenties
111 https://eh.net/encyclopedia/the-u-s-economy-in-the-1920s/
112 https://eh.net/encyclopedia/the-u-s-economy-in-the-1920s/
113 http://en.wikipedia.org/wiki/Economic_history_of_the_United_States
114 https://eh.net/encyclopedia/the-u-s-economy-in-the-1920s/
115 Nelson, Daniel. "Mass Production and the U.S. Tire Industry." *The Journal of Economic History 48 (1987): 329-40*
116 http://austrianeconomics.wikia.com/wiki/Great_Depression
117 http://www.bis.org/publ/work137.pdf
118 http://austrianeconomics.wikia.com/wiki/Great_Depression
119 https://eh.net/encyclopedia/the-u-s-economy-in-the-1920s/
120 http://www.bis.org/publ/work137.pdf
121 http://www.bis.org/publ/work137.pdf
122 http://www.bis.org/publ/work137.pdf
123 http://www.bis.org/publ/work137.pdf
124 Field, A.J., 1992. *Uncontrolled land development and the duration of the Depression in the United States*. Journal of Economic History 52, pp 785-805
125 http://www.bis.org/publ/work137.pdf
126 http://www.bis.org/publ/work137.pdf
127 http://www.bis.org/publ/work137.pdf
128 http://www.bis.org/publ/work137.pdf
129 https://eh.net/encyclopedia/the-u-s-economy-in-the-1920s/
130 https://eh.net/encyclopedia/the-u-s-economy-in-the-1920s/
131 https://eh.net/encyclopedia/the-u-s-economy-in-the-1920s/
132 http://www.history.com/topics/roaring-twenties

133 "Film History of the 1920s". Retrieved 31 January 2017
134 "Film History of the 1920s". Retrieved 31 January 2017
135 http://learningenglish.voanews.com/a/american-history--roaring-twenties-a-time-of-economic-and-social-change-112612204/115985.html
136 "Index of /web". dreamwell.com
137 Julian Jackson (2009). Living in Arcadia: Homosexuality, Politics, and Morality in France from the Liberation to AIDS. University of Chicago Press. p 32
138 http://www.history.com/topics/roaring-twenties
139 http://www.history.com/topics/roaring-twenties
140 Murrin, John M.; Hämäläinen, Pekka; Johnson, Paul E.; Brunsman, Denver; McPherson, James M. (2015). Liberty, Equality, Power: A History of the American People, Volume 2: Since 1863. Cengage Learning.
141 https://history.state.gov/milestones/1921-1936/immigration-act
142 https://mises.org/library/forgotten-depression-1920
143 https://eh.net/encyclopedia/the-u-s-economy-in-the-1920s/
144 http://www.bbc.co.uk/schools/gcsebitesize/history/tch_wjec/usa19101929/2riseandfall1.shtml
145 http://www.frbsf.org/economic-research/publications/economic-letter/1999/march/monetary-policy-and-the-great-crash-of-1929-a-bursting-bubble-or-collapsing-fundamentals/
146 https://mises.org/library/great-depression
147 https://eh.net/encyclopedia/the-u-s-economy-in-the-1920s/
148 http://www.frbsf.org/economic-research/publications/economic-letter/1999/march/monetary-policy-and-the-great-crash-of-1929-a-bursting-bubble-or-collapsing-fundamentals/
149 https://en.wikipedia.org/wiki/Wall_Street_Crash_of_1929
150 Weeks, Linton. "History's Advice During a Panic? Don't Panic". NPR. Retrieved October 1, 2008
151 Jerome Blum, Rondo Cameron, Thomas G. Barnes, *The European world: a history* (2nd ed 1970) p 885
152 https://fred.stlouisfed.org/series/M1109BUSM293NNBR
153 Herbert Hoover, *The Memoirs of Herbert Hoover: The Great Depression, 1929-41*, (New York: Macmillan, 1952) pp 44–45
154 John T. Woolley and Gerhard Peters, The American Presidency Project [online]. Santa Barbara, CA. Available from World Wide Web: http://www.presidency.ucsb.edu/ws/?pid=22005.
155 http://www.frbsf.org/economic-research/publications/economic-letter/1999/march/monetary-policy-and-the-great-crash-of-1929-a-bursting-bubble-or-collapsing-fundamentals/
156 Murray N. Rothbard. "America's Great Depression" (pdf), The New Deal Farm Program, pp 217-237, referenced 2009-11-21

157 Taussig, FW (1931), The Tariff History of the United States (PDF) (8th ed.), New York: G.P. Putnam's Sons
158 https://fee.org/articles/the-smoot-hawley-tariff-and-the-great-depression/?gclid=CJ_vzurqjtICFYSYvAodKvYMeg
159 Bureau of the Census, *Historical Statistics* series F-1
160 "Smoot–Hawley Tariff", U.S. Department of State, June 21, 2003, ISBN 0-8240-5367-2
161 https://mises.org/library/great-depression
162 https://fee.org/articles/the-smoot-hawley-tariff-and-the-great-depression/?gclid=COuDgczxjtICFVYGvAod5AsKkw
163 https://fee.org/articles/the-smoot-hawley-tariff-and-the-great-depression/?gclid=COuDgczxjtICFVYGvAod5AsKkw
164 "Drought: A Paleo Perspective – 20th Century Drought". National Climatic Data Center. Retrieved April 5, 2009
165 Hamilton, James (1987). "Monetary Factors in the Great Depression". Journal of Monetary Economics. 19 (2): 145–169. doi:10.1016/0304-3932(87)90045-6
166 http://www.frbsf.org/economic-research/publications/economic-letter/1999/march/monetary-policy-and-the-great-crash-of-1929-a-bursting-bubble-or-collapsing-fundamentals/
167 Murray N. Rothbard. "America's Great Depression" (pdf), 10. 1931—"The Tragic Year", pp 257-284, referenced 2009-11-27
168 Herbert Hoover, *The Memoirs of Herbert Hoover: Volume 2, The Cabinet and the Presidency, 1920-33*, (New York: Macmillan, 1952) p 108
169 "Norris-Laguardia Act (1932): Major Acts of Congress", accessed 2011-02-01
170 Murray N. Rothbard. "America's Great Depression" (pdf), 12. The Close of the Hoover Term, p. 321-337, referenced 2010-06-20
171 Peter Clemens, *Prosperity, Depression and the New Deal: The USA 1890–1954*, Hodder Education, 4. Auflage, 2008, ISBN 978-0-340-965887, p 114
172 http://austrianeconomics.wikia.com/wiki/Great_Depression
173 http://austrianeconomics.wikia.com/wiki/Great_Depression
174 https://wiki.mises.org/wiki/Great_Depression
175 https://wiki.mises.org/wiki/Great_Depression
176 http://great-depression-facts.com/
177 "The American Experience: Drought". PBS. Retrieved March 15, 2015
178 John T. Woolley and Gerhard Peters. "Democratic Party Platform of 1932", June 27, 1932, from The American Presidency Project [online]. Referenced 2010-06-20
179 Carol Berkin; et al. (2011). Making America, Volume 2: A History of the United States: Since 1865. Cengage Learning. pp. 629–32. ISBN 0495915246.

180 http://thegreatdepressioncauses.com/facts/
181 George F. Smith. "The Virtue of Hoarding", Mises Daily, posted on October 09, 2009, referenced 2009-11-18
182 Murray N. Rothbard. "America's Great Depression" (pdf), 11. The Hoover New Deal of 1932, p. 325-326, referenced 2013-04-12
183 http://www.federalreservehistory.org/Events/DetailView/25
184 https://en.wikipedia.org/wiki/National_Recovery_Administration
185 Reed, Lawrence W. Great Myths of the Great Depression Mackinac Center for Public Policy
186 Clapper in *Washington Post,* Dec. 4, 1934, quoted in Best, 79–80 (1991)
187 Thomas J. DiLorenzo. "A New, New Deal", Mises Daily, October 1998, referenced 2010-06-20
188 Rasmussen, Wayne D., Gladys L. Baker, and James S. Ward, "A Short History of Agricultural Adjustment, 1933-75." Economic Research Service, United States Department of Agriculture, Agriculture Information Bulletin No. 391 (March 1976), p4
189 Rasmussen, Wayne D., Gladys L. Baker, and James S. Ward, "A Short History of Agricultural Adjustment, 1933-75." Economic Research Service, United States Department of Agriculture, Agriculture Information Bulletin No. 391 (March 1976), p2
190 Hamilton, David. *Agricultural Adjustment Act: An entry from Macmillan Reference USA's Encyclopedia of the Great Depression. s.v. "Sharecroppers"*. 1. Macmillan Reference USA.
191 http://austrianeconomics.wikia.com/wiki/Great_Depression
192 http://www.u-s-history.com/pages/h1528.html
193 https://wiki.mises.org/wiki/Great_Depression
194 http://www.history.com/topics/new-deal
195 http://www.u-s-history.com/pages/h1528.html
196 Arnesen, Eric (2007). *Encyclopedia of U.S. Labor and Working-Class History*. 1. New York: Routledge. p 1540. ISBN 9780415968263
197 Leighninger, Robert D. (2007*). Long-Range Public Investment: The Forgotten Legacy of the New Deal.* Columbia, S.C.: University of South Carolina Press. ISBN 9781570036637
198 Leighninger, Robert D. (May 1996). "*Cultural Infrastructure: The Legacy of New Deal Public Space*". Journal of Architectural Education. 49 (4): 226–236. JSTOR 1425295
199 Thomas J. DiLorenzo. "A New, New Deal", Mises Daily, October 1998, referenced 2010-06-20
200 Robert Goldston, *The Great Depression*, Fawcett Publications, 1968, p 228
201 *Business Cycles*, James Arthur Estey, Purdue University, Prentice-Hall, 1950, pp 22–23 chart

202 *Economic Fluctuations*, Maurice W. Lee, Chairman of Economics Dept., Washington State College, published by R. D. Irwin Inc, Homewood, Illinois, 1955, p 236
203 Maurice W. Lee, 1955
204 A Century of Change in the Australian Labour Market, Australian Bureau of Statistics
205 1929–1939 – The Great Depression, Source: Bank of Canada
206 Unemployment During The Great Depression, thegreatdepression.co.uk
207 Jerome Blum, Rondo Cameron, Thomas G. Barnes, *The European world: a history* (2nd ed 1970) p 885
208 https://en.wikipedia.org/wiki/Great_Depression
209 Myung Soo Cha, "Did Takahashi Korekiyo Rescue Japan from the Great Depression?" *The Journal of Economic History* 63, No. 1 (March 2003): pp 127–144
210 https://en.wikipedia.org/wiki/The_General_Theory_of_Employment,_Interest_and_Money
211 https://en.wikipedia.org/wiki/John_Maynard_Keynes
212 http://www.econlib.org/library/Enc1/KeynesianEconomics.html
213 Keynes, John Maynard (1924). "*The Theory of Money and the Foreign Exchanges*". A Tract on Monetary Reform.
214 https://en.wikipedia.org/wiki/Keynesian_economics
215 https://en.wikipedia.org/wiki/Keynesian_economics
216 O'Sullivan, Arthur; Sheffrin, Steven M. (2003). Economics: Principles in Action. Upper Saddle River: Pearson Prentice Hall. ISBN 0-13-063085-3
217 http://www.econlib.org/library/Enc1/KeynesianEconomics.html
218 http://www.econlib.org/library/Enc/bios/Keynes.html
219 W. H. Greenleaf, *The British Political Tradition. Volume II: The Ideological Heritage* (London: Methuen, 1983), p 143
220 https://fee.org/articles/henry-hazlitt-and-the-failure-of-keynesian-economics/
221 https://fee.org/articles/henry-hazlitt-and-the-failure-of-keynesian-economics/
222 https://fee.org/articles/henry-hazlitt-and-the-failure-of-keynesian-economics/
223 https://fee.org/articles/henry-hazlitt-and-the-failure-of-keynesian-economics/
224 Robert D. McFadden, James M. Buchanan, Economic Scholar and Nobel Laureate, Dies at 93, New York Times, January 9, 2013
225 Tyler Cowen, It's Time to Face the Fiscal Illusion, New York Times, March 5, 2011
226 Feldstein, Martin (Summer 1981). "The retreat from Keynesian economics". The Public Interest: pp 92–105

227 Friedman, Milton (1997). "John Maynard Keynes". FRB Richmond Economic Quarterly. **83**: 1–23.
228 https://www.federalreserve.gov/boarddocs/speeches/2004/200403022/
229 https://fee.org/articles/the-depression-youve-never-heard-of-1920-1921/
230 http://austrianeconomics.wikia.com/wiki/Austrian_Business_Cycle_Theory
231 Manipulating the Interest Rate: a Recipe for Disaster, Thorsten Polleit, 13 December 2007
232 "The weeds of destruction". Economist. 2006-05-04. Retrieved 2008-10-08
233 Human Action, Ludwig von Mises, Chapter XX, section 8
234 https://wiki.mises.org/wiki/Murray_Rothbard
235 George C. Leef, Book Review of Egalitarianism as a Revolt Against Nature and Other Essays by Murray Rothbard, edited by David Gordon (2000 edition), The Freeman, July 2001
236 Rothbard, Murray (1997). "*The Myth of Neutral Taxation*". The Logic of Action Two: Applications and Criticism from the Austrian School. Cheltenham, UK: Edward Elgar. p 67. ISBN 1-85898-570-6. First published in The Cato Journal, Fall 1981
237 *For a New Liberty, Chapter 3*
238 White, Lawrence H. (2008). "*The research program of Austrian economics*". Advances in Austrian Economics. Emerald Group Publishing Limited: 20
239 Skousen, Mark (2001). *The Making of Modern Economics*. M.E. Sharpe. p 284. ISBN 978-0-7656-0479-8
240 Steele, G. R. (2001). *Keynes and Hayek*. Routledge. p 9. ISBN 978-0-415-25138-9
241 Fisher, Irving (October 1933). '*The Debt-Deflation Theory of Great Depressions*'. Econometrica. The Econometric Society. 1 (4): 337–357. doi:10.2307/1907327. JSTOR 1907327
242 Bernanke, Ben (1995), "The Macroeconomics of the Great Depression: A Comparative Approach" (PDF), Journal of Money, Credit, and Banking, 27 (1): 1–28, doi:10.2307/2077848, JSTOR 2077848
243 http://www.debtdeflation.com/blogs/2009/01/11/bernanke-an-expert-on-the-great-depression/
244 http://www.levyinstitute.org/pubs/wp74.pdf

Part 3

245 http://www.conference-board.org/data/economydatabase/
246 http://www.conference-board.org/data/economydatabase/
247 http://www.mckinsey.com/global-themes/employment-and-growth/debt-and-not-much-deleveraging
248 https://www.independent.co.uk/news/business/analysis-and-features/global-debt-crisis-explained-all-time-high-world-economy-causes-solutions-definition-a8143516.html
249 The Conference Board. 2016. The Conference Board Total Economy Database™ (Original version), November 2016, http://www.conference-board.org/data/economydatabase/
250 https://www.britannica.com/place/Japan/Demographic-trends#toc23255
251 http://www.grips.ac.jp/teacher/oono/hp/lecture_J/lec10.htm
252 https://history.state.gov/milestones/1945-1952/japan-reconstruction
253 http://www.grips.ac.jp/vietnam/VDFTokyo/Doc/EDJ_Chap10-11.pdf
254 http://www.grips.ac.jp/vietnam/VDFTokyo/Doc/EDJ_Chap10-11.pdf
255 http://www.lehigh.edu/~rfw1/courses/1999/spring/ir163/Papers/pdf/mat5.pdf
256 https://history.state.gov/milestones/1945-1952/japan-reconstruction
257 http://www.lehigh.edu/~rfw1/courses/1999/spring/ir163/Papers/pdf/mat5.pdf
258 https://history.state.gov/milestones/1945-1952/japan-reconstruction
259 http://www.grips.ac.jp/teacher/oono/hp/lecture_J/lec10.htm
260 https://en.wikipedia.org/wiki/Ministry_of_International_Trade_and_Industry
261 http://www.iun.edu/~hisdcl/h207_2002/jecontakeoff.htm
262 https://www.gsid.nagoya-u.ac.jp/sotsubo/Postwar_Development_of_the_Japanese%20Economy(Otsubo_NagoyaU).pdf
263 https://www.gsid.nagoya-u.ac.jp/sotsubo/Postwar_Development_of_the_Japanese%20Economy(Otsubo_NagoyaU).pdf
264 http://www.iun.edu/~hisdcl/h207_2002/jecontakeoff.htm
265 http://www.iun.edu/~hisdcl/h207_2002/jecontakeoff.htm
266 https://www.gsid.nagoya-u.ac.jp/sotsubo/Postwar_Development_of_the_Japanese%20Economy(Otsubo_NagoyaU).pdf
267 https://www.gsid.nagoya-u.ac.jp/sotsubo/Postwar_Development_of_the_Japanese%20Economy(Otsubo_NagoyaU).pdf
268 https://en.wikipedia.org/wiki/Plaza_Accord
269 http://www.investopedia.com/articles/forex/09/plaza-accord.asp

270 https://www.gsid.nagoya-u.ac.jp/sotsubo/Postwar_Development_of_the_Japanese%20Economy(Otsubo_NagoyaU).pc
271 http://www.thebubblebubble.com/japan-bubble/
272 https://pdfs.semanticscholar.org/564b/615839b3761f2902c5cb6c8086ded6f9e4fa.pdf
273 https://www.gsid.nagoya-u.ac.jp/sotsubo/Postwar_Development_of_the_Japanese%20Economy(Otsubo_NagoyaU).p
274 http://www.nytimes.com/2008/10/19/weekinreview/19impoco.html
275 https://pdfs.semanticscholar.org/564b/615839b3761f2902c5cb6c8086ded6f9e4fa.pdf
276 https://en.wikipedia.org/wiki/Nikkei_225
277 http://www.tradingeconomics.com/japan/government-budget
278 https://fred.stlouisfed.org/graph/?id=GGGDTAJPA188N,
279 https://krugman.blogs.nytimes.com/2010/03/17/how-much-of-the-world-is-in-a-liquidity-trap/?_r=0
280 Koo, Richard (2009). *The Holy Grail of Macroeconomics-Lessons from Japan's Great Recession.* John Wiley & Sons (Asia) Pte. Ltd. ISBN 978-0-470-82494-8
281 Sumner, Scott. "Why Japan's QE didn't 'work'". The Money Illusion. Retrieved November 24, 2014
282 https://fred.stlouisfed.org/tags/series?t=interest+rate%3Bjapan
283 https://en.wikipedia.org/wiki/Lost_Decade_(Japan)
284 Amyx, Jennifer (2004). *Japan's Financial Crisis: Institutional Rigidity and Reluctant Change.* Princeton University Press. pp 17–18
285 https://www.gsid.nagoya-u.ac.jp/sotsubo/Postwar_Development_of_the_Japanese%20Economy(Otsubo_NagoyaU).p
286 http://www.nber.org/papers/w15052.pdf p 32
287 Okina, Kunio, Masaaki Shirakawa and Shigenori Shiratsuka (2001): "The asset price bubble and monetary policy: experience of Japan's economy in the late 1980s and its lessons", *Monetary and Economic Studies*, 19 (S-1), Institute for Monetary and Economic Studies, Bank of Japan, pp 395-450.
288 https://www.gsid.nagoya-u.ac.jp/sotsubo/Postwar_Development_of_the_Japanese%20Economy(Otsubo_NagoyaU).pdfHG
289 https://fred.stlouisfed.org/graph/?id=JPNCPIALLQINMEI,
290 https://fred.stlouisfed.org/series/FPCPITOTLZGJPN
291 https://fred.stlouisfed.org/graph/?id=JPNRGDPEXP,
292 The Conference Board. 2016. The Conference Board Total Economy Database™ (Original version), November 2016, http://www.conference-board.org/data/economydatabase/
293 The Conference Board. 2016. The Conference Board Total Economy Database™ (Original version), November 2016, http://www.conference-board.org/data/economydatabase/

294 http://www.bis.org/publ/bppdf/bispap21e.pdf
295 https://fred.stlouisfed.org/graph/?id=MKTGDPCNA646NWDB,
296 http://www.populstat.info/Asia/chinac.htm
297 http://alphahistory.com/chineserevolution/
298 http://alphahistory.com/chineserevolution/first-five-year-plan/
299 http://www.liberation.fr/planete/2011/06/17/la-chine-creuse-ses-trous-de-memoire_743211
300 Dikötter, Frank (2010). pp. x, xi. ISBN 0-8027-7768-6
301 Jones, Adam (2010). *Genocide: A Comprehensive Introduction.* Routledge, 2nd edition (August 1, 2010). p 96. ISBN 0-415-48619-X
302 The Conference Board. 2016. The Conference Board Total Economy Database™ (Original version), November 2016, http://www.conference-board.org/data/economydatabase/
303 http://www.shsu.edu/~his_ncp/PWChina.html
304 Jasper Becker. Systematic genocide Archived 2012-04-11 at the Wayback Machine.. The Spectator, September 25, 2010
305 https://fred.stlouisfed.org/graph/?id=MKTGDPCNA646NWDB,
306 https://en.wikipedia.org/wiki/Cultural_Revolution
307 Joel Andreas (2009). Rise of the Red Engineers: The Cultural Revolution and the Origins of China's New Class. Stanford University Press. p. 164. ISBN 978-0804760782
308 Ebrey, Patricia Buckley (2005). *China: A Cultural, Social, and Political History* (1st ed.). Wadsworth Publishing. p 294. ISBN 978-0618133871
309 https://en.wikipedia.org/wiki/China
310 http://data.worldbank.org/indicator/SP.DYN.LE00.IN
311 "China's growing middle class" CNN. 26 April 2012
312 "Richest People in China Got Poorer, Says Hurun Rich List 2012". Ibtimes. 25 September 2012. Retrieved 31 May 2015
313 https://www.cia.gov/library/publications/the-world-factbook/geos/ch.html
314 "Urbanisation: Where China's future will happen". The Economist. 19 April 2014. Retrieved 18 February 2015
315 "China Now Has More Than 260 Million Migrant Workers Whose Average Monthly Salary Is 2,290 Yuan ($374.09)". International Business Times. 28 May 2013. Retrieved 18 February 2015
316 H., Hunt, Michael. The world transformed: 1945 to the present. p 355. ISBN 9780199371020. OCLC 907585907
317 Naughton, Barry. (2007). *The Chinese Economy: Transitions and Growth.* Cambridge: MIT Press
318 Brandt, Loren; et al. (2008), "*China's Great Transformation*", in Brandt, Loren; Rawski, G. Thomas, China's Great Transformation, Cambridge: Cambridge University Press p116

319 Perkins, Dwight; et al. (2008), "*Forecasting China's growth to 2025*", in Brandt, Loren; Rawski, G. Thomas, China's Great Transformation, p 862 Cambridge: Cambridge University Press

320 https://en.wikipedia.org/wiki/Chinese_economic_reform

321 Scissors, Derek (May–June 2009). Deng Undone: The Costs of Halting Market Reform in China". Foreign Affairs. 88 (3).

322 http://www.aeconf.com/Articles/May2004/aef050107.pdf

323 https://www.imf.org/external/pubs/ft/weo/2016/02/weodata/weoselgr.aspx

324 "Literacy rate, adult total (% of people ages 15 and above)". World Bank. Retrieved 9 July 2013

325 Plafker, Ted. "China's Long—but Uneven—March to Literacy". International Herald Tribune. 12 February 2001. Retrieved 22 December 2012

326 "Desperately seeking math and science majors" CNN. 29 July 2009. Retrieved 9 April 2012

327 "China publishes the second most scientific papers in international journals in 2010: report". Xinhua. 2 December 2011. Retrieved 25 April 2012

328 The Controversial Chinese Economist Uncovering Tough Truths, Bloomberg Businessweek, 24 March 2017

329 https://www.washingtonpost.com/news/wonk/wp/2017/05/01/chinas-economic-miracle-has-an-ugly-underbelly/?utm_term=.769c31a14ff5

330 http://www.aeconf.com/Articles/May2004/aef050107.pdf

331 https://www.transparency.org/news/feature/corruption_perceptions_index_2016

332 https://www.smh.com.au/world/chinese-leaders-family-worth-a-billion-20120629-218qi.html

333 "Can Xi Jinping's Anti Corruption Campaign Succeed?". ChinaPowerCSIS.

334 "Robber barons, beware". The Economist. 24 October 2015.

335 http://www.ipcommission.org/report/ip_commission_report_052213.pdf

336 https://www.nytimes.com/2017/04/11/business/economy/trump-china-currency-manipulation-trade.html

337 https://www.uscc.gov/sites/default/files/Research/The%2013th%20Five-Year%20Plan.pdf

338 http://www.mckinsey.com/global-themes/employment-and-growth/debt-and-not-much-deleveraging

339 http://www.mckinsey.com/global-themes/employment-and-growth/debt-and-not-much-deleveraging

340 https://www.marketsandmoney.com.au/janet-yellens-shadow-banking-crisis/2017/05/23/
341 http://www.mckinsey.com/global-themes/employment-and-growth/debt-and-not-much-deleveraging
342 https://www.uscc.gov/Research/13th-five-year-plan
343 http://www.afr.com/news/politics/world/white-house-to-prepare-trade-case-against-china-20170802-gxnw4m
344 http://www.news.com.au/finance/economy/world-economy/chinas-belt-and-road-initiative-could-redraw-the-map-on-global-trade/news-story/eb752b6332e24ea219e36d0f16742463
345 http://www.news.com.au/finance/economy/world-economy/chinas-belt-and-road-initiative-could-redraw-the-map-on-global-trade/news-story/eb752b6332e24ea219e36d0f16742463
346 https://www.ft.com/content/3cdcbf42-4814-11e6-8d68-72e9211e86ab
347 http://www.afr.com/news/economy/trade/beijing-strikes-back-after-trump-targets-china-with-us60b-of-tariffs-20180323-h0xv68
348 The Conference Board. 2016. The Conference Board Total Economy Database™ (Original version), November 2016, http://www.conference-board.org/data/economydatabase/
349 https://history.state.gov/milestones/1937-1945/bretton-woods
350 https://www.federalreservehistory.org/essays/gold_convertibility_ends
351 https://www.federalreservehistory.org/essays/gold_convertibility_ends
352 https://en.wikipedia.org/wiki/1973%E2%80%9374_stock_market_crash
353 https://en.wikipedia.org/wiki/1973_oil_crisis
354 http://www.zerohedge.com/news/2016-05-31/secret-story-how-saudi-petrodollar-deal-was-born
355 http://www.econlib.org/library/Enc1/Reaganomics.html
356 Gregg Jackson, "Conservative Comebacks to Liberal Lies" (2011)
357 "CBO Historical Tables" (PDF). Retrieved 2012-01-04.
358 http://www.history.com/this-day-in-history/reagan-signs-economic-recovery-tax-act-erta
359 http://www.taxhistory.org/www/features.nsf/Articles/2BEBD14445F182F1852579F10058AA9F?OpenDocument
360 http://www.econlib.org/library/Enc1/Reaganomics.html
361 https://mises.org/library/myths-reaganomics
362 https://www.bea.gov/
363 https://fred.stlouisfed.org
364 https://www.govinfo.gov/content/pkg/ERP-2017/pdf/ERP-2017.pdf Table B-14

365 The Conference Board. 2016. The Conference Board Total Economy Database™ (Original version), November 2016, http://www.conference-board.org/data/economydatabase/
366 https://www.gmo.com/docs/default-source/research-and-commentary/strategies/asset-allocation/the-deep-causes-of-secular-stagnation-and-the-rise-of-populism.pdf?sfvrsn=11
367 http://money.cnn.com/2017/09/27/news/economy/inequality-record-top-1-percent-wealth/index.html
368 http://time.com/money/5054009/stock-ownership-10-percent-richest/
369 https://www.govinfo.gov/content/pkg/ERP-2017/pdf/ERP-2017.pdf Table B-14
370 https://www.bls.gov/news.release/empsit.t12.htm
371 https://www.govinfo.gov/content/pkg/ERP-2017/pdf/ERP-2017.pdf Table B-9
372 http://www.newsweek.com/people-food-stamps-snap-decline-participation-640500
373 http://money.cnn.com/2017/09/27/news/economy/inequality-record-top-1-percent-wealth/index.html
374 https://www.theatlantic.com/business/archive/2015/04/how-corporate-lobbyists-conquered-american-democracy/390822/
375 http://letsfixthiscountry.org/2018/08/24/whats-creating-all-these-socialists-thats-easy-capitalism/
376 Blinder, Alan S.; *Studies, International Center for Monetary and Banking* (2001). How do central banks talk?. Centre for Economic Policy Research. p. 66. ISBN 978-1-898128-60-1. Retrieved 5 August 2010.
377 https://www.wsj.com/articles/paying-professors-inside-googles-academic-influence-campaign-1499785286
378 http://www.nytimes.com/1970/09/13/archives/a-friedman-doctrine-the-social-responsibility-of-business-is-to.html
379 https://hbr.org/1990/05/ceo-incentives-its-not-how-much-you-pay-but-how
380 https://knowledge.insead.edu/blog/insead-blog/the-economic-consequences-of-shareholder-value-maximisation-5646
381 James, Paul (et al) (2—7) Globalization and Economy, Vols 1-4: London: Sage Publications.
382 http://data.worldbank.org/indicator/NY.GDP.MKTP.CD; http://stat.wto.org/StatisticalProgram/WSDBViewData.aspx?Language=E
383 https://founders.archives.gov/documents/Jefferson/03-10-02-0053
384 https://www.goodreads.com/quotes/tag/banks
385 https://www.fool.com/investing/general/2015/02/04/my-50-favorite-quotes-about-banking.aspx

386 Epstein, G. 2001. “Financialization, Rentier Interests, and Central Bank Policy,” manuscript, Department of Economics, University of Massachusetts, Amherst, MA, December. p 1
387 https://www.govinfo.gov/content/pkg/ERP-2017/pdf/ERP-2017.pdf. Tables B-6 and B-14
388 https://fred.stlouisfed.org/series/DDDM01USA156NWDB, March 15, 2018
389 https://fred.stlouisfed.org/series/CMDEBT, March 15, 2018
390 https://fred.stlouisfed.org/graph/?id=SLOAS,
391 http://bankruptcy.findlaw.com/debt-relief/your-options-when-you-can-t-repay-student-loans.html
392 https://www.newyorkfed.org/microeconomics/hhdc.html
393 https://www.forbes.com/sites/zackfriedman/2017/10/06/student-loan-default/#249116ec28de
394 https://fred.stlouisfed.org/graph/?id=TDSP,
395 https://fred.stlouisfed.org
396 https://www.reuters.com/article/us-usa-fed-inflation-target-idUSU.S.TRE80O25C20120126
397 https://en.wikiquote.org/wiki/Milton_Friedman
398 https://wiki.mises.org/wiki/Inflation
399 https://fred.stlouisfed.org/graph/?id=DDDM01USA156NWDB,#0
400 https://fred.stlouisfed.org/graph/?id=CSUSHPISA,
401 http://www.socionomics.net/2011/04/social-mood/
402 https://fred.stlouisfed.org/series/GS10
403 https://fred.stlouisfed.org/graph/?id=DISCNTD8,
404 http://ritholtz.com/2012/01/222-years-of-long-term-interest-rates/
405 https://fred.stlouisfed.org/graph/?id=DGS30,
406 https://www.reuters.com/article/us-usa-fed-inflation-target-idUSTRE80O25C20120126
407 A. Gary Shilling & Co: Insight October 2009 - InflationDeflation: 7 Varieties.pdf
408 https://www2.census.gov/library/publications/1975/compendia/hist_stats_colonial-1970/hist_stats_colonial-1970p1-chF.pdf
409 https://fred.stlouisfed.org/graph/?id=CPIAUCNS,
410 https://www.bis.org/publ/qtrpdf/r_qt1503e.htm
411 https://www.bea.gov/
412 https://www.census.gov/foreign-trade/balance/c5700.html
413 http://www.shadowstats.com/
414 http://www.reuters.com/article/us-usa-economy-geithner/financial-crises-caused-by-stupidity-and-greed-geithner-idUSBRE83P01P20120426
415 http://www.washingtonpost.com/wp-dyn/content/article/2007/08/31/AR2007083100506.html

416 http://www.washingtonpost.com/wp-dyn/content/article/2007/08/31/AR2007083100506.html
417 https://www.ft.com/content/ae19e60e-81b0-11e7-94e2-c5b903247afd
418 https://www.mises.ca/bernanke-thinks-he-saved-the-world/
419 https://www.rba.gov.au/publications/bulletin/2011/jun/pdf/bu-0611-8.pdf
420 https://fred.stlouisfed.org/graph/?id=SAVINGS,
421 http://www.bbc.com/news/business-19356665
422 http://www.afr.com/opinion/columnists/top-european-officials-fret-openly-about-the-potential-for-fresh-financial-crisis-20171009-gyxirr
423 http://www.afr.com/opinion/columnists/top-european-officials-fret-openly-about-the-potential-for-fresh-financial-crisis-20171009-gyxirr
424 https://www.cnbc.com/2017/06/27/yellen-banks-very-much-stronger-another-financial-crisis-not-likely-in-our-lifetime.html
425 https://www.cnbc.com/2017/09/19/fed-economist-no-evidence-qe-works-as-balance-sheet-unwind-starts.html
426 https://www.wsj.com/articles/former-fed-chief-greenspan-worried-about-future-of-monetary-policy-1414597627
427 http://www.businessinsider.com/underlying-inflation-just-reached-an-11-year-high-2017-11?IR=T
428 http://www.afr.com/opinion/columnists/ben-bernankes-pricetargeting-masters-of-the-universe-20171015-gz1gy5
429 http://www.abc.net.au/news/2017-10-27/rba-wants-more-timely-data-from-abs/9090752
430 http://www.abc.net.au/news/2017-11-21/cost-cutting-hurting-workers-and-the-economy-rba-says/9177564
431 http://www.afr.com/opinion/columnists/ben-bernankes-pricetargeting-masters-of-the-universe-20171015-gz1gy5
432 https://www.thenational.ae/business/ecb-chief-s-dire-warning-of-lasting-damage-for-europe-1.171158
433 The Conference Board. 2016. The Conference Board Total Economy Database™ (Original version), November 2016, http://www.conference-board.org/data/economydatabase/
434 Hogan, Michael J. *The Marshall Plan: America, Britain, and the Reconstruction of Western Europe, 1947–1952*. Cambridge: Cambridge University Press, 1987 p30
435 Pas de Pagaille! Time 28 July 1947
436 Gaddis, John Lewis. We Now Know: Rethinking Cold War History. New York: Oxford University Press, 1997
437 Hogan, Michael J. *The Marshall Plan: America, Britain, and the Reconstruction of Western Europe, 1947–1952*. Cambridge: Cambridge University Press, 1987

438 Wettig, Gerhard (2008). *Stalin and the Cold War in Europe.* Rowman & Littlefield. ISBN 0-7425-5542-9 p142
439 "Milestones: 1945–1952 - Office of the Historian". history.state.gov. *Retrieved 2016-06-06*
440 Barry Eichengreen, *The European Economy since 1945: Coordinated Capitalism and Beyond,* (2008) p. 57; West Germany was 6% higher, the other countries 45% higher.
441 Milward, Alan S. The Reconstruction of Western Europe, 1945–51. (1984) p 466
442 R. R. Palmer. *A History of the Modern World.* p 461
443 Ben Rosamond, Theories of European Integration, Palgrave Macmillan, 2000, pp 21–22
444 "Ein britischer Patriot für Europa: Winston Churchills Europa-Rede, Universität Zürich, 19. September 1946" [A British Patriot for Europe: Winston Churchill's Speech on Europe University of Zurich, 19 September 1946]. Zeit Online. Retrieved 13 January 2010
445 https://www.britannica.com/topic/European-Coal-and-Steel-Community
446 https://en.wikipedia.org/wiki/European_Coal_and_Steel_Community
447 https://www.britannica.com/topic/European-Coal-and-Steel-Community
448 Mathieu, Gilbert (9 May 1970). "The history of the ECSC: good times and bad". Le Monde. France, accessed on CVCE. Retrieved 4 March 2013
449 https://en.wikipedia.org/wiki/Common_Agricultural_Policy
450 *The Economics of Europe* – Dennis Swann p 232
451 https://en.wikipedia.org/wiki/European_Economic_Community
452 https://en.wikipedia.org/wiki/Enlargement_of_the_European_Union
453 https://en.wikipedia.org/wiki/Treaty_of_Lisbon
454 https://en.wikipedia.org/wiki/European_Parliament_election,_1979
455 http://news.bbc.co.uk/2/hi/europe/6901353.stm
456 The Conference Board. 2016. The Conference Board Total Economy Database™ (Original version), November 2016, http://www.conference-board.org/data/economydatabase/
457 The Conference Board. 2016. The Conference Board Total Economy Database™ (Original version), November 2016, http://www.conference-board.org/data/economydatabase/
458 The Conference Board. 2016. The Conference Board Total Economy Database™ (Original version), November 2016, http://www.conference-board.org/data/economydatabase/
459 https://ourworldindata.org/grapher/social-spending-oecd-longrun

460 The Conference Board. 2016. The Conference Board Total Economy Database™ (Original version), November 2016, http://www.conference-board.org/data/economydatabase/
461 The Conference Board. 2016. The Conference Board Total Economy Database™ (Original version), November 2016, http://www.conference-board.org/data/economydatabase/
462 http://appsso.eurostat.ec.europa.eu/nui/setupDownloads.do
463 http://ec.europa.eu/eurostat/statistics-explained/index.php/File:Youth_unemployment_figures,_2007-2016_(%25)_T1.png
464 http://ec.europa.eu/eurostat/statistics-explained/index.php/File:Youth_unemployment_figures,_2007-2016_(%25)_T1.png
465 https://www.ecb.europa.eu/stats/policy_and_exchange_rates/key_ecb_interest_rates/html/index.en.html
466 https://www.ecb.europa.eu/mopo/implement/omt/html/index.en.html
467 http://www.safehaven.com/article/41282/negative-interest-rates-claim-more-victims-today-its-deutsche-bank-tomorrow-german-insurers
468 https://en.wikipedia.org/wiki/European_Stability_Mechanism
469 Editorial (24 May 2012). "Hey, Germany: You Got a Bailout, Too". Bloomberg. Retrieved 9 November 2012.
470 "Corruption perception survey". Transparency International
471 http://dailycaller.com/2015/07/03/retirement-at-45-and-8-other-simple-reasons-greece-is-imploding-right-now/
472 http://www.smh.com.au/comment/head-20150629-gi0erc.html
473 http://www.afr.com/opinion/the-greek-values-that-have-led-to-its-mendicant-economy-20150906-gjgipr
474 "State collected less than half of revenues due last year". Ekathimerini. 5 November 2013. Retrieved 7 November 2013
475 "Will Euro Austerity Push the Shadow Economy Even Deeper into the Dark?". Bloomberg. 6 December 2012. Retrieved 8 January 2014
476 "Greek minister slams Swiss over tax evasion". The Local ch. 24 June 2015
477 Balzli, Beat (2 August 2010). "How Goldman Sachs Helped Greece to Mask its True Debt". Der Spiegel. Retrieved 1 August 2012
478 Melander, Ingrid; Papchristou, Harry (5 November 2009). "Greek Debt to Reach 120.8 Pct of GDP in '10 – Draft". Reuters. Retrieved 5 August 2011
479 "Eurostat – Tables, Graphs and Maps Interface (TGM) table". europa.eu. Retrieved 3 July 2015
480 https://en.wikipedia.org/wiki/Greek_government-debt_crisis
481 http://www.smh.com.au/comment/real-reasons-behind-the-greek-crisis-inefficiency-and-a-fudged-budget-deficit-20150706-gi5xca.html

482 "FRED Graph". stlouisfed.org. Retrieved 3 July 2015
483 "Government debt-to-GDP ratio". Eurostat. 22 October 2012. Retrieved 22 October 2012
484 Higgins, Matthew; Klitgaard, Thomas (2011). "Saving Imbalances and the Euro Area Sovereign Debt Crisis" (PDF). Current Issues in Economics and Finance. Federal Reserve Bank of New York. 17 (5). Retrieved 11 November 2013
485 https://fred.stlouisfed.org/graph/?id=IRLTLT01GRA156N,
486 "Revisiting Greece". The Observer at Boston College. 2 November 2011. Archived from the original on 5 September 2012
487 "*OECD Economic Surveys: Greece 2013*". OECD. 27 November 2013
488 "OECD Economic Surveys: Greece 2013 overview" (PDF). November 2013. Retrieved 28 May 2017
489 "Should other Eurozone programme countries worry about a reduced Greek primary surplus target?". 25 February 2015. Retrieved 28 May 2017
490 (Keeptalkinggreece) "Marianne: The incredible errors by IMF experts & the wrong multiplier". 22 January 2013. Retrieved 29 May 2017
491 "Barroso: Europe 'closer to resolving eurozone crisis'". BBC. 27 October 2011. Retrieved 27 October 2011
492 http://appsso.eurostat.ec.europa.eu/nui/setupDownloads.do
493 Kerin Hope (17 February 2012). "Grim effects of austerity show on Greek streets". The Financial Times. Retrieved 19 February 2012
494 Sakellari, E., & Pikouli, K. (2013). Assessing the impact of the financial crisis in mental health in greece. Mental Health Nursing (Online), 33(6), 19
495 https://en.wikipedia.org/wiki/Greek_government-debt_crisis
496 "Database – Eurostat". europa.eu.
497 https://en.wikipedia.org/wiki/Greek_government-debt_crisis
498 http://news.bbc.co.uk/2/hi/business/8642399.stm
499 OECD (2017), General government debt (indicator). doi: 10.1787/a0528cc2-en (Accessed on 26 October 2017)
500 "Greece: Preliminary Draft Debt Sustainability Analysis". imf.org.
501 http://www.telegraph.co.uk/business/2016/07/28/imf-admits-disastrous-love-affair-with-euro-apologises-for-the-i/
502 https://www.lewrockwell.com/2015/07/david-stockman/good-on-you-greece/
503 https://www.lewrockwell.com/2015/07/david-stockman/good-on-you-greece/
504 Ivana Kottasova (28 January 2015). "Greek debt crisis: Who has most to lose?". CNNMoney. Retrieved 3 July 2015
505 https://www.lewrockwell.com/2015/07/david-stockman/good-on-you-greece/

506 https://www.lewrockwell.com/2015/07/david-stockman/good-on-you-greece/

507 https://data.worldbank.org/indicator/BN.CAB.XOKA.GD.ZS?end=2016&locations=DE-GR&start=1971

508 https://www.economist.com/news/leaders/21724810-country-saves-too-much-and-spends-too-little-why-germanys-current-account-surplus-bad

509 http://www.reuters.com/article/us-eurozone-greece-germany/euro-zone-no-longer-obliged-to-rescue-greece-merkel-ally-says-idUSKBN0K90LM20141231

510 The Conference Board. 2016. The Conference Board Total Economy Database™ (Original version), November 2016, http://www.conference-board.org/data/economydatabase/

511 "Cracks in the crust". The Economist. 11 December 2008. Retrieved 4 February 2013

512 https://www.washingtonpost.com/news/wonk/wp/2015/06/17/the-miraculous-story-of-iceland/?utm_term=.c22a71df2691

513 "Kreppanomics". The Economist. 9 October 2008. Archived from the original on 12 October 2008. Retrieved 10 October 2008

514 Central Bank of Iceland (September 2008). "Economic Indicators". Retrieved 11 October 2008

515 The policy rate was raised from 13.75 percent to 15 percent on 25 March 2008, and to 15.5 percent on 10 April 2008: Central Bank of Iceland (2008). "Monetary Bulletin Q2". Retrieved 11 October 2008

516 "Economic Indicators". Central Bank of Iceland. November 2008. Archived from the original (PDF) on 18 December 2010. Retrieved 4 February 2013. GDP growth is for the second quarter 2008 (annualised); Q3 growth was –0.8% (annualised).

517 https://en.wikipedia.org/wiki/2008%E2%80%932011_Icelandic_financial_crisis

518 Central Bank of Iceland. "Exchange rate". Archived from the original on 12 October 2008. Retrieved 15 October 2008

519 BRUEGEL policy contribution Dezember 2011, Zsolt Darvas, A Tale of Three Countries: Recovery after Banking Crises, pp 6-7

520 https://www.nytimes.com/2017/03/14/business/iceland-economy-finance-capital-controls.html?_r=0

521 https://en.wikipedia.org/wiki/Icesave_dispute

522 https://en.wikipedia.org/wiki/2008%E2%80%932011_Icelandic_financial_crisis

523 Marshall, Chris; Martin, Iain (8 October 2008). "UK govt launching legal action against Iceland". Citywire. Retrieved 8 October 2008

524 McGagh, Michelle (29 January 2013). UK loses out as Iceland escapes Icesave repayment". CityWire. Retrieved 15 February 2016

525 "Stock exchange update". IceNews. 14 October 2008. Archived from the original on 16 October 2008. Retrieved 15 October 2008
526 https://www.nytimes.com/2017/03/14/business/iceland-economy-finance-capital-controls.html?_r=0
527 https://en.wikipedia.org/wiki/2008%E2%80%932011_Icelandic_financial_crisis
528 https://www.nytimes.com/2017/03/14/business/iceland-economy-finance-capital-controls.html?_r=0
529 https://fred.stlouisfed.org/series/DEBTTLISA188A
530 https://www.nytimes.com/2017/03/14/business/iceland-economy-finance-capital-controls.html?_r=0

Part 4

531 http://www.mckinsey.com/insights/economic_studies/debt_and_not_much_deleveraging
532 http://www.mckinsey.com/insights/economic_studies/debt_and_not_much_deleveraging
533 https://www.bloomberg.com/news/articles/2018-01-05/global-debt-hits-record-233-trillion-but-debt-to-gdp-is-falling
534 http://www.rba.gov.au/statistics/tables/xls/e02hist.xls
535 http://www.abs.gov.au/ausstats/abs@.nsf/Lookup/by%20Subject/6523.0~2015-16~Feature%20Article~Household%20Debt%20and%20Over-indebtedness%20(Feature%20Article)~101
536 http://www.afr.com/news/economy/rba-flags-dangers-of-480b-in-interestonly-loan-resets-over-the-next-four-years-20180413-h0yppv
537 https://worldview.stratfor.com/article/dim-chances-european-banking-union-breakthrough
538 https://fred.stlouisfed.org/graph/?id=DDDM011WA156NWDB,
539 http://www.multpl.com/shiller-pe/
540 https://safehaven.com/article/45341/Investor-Debt-Outpaces-SP-500-Growth
541 http://www.afr.com/news/world/imf-warns-that-volatility-bets-loom-as-next-big-financial-shock-20171030-gzbgre
542 http://www.newsmax.com/Finance/StreetTalk/Jamie-Dimon-JPMorgan-Federal-Reserve-debt/2017/07/11/id/801047/
543 https://www.hoover.org/news/hoover-institution-releases-2017-study-highlighting-unfunded-liabilities-state-and-local
544 https://www.bloomberg.com/gadfly/articles/2016-09-13/low-rates-put-pension-plans-in-worst-shape-in-15-years
545 https://www.bloomberg.com/gadfly/articles/2016-09-13/low-rates-put-pension-plans-in-worst-shape-in-15-years

546 United Nations, Department of Economic and Social Affairs, Population Division (2017). World Population Prospects: The 2017 Revision, DVD Edition
547 United Nations, Department of Economic and Social Affairs, Population Division (2017). World Population Prospects: The 2017 Revision, DVD Edition
548 https://www.bloomberg.com/news/articles/2017-10-15/what-global-finance-chiefs-are-saying-about-the-global-economy
549 https://www.marketwatch.com/story/why-larry-summers-wants-to-take-away-the-100-bill-2016-02-16
550 https://www.infowars.com/report-jpmorganchase-bans-storage-of-cash-in-its-safety-deposit-boxes/
551 http://www.investopedia.com/terms/c/credit.asp
552 Francois Louis Ganshof (1944). Qu'est-*ce que la feodalite* 1st edn. New York and London, 1952.
553 https://economictimes.indiatimes.com/definition/microeconomics